ICONS OF AMERICAN COOKING

ICONS OF AMERICAN COOKING

Victor W. Geraci and
Elizabeth S. Demers, Editors

GREENWOOD ICONS

GREENWOOD

AN IMPRINT OF ABC-CLIO, LLC
Santa Barbara, California • Denver, Colorado • Oxford, England

Library of Congress Cataloging-in-Publication Data

Icons of American cooking / Victor W. Geraci and Elizabeth S. Demers, editors.
   p. cm. — (Greenwood icons)
Includes bibliographical references and index.
ISBN 978-0-313-38132-4 (hard copy : alk. paper)—ISBN 978-0-313-38133-1 (ebook)
1. Chefs—United States—Biography. I. Geraci, Victor W. (Victor William), 1948– II. Demers,
Elizabeth S.
   TX649.A1I26   2011
   641.5092—dc22   2010041392
   [B]
ISBN: 978-0-313-38132-4
EISBN: 978-0-313-38133-1

15 14 13 12 11   1 2 3 4 5

This book is also available on the World Wide Web as an eBook.
Visit www.abc-clio.com for details.

Greenwood
An Imprint of ABC-CLIO, LLC

ABC-CLIO, LLC
130 Cremona Drive, P.O. Box 1911
Santa Barbara, California 93116-1911

This book is printed on acid-free paper ∞

Manufactured in the United States of America

We praise the icons in this book who persuaded us to cook,
but, more important, we dedicate this work
to those icons not mentioned,
including our colleagues, friends, and family,
with whom we have shared many a nurturing meal.

Contents

Series Foreword

Worshiped and cursed. Loved and loathed. Obsessed about the world over. What does it take to become an icon? Regardless of subject, culture, or era, the requisite qualifications are the same: (1) challenge the status quo, (2) influence millions, and (3) impact history.

Using these criteria, Greenwood Press introduces a new reference format and approach to popular culture. Spanning a wide range of subjects, volumes in the Greenwood Icons series provide students and general readers a port of entry into the most fascinating and influential topics of the day. Every title offers an in-depth look at 24 iconic figures, each of which captures the essence of a broad subject. These icons typically embody a group of values, elicit strong reactions, reflect the essence of a particular time and place, and link different traditions and periods. Among those featured are artists and activists, superheroes and spies, inventors and athletes, the legends and mythmakers of entire generations. Yet icons can also come from unexpected places: as the heroine who transcends the pages of a novel or as the revolutionary idea that shatters our previously held beliefs. Whether people, places, or things, such icons serve as a bridge between the past and the present, the canonical and the contemporary. By focusing on icons central to popular culture, this series encourages students to appreciate cultural diversity and critically analyze issues of enduring significance.

Most importantly, these books are as entertaining as they are provocative. Is Disneyland a more influential icon of the American West than Las Vegas? How do ghosts and ghouls reflect our collective psyche? Is Barry Bonds an inspiring or deplorable icon of baseball?

Designed to foster debate, the series serves as a unique resource that is ideal for paper writing or report purposes. Insightful, in-depth entries provide far more information than conventional reference articles but are less intimidating and more accessible than a book-length biography. The most revered and reviled icons of American and world history are brought to life with related sidebars, time lines, fact boxes, and quotations. Authoritative entries are accompanied by bibliographies, making these titles an ideal starting point for further research. Spanning a wide range of popular topics, including business, literature, civil rights, politics, music, and more, books in the series provide fresh insights for the student and popular reader into the power and influence of icons, a topic of as vital interest today as in any previous era.

Preface

The 24 icons profiled here are some of the most popular and respected individuals and institutions in the food business, both today and in the recent past. The broad selection is meant to be representative of different cooking styles, regions, approaches to food, and areas of endeavor.

The explosion of widespread, mainstream interest in cooking is manifested most explicitly in the television cooking shows that Americans of all ages are exposed to. Cooks, chefs, food mavens, and food writers are media celebrities. Americans use their cookbooks, buy their products, watch their shows, and read their books, or at least have heard about them. The stories of these icons are told so that their audience and the general public can put their works into a more personal context and also understand why and how they became icons. Everyone, from students writing reports to dedicated foodies or food scholars, will come away enlightened and inspired.

Each authoritative biographical profile, presented in alphabetical order, covers early life and family, education, career hurdles, personal details, accomplishments, and impact or legacy. Some of the profiles contain original quotations from interviews that were conducted especially for this work or never published before. At the end of each profile, further reading, including books, articles, and Web sites, allows for more in-depth research. Some entries include a list of works by the icons. Interspersed sidebars present interesting quotations, menus, excerpts, and the like.

ACKNOWLEDGMENTS

We would like to thank the contributors who graciously gave of their time and expertise to make this project possible. Thank you to our editor, Wendi Schnaufer, and the production staff at Greenwood/ABC-CLIO, whose hard work kept us on track and helped make us look good.

Introduction

During the latter half of the 20th century, a revolution occurred in the United States in how we cook, eat, and think about food. In the 19th century, kitchens were large and cooks had many hands to help them put food on the table. Ingredients were local by necessity; the lack of consistent refrigeration meant that the food people ate was seasonal and fresh or was preserved by such methods as canning, pickling, or salting. In the 20th century, scientific innovations in agribusiness, transport, and refrigeration, as well as food processing, made mass-produced out-of-season food available to all Americans. Kitchens became smaller and servants began to vanish in the everyday home, and the smaller kitchen meant that the lone cook, increasingly the lady of the house, could be more efficient, with ingredients close at hand. Canned soups and other convenience foods seemed to become the norm, leaving many Americans with a memory of American diets as bland, thoughtless, and unvaried across the board.

Yet, in the last half of the 20th century, a small group of cooks, chefs, and writers began to question the way Americans ate. Postwar travel to Europe introduced them to other models of eating. The French, for example, went to market every day and bought whatever looked good. They took long lunches and savored their meals, pairing wine with food and finishing with heady cheeses to settle the palate. Additionally, new immigrant streams from Asia, Central and South America, and other parts of the world made new flavors available to the American palate. Americans increasingly sought out new tastes and new techniques. A number of the 24 icons of American cooking who are profiled here were at the vanguard of this revolution in eating. They traveled, studied, and ate, and they brought back to their hometowns everything they learned, recreating their experiences in situ and, in the process, transforming all of American cooking. Seemingly overnight, Americans went from a nation addicted to can openers to a nation where *foie gras*, cilantro, heirloom tomatoes, lemongrass, unpasteurized cheeses, and grass-fed beef became nearly mainstream.

What is most striking about these new food pioneers is how many of them knew, and still know, each other. They were truly a community of diners who collaborated, wrote, ate, and appeared on television together to spread the gospel of good food, made well. James Beard famously mentored and befriended many of these icons, including Marion Cunningham, Cecilia Chiang, Julia Child, and Alice Waters. Many of these cooks and writers shared the same editor, the famous Judith Jones at Knopf (another good friend of Beard's), whose authors included Cunningham as well as Joan Nathan, Edna Lewis, and Lidia Bastianich.

Several icons also shared the experience of culinary school and/or the rough-and-tumble world of restaurant kitchens on their way up the ladder to celebrity chefdom. These chefs tend to be men, including Mario Batali, Anthony Bourdain, Charlie Trotter, and Jacques Pépin. However, most of the icons featured here are women who came to cooking either later in life or by accident, such as Julia Child, Diana Kennedy, Irma Rombauer, Marion Cunningham, and Rachael Ray.

Region has also played a central role in the food revolution of the mid-20th century. James Beard, Marion Cunningham, Alice Waters, Chuck Williams, Cecilia Chiang, Ruth Reichl, Mario Batali, M. F. K. Fisher, and Charlie Trotter were all from the West Coast or had formative culinary experiences there. New York and the East Coast form the other hotbed of American gastronomy, claiming Martha Stewart, Anthony Bourdain, Rachael Ray, Joan Nathan, Lidia Bastianich, the Zagats, and the Culinary Institute of America. Several icons have lived or worked extensively on both coasts, such as James Beard, Ruth Reichl, and Mario Batali. Because these cooks and writers know each other well, work together often, and share the same values, their influence on American cooking is unparalleled.

Yet, the outliers in the book are, in their own way, perhaps even more iconic than their professional counterparts. In an ironic twist reflective of American exceptionalism, midwesterner Irma Rombauer's *Joy of Cooking* became the most popular American cookbook of all time, beating out even Cunningham's *Fannie Farmer* revision. Betty Crocker and Rachael Ray have had a similar audience and appeal—in many ways, they represent the way Americans really cook on a day-to-day basis, versus how they eat in restaurants or how they might cook for special occasions. Martha Stewart, on the other hand, is both a member of the foodie community and an extremely influential outlier whose connections, adventures in prison, and meteoric business success put her in an iconic class by herself.

Finally, the recent phenomenon of the Food Network and other food-focused programming has catapulted culinary personalities such as Rachael Ray, Anthony Bourdain, Mario Batali, Martha Stewart, and Lidia Bastianich to an unprecedented level of fame. Personality has, in these instances, become as important as recipes, ingredients, or philosophy in the American food revolution.

The irony of icons is that, although they are deeply rooted in historical circumstances, they ultimately transcend time and place. How else could a housewife from southern California refashion herself as one of the most famous experts on French cooking in the United States or a failed actor from Oregon become "the Dean of American cuisine," a symbol of excellence and taste so recognizable that his name is invoked in awarding the highest honors in American cooking? Both Julia Child and James Beard became icons through their talent, energy, creativity, and drive, as much as through the unique elements of their lives. If Child had not moved with her husband to Paris during the postwar period, she may never—as a cure for boredom—have taken the French cooking classes that changed history. If Beard had been able to land more acting roles in New York, he may never have turned to catering to pay the bills, drawing on the rich food culture of his native Pacific Northwest.

All the icons in this book have likewise transformed or epitomized American cooking. They represent various regions and styles. They come from the ranks of professional chefs and cooks, as well as hugely talented amateurs. Many of them were and are friends and colleagues, collaborating on the books, television shows, and restaurants that Americans have grown to love. Immigrant Lidia Bastianich's love of Italian food resulted in restaurants that celebrate the many culinary styles of Italy and of Italian Americans, as well as several best-selling cookbooks and popular television shows. If she did not single-handedly bring real Italian food to Americans, she has made the diversity of Italian cuisine accessible to everyone. Like Bastianich, Mario Batali has made real Italian restaurant food and Iberian cuisine wildly popular, thanks to his large personality, unstinting commitment to excellence, and enthusiasm for good cooking. He is a "rock star" among chefs. James Beard is the grandfather of American cooking. His books, teaching, and befriending of other cooks, many of whom are icons in this book, have completely transformed the American culinary landscape. Anthony Bourdain is also a "rock star" chef. Having written the ultimate insiders' guide to restaurant kitchens, Bourdain now travels the world, presenting unique and fabulous foods with his biting wit and canny charm. In an immigrant story similar to Bastianich's, Cecilia Chiang brought Mandarin Cuisine to a nation convinced that all Asian food was Cantonese. Her restaurant, classes, cookbooks, and friendship assisted in the mentoring of Cunningham, Waters, Chuck Williams, and her personal friend James Beard.

Julia Child almost needs no introduction. She is credited, perhaps somewhat erroneously, with bringing Americans back to the kitchen, away from the convenience foods that stereotype midcentury American cuisine. Her "bible" of French cooking is as much a pop culture icon as is Child herself, and for many Americans it is the epitome of *haute cuisine*. Betty Crocker is one of two icons in this book who is not a real person; nevertheless, Betty represents the way American women really cook—the Betty Crocker brand includes cookbooks, recipes, a radio show, and convenience foods. As an icon, she has been a companion in the kitchen and a role model both for cooking and for American womanhood. Like Betty, the Culinary Institute of America is both an entity and an idea. The CIA, as it is familiarly known, is the most famous culinary school in the United States and has set the standard of excellence for all others. Its graduates staff restaurants all over the United States and the world, thus making the school's vision and mission a formidable influence.

At first glance, Fannie Farmer and Marion Cunningham seem an unlikely pairing. Both were women who sought out careers in food after overcoming physical adversities. Farmer wrote the original *Boston Cooking-School Cookbook*, which later became the *Fannie Farmer Cookbook*. Marion Cunningham, a close friend, student, and assistant of James Beard, transformed Farmer's iconic book in the late 20th century, creating an excellent everyday bible for the home cook in search of an excellent meal. Like Cunningham and Julia Child, M. F. K. Fisher came to cooking by accident. She considered herself a writer first and began to write about food as a metaphor for life when she moved to France. She is the quintessential food writer, whose books and recipes have influenced successive generations of American cooks and writers.

Addressing a more specific area, Mollie Katzen's Moosewood Restaurant and cookbooks brought vegetarian cooking into the mainstream. Her creative and delicious recipes made it hip to give up meat and forged an enduring model for American vegetarian cuisine. Diana Kennedy, a British expatriate, fell in love with Mexican culture and unexpectedly became the grande dame of Mexican cooking, who with her books and research brought the traditional cuisines of Mexico to the level of *haute cuisine* for American audiences.

Like James Beard, Marion Cunningham, and many of the other icons in this book, Edna Lewis fell into cooking as a way to make money. Originally from the South, she moved to New York, where she opened a restaurant so special it soon became the favorite of famous Southerners who lived in the city. Her books, published with legendary Knopf cookbook editor Judith Jones, and her commitment to Southern, African American culinary traditions have cemented her place as a true American icon. Joan Nathan likewise celebrates American food as the chronicler of Jewish foods, both in the United States and in Israel, and as an ethnographer of American folk foodways and regional cooking.

French immigrant Jacques Pépin, like Julia Child, has been extremely influential in interpreting classic French food for American audiences. Paul Prudhomme, in a similar fashion, has created the craze for New Orleans and Louisiana cooking, popularizing blackened redfish, gumbo, and *etouffé* not just in his home state, but all over the country. TV cook and host Rachael Ray, with her bubbly personality, enthusiasm, and confidence, brought a new sense of fun to the kind of cooking Americans do every night—fast, fresh, and fabulous. Her personal brand represents the everywoman sensibility of a younger, more blue-collar Martha Stewart, a woman who wants to make a great home and a great meal for her family, both for special occasions and every day.

Food writer and editor Ruth Reichl is, in many ways, like the lovechild of M. F. K. Fisher and Craig Claiborne. Although she has written and edited cookbooks and worked in a restaurant, she is not really a chef herself. Nevertheless, Reichl's memoirs and reviews have reshaped not only food writing, but the way we choose restaurants and how we evaluate taste. Irma Rombauer and her daughter Marion Rombauer Becker, on the other hand, represent midwestern cooking at its finest—their *Joy of Cooking* is the best-selling American cookbook of all time. The book gives cooks the tools they need for every eventuality in the kitchen, from an emergency pantry dinner of tuna noodle casserole to a fancy dinner party for 20.

Martha Stewart is an icon who, like Julia Child, almost needs no introduction. Unlike Child, Stewart is not at heart a chef, though food and cooking remain the quintessential core of her ethos. Her brand includes high-end recipes and cookbooks, decorating, magazines, television, and new media. A former housewife, model, and stockbroker turned caterer, Martha has parlayed her talents into a media empire and is so famous that many people do not even bother to use her last name.

Charlie Trotter, conversely, is a trained chef and restaurateur with a commitment to fresh seasonal ingredients and exceptional customer service. Yet, perhaps the most influential proponent of the fresh and seasonal movement in American food culture is Alice Waters, whose Chez Panisse restaurant and cookbooks have set the standard for fine dining and for California cuisine. Chuck Williams further revolutionized the way Americans cook by making French and European cookware available in this country, thus allowing home cooks to recreate their favorite restaurant meals with the proper tools and with imported and exotic ingredients. Finally, Nina and Tim Zagat have demystified restaurants with their unique guidebook system. Whereas before diners had to be "in the know," with the Zagat guides, any food lover can seek out the best restaurants, all over the world.

Elizabeth S. Demers

Lidia Matticchio Bastianich poses in the dining room of Felidia, one of her restaurants in New York City, April 19, 2004. Bastianich is renowned for her Italian and Italian American cooking, whose traditions are part of her family's way of life. (AP/Wide World Photos)

Lidia Bastianich

Lidia Matticchio Bastianich, chef, restaurateur, author, television personality, and humanitarian, is an icon of American cooking who also embodies the American dream. Twelve years after immigrating to the United States in 1970, Bastianich entered the restaurant business at a time when there were few women chefs and garnered much respect in what was a male-dominated industry. She has played a major role in introducing Americans to authentic Italian cooking.

EARLY LIFE

Bastianich was born on February 21, 1947, in Pula, a city located on the tip of Istria, a peninsula that lies on the Adriatic Sea 90 miles east of Venice. Having been occupied by many powers, including Austro-Hungary, Italy, Yugoslavia, Croatia, and Slovenia, Istria contains elements of Italian, Croatian, German, and Hungarian food cultures. The geography also makes possible unlimited variations: fish from the Adriatic Sea, game from inland areas, and traditional Mediterranean crops like grapes, olives, and figs that thrive in warmer climates. This complex history helps to explain how Bastianich developed her culinary interests.

Childhood in Istria and Italy

Bastianich's passion for the culinary arts began during her childhood in Istria, where much of her life was centered on family and food. She was born shortly after the end of World War II, when Istria was given to the new country of Yugoslavia via the terms of the peace treaty with Italy in 1947. Bastianich lived and attended school in Pula but spent most of her free time with her maternal grandparents, who lived in the nearby village of Busoler in a court-yard that they shared with neighbors and relatives. Resources were scarce in the region just after the war, and because few people had fishing equipment or guns for hunting, they had little meat. Like their neighbors, Bastianich's frugal family could afford to waste nothing. If they were fortunate enough to have a small bird, it was considered a luxury and had to be stretched to supply food for many meals.

Despite the family's poverty, Bastianich has rich memories of the time spent with her grandparents. They produced most of their own food, raising animals, growing fruits and vegetables, making olive oil and wine, distilling *grappa*, curing meats, and drying beans, herbs, and fruit. They bartered for ingredients that they did not have, and they even ground their own wheat at a communal mill. Any surplus was carefully preserved for the winter months. Bastianich's grandparents served food to the seasonal workers in the Osteria, a small eatery that they set up in their communal courtyard; when it rained, the seating was moved to the family's wine cellar. Her large extended family also gathered here for meals. The young Bastianich loved this time with her family and delighted in being involved with every element of the culinary process.

Easter in Istria

I remember most fondly the ritual of making pinza (Easter bread) at Grandma Rosa's house. The communal oven was in the courtyard in the middle of town. Maria was the official keeper, and it would be lit every second day. The townswomen would knead their breads according to their places in line, each one having to bring her own supply of wood in advance—always enough to bake her own bread.

We kids would run from house to house to advise our mothers and grandmothers of the readiness of the ovens for the next batch. Between batches the oven was brushed with a broom made out of bussolo, or branches tied to a long stick with wire. Their leaves would crackle like popcorn under the intense heat of the oven.

The women came—one by one—with the kneading boards lined with the puffy loaves of bread wrapped like babies. If it was cool, they would cover them with a blanket. "Risen bread should never 'catch a cold' or be in a draft," said Grandma. The women used the same board to take the baked bread home. If the loaves were well risen and high, they would carry them home uncovered for everyone to see and praise. If the bread was not perfect, you can bet it was wrapped tightly and taken home quickly.

The day before Easter Sunday was the best day to be near the oven— everybody was baking their Easter bread and the children made little dough dolls called titole or puppa con uova, with a colored boiled egg for the head surrounded by dough that was braided into a body. We played "mommy" with our puppa dolls, wrapping them in blankets and caring for them, but slowly our maternal instincts gave way to hunger and we would begin to nibble the puppa doll under its little blanket, beginning at the feet, until we were left with just the egg.

—Lidia Matticchio Bastianich, *Lidia's Italian Table*.
New York: William Morrow, 1998, p. 340

For the Matticchios, who were not communists, living under communist rule meant that they were not permitted to practice their Catholicism or speak their native Italian. They felt like second-class citizens; authorities even changed their name from Matticchio to Motika. In 1956, when Bastianich was 11, her parents, Erminia and Vittorio, decided to escape the oppressive dictatorial government, but leaving the Iron Curtain proved to be a challenge. Bastianich and her mother and older brother, Franco, left first, under the pretense of going to visit a sick aunt in Italy, and fled to Trieste, which, like Istria, has a complex history and has been an oasis for refugees. Here they lived with Bastianich's great aunt Nina, a personal chef, and nervously awaited the arrival of Vittorio, who eventually joined them after being shot at while secretly crossing the border during the night. However, Bastianich's Aunt Nina could only give the family temporary shelter because everyone was struggling financially in post–World War II Italy.

Because it was difficult to find work, the family reluctantly moved to San Saba, a refugee camp in Trieste, where they remained for two years. The camp was housed in a facility that originally stored and packaged rice but had been used as a concentration and deportation camp by the Germans during World War II. Although the camp's living conditions were rudimentary, Bastianich has pleasant memories of experiencing with her Aunt Nina the bounty of Trieste's market, the Ponte Rosse, or "red bridge." She also spent time in her aunt's kitchen, where she began to refine the rudimentary knowledge of cuisine that she had acquired at her grandparents' home in Istria.

During this time, Bastianich's mother, who had been employed as an elementary school teacher in Istria, worked as a domestic and cook, and her father, who was trained to be a mechanic, worked as a chauffeur. Bastianich attended a convent school, where she was first introduced to a well-equipped, industrial kitchen. She helped in the kitchen in exchange for her tuition. While the other children were outside playing, Bastianich could be found in the kitchen peeling potatoes and apples. This was her introduction to preparing food in large quantities.

Immigration to the United States

Bastianich's parents dreamed of a better life for themselves and their children, and when the United States lifted its immigration quotas, the family moved to New York as political refugees. They arrived in 1958 when Bastianich was 12 years old. Catholic Charities financed their trip and helped them find jobs and housing. Initially, they stayed at a New York hotel, but when her father found employment as an automobile mechanic with Chevrolet, the family moved to North Bergen, New Jersey, where her mother began working as a tailor at the Evan Picone factory. Eventually the family relocated to join relatives in the Astoria neighborhood of Queens, New York, where other Istrians had clustered. Like most immigrants, the Matticchios yearned for the security of the familiar, and Astoria offered some solace.

Bastianich became a naturalized American citizen in 1965 at the age of 18 and quickly learned English. While she was adapting to life in the United States, the memories of the food and rich culture from her childhood in Istria remained with her and helped to shape her career. However, as an adolescent she cooked for more practical reasons. Because her parents continued to work in New Jersey and had a lengthy commute, Bastianich was responsible for preparing the family's dinner each night. She was fascinated by the ingredients of her new land: canned, packaged, and frozen foods such as peanut butter, instant puddings, cake mixes, and the ubiquitous Wonder Bread. But the novelty of many of these items quickly wore off as Bastianich went on to develop a greater appreciation for the diverse food of her homeland.

Bastianich's mother valued education and she saw it as the key to her children's success in the United States. Thus, it is not surprising that Bastianich's brother, Franco, went on to earn a Ph.D. in electrical engineering. Being interested in the sciences, especially biology, Bastianich imagined that she would become a pediatrician, but she always gravitated toward her true love: food. Even her part-time jobs as a teenager eventually drew her to the kitchen. She worked as a clerk in a bakery and ended up baking bread and decorating cakes. She also worked as a hostess in a restaurant and ended up preparing salads. Later, she sought employment in Italian American restaurants as a hostess and waitress, but these front-of-the-house positions invariably led her to the kitchens. During that period, Bastianich became more familiar with Italian American cuisine. Although she knew many of the ingredients, the preparation of the dishes was quite different. For example, in Istria, spaghetti and meatballs would be served separately, and the meatballs, which were flat, were fried and served as a main dish.

When she was 16, Bastianich met her future husband, Felice, from whom she is now divorced. They met when he was hired by her friends to play the accordion at her birthday party. Felice, who was also from Istria, was working as a waiter and shared her interest in food. Although Bastianich received a full scholarship to attend Hunter College, where she planned to major in biology, she dropped out of college as a freshman, and the two married in 1966 when she was 19. For their honeymoon, they traveled throughout Europe and returned to Istria, where the economy had come to rely on tourism and welcomed its former residents. Here Bastianich had a joyful reunion with her grandparents. They also spent time with Felice's family. After returning to Astoria, Bastianich gave birth to their first child, Joseph, in 1968, and in 1972 she had a daughter, Tanya.

RESTAURANTS

The United States presented Bastianich with many opportunities, and she was quick to take advantage of them. In 1971, when she was only 24, she and Felice opened their first restaurant using their savings and money borrowed from her parents. It was a small establishment in the Forest Hills section of Queens that they named Buonavia, Italian for "on the good road." Bastianich hired a chef who was knowledgeable about Italian American food, which was what their American clientele expected to see on the menu. She worked as the sous-chef so that she could learn about Italian American cooking while also offering some traditional, northern Italian dishes such as *risotto, gnocchi*, and *polenta*. The restaurant was an enormous success, and they enlarged it twice. Buonavia's popularity enabled them to open a second restaurant in 1973, Villa Secondo, in the nearby Fresh Meadows neighborhood.

During this time, Bastianich remained a student of food and took food-related courses in chemistry, physiology, history, and anthropology at local colleges. When they had the financial resources, she and her husband traveled extensively to familiarize themselves with foreign food and techniques to use in their restaurants. While raising two children and running two successful restaurants, she also took trips to Italy to further her culinary education.

Despite the overwhelming success of both establishments, or perhaps because of it, Bastianich was eager to attempt the business in the more competitive, upscale Manhattan. To raise the funds for this next venture, the couple sold both restaurants. It was then that Bastianich and her husband opened what is considered to be her flagship restaurant.

The move was a tremendous financial risk, for they invested everything they had. The restaurant that they purchased required extensive remodeling, and because of limited capital, the couple did much of the work themselves. Felidia opened in 1981 on Manhattan's East 58th Street and featured Bastianich as the chef. It remains open today, offering authentic food from all regions of Italy. In some respects, Felidia was groundbreaking. At that time, Italian restaurants were serving Italian American food to meet the tastes of their clientele, and many of the traditional Italian ingredients were not available in the United States. Italian restaurants served mostly southern Italian food that Americans equated with an uncomplicated plate of spaghetti and meatballs. Although a few restaurants were just beginning to serve classic fare such as *risotto* and *polenta*, Felidia was innovative in its authentic approach to the diverse regional dishes of Italy. In a short time, it garnered much acclaim as a genuine Italian restaurant. Over the years, it has earned three stars from *The New York Times*, was identified by *Wine Spectator* as one of the top Italian restaurants in the United States, and was nominated as "outstanding restaurant" by the James Beard Foundation. Eventually, wanting time to pursue other projects, Bastianich hired an executive chef, Fortunato Nicotra, to operate Felidia. Nicotra has brought his own more contemporary touch to the restaurant while continuing to prepare the traditional cuisine that the restaurant's longtime enthusiasts expect.

Everything is a family affair for Bastianich. While she and her husband worked the grueling hours required of restaurant operators, their children were always with them or with family. It was not unusual for her children to do their homework at the restaurant while Bastianich's mother helped her make pasta. The family had their holiday dinners at the restaurant, and then the children would go home with their grandmother. Although Bastianich and Felice divorced in 1997 after being married for 31 years, they remain friends. Their children were raised to understand the importance of family and to appreciate their Italian heritage. In fact, when they were growing up, each summer the family returned to Istria to visit Bastianich's childhood home. Today, Bastianich owns her grandmother's home in the courtyard. Chickens and rabbits can be found in the back, near the huge pine tree forest that Bastianich played in as a child.

Bastianich encouraged her children to pursue a line of work other than the food industry. Joseph attended Boston College and worked on Wall Street, and Tanya earned a Ph.D. in Italian Renaissance art from Oxford University. They have become involved with their mother's many enterprises. In 1993 Bastianich and Joseph opened a restaurant in New York's theater district named Becco, which is derived from the Italian word *beccare*, meaning "to savor, peck, or nibble." The restaurant, designed to resemble a country home in Italy, is well known for its hearty, generous portions and fixed-price lunch and dinner menus. At Joseph's recommendation, the restaurant offers reasonably priced wines to encourage customers to purchase a bottle rather than a glass, and people have responded with enthusiasm.

Bastianich and her children then began to look for smaller cities where they could bring what they envisioned as a multiunit restaurant concept that could be easily replicated in multiple cities, and they opened Bastianich's Kansas City in 1998. This was followed by Bastianich's Pittsburgh in 2001. Both restaurants' menu offerings have been influenced by Felidia and Becco and include dishes from Istria as well as regional Italian fare.

Bastianich's next restaurant venture in Manhattan was Esca, the Italian word for "bait." Esca was opened by Bastianich, her son, and acclaimed chef Mario Batali in 2000. Under the restaurant's chef, David Pasternack, who is also a partner, Esca earned three stars from *The New York Times*. The restaurant serves southern Italian cuisine, emphasizes an uncomplicated preparation of fresh seafood, and offers an exclusively Italian wine list that showcases regional wines.

In late 2005, along with her son and Batali, Bastianich opened her sixth and most recent restaurant, Del Posto, from the Italian phrase meaning "of the place." The elegant restaurant, situated in New York's trendy meatpacking district, is meant to evoke memories of the past by reminding its diners of Italy's once formal hotel dining rooms. It is built on a grand scale, with rich mahogany, imposing columns, and a prominent staircase. Its cuisine, which is intended to match the grandeur of the restaurant's dining rooms, is identified as being transgenerational, meaning that it unites classic Italian cuisine with contemporary culinary techniques. The restaurant uses only the finest ingredients. It offers freshly baked bread, house-cured *lardo*, and made-in-house artisanal pasta. The seasonal menu gives the customer the option of choosing from multiple courses, and the seven-course tasting menu is pure decadence. Although many anticipated that Del Posto would earn the much-sought-after four stars from *The New York Times*, it earned a noteworthy, but nonetheless disappointing, three stars. It was also given an impressive two-star rating from *Michelin*. Del Posto, in keeping with the times, is certified by the Green Restaurant Association, which means that the restaurant works with the Association to determine the most eco-friendly way to conduct business.

TELEVISION SHOWS

Bastianich's success with preparing authentic Italian food at Felidia caught the attention of many food enthusiasts, including Julia Child, who invited her to appear on *Cooking with Master Chefs*, a series that featured celebrated chefs cooking in their homes rather than restaurant kitchens. Bastianich prepared her signature dish, *risotto*. Her appearance attracted the interest of producers, who recognized that she would be a sensation if given her own show. Their predictions were accurate, as audiences gravitated to her maternal demeanor and her genuine love for her craft. Bastianich's public television cooking shows have garnered a worldwide audience. Filming the shows in her home kitchen seemed like a natural choice. Bastianich has always combined work and family, a characteristic of her warm personality; in fact, her entire family has appeared on her shows at one time or another.

The cooking series includes *Lidia's Italian Table* (1998), which has a companion cookbook, *Lidia's Italian-American Kitchen* (1998), and *Lidia's Family Table* (2004), which explores the traditional northern Italian food of Istria. The James Beard Foundation nominated *Lidia's Family Table* as the best national television food show in 2007. Her most recent program, *Lidia's Italy*, debuted in 2007 and also has a companion cookbook. In it Bastianich prepares traditional, regional Italian food, but the show takes Bastianich out of the kitchen and places her in Italy as she explores the bountiful markets and selects ingredients for her dishes. She then demonstrates the preparation of two to three recipes per show in her home kitchen. Her most recent shows have cultural segments produced by Tanya.

COOKBOOKS

Eager that her fans share her understanding of and appreciation for the cuisine of Italy, Bastianich gives a wealth of information in her five cookbooks. In addition to detailed recipes, they contain personal anecdotes about her family history as well as treasured family photos.

Bastianich's debut cookbook, *La Cucina di Lidia: Distinctive Regional Cuisine from the North of Italy* (1990), is considered by many to be her most personal cookbook in that she shares many memories and photos from her childhood along with the traditional, regional recipes. *Lidia's Italian Table: More Than 200 Recipes from the First Lady of Italian Cooking* (1998), the companion book to the public television show of the same name, emphasizes her childhood and how it influenced her love of food. Bastianich offers seasonal recipes that she has been collecting since she was a young girl, explains the importance of quality ingredients, and provides anecdotes, sometimes exceptionally detailed, on every aspect of food, from growing and harvesting to preparing, preserving, and storing. For example, she includes tips for cooking fresh and dried pasta and a list of 13 rules for preparing *risotto*. The book also contains a more detailed discussion of the key elements in Italian cuisine, such as *Parmigiano-Reggiano*, truffles, olive oil, salt, and wine.

Whereas *Lidia's Italian Table* focuses on Bastianich's childhood, *Lidia's Italian-American Kitchen* (2001) is about the food that Bastianich encountered as an adolescent in America. Although some are quick to criticize Italian American cooking for bastardizing authentic Italian cuisine, Bastianich defends it by noting that it was the way Italian immigrants adapted to an unfamiliar environment. They sought the comforting familiarity of the dishes from their homeland but often had to find substitutions for ingredients that were not available in their new country. The book pays homage to those dishes created by Italian immigrants, but the recipes have been updated so that they require authentic ingredients that are now available in gourmet markets and even local grocery stores. It also includes recipes for more traditional Italian dishes that have become an accepted part of American cuisine, ranging from stuffed shells to lobster *Fra Diavolo*. The book, which helps to validate Italian American cuisine, won the International Association of Culinary Professionals cookbook award in 2002.

Bastianich's fourth cookbook, *Lidia's Family Table: More Than 200 Fabulous Recipes to Enjoy Every Day—with Wonderful Ideas for Variations and Improvisations* (2004), includes recipes for preparing everyday Italian food for one's family as well as valuable notes about cooking techniques. *Lidia's Italy: 140 Simple and Delicious Recipes from the Ten Places in Italy Lidia Loves Most* (2007), another companion book for the public television show by the same name, is part cookbook and part travel guide. While offering traditional recipes from her favorite locations in Italy, including Istria, Trieste, Rome, Naples, and Sicily, it also includes highlights of cultural sights contributed by Tanya. Together, Bastianich and her daughter describe a rich culture. The book also provides resources for locating hard-to-find ingredients.

Bastianich's most recent cookbook, *Lidia Cooks from the Heart of Italy: A Feast of 175 Regional Recipes* (2009), contains recipes from Trentino-Alto Adige to Sardinia. It covers the ten regions of Italy that Bastianich's previous book did not cover, so that together the two books cover all of Italy and Istria. *Lidia Cooks from the Heart of Italy* also has interesting cultural notes by Tanya, as well as Bastianich's stories of the people she met and foods she enjoyed during her travels.

OTHER ENDEAVORS

Bastianich's entrepreneurial spirit has extended beyond restaurant ownership, cooking shows, and cookbook publishing. She is the founder and president of Tavola Productions, the company responsible for her acclaimed show *Lidia Bastianich's Italy*. She has also created a line of specialty pasta sauces, named Lidia's Flavors, that are made with imported San Marzano tomatoes and freshly cut vegetables. The six sauces—Italian Tomato and Fresh Herb, Garden Vegetable and Herb, Zesty Onion and Tuscan Pepper, Marinara, Artichoke Marinara, and Chunky Eggplant Sauce—are sold by high-end retailers nationwide and are available through her Web site. Bastianich and Tanya, along with Tanya's friend Shelly Burgess Nicotra, also own a travel company, *Esperienze*

Italiane, that offers high-end, customized trips for groups of all sizes that explore the food, wine, and culture of Italy. Bastianich and Tanya are working on developing cookware and tabletop items.

Bastianich also co-owns two successful vineyards with Joseph. Their first wine business, *Azienda Agricla Bastianich*, is located in the Colli Orientali region of Friuli in northeastern Italy, a region known for its white wines. Bastianich Vineyards produces Tocai Friulan, Tocai Plus, and Vespa Bianco. Recently the area has begun to make red wines, and Bastianich Vineyards turns out an impressive Vespa Rossa and Calabrone. In its first seven years of business, the winery was given the prestigious Italian wine award, *Tre Bicchieri*, five times. Along with Batali, Bastianich and Joseph purchased a second winery, La Mozza, in Maremma, Tuscany.

HUMANITARIAN CONTRIBUTIONS

In 1999 Bastianich created the Lidia Matticchio Bastianich Foundation, a nondiscriminatory organization that provides academic and vocational development to those in need. It is no doubt because of her own generosity as well as the role that Catholic Charities played in enabling Bastianich's family to come to the United States that Bastianich feels the desire to aid the disadvantaged.

Bastianich uses her talent and clout as a chef to organize benefits and to support humanitarian causes. In the nation's capital, Bastianich participated in a series of charitable dinners for "Art. Food. Hope," raising $100,000 for D.C. Central Kitchen, Martha's Table, and Fresh Farm Markets.

In April 2009, the women in Bastianich's family became the public faces of UNIFEM's national campaign, "Say No to Violence against Women." As co-chair of numerous events sponsored by UNICEF and UNIFEM, Bastianich has raised funds to increase awareness about female refugees in war-torn Kosovo, all the while advocating for greater recognition of the integral roles performed by women worldwide within families, communities, and society. Accordingly, Bastianich helped launch "The UNIFEM/International Alert Millennium Peace Prize for Women" to honor organizations and women engaging in conflict prevention and resolution.

AWARDS AND HONORS

Bastianich has won many awards, including the prestigious James Beard Foundation's Outstanding Chef award in 1999, Best Chef in New York City in 1999, and *Wine Spectator*'s Grand Award in 2006. In 2007, she was identified as one of Crain's 100 Most Influential Businesswomen in New York. Additional honors have included acting as grand marshall of New York City's Columbus Day Parade in 2007. In 2008, she prepared dinner for Pope Benedict XVI when he visited New York. In 2009, Bastianich was named "Humanitarian of the Year" at the National Italian American Foundation's 34th Anniversary Gala in Washington, D.C. Also in 2009, *Entertainment Weekly* identified *Lidia's Italy* as one of the top food shows on television, and it was celebrated by James Beard as the best cooking television series.

CONCLUSION

Today, Bastianich lives in a Tudor-style home in Queens overlooking Long Island Bay. Her mother, who has always lived with her, resides near her in a separate apartment, and her children and her five grandchildren visit frequently. Bastianich personifies the American dream in that she has become an American success story by acquiring wealth and achieving critical acclaim. More significant, however, is that she has maintained a lifelong love affair and an unbreakable bond with her homeland that she has, in turn, shared with her children and her millions of fans. Indeed, Bastianich is an American icon who has brought authentic Italian cuisine to the gourmands of America. Her tagline, *tutti a tavola a mangiare,* "everyone to the table to eat," commands that all join her in her love affair with Italian food.

FURTHER READING

Bastianich, Lidia Matticchio. *Lidia's Italian Table: More Than 200 Recipes from the First Lady of Italian Cooking.* Ed. Christopher Styler. New York: William Morrow, 1998.

Bastianich, Lidia Matticchio. *Lidia's Italian-American Kitchen.* 2nd ed. New York: Knopf, 2005.

Bastianich, Lidia Matticchio. *Lidia's Family Table: More Than 200 Fabulous Recipes to Enjoy Every Day—with Wonderful Ideas for Variations and Improvisations.* New York: Knopf, 2004.

Bastianich, Lidia Matticchio, and Jay Jacobs. *La Cucina di Lidia: Distinctive Regional Cuisine from the North of Italy.* New York: Doubleday, 1990.

Bastianich, Lidia Matticchio, Tanya Bastianich Manuali, and David Nussbaum. *Lidia's Italy: 140 Simple and Delicious Recipes from the Ten Places in Italy Lidia Loves Most.* New York: Knopf, 2007.

Bastianich, Lidia and Tanya Bastianich Manuali. *Lidia Cooks from the Heart of Italy: A Feast of 175 Regional Recipes.* New York: Knopf, 2009.

Ciceran, Marisa, and Guido Villa. "Lidia Bastianich." www.istrianet.org

Cloud, John. "The Matron Saint of Pasta." *Time.* October 3, 2005, W19–W22.

DeLucia, Matt. "Lidia Bastianich: New York's First Lady of Italian Cuisine." www.newyorkrestaurantinsider.com

Manuali, Tanya Bastianich. "Lidia's Italy." www.lidiasitaly.com

Witchel, Alex. "At Home with Lidia Bastianich: A Recipe Kept Warm for 55 Years." *New York Times.* November 15, 2001, NY edition, F1.

Diane Todd Bucci

Chef Mario Batali attends the grand opening of Eataly in New York, August 31, 2010. (AP/Wide World Photos)

Mario Batali

Mario Batali is a celebrity chef renowned both for his dedication to authentic regional Italian cuisine and for his signature ensemble: shorts and bright orange Crocs with equally bright orange hair pulled back in a long ponytail. As one of the top chefs in the United States, Batali has graced the morning talk shows, held forth on his own television show, opened numerous successful restaurants, published eight cookbooks, and enchanted Americans with his culinary acumen and exuberant personal charm.

EARLY LIFE

Cooking Experiences

Born on September 9, 1960, Batali grew up outside Seattle, Washington. His father, Armandino Batali, an executive with Boeing and a second-generation Italian American, came from a long line of culinary mavens from the Abruzzo region. Armandino's mother ran an Italian import store founded by her parents in 1903. Under her tutelage, the Batali children—Mario, his sister Gina, and his brother Dana—learned how to eat like Italians, with an *antipasti* course, followed by a *primo piatto*, an opening course of pasta like their grandmother's famed ravioli, and then a *secondo piatto*, a gracious serving of meat or fish. Batali's mother Marilyn, a half-French Canadian, gave her son his signature red hair and a home life filled with cooking. Each child in the family was tasked with preparing one meal a week.[1]

After Boeing transferred Armandino in 1975, the Batali family moved to Spain, where they embraced the sites and traditions of their temporary home and where Batali discovered his insatiable desire for all things edible. As Bill Buford, Batali's biographer and volunteer "kitchen slave," reports, "For Batali, Madrid, in the years after dictator Francisco Franco's death, was a place of exhilarating license: bars with no minimum wage, hash hangouts, and flirtations with members of the world's oldest profession."[2]

In 1978 Batali returned to the United States to attend Rutgers University in New Jersey. Despite an early desire to be a Spanish banker, he soon settled on a joint degree in Spanish theater and business management. After being expelled from his dormitory for an alleged drug sale,[3] he remained in school and eventually found a job at the student stomping ground Stuff Yer Face, where he worked his way up from a dishwasher to a line cook and finally to a pizza maker. According to lore, Batali could throw the most pies in an hour. Finally, in his junior year, at a career conference dotted with corporate recruiters, Batali realized he would never succeed as a banker. After graduation in 1982 and years of prodding from his mother and grandmother, he decided that cooking would be his life's work and returned to Europe to attend the Cordon Bleu in London.

During the day, Batali studied classical technique; at night, he tended bar at a small pub on King's Road in Chelsea. When Marco Pierre White was hired to run the fancy dining room in the back of the pub, Batali quit the Cordon Bleu and began four months of grueling labor as White's kitchen serf. Known for his brutal temper, White made titanic demands and the relationship soured after a short four months. Despite their tempestuous relationship, Batali learned about the value of presentation and the need for athletic speed and stamina in the restaurant business.

After stints at college and cooking school and in kitchens, Batali finally decided to get the education he wanted by touring the great restaurants in Europe, mastering crafts on the job rather than in the classroom. No matter how grotesque the task he had to do, such as "squeezing duck carcasses for twelve hours," he felt he was on the right track. "You learn by working in the kitchen," he said, "not by going to cookery school. That's how it's done."[4]

In 1985, Batali finished his whirlwind tour of famed European kitchens and settled down in the Haight-Ashbury district of San Francisco at the "height of the California food revolution."[5] After an unfortunate stint at a catering firm, Batali became the sous-chef at the San Francisco Clift Hotel. During the day he worked as a cook and at night he ate like one, sampling and discussing the best of what California food gurus like Alice Waters and Jeremiah Tower had to offer. In California, Batali "first met chefs who wanted to talk about their craft."[6] From these California chefs he cultivated a taste for acidity. "Since then my food has always been on the upper edge of acidity," he has commented. "I tune things up with acidity, I fix things with acidity."[7] After two years at Clift, at the young age of 27, he was given his own restaurant, La Marina, at the Biltmore Santa Barbara.

Return to Italy

However, after only 12 months in Santa Barbara, Batali quit his job and the state of California and phoned his father. Bored by his cuisine and exhausted by too many late nights spent in gluttonous abundance, he wanted to leave the country and master the recipes of his beloved grandmother, Leonetta Merlino Batali. He asked his father whether he knew of a place where he could learn to cook true Italian food and receive room and board. Armandino, through his Boeing connections, found La Volta, a seemingly modest trattoria in Borgo Capanne, a small village between Bologna and Florence.[8]

Batali arrived in Italy in 1989 and lived in a small room above La Volta for three years, studying recipes that had been in the Valdiserri family for hundreds of years. Under their tutelage, Batali learned how to roll and craft homemade pasta, to master the various sauces, and, perhaps, most importantly, to appreciate the value of local, fresh, and seasonal ingredients. In Borgo Capanne, he scavenged for local mushrooms, berries, and greens; traveled across the region to sample the best *prosciutto*, cuts of beef, and *vino*; and lived the philosophy he so often preaches: "What grows together goes together."[9]

According to Armandino, "Italy changed Mario. . . . It made him serious; it gave him his culture."[10] La Volta and Italy gave Batali a culinary tradition that was Italian in both form and content. It was a philosophy that prized land, seasons, and the time that went into cooking something right. Batali came to appreciate why Italian staples like *Prosciutto di Parma* or *Pecorino Romano* were prized in their region of origin: because they were the best the land and the people could produce together. He felt emboldened to adapt Italian cuisine to an American landscape, replete with its own local ingredients and culinary history.

RESTAURANTS

In 1992, with an invigorated sense of self, a coherent culinary philosophy, and an irrepressible drive to succeed, Batali left Italy. At the age of 32, with "two hundred dollars, a duffle bag, and a guitar," he arrived in New York City ready to cook.[11]

Batali's career as a New York chef began at an old New York mainstay, Rocco. A college friend from Rutgers, Arturo Sighinolfi, hired Batali to take over the restaurant upon the elder Sighinolfi's retirement.[12] Rocco was the kind of Sunday evening restaurant renowned for its Italian American staples and comforting consistency. Batali's authentic, regional Italian recipes and penchant for experimentation were a poor fit. According to Buford, "The dishes Mario prepared in 1992 at the new Rocco read like episodes in an autobiography; each one is so intimately associated with a specific moment in Mario's life that the menu is more literary than culinary—cooking as memoir. Ravioli stuffed with brains and Swiss chard is his grandmother's recipe."[13] But whereas Batali's cooking dismayed most customers, it managed to charm his wife to be, Susan Cahn.

The Cahns, who own Coach farm and sell artisanal goat cheese, arrived at Rocco to celebrate their daughter Susan's birthday. The Batali family also had a special occasion that night, the birthday of Batali's mother, Marilyn. "The dinner didn't finish until three," reported Buford. "For Susi, it was a drunken, energetic blur of festivities, Mario's rushing back and forth from the kitchen, returning each time with a surprise—another course, another bottle of wine, another grappa, and, finally, an accordion, which his father played, leading everyone in Italian drinking songs."[14] The merriment continued, Batali and Susi got married in 1994, and they now have two sons, Benno and Leo.

Despite that auspicious evening, Rocco's loyal customer base rapidly declined. Arturo and Batali had a less than amicable split and Batali soon opened a restaurant where he could define the tenor of the cuisine and the expectations of the diners. In 1993, he opened Pó with his late-night compadre from San Francisco, waiter-turned-restaurateur Steven Crane. Tucked into a charming West Village street, Pó, from the outset, became a favorite late-night haunt of New York chefs and downtown artists. With a six-course tasting menu for only $29 and a menu filled with unexpected seasonal delicacies, Pó beguiled *New York Times* food critic Eric Asimov, who published a rave review in 1993 that highlighted Batali's unusual flare for Italian cuisine: "Take the pasta, for example. Instead of bland linguine with white clam sauce, a sacrosanct dish most restaurants do not tamper with, Pó's version includes tiny Manila clams, bits of crunchy pancetta, and a jolt of hot chili pepper, creatively breathing new life into this staple. Or try the terrific white-bean ravioli, triangular pockets of pasta infused with tomato, stuffed with savory mashed Tuscan beans and drizzled with balsamic vinegar and butter. Or tagliatelle dotted with black pepper in a delicious sauce of eggplant and spicy chili, made fragrant with mint. Or spinach spaghettini, with tender little shrimp, olive oil and garlic. You get the idea."[15] Three years after Batali became a television chef the lines outside the restaurant became so long that he reluctantly sold Pó to his partner Crane.

In 1998, Batali opened Babbo, again in Greenwich Village. With his new partner, veteran restaurateur and wine maker Joseph Bastianich, son of famed Italian chef Lidia Bastianich, Batali took his culinary attitude to unprecedented heights. Together they revamped one of New York's classic restaurants, the Coach House, into a cozy Italian restaurant where high-end food is complemented by casual attitudes and never-ending rock music. In 1998, *The New York Times* awarded Babbo a coveted three stars. The restaurant critic Ruth Reichl noted that "Mario Batali and Joseph Bastianich are not playing it safe. They have taken one of the city's most beloved old restaurants, the Coach House on Waverly Place, and completely gutted its interior. . . . Mr. Batali's menu isn't safe, either. He has loaded it with dishes that Americans are not supposed to like. Fresh anchovies and warm testa (that's headcheese) are among the appetizers, and pastas include bucatini with octopus, and ravioli filled with beef cheeks and topped with crushed squab livers. . . . My all-time favorite is a ravioli that tastes like clouds wrapped in tender sheets sprinkled with fragrant flowers of sage and thyme. The clouds, in this case, turn out to be calf's brains, and they are extraordinary." In addition to the rave reviews, Babbo received the Best New Restaurant Award from the James Beard Foundation.

In 2004, the *New York Times* critic Frank Bruni returned to Babbo to see whether Reichl's original review still held. After sampling the full array of Batali's carnivorous comestibles, Bruni gushed, "Some restaurants revel in exquisite subtleties, while others simply go for the gut. Babbo, blessedly, hangs with the latter crowd. . . . Mr. Batali is not much for restraint (except with prices, which are reasonable for food of this quality). The warm lamb's tongue, my favorite appetizer, has a delightfully funky flavor on its own, but Mr. Batali dressed it with a black truffle vinaigrette and doesn't stop there. Upon the summit of the dish teeters a three-minute egg; tap it and the ruptured yolk runs like lava down the slopes of the meat, bringing extra excitement to the landscape." Batali's cuisine was luscious, bold, and consistently attractive to epicureans across the globe. In line with Reichl and Bruni's assessment, The *New York Michelin Guide* has consistently awarded Babbo a coveted one star.

Tasting Menus from Babbo, Winter 2010

PASTA TASTING MENU

Black Tagliatelle *with Parsnips and Pancetta*
Chardonnay "Strade del Sole," Michelotti 2007
"Casunzei" *with Poppy Seeds*
Colli Scaligeri Soave "Vigne della Brà," Filippi 2006
Garganelli *with "Funghi Trifolati"*
Cesanese di Olevano Romano "Corte alla Luna," Proietti 2007
Domingo's Pyramids *with "Passato di Pomodoro"*
Ronco dei Roseti, Vigne di Zamó 1997
Pappardelle Bolognese
Taurasi Riserva "Radici," Mastroberardino 1999
"Castagnaccio"
"Le Passule," Librandi 2007
Chocolate "al Diavolo"
"Sibilla Appeninica," Le Caniette 1999
Tyrolean Carrot and Poppyseed Cake *with Olive Oil and Orange Gelato*
Passito di Pantelleria, Abraxas 2003

TRADITIONAL TASTING MENU

Duck Bresaola *with Parmigiano and Aceto Manodori*
Colline Teatine, Di Sipio 2007
Pappardelle *with Chanterelles and Thyme*
"Vespa Bianco," Bastianich 2007
Duck Tortelli *with "Sugo Finto"*
Breganze Merlot, Gastaldía 2003
Pork Tenderloin *with Pumpkin Fregula and Black Truffle Vinaigrette*
Morellino di Scansano "I Perazzi," La Mozza 2007
Coach Farm's Finest *with Fennel Honey*
Franciacorta Blanc des Blanc, Cavalleri NV
"Fico in Mosto"
"Nanerone," Piandibugnano 2006
Chocolate "Tartufino"
"Ninive," Ermes Pavese NV
Lavender Honey Spice Cake *with Sweet Potato Gelato*
Moscato Dolce "Cuvèe Speciale," Canevari NV

Despite his sprawling food empire today, Batali still considers Babbo his culinary home and the centerpiece of his particular style of rustic Italian cooking. According to Bruni, "Babbo remains his throne, from which he bestows his most lavish favors and intense flavors upon an appropriately grateful dining public."

In 1999, Batali opened Lupa, a casual Roman-style trattoria that became yet another downtown New York culinary sensation. Glowing reviews matched impossibly long lines at this hot spot of pared-down Italian dishes. "Antipasti, though stripped down to the basics, are anything but artless," notes food critic Daniel Young. "A delicately bound headcheese of octopus and preserved lemon collapses upon fork contact. Citrus-curing blunts the fishiness but not the character of iridescent sardines dangling over a pilaf-like pillow of cracked wheat. And cacciatorini sausage you could nibble on all afternoon is sided with artichokes and anchovy vinaigrette."

Batali did not stop there. In 2000, he helped open the southern-Italian-style seafood restaurant Esca. Otto Enoteca Pizzeria soon followed. Modeled after an Italian train station, Otto's décor, pizza, and extended wine list seduced its visitors. In 2003, Batali finally turned his attention back to Spain with Bar Jamon and Casa Mono, two adjacent restaurants in the Flatiron District of New York devoted to tapas, Catalan fare, and other Spanish specialties. With their substantial *vino* and *carne* lists, Batali's Spanish ventures proved another win. He went on to open the French restaurant Bistro Du Vent, which never inspired the same adoration as his Italian and Spanish eateries, and restaurants in Las Vegas, Los Angeles, and even Port Chester, New York. By 2003, Batali had officially progressed from chef to restaurateur, and in 2009 he claimed a partnership in 15 restaurants nationwide. He even joined forces to open a wine store, purchase a vineyard in Italy, and launch his own kitchen products.

From casual eateries like Pizzeria Mozza, where an average pizza costs $13, to luxury outposts, like New York's Del Posto, where diners can share a rack of veal for $240, Batali's vast culinary empire runs the full edible and economic gambit.

TELEVISION SHOWS

Batali's success as a restaurateur is due in no small part to his fame as a Food Network star. Julia Child's popular 1960s television show launched the era of the chef cum television star. In 1995, a modest article on a "cabal of chefs hanging out at a downtown restaurant," published in *The New York Observer*, transformed Batali from a hero of downtown bohemia to an all-American celebrity. An office assistant at the recently launched Food Network brought the *Observer* article to the attention of Jonathan Lynne, the head of development. Lynne recognized the appeal of watching "a group of friends hanging out together," phoned Batali, and after a lunch of "tortelloni with sage and butter, served with wilted endives," invited him to be a TV star. On January 8, 1996, the program *Molto Mario* appeared on television. Within three weeks, Batali's flaming crop of hair and robust frame were recognizable to a growing audience of American food enthusiasts. Along with Emeril Lagasse, he became one of the Food Network's first signature chefs. *Time* magazine reported that Batali "turned out to be an incredibly productive TV cook, able to shoot as many as eight back-to-back episodes of Molto Mario. . . . Because of his speed, Batali was able to deliver 517 episodes of the show in just six seasons of shooting."[16]

Molto Mario was an instant sensation and provided a platform for Batali to evangelize about the theory of regional Italian cooking: Ingredients must be fresh, local, and put together with an attention to balance. The Food Network's short biography of Batali notes that "Mario Batali believes that olive oil is as precious as gold, shorts are acceptable attire for every season and food, like most things, is best when left to its own simple beauty."[17] Each episode opened with Batali ribbing his guests and pronouncing the menu in exuberant Italian. To an American audience, his dishes contained unfamiliar ingredients, combinations, and techniques. In one episode, "Simple Harvest Meal," Batali matched *sformato di cardi* with *bracioli di vitelo* and *insalata di finocchio e olive* to highlight the cuisine of Campagna. First, exposed his audience to the Italian vegetable cardoons, then to the technique of cooking the *sformato* pudding, then to picking the right cut of veal, tying a butcher's knot, and finally correctly chopping a fennel. Batali closed each show with a humble gesture of thanks and a winning smile. With his generous form, gregarious persona, and eagerness to teach, he was a perfect television personality, someone everyone wanted as a favorite uncle or a best friend.

The Food Network also refined Batali's wild guy image. His late nights, excessive drinking, and gluttonous tendencies were carefully given a patina of all-American charm. Even his standard outfit of orange Crocs and shorts became aligned with a down-to-earth personality that had a dash of harmless eccentricity. From *Molto Mario*, Batali went on to star in the travel shows *Mario Eats Italy* and *Ciao America*, food tourism shows set in Italy and the United States, respectively. In one episode, Batali returned to his beloved Borgo Capanne for chestnut season.[18] Yet these travel shows never inspired the following of *Molto Mario*, and it seemed that Batali's tenure at the Food Network might be at a close—that is, until he suddenly rose up as the unbeatable *Iron Chef*. Buford noted, "When Mario appeared as a contestant on a spin-off, *Iron Chef America*—fast, spontaneous, dazzling, improvisational, both large and larger than life—network executives realized that they'd *finally* found a venue for him: no script, just a stage."[19] With *Iron Chef America*, Batali and his brand unzipped. Eschewing the sedate all-American chef beloved by scripted television, Batali finally came out as himself, a chef with a boisterous grin, ample skills, and an almost magical ability to turn any ingredient into a decadent bite. Batali was the great American "peddler of excess,"[20] seducing America with his winning combination of childlike awe and bad-boy desires.

With a little more gusto and a little more *lardo*, Batali dominates Kitchen Stadium, the arena where *Iron Chef America* stages its athletic culinary contests. His larger-than-life personality adds pizzazz to what is otherwise a calm, collected, and graceful performance. As Buford noted, "In the kitchen Mario is different. He is no longer Molto Mario. . . . In most situations, Mario has the impish look of a class clown, slightly mischievous, teasing: Whatever he's going to do next, it's going to charm you, and he knows that it will. In the kitchen, there's no clown act, no clown mask, and no charm. His face is relaxed, transparent."[21] With an encyclopedic knowledge of almost every edible offered and an ability to lovingly describe the regional origins and whimsical inspirations of his dishes, Batali is hard to beat. While some chefs have come close, few have outmaneuvered him in Kitchen Stadium.

The vigorous, improvisational, and gutsy performance demanded in *Iron Chef America* fit neatly into Batali's evolving brand. In 2005, he pushed his athletic kitchen persona to a new level by becoming NASCAR's "superchef." Then in 2009 he continued his tradition of cars and comestibles with the eat-and-drink-everything-you-can documentary *On the Road Again: Spain* with actress Gwyneth Paltrow. No longer tamed, Batali came out as the edgy, rustic glutton that every American wants to eat with.

In 2005, Batali addressed the graduating class of Rutgers University, where he "urged the graduates to 'get a brand.'" "'For better or worse,'" he said, "'I've got a brand. . . . The orange clogs, the ponytail, the attitude, my seeming fluency in Italian—it's instantly recognizable. But what matters to me is, it's not fake.'"[22] Batali's brand is so successful because it has grown into an accurate and full expression of his personality. "Pay attention to the truth," he warned students. "It's not an intellectual thing. It's a gut thing. My truth is that I love real, honest, passionate, intense experiences. Experiences that don't apologize for themselves or claim to be something they aren't."[23] In his life, in his shows, and, most of all, in his cooking, Batali looks beyond what is complex, overdone, and counterfeit to locate the simple perfection of what is raw and pure.

COOKBOOKS

Batali's cookbooks express his wide culinary range and flair for entertaining. They include *Simple Italian Food: Recipes from My Villages* (1998); *Holiday Food: Family Recipes for the Festive Time of Year* (2000); *The Babbo Cookbook* (2002); *Molto Italiano: 327 Simple Italian Recipes to Cook at Home* (2005); *Mario Tailgates NASCAR Style* (2006); *Dolce Italiano: Desserts from the Babbo Kitchen* (2007); *Italian Grill* (2008); and *Spain: A Culinary Road Trip* (2008). These works combine five-course Italian meals, evenings of Spanish tapas, American grill parties, and even NASCAR tailgates. In the midst of these exuberant recipes, Batali articulates and sustains his unique philosophy. Ingredients should be "perfectly pristine," "combined sensibly," and "cooked properly."[24] It is not about following an Italian or a Spanish recipe perfectly but rather about understanding the supremacy of local ingredients and integrating Italian or Spanish flavor combinations and techniques. In his opening to *The Babbo Cookbook*, Batali says, "Like Italian cooks, we use locally grown products with a near fanaticism to express the flavor of our dirt, our wind, our rain."[25]

AWARDS AND HONORS

Batali's hard work, innovation, and culinary acumen have been amply rewarded. In 1998 *GQ Magazine* named him "Man of the Year" within the chef category. In 1999 the James Beard Foundation deemed Babbo "Best New Restaurant." In 2001 Batali received "Who's Who of Food and Beverage in America," the lifetime achievement award from D'Artagnan Cervena. In 2002, the James Beard Foundation awarded him "Best Chef: New York City." In 2005, Babbo received the Ivy Award and Batali the Outstanding Chef in America Award from the James Beard Foundation. In 2006, the James Beard Foundation deemed Batali's cookbook *Molto Italiano* the "Best International Cookbook." And, in 2008, the James Beard Foundation granted Batali and Bastianich the prize "Outstanding Restaurateur."

CONCLUSION

Batali and his growing empire have convinced professional gourmands and amateur home cooks that Italian food is equally suited to elegant fine dining and rustic home-prepared feasts. Fans can consume an array of Batali products. They can savor his cuisine at one of 15 restaurants nationwide, enjoy his penchant for excess on the Food Network and PBS, and purchase his cast iron cookware at stores nationwide. Batali's gutsy, unrestrained, and inventive kitchen persona continues to transform American eating habits, inspiring a devoted gaggle of foodies to wonder—what will he cook next?

NOTES

1. John Cloud, "Super Mario!" *Time*, April 2, 2006.

2. Bill Buford, "The Secret of Excess: How a Life Became Cooking," *The New Yorker* (August 19, 2002).

3. Bill Buford, *Heat: An Amateur's Adventures as Kitchen Slave, Line Cook, Pasta-maker, and Apprentice to a Dante-quoting Butcher in Tuscany* (New York: Alfred A. Knopf, 2006), 7.

4. Buford, "The Secret of Excess."

5. Buford, "The Secret of Excess."

6. Mario Batali quoted in Buford, "The Secret of Excess."

7. Mario Batali quoted in Buford, "The Secret of Excess."

8. Bill Buford, "The Secret of Excess."

9. Mario Batali quoted in Gwyneth Paltrow, Mario Batali, et al., *On the Road Again: Spain* (New Video Group, 2008).

10. Buford, "The Secret of Excess."

11. Buford, "The Secret of Excess."

12. Buford, "The Secret of Excess."

13. Buford, "The Secret of Excess."

14. Buford, *Heat,* 52.

15. Eric Asimov, "$25 and Under," *The New York Times* (August 20, 1993).

16. Cloud, "Super Mario!"

17. "Bio," Food Networks Hosts and Chefs: Mario Batali, http://www.food network.com/mario-batali/bio/index.html (August 30, 2009).

18. "A Visit to Borgo Capanne," *Mario Eats Italy,* http://www.foodnetwork.com/mario-eats-italy/a-visit-to-borgo-capanne/index.html (August 30, 2009).

19. Buford, *Heat,* 144.

20. See Cloud, "Super Mario!" and Buford, *Heat.*

21. Buford, "The Secret of Excess."

22. Cloud, "Super Mario!"

23. Mario Batali quoted in Sam Dillon, "Commencement Speeches; War on Terror Dominates Talks Given at Graduations," *The New York Times* (June 12, 2005).

24. Mario Batali, *Simple Italian Food: Recipes from My Villages* (New York: Clarkson Potter, 1998).

25. Mario Batali, *The Babbo Cookbook* (New York: Clarkson Potter, 2002).

FURTHER READING

Batali, Mario. *The Babbo Cookbook.* New York: Clarkson Potter, 2002.

Batali, Mario. *Dolce Italiano: Desserts from the Babbo Kitchen.* New York: W.W. Norton, 2007.

Batali, Mario. *Holiday Food: Family Recipes for the Festive Time of Year.* New York: Clarkson Potter, 2000.

Batali, Mario. *Mario Tailgates NASCAR Style.* New York: HarperCollins, 2006.

Batali, Mario. *Molto Italiano: 327 Simple Italian Recipes to Cook at Home.* New York: HarperCollins, 2005.

Batali, Mario. *Simple Italian Food: Recipes from My Villages.* New York: Clarkson Potter, 1998.

Batali, Mario, Judith Sutton, and Beatriz Da Costa. *Italian Grill.* New York: Ecco, 2008.

Batali, Mario, Judith Sutton, and Beatriz Da Costa. Bio. http://www.foodnetwork.com/mario-batali/index.html

Batali, Mario, Judith Sutton, and Beatriz Da Costa. Official Web site. http://www.mariobatali.com/

Batali, Mario, Gwyneth Paltrow, Moses Saman, et al. *Spain: A Culinary Road Trip.* New York: Ecco, 2008.

Buford, Bill. *Heat: An Amateur's Adventures as Kitchen Slave, Line Cook, Pasta-maker, and Apprentice to a Dante-quoting Butcher in Tuscany.* New York: Alfred A. Knopf, 2006.

Buford, Bill. "The Pasta Station: How Can Something Simple Be So Difficult?" *The New Yorker,* September 6, 2004.

Buford, Bill. "The Secret of Excess: How a Life Became Cooking." *The New Yorker*, August 19, 2002.

Cloud, John. "Super Mario!" *Time*, April 2, 2006.

Pasternack, David, Ed Levine, Christopher Hirsheimer, and Mario Batali. *The Young Man & the Sea: Recipes & Crispy Fish Tales from Esca.* New York: Artisan, 2007.

VIDEOS

Batali, Mario. *Molto Mario.* Food Network, 2000, 2001, 2003.

Paltrow, Gwyneth, Mario Batali, et al. *On the Road Again: Spain.* New Video Group, 2008.

Stewart, Martha, Mario Batali, et al. *Martha's Guests. Master Chefs.* Warner Home Video, 2006, 1993.

Tamara Mann

American chef, author, and food critic James Beard in October 1973. (AP/Wide World Photos)

James Beard

James Beard was a celebrity chef, master chef, prolific cookbook author, teacher, and television host who was highly influential in advocating better American cooking. Julia Child, who called him "the Dean of American Cuisine," viewed him as a "living encyclopedia of culinary lore and history" and as a teacher who loved his work, people, gossip, and above all good food.[1] When American foodways collapsed in the post–World War II era, he stood as a food guru with the ability to bring people from all areas of food together in an intellectual and hedonistic celebration of quintessentially American cuisine. During the 1960s and 1970s, his western American upbringing with everyday food served as the basis for what is now referred to as the American food revolution, and his influential teaching, mentoring, writing, television shows, and network building sparked the energy of many of the great food pioneers. Included in his mentoring circle were numerous food greats, including Julia Child and Craig Claiborne. Above all, he was a celebrity chef before there was such a category. His friend Joe Baum said of Beard, "It's hard to separate myth and legend, but with Jim I think it's not necessary. There was elegance in all that lusty strange self-irony—and maleness that made it all right for men to cook."[2]

Although Beard was famous as a master chef, as a teacher he often reached out to everyday cooks. He embraced educational tensions in the classroom and always enjoyed the first day of new classes when students challenged each other for instructor recognition. He wrote, "The students eye each other, and there is a chill in the air." Instead of feeling pressured, he encouraged students to have fun.[3] In the foreword to one of his books, he wrote, "In my twenty-five years of teaching I have tried to make people realize that cooking is primarily fun and that the more they know about what they are doing, the more fun it is."[4] Although he appreciated good food, he was unpretentious in his approach to cooking. Evan Jones, his biographer, wrote, "The word 'fun' came as close as any to defining Jim's notions about dealing with food. His strength was that he was both well informed and amusing in person."[5] Students learned not to make cooking too complex

---

There is absolutely no substitute for the best. Good food cannot be made of inferior ingredients masked with high flavor. It is true thrift to use the best ingredients available and to waste nothing.
—James Beard, *The Fireside Cook Book: A Complete Guide to Fine Cooking for Beginner and Expert.* New York: Simon and Schuster, 1949, p. 13

I'm going to break one of the rules of the trade here. I'm going to tell you some of the secrets of improvisation. Just remember—it's always a good idea to follow the directions exactly the first time you try a recipe. But from then on, you're on your own.
—James Beard, *The Best of Beard: Great Recipes from a Great Cook.* New York: Western Publishing Company, 1974, p. 6

In a time when serious cooking meant French cooking, Beard was quint-essentially American, a Westerner whose mother ran a boardinghouse, a man who grew up with hotcakes and salmon and meatloaf in his blood. A man who was born a hundred years ago on the other side of the country, in a city, Portland, that at the time was every bit as cosmopolitan as, say, Allegheny PA.

—Mark Bittman, from Mark Bittman and James Beard,
*James Beard on Food: The Best Recipes and Kitchen Wisdom from
the Dean of American Cooking.* 3rd ed. New York: Bloomsbury, 2007, p. viii

---

and difficult, to use good-quality, fresh, and often simple ingredients, and to not be afraid of tweaking a recipe to suit the cook's needs. Beard helped bring novice and professional cooks alike to believe in themselves and good cuisine.

EARLY LIFE

Food and Theater

Beard was born on May 5, 1903, in Portland, Oregon. As an only child, he relished the attention he received from his mother, Elizabeth Beard, who ran a hotel and boarding house where she also served as cook. His father, John Beard, processed paperwork as a political appointee at a custom house. His parents did not have a happy marriage, and Beard noted in his memoir that his mother's feelings for her husband were not strong and they lessened when she learned of his debts after their wedding. Elizabeth Beard later paid off her husband's loans, and she never openly admitted her disappointment in the relationship. She did, however, dote on her son and taught him a love for food and cooking.

Like many great chefs and food impresarios who draw on their background, Beard was heavily influenced by his early years in the rich food-ways of the Pacific Northwest. His early love of regional fruits, fish, and nuts was the basis for his later work. He also learned to appreciate a variety of foods. In one childhood story, he recalled finding an onion and eating it like an apple. In another, he traced his love of chicken jelly and his hatred of milk to experiences at age three. Those feelings lingered: "I am still revolted when I see people drinking milk with a good meal."[6] Beard later noted of his childhood, "The Oregon coast left [its] mark on me, and no place on earth, with the exception of Paris, has done as much to influence my professional life."[7]

Beard's culinary education included many influences from his mother and household helpers. Elizabeth Beard was a strong woman with high standards, and in one biographical anecdote, James reminisced about a nursemaid who went to the market to buy a piece of meat. After the butcher learned that the package was for Elizabeth Beard, he asked to replace the meat with a better cut: "For God's sake, give me that package. If I sent that to her, she'd kill me."[8] Beard's food education also benefited from the household cook and his unofficial caretaker Jue Let, who exposed the young Beard to Chinese cooking. In later years, he wrote in the introduction to *The Fireside Cook Book* (1949), "It is to the highly developed civilization of the Chinese that we owe our greatest cookery debt."[9]

Beginning in 1921, Beard briefly attended Reed College in Portland. It has been noted that poor grades led to his dropping out of school in 1922, but other sources indicate that college officials dismissed Beard for his homosexual activities. In his later years Beard recalled in his memoir, "By the time I was seven, I knew that I was gay."[10] Regardless, the antihomosexual position of the university left him bitter over his treatment and subsequent dismissal. The anger softened over the years, and eventually he accepted recognition awards from the college.

With college seemingly out of the question, Beard journeyed to France in 1923, where he supported himself by traveling with a theatrical troupe and took advantage of opportunities to study voice and theater. After a few years he tired of this lifestyle and longed for home, and in 1927 he returned to the United States, where he eventually settled in New York City. Here he attempted to further his acting career and even tried his hand at singing but quickly realized that his size and looks precluded him from being cast in plays. Without success in the theater, he turned to cooking and in 1937, with his friend Bill Rhodes, opened a catering service called Hors d'Oeuvre that specialized in cocktail food, a popular trend at the time. In 1940 he published his first book, *Hors d'Oeuvre and Canapés,* and also lectured, taught, and wrote articles about his newfound food passions. Although World War II and rationing brought an end to the catering company in 1940, Beard's passion for food did not ebb and proved to be the roots of a new career.

COOKBOOKS

In 1942 Beard wrote *Cooking It Outdoors*, a groundbreaking book that was one of the first to look at food from a truly culinary perspective. The text piqued the interest of a hungry audience, and Beard quickly gained a following of both professional cooks and home cooks. In 1949, he wrote one of his best-known works, *The Fireside Cook Book*, in which he wrote, "Do not neglect to take advantage of new developments in the growing, shipping, preserving, and cooking of food. Take time both to cherish the old and to investigate the new."[11] He went on to write and coauthor a total of 22 books on numerous culinary subjects, many of which became timeless classics. Beard's dedication to good or gourmet food became enmeshed with the idea that quality cuisine is a timeless practice. Two decades later, when he updated his book *Hors d'Oeuvre and Canapés,* he noted that few changes were needed. *Publishers Weekly* supported his philosophy when it noted, "More than any other author of cookbooks, perhaps, Beard had introduced Americans to gourmet food, though he says he dislikes the word 'gourmet' and wishes he could invent another word for imaginative, well-cooked meals. He favors what he calls a 'narrative type of recipe,' and he writes in a rather chatty style."[12]

As the United States entered World War II, Beard tried to get into the different branches of military service, but his age stood in the way. Not to be deterred by this roadblock, he turned to his food passion as a means to support the troops and his nation and began setting up canteens for the United Seamen's Service in Puerto Rico, Rio de Janeiro, Marseilles, and Panama. Beard found this enterprise a challenge, stating, "I have always felt that food in the Caribbean is perhaps the worst in the world, and this experience did nothing to change my opinion."[13] This opinion remained the same in later years as well.

After the war and throughout the 1950s, Beard continued to devote his time to cooking and writing. His culinary articles for women's magazines, including *Woman's Day, Gourmet*, and *House & Garden*, furthered his name recognition, and many began to see him as an American food guru. During this period Beard established himself as an expert: "His knowledge of European cuisines was as good as or better than that of the few other people writing about food. Most were entrenched home economists who were taught that they must have a scientific approach to food, that food wasn't supposed to be fun."[14] Because writing alone did not financially support him, Beard also managed the restaurant Lucky Pierre's on Nantucket for a summer. This experience was as close as he would ever come to running his own restaurant. However, for most of his life he served as a consultant to restaurateurs interested in gourmet menus and helped them select the best locations for new establishments.

TELEVISION SHOWS

Beard spent much of his life lamenting the loss of his dream career in the theater, and so in 1946 he jumped at the opportunity to work with the new television format. Most people remember Julia Child as the queen of French cooking because of her television show *The French Chef* and her cookbook *Mastering the Art of French Cooking* (1961). Yet it was Beard who prepared the American audience to accept new food ideas. His brief career as a television chef helped bridge his two loves, acting and cooking. His 15-minute NBC program, sponsored by the Borden Company, was called *I Love to Eat*. Like many of the small screen programs of the period, it quickly became popular. "Unlike the purely instructional shows that were more prevalent at the time, Beard's was meant to be entertaining to watch, perhaps enough to capture the attention of even those whose only relationship to the stove was passing it on the way to the refrigerator or some of those fellows who claimed cooking was a hobby."[15]

Despite his training as an actor, however, Beard did not appear comfortable on camera and clashed with the producers. Thus, the program did not last long. By Beard's own admission, he possessed "until I was about forty-five, I guess a really violent temper."[16] What did continue was his interest in instructing others on how to cook.

OTHER ENDEAVORS

Cooking School

At this point in his life Beard shifted his career goals to become a food educator, writer, and mentor. From his earliest cooking years he had always focused on food education, and it was logical that his next move in 1955 included the establishment of his New York City James Beard Cooking School. His role as one of the first chefs to introduce French cooking to an American middle- and upper-class audience had made him eminently qualified for this endeavor. Yet, at the same time, he rejected the idea of American gourmet food and began loudly vocalizing his strong opinions about his favorite American recipes and his deep appreciation of home-style American cuisine. He quickly became known in food circles as a giant in the field, both literally and figuratively. As an adult, Beard stood 6 feet 2 inches tall and weighed more than 300 pounds. His career as an American food pioneer was in full swing.

Although the school project was a struggle for the first few years, it eventually became a success. The school's student body grew to include everyday cooks who had other daytime professions, hobbyists, and later food professionals. The weekly classes concluded with eating the meal prepared as part of the lesson along with a bottle of wine. Beard said of the school, "We have been attacked by one or two people for not being classic. We're not."[17] Like many business endeavors, the school faced a slow start, and to make ends meet Beard agreed to endorse the Green Giant Company with its canned and frozen food lines. Being a representative for industrial processed foods presented an ethical conundrum. It has been noted that Beard probably thought he was a "gastronomic whore" for endorsing this food, which was not fresh, local, or seasonal.[18] Nevertheless, Beard continued the endorsement because it was the only means to support his cooking school. This would not be the last of his corporate endorsements, all promulgated by a need for cash flow to pursue his food dreams.

Traveling, Teaching, and Advising

Beard also traveled the country training citizen cooks at women's clubs and civic events. Despite his success on the lecture circuit and his new culinary stature, he continued to have financial problems. His educational work and industry involvement did not pay, forcing him to fund his educational dream through further endorsements. Over the years, he attached his name to numerous other products and services, including Adolph's Meat Tenderizer and Planters Peanuts. He also endorsed nonfood corporations such as Air France and American Airlines. These corporate attachments resulted in criticism from many home and professional food enthusiasts. His defense was that he tested the products he endorsed and rejected many of the offers he received.[19] He not only endorsed products but was also involved in product development. For example, as a frequent adviser to the Green Giant Company, he helped to develop a butter sauce for packaging with peas and also created recipes to accompany other vegetables.[20]

Beard led the charge of the new American culinary revolution as an early pioneer throughout the 1950s and took advantage of changing and more experimental American tastes following World War II. The public and professionals alike raved about his new dishes and recipes for spaghetti carbonara, lobster à l'Americaine, potatoes Anna, and soufflé. Beard successfully transformed European dishes that he experienced abroad into American favorites. As his fame increased, his speaking and writing projects multiplied, and one of his cookbook coauthors, Helen Brown, believed that Beard was becoming "the foremost authority on cooking in the country."[21]

To further his personal food knowledge, Beard traveled widely and dined at restaurants internationally. At one such trip in 1961, he visited all the three-star restaurants and some smaller establishments in France. He then wrote about those he admired, such as L'Auberge de Pere Bise at Talloires, and those that failed to meet his standards, such as Robinson outside of Paris. He also critiqued restaurants at home, continuously lamenting the lack of quality, the dearth of trained chefs, and the use of substandard foods. In an effort to overcome this problem, he would throughout his life serve as a consultant to numerous American restaurants.

Beard experimented regularly with recipes to keep them fresh and updated with the newest in processes, cooking equipment, and taste trends. A good example is the lobster pizza recipe that he originally published in 1954 in *James Beard's Fish Cookery*. Twenty-five years later, he updated the recipe using a food processor and substituted processed lobster, which markets had just started carrying.[22] In another example of food experimentation, he introduced Americans to Cepes a la Cuisine de l'Enfant Barbie, a casserole-type dish with green vegetables, garlic, cod, and cheese that he created with Julia Child in her kitchen in Provence. Beard described the dish in this way: "Contrary to the Bordelaise fashion, we sliced the mushroom caps rather thinly and chopped the stems fairly coarsely and they were absolutely divine eating."[23] His experimentation also included exotic dishes that he had introduced as early as 1944 in his book *Fowl and Game Cookery*, which included recipes for squirrel and muskrat.

The exotic dishes were only part of Beard's culinary concerns. He was also a fan of farmers' markets, having visited them often as a child. He visited his first European farmers' market at age 19 when he traveled alone to Europe. As an adult, he sought them out when he traveled and enjoyed getting to know a country through its native fruits, vegetables, and nuts. In his memoir, he wrote, "No market is too small to captivate me. In each I discover new foods, new challenges."[24]

Those trips to the market led Beard to be an advocate for simple dishes. He advised cooks to take as much care with humble foods as they did with elaborate dishes and ambitious menus. For example, he respected a well-grilled hamburger, writing, "With some mustard or coarse pepper, this can be a succulent treat."[25] His books contain recipes with basic ingredients and techniques. For Beard even a simple potato could be a glorious experience, as he expressed in his 1964 book *Delights and Prejudices*: "Certainly a baked Idaho potato is a great gastronomic experience if it is rushed from oven to plate and then split, buttered and seasoned with freshly ground pepper and salt."[26]

One of Beard's greatest pleasures was cooking for the many friends he came to know and mentor over the years. He preferred a simple but elegant menu for a dinner of six to eight people, and when entertaining friends from abroad, he would prepare dishes that were not available in their home countries. For example, he planned a menu of clam bisque, made with canned clams from Oregon, and grilled beef with new potato and peas for friends visiting from England. The meal concluded with a skillet soufflé that was flambéed at the table.[27]

By the 1970s, Beard was being described as the "champion of American cuisine."[28] During that decade his syndicated newspaper column, "Beard on Food," greatly influenced many American food revolution pioneers. He continued to experiment with classic recipes and embraced the new convenience cooking trends that became popular as more women entered the workforce. It was a transitional time in the country, and some chefs were critical of the new shortcuts being offered. Beard was more accepting. "If we want to do it from scratch, we can. If we want to serve convenience foods which take little time, we can go that way."[29]

AWARDS AND HONORS

On January 21, 1985, Beard died at the age of 81 from a heart attack in his beloved New York City. His ashes were later scattered over the Gearhart, Oregon, beach where he played as a child. His influences on American foodways were duly noted in numerous obituaries in newspapers across the country. *The Los Angeles Times* described Beard as a "food authority, chef and columnist—and the acknowledged dean of American cooking who long ago declared this country's culinary independence from decades of European influence and pretension."[30] When he died, his reputation as a food household name continued, and several of his books are still in print. Beard's estate donated a small collection of his papers to the Fales Library and Special Collections at New York University.

After a request by Julia Child, Beard's New York house was dedicated as a place for chefs and their students to study, share, and mentor American food-ways as a way of continuing the tradition that Beard had established in his kitchen, in his writing and lecturing, and in his school. Later, a fund-raiser was held to buy the house from Reed College, and the James Beard Foundation opened at the Greenwich Village townhouse in November 1986. Every May, on Beard's birthday, the foundation gives out the prestigious James Beard Awards, which *Time* magazine described as the "Oscars of the food world."

James Beard's Cookbooks

Hors d'Oeuvre and Canapés, 1940; revised in 1963, 1985

Cook It Outdoors, 1941

Fowl and Game Cookery, 1944; retitled in 1979 as James Beard's Fowl and Game Bird Cookery, and in 1989 as Beard on Birds

The Fireside Cook Book: A Complete Guide to Fine Cooking for Beginner and Expert, 1949; retitled in 1982 as The Fireside Cookbook

Paris Cuisine, 1952, with coauthor Alexander Watt

The Complete Book of Barbecue & Rotisserie Cooking, 1954; retitled in 1958 as New Barbecue Cookbook, in 1966 as Jim Beard's Barbecue Cookbook, and in 1967 as James Beard's Barbecue Cookbook

Complete Cookbook for Entertaining, 1954

How to Eat Better for Less Money, 1954; revised in 1970

James Beard's Fish Cookery, 1954; retitled in 1976 and 1987 (paperback) as James Beard's New Fish Cookery

Casserole Cookbook, 1955

The Complete Book of Outdoor Cookery, 1955

The James Beard Cookbook, 1959; revised in 1961, 1970, 1987 (paper-back), 1996

Treasury of Outdoor Cooking, 1960

Delights & Prejudices: A Memoir with Recipes, 1964; revised in 1981, 1990

James Beard's Menus for Entertaining, 1965; revised in 1970, 1975, 1996, 2004 (paperback)

How to Eat (and Drink) Your Way through a French (or Italian) Menu, 1971

James Beard's American Cookery, 1972; revised in 1980, 1996 (paperback)

Beard on Bread, 1973; revised in 1995 (paperback)

James Beard Cooks with Corning, 1973

Beard on Food, 1974; revised in 2000, 2007

New Recipes for the Cuisinart Food Processor, 1976
James Beard's Theory and Practice of Good Cooking, 1977; revised in 1978, 1986, 1990
The New James Beard, 1981; revised in 1989
Beard on Pasta, 1983; retitled in 1995 as Beard on Pasta: A James Beard Cookbook
James Beard's Simple Foods, 1993
Love and Kisses and a Halo of Truffles, 1994, edited by John Ferrone
The James Beard Cookbooks, 1997, edited by John Ferrone
The Armchair James Beard, 1999, edited by John Ferrone

The foundation also hosts educational conferences, sponsors scholarships, and publishes *Beard House*, a quarterly magazine dedicated to the best in culinary journalism. Other foundation publications include the James Beard Foundation Restaurant Directory, which lists chefs who have cooked at the Beard House or raised funds for the house.

Beard's contribution to American culinary history continues. In Portland, the James Beard Public Market has been established on a property near Morrison Bridge as a way to recognize Beard's experiences as a child shopping in farmers' markets with his mother. When the 2009 film *Julie and Julia* brought Julia Child back into popular consciousness, *Time* magazine published a retrospective of top television chefs in which James Beard was featured prominently. Beard's legacy helped establish American cookery at a time when European dishes dominated the culinary world. He also was a pioneer in food television, setting the foundation for later celebrity chefs on the popular Food Network. *The New York Times* obituary used words such as innovator, experimenter, and missionary to describe Beard's influence on American home cuisine. The awards given in his name continue to be the highest honors in the field, his recipes have stood the test of time, and he continues to influence the next generation of cooks. His role as an icon of American cooking will continue to influence food enthusiasts and advocates for generations to come.

NOTES

1. James Beard, *Delights and Prejudices* (Philadelphia: Running Press Book Publishers, 1964), vii.

2. Evan Jones, *Epicurean Delights: The Life and Times of James Beard* (New York: Alfred A. Knopf, 1990), 214.

3. Beard, *Delights and Prejudices*, 210.

4. James Beard, *Theory and Practice of Good Cooking* (New York: Wing Books, 1977), vii.

5. Jones, *Epicurean Delights*, 141.

6. Beard, *Delights and Prejudices*, 2.

7. Jones, *Epicurean Delights,* 20.

8. Beard, *Delights and Prejudices,* 32–33.

9. James Beard, *The Fireside Cook Book* (New York: Simon and Schuster, 1949), 8.

10. James Beard, *A James Beard Memoir; The James Beard Celebration Cookbook,* ed. Barbara Kafka (William Morrow & Company, 1990), 24.

11. James Beard, *The Fireside Cook Book,* 13.

12. Jones, *Epicurean Delights,* 236.

13. Beard, *Delights and Prejudices,* 198.

14. Jones, *Epicurean Delights,* 141.

15. Kathleen Collins, *Watching What We Eat: The Evolution of Television Cooking Shows* (New York: Continuum Books, 2009), 27.

16. Beard, *A James Beard Memoir,* 20–21.

17. Beard, *Delights and Prejudices,* 209.

18. David Kamp, *The United States of Arugula: The Sun Dried, Cold-Pressed, Dark-Roasted, Extra Virgin Story of the American Food Revolution* (New York: · Broadway Books, 2006), 62–63.

19. Jones, *Epicurean Delights,* 314.

20. Jones, *Epicurean Delights,* 243.

21. James Beard, *Love and Kisses and a Halo of Truffles: Letters to Helen Evans Brown,* ed. John Ferrone (New York: Arcade Publishing, 1994), xi.

22. Jones, *Epicurean Delights,* 228.

23. Jones, *Epicurean Delights,* 265.

24. Beard, *Delights and Prejudices,* 40.

25. Beard, *Delights and Prejudices,* 176.

26. Beard, *Delights and Prejudices,* 43.

27. Beard, *Delights and Prejudices,* 214.

28. Jeanne Voltz, "James Beard Rolls with Culinary Punches," *The Los Angeles Times* (October 19, 1972).

29. Voltz, "James Beard Rolls."

30. Daniel Puzo, "James Beard, Dean of U.S. Cookery, Dies," *The Los Angeles Times* (January 24, 1985).

FURTHER READING

Beard, James. *The Fireside Cook Book.* New York: Simon and Schuster, 1949.

Beard, James. *Delights and Prejudices.* Philadelphia: Running Press Book Publishers, 1964.

Beard, James. *Love and Kisses and a Halo of Truffles: Letters to Helen Evans Brown,* ed. John Ferrone. New York: Arcade Publishing, 1994.

Beard, James. *Beard on Food: The Best Recipes and Kitchen Wisdom from the Dean of American Cooking.* New York: Bloomsbury, 2007.

Collins, Kathleen. *Watching What We Eat: The Evolution of Television Cooking Shows.* New York: Continuum Books, 2009.

James Beard Foundation http://www.jamesbeard.org

James Beard Papers at the Fales Library http://dlib.nyu.edu/findingaids/html/fales/beard.html

Jones, Evan. *Epicurean Delights: The Life and Times of James Beard.* New York: Alfred A. Knopf, 1990.

Kamp, David. *The United States of Arugula: The Sun Dried, Cold-Pressed, Dark-Roasted, Extra Virgin Story of the American Food Revolution.* New York: Broadway Books, 2006.

Puzo, Daniel. "James Beard, Dean of U.S. Cookery, Dies." *The Los Angeles Times.* January 24, 1985.

Voltz, Jeanne. "James Beard Rolls with Culinary Punches." *The Los Angeles Times.* October 19, 1972.

Kimberly Wilmot Voss
Victor W. Geraci

Anthony Bourdain, the owner and chef of Les Halles restaurant, sits at one of its tables in New York, December 19, 2001. (AP/Wide World Photos)

Anthony Bourdain

Anthony Bourdain is a chef and food writer who became famous after publishing the best-selling book *Kitchen Confidential: Adventures in the Culinary Underbelly* in 2000. Bourdain's candid, colorful language gave the world a glimpse into the seedy, sexy, and sometimes self-destructive life of a modern chef. This book led to Bourdain's career as a food and travel show host, first with his show *A Cook's Tour* on the Food Network and later with his show *Anthony Bourdain: No Reservations* on the Travel Channel. On *No Reservations*, he is filmed as he travels around the world eating expensive specialties, dirt-cheap street food, and other odd delicacies like a still-beating snake heart in Vietnam, all while sharing whatever is on his mind.

Bourdain's writing and shows have been called offensive and funny, truthful and insightful. His characteristic outspokenness has caused reporters to brand him as the "anticelebrity chef." Drinking, smoking, swearing, and ranting about whatever celebrity, chef, or person is annoying him at the moment, Bourdain breaks away from the standard celebrity chef/food show host model, where most chefs have memorable catchphrases and everything they taste is delicious. He prefers to be more honest and candid. He is not afraid to call Food Network star Emeril Lagasse names or to say that the gelatinous bird's nest soup

---

We flew to Curaçao, where we were met by a ResidenSea representative and soon got our first look at The World, an impressively sharp-looking version of the floating cities you see disgorging day-trippers all over the Caribbean.

During a tour, I learned that though The World may be a floating enclave of rich people who demand the very best, in this case, the rich eat a lot of frozen food. Until I saw a sushi chef hanging a fishing line off the far end of the putting green, I was staying away from the sushi bar, thank you very much.

When Nancy and I were summoned to meet with Stig, the safety officer, I told him that I'd be doing a lot of cooking. His face immediately took on a look of horror. He explained that at the first sign of smoke, our kitchen would automatically seal itself up behind Bond-like sliding fire doors that would emerge from tasteful concealment in the walls. Overhead sprinklers would discharge; an alarm would alert the bridge. Stig seemed like a nice man, but I did not want to see him wielding a fire extinguisher in his pajamas in the middle of the night as I stood with a scorched pan in my hand.

I decided to keep it simple. Steak and potatoes. Pan-seared entrecôte, perhaps, with a baked potato.

—Anthony Bourdain, "Cruise Ship Confidential," *Gourmet* 23 (September 2003): http://www.gourmet.com/ magazine/2000s/2003/09/cruiseship?currentPage=1

---

he just ate made him vomit. Colorful language and enthusiasm are key traits for Bourdain, and it is a personality that many people across the world have come to love. Bourdain has managed to use his popularity to speak out about causes he believes in, from the rights of Latin America kitchen workers to the delights of a maple bacon doughnut. He is known for the unique topics he covers and the passion he brings to his work.

EARLY YEARS

Childhood Adventures

Anthony Michael Bourdain was born on June 25, 1956, in New York City. His father was the late Pierre Bourdain, an executive in the classical music recording industry, and his wife, Gladys, was a stay-at-home mom who later worked as a copyeditor for *The New York Times*. Bourdain and his younger brother Christopher had a privileged upbringing in Leonia, New Jersey. His family would often take trips to the New Jersey shore and to the Bourdain family home in the south of France, which almost always included trips to the beach. He credits his father with his love of traveling, and both of his parents for his adventurous eating habits. One of Bourdain's earliest food memories was a yearly birthday ritual of his mother making him roast beef and York-shire pudding. He also remembers his parents taking him and his younger brother to New York to try new cuisines, such as Japanese food, but Bourdain claims he never paid much attention to the fact that his parents loved food so much.

Bourdain's parents' love of books encouraged the boy to feed his overactive imagination with comic books and pirate stories. As a defiant, intelligent, and well-read boy, Bourdain enjoyed adventures. He loved breaking the rules, whether he was setting off fireworks to blow up army men or sneaking off for a pilfered cigarette and wine in France. He reportedly was smart, angry, and articulate growing up, and he would often use his wide vocabulary to manipulate adults into giving him whatever he wanted.

On a family trip to Europe, the nine-year-old Bourdain tasted the first of several life-altering food experiences: vichyssoise, a cold soup of leek and potato. Up to this point he had never had anything but hot soup. The intense flavor of the soup combined with its cool temperature challenged his precon-ceptions of soup and made him realize that food could be more than just fuel for the body—it could be exciting.

Bourdain's second early gastronomic experience occurred when his parents left him and his brother locked in the car with comic books while they dined at the famous and expensive La Pyramide in France during the same trip. His parents had always included him when dining out despite his finicky eating habits, so this banishment warned him that picky eating could equal exclusion.

This event inspired him to be a more adventurous eater and led to another life-altering food experience on the trip: Bourdain was the only member of his family brave enough to eat a raw oyster on an oyster boat. When he saw how the raw oyster completely disgusted his younger brother, and even his adventurous parents, he had a revelation: By eating the oyster, he could both shock his brother and have a stronger stomach than his parents. These thoughts motivated him to eat the raw oyster, and he loved the salty, briny taste. That one experience taught Bourdain that food could cause people to have strong emotions: joy, motivation, shock, and power. His early understanding of food as a medium for other feelings would help inspire his kitchen career years later.

Entering the Kitchen

In 1973, Bourdain graduated from his New Jersey high school a year early to follow his love, Nancy Putkoski, to Vassar College. He lasted only two years at Vassar, where he skipped classes, drank too much, did drugs, and played practical jokes on his friends. Bourdain paints a distinct portrait of himself at that time in *Kitchen Confidential*: "I was—to be frank—a spoiled, miserable, narcissistic, self-destructive and thoughtless young lout, badly in need of a good ass-kicking."[1] In the summer, he joined his friends in Provincetown, Cape Cod, Massachusetts, where they helped him land his first real job as a dishwasher at a local restaurant. He eventually moved up to work on the line as a salad cook, and later as a fry cook and broiler cook.

Bourdain loved working with the other cooks, all of whom seemed like criminals with dirty mouths and drug problems. He enjoyed watching them put out 300 plates of food in one night without breaking a sweat. They would work long hours, smoke marijuana, and snort cocaine during and after work, and Bourdain admired their stamina. Casual sex with waitresses and customers also seemed to be the norm among the cooks, and this further convinced Bourdain that the kitchen was a fun place to be.

When the restaurant came under new ownership, Bourdain showed up to the interview feeling cocky, expecting to receive a good position in the kitchen. Part of the interview involved working a shift; however, Bourdain showed up overdressed in a suit instead of traditional chef clothing and could not keep up with the fast pace of the restaurant. His poor performance caused management to knock him down to prep cook (only one step above a dishwasher), which led to merciless mocking from the rest of the kitchen crew. Much like when his parents excluded him for being a picky eater, this experience inspired the defiant Bourdain to become a better chef. He quit Vassar and enrolled in the Culinary Institute of America (CIA), the premier American school for chefs, in Hyde Park, New York, in 1975.

Classes at the CIA were fairly easy for Bourdain given his previous kitchen experience. While the rest of his class made stock from scratch, he stayed true to his rebel character and made the best stock in class thanks to the powdered bouillon he smuggled in. When Bourdain heard that a few fellow classmates wanted to construct a sculpture of chocolate, marzipan, pastries, and cakes in homage to someone famous for graduation, he convinced the school to ban any food sculptures by suggesting one so over the top (a beef fat sculpture of baby Jesus and Mary) that they had to prevent others from going that far.

While attending school, Bourdain worked a weekend job at a West Village saloon in New York City. Here he polished his line skills and met one of his culinary mentors, a man he called Bigfoot but whom he has never officially identified. Bourdain admired Bigfoot because he inspired fear and loyalty among his staff. In a professional kitchen, a head chef has to watch out for many traps, including employees frequently quitting and vendors sending incorrect orders, both of which could easily affect profits. Bigfoot would work his employees hard but reward them when they were just about to break. He would scrutinize every food order that came in and wreak havoc on any vendor who brought him the wrong food. Bourdain called this management style the Bigfoot System, a combination of street smarts and micromanagement that prevented Bigfoot from being taken advantage of by anyone. Bourdain would later use this system when he was the head of his own kitchen.

Halfway through his time at the CIA, Bourdain returned to the restaurant in Provincetown for the summer. There he was inspired by an older chef called Dimitri. Both he and Dimitri shared a love of classic French cooking and particularly enjoyed the works of chef Marie-Antoine Carême (1784–1833), who had cooked for royalty and was known for creating elaborate, architectural food pieces for dinner parties and functions. Bourdain and Dimitri started a catering company in their free time called Moonlight Menus, and they became known in the area for delivering delicious, overpriced Carême-esque food displays. Amid a whirlwind of drugs, debauchery, and catering, Bourdain made so much money that he was able to quit his restaurant job that summer.

RESTAURANTS

Early Chef Experiences

After graduating from the CIA in 1977, Bourdain got a job at the Rainbow Room, a restaurant atop Rockefeller Center. He worked as a lunch buffet chef for a year and a half, turning the previous night's leftovers into a delicious, expensive buffet frequented by the rich and elderly. After he ran for shop steward of the local union and won, he was quickly told to step down by management at the restaurant. Bourdain speculated in *Kitchen Confidential* that the previous person in the position had dabbled in organized crime. Bourdain left the Rainbow Room shortly after that.

From there, Bourdain moved through a series of cooking jobs, consistently moving up to better positions—from dishwasher to line chef to sous-chef and eventually executive chef—but he was unhappy. As he reminisces in *Kitchen*

Confidential, he had an undesirable habit of entering a restaurant when it was already failing, and he blamed his desire for money for keeping him in unfulfilling positions. Instead of trying to get a low-paying job with one of America's culinary masters to learn as much as he could, he went after high-paying jobs with less than ideal bosses, mainly to fund his growing drug habit, which now included heroin. Years later, Bourdain reflected on his drug addiction, calling it a love affair. He recalled reading as a boy about LSD and the drug scene in San Francisco's Haight-Ashbury, and all of the artists he loved were into drugs, so he had his mind set on trying drugs from a young age.

At the tender age of 22, Bourdain became the chef of a new but failing restaurant in the theater district of New York City. He did what he could, but the place was unsalvageable. It was there that Bourdain learned an important lesson: how to recognize failure. However, it would be years before he knew how to respond to and avoid failing restaurants.

In 1981, a good friend from both high school and Provincetown became the chef of a trendy Soho restaurant that was going under. Bourdain and his former mentor Dimitri assumed sous-chef positions, and numerous friends and former coworkers joined them. The young chefs did whatever they wanted, which mainly involved doing a lot of drugs and listening to rock and roll. In a memorable scene from *Kitchen Confidential*, Bourdain explains how they would ignite the range top with brandy before each shift started and do lines of cocaine that were the entire length of the bar after work, crawling on all fours across the bar top. Bourdain jumped ship before the restaurant failed.

Personal Transformations

Bourdain slowly straightened up his life. He began courting Nancy Putkoski, whom he had been dating off and on since high school, and in 1985 the couple married. Eventually, Bourdain managed to get off heroin, but he continued doing cocaine and worked another string of terrible jobs while using methadone to detoxify his body. In *Kitchen Confidential,* he called these his "Wilderness Years," when he lost all desire to cook and worked so many different jobs he could hardly keep them straight. He eventually sobered up and worked at several well-known restaurants in the 1990s, including Coco Pazzo Teatro (an Italian restaurant run by famous restaurateur Pino Luongo), Sullivan's, and the Supper Club. While serving as the executive chef of the Supper Club, Bourdain met Steven (whom he has never officially identified), who would soon become his best friend and longtime sous-chef. Bourdain also cooked for several celebrities while working at this restaurant, a far cry from his days as a dishwasher in Provincetown.

Restaurant Writings

Deciding to dabble in writing, Bourdain published two crime fiction novels while still working as a chef: *Bone in the Throat* (1995), which was set in a kitchen, and *Gone Bamboo* (1997). The books were not overwhelmingly popular, but they gave Bourdain a taste of what life as a writer could be like. He has called fiction writing his release from constantly writing about food and his own life. In 1998, Bourdain was named the executive chef of Les Halles, a French bistro on Lower Park Avenue in Manhattan. A year later, his bosses sent him to Tokyo to open up a Japanese branch of Les Halles.

COOKBOOKS

Bourdain's writing career really took off in 1999, when he wrote an article for *The New Yorker* entitled "Don't Eat before Reading This," which provided an explicit look inside the New York restaurant industry. The article was so popular that Bourdain turned it into the book *Kitchen Confidential: Adventures in the Culinary Underbelly* in 2000. Part autobiography, part down-and-dirty look at the life of a chef, the book outlined Bourdain's honest opinions about the strenuous work and overload of sex, drugs, and rock-and-roll found in a modern American restaurant kitchen. This book became a *New York Times* bestseller and cemented his public persona as a rebel chef without a cause. Fellow cooks and chefs were grateful to find that an insider had written about their world and could commiserate with them. Customers were grateful for the dining rules it provided, such as do not order fish on Mondays and never order a well-done steak.

The year 2001 was also successful for Bourdain, who was named Food Writer of the Year by *Bon Appétit* magazine for his book *Kitchen Confidential*. He also published two very different books that year. The first book, *Typhoid Mary: An Urban Historical*, retells the story of Mary Mallon, or Typhoid Mary, a cook who infected more than 30 people with typhoid at the beginning of the twentieth century. He tells the story from a chef's perspective, adding his own narrative where history left off. He hypothesizes that she became infected and passed the infection on to others rather than take time off because chefs often risk losing their jobs when they stay home sick. His perspective as a chef put an entirely new spin on the historical story. The second book he published that year was another crime novel, *The Chronicles of Bobby Gold*, which tells the story of a man who dates a sous-chef and gets on the wrong side of the mob.

TELEVISION SHOWS

A Cook's Tour

Because of *Kitchen Confidential*'s popularity, Bourdain was able to pitch and sell another book idea: He would travel around the world in search of the perfect meal. He managed to double-sell the idea to the Food Network as a television series, so he would be eating, writing, and filming all at the same time, something he had never done before. The book, published in 2001, and the show, produced in 2002, were called *A Cook's Tour*. Among the countries visited while filming were Portugal, Vietnam, Russia, Morocco, China, Cambodia, Mexico, and Scotland. In 2002, the British Guild of Food Writers named *A Cook's Tour* the Food Book of the Year.

In the book version of *A Cook's Tour*, Bourdain's writing shifted from funny and honest stories about a chef's life to travel and eating stories. Showing a new side of his storytelling skill, Bourdain shared the fascination and horror he experienced in exotic countries. When writing about the ancient city of Fez in Morocco, for instance, Bourdain offered a more complex look as he weaved his personal experiences in the city with a vivid and engaging gastronomic history of Fez, describing how its existence as a walled city has influenced the citizens' eating habits and cuisine to this very day.

The television series also depicts his first animal slaughter. He killed a pig in Portugal and was shocked to find that, despite his typical lust for adventure, he did not enjoy killing animals. Other uncomfortable moments during the recording of the show included eating his first live snake heart in Vietnam and his first, and probably last, vegan dinner party in San Francisco (both suggested by his producers). Bourdain has always been quite vocal about his dislike of vegans and vegetarians. As he says in *Kitchen Confidential*, "the only people who seem to really hate me for this book are . . . vegetarians, but they don't get enough animal protein to get really angry."[2]

Despite the book and series' success, Bourdain did not enjoy working on television shows. He disliked having a camera crew around constantly and resented being controlled by the Food Network. He found that the network sometimes forced him to get something out of a scene that was not there, made him repeat actions, or required him to eat disgusting food, such as the gelatinous bird's nest soup in Vietnam, just to get a good shot. They were even there to tape him when the food made him sick.

During this time, Bourdain was named Les Halles's official "chef-at-large," which meant that his name was still associated with the restaurant while he traveled and filmed the show. In 2004, he helped publish *Anthony Bourdain's Les Halles Cookbook*. The book, which was full of the restaurant's popular recipes, featured the witty and forward writing style Bourdain had become known for. He wrote the introduction and opening "basics" chapters as if he were training a new employee in his own kitchen, and his language matches that of a typical busy chef, meaning it is littered with curse words and insults. For example, the section about the history of the restaurant is mockingly entitled "Les Halles: What the Hell Is It?"[3]

After taping two seasons, comprising 22 shows, with the Food Network, Bourdain opted out of doing a third season. He had wanted to tape an entire episode about Spanish chef Ferran Adria, who at that time was the world's leading chef in molecular gastronomy, a new style of cooking based on the science behind traditional cooking preparations. Bourdain had gained permission from Adria to tape a show in Adria's secret workshop and in the restaurant, something no one had done before. The Food Network turned down the idea because, according to Bourdain, it wanted to focus on barbecues and tailgating in the third season. Bourdain and his crew, including camera people/producers Lydia Tenaglia and her husband Chris Collins, parted ways with their production company and the Food Network and paid for the week of filming with Adria out of their own pockets. In 2006 they packaged the footage as a DVD called *Decoding Ferran Adria,* which has since been viewed worldwide.

No Reservations

After parting ways with the Food Network, Bourdain went through a few life changes. First, in 2005 he split up with his wife of 20 years, Putkoski, and alluded to his traveling around the world as the cause for the divorce. That same year, Bourdain and his crew produced a new show with the Travel Channel entitled *Anthony Bourdain: No Reservations*. Much like the chefs who had followed him earlier in his career, the crew from *A Cook's Tour* remained loyal to Bourdain and followed him onto the set of *No Reservations*.

Bourdain has had more creative liberty with his show *No Reservations*, and although the concept of traveling around the world and eating is similar to the first series, the end product is very different. Instead of focusing on "the best of" or "the real" story about a country as most food travel shows do, this show concentrated on whatever Bourdain and the crew experienced. They understood they could not cover everything, so they focused on making the viewers feel as if they were traveling with the crew. They occasionally shot or edited a show to mimic their favorite directors, such as John Woo and Martin Scorsese, and strove to make each show different from the last. The same year *No Reservations* was created, Bourdain wrote a sitcom for Fox Network based on and titled after his first book, *Kitchen Confidential*. Several episodes aired in 2006, but the show was canceled before the first season finished.

Bourdain and the *No Reservations* crew were filming in Beirut, Lebanon, in July 2006 when the 2006 Lebanon War broke out, a military conflict between Lebanon and northern Israel that lasted just over a month. He and his crew had enjoyed a few delicious meals and were overwhelmed by the proud and happy citizens who wanted to show off their newly restored country. Yet, as the days passed and he saw the airport bombed multiple times, Bourdain knew this would be a very different show, and he worried about how they would get home. They were evacuated to a hotel near the American Embassy for a week, where they were close enough to hear the bombings day and night. Bourdain and his crew, along with other Americans, evacuated to the USS *Nashville*, where they stayed for another week.

According to Bourdain, he and the crew looked for hope from then-President George W. Bush, but the only news clip they received was of Bush eating a buttered roll and ignoring British prime minister Tony Blair, who Bourdain claims was trying to get Bush to focus on the events in Lebanon. This one clip destroyed the hopes of Bourdain and his crew. They attempted to film as much as they could, but primarily they sadly watched as the city of Beirut suffered terrible loses and damage. They eventually made it home safely, and in August 2006 their footage was aired. It was not a happy episode, but according to Bourdain, it was honest.

OTHER ENDEAVORS

Bourdain published his seventh book in 2006, *The Nasty Bits*, a collection of essays written for various publications such as *The New Yorker, The New York Times, Gourmet Magazine, The Observer*, and the *Financial Times*. This book covers a wide range of food-related topics. In it, Bourdain discusses current restaurant trends, such as famous chefs opening casual eateries, and offers a few profiles of especially intriguing chefs. He tells a few tales from the kitchen, outlines his favorite books to read for motivation in the kitchen, and, of course, mocks other celebrity chefs. This time, chef-turned-reality-TV-star Rocco Dispirito and raw food received the brunt of his anger.

One of the articles in *The Nasty Bits* showcases a cause Bourdain adamantly supports: rights for Latinos and immigrants in the kitchen. In *Kitchen Confidential*, he often speaks about how Mexican immigrants make up a majority of the staff in the kitchens of restaurants all around the United States. In *The Nasty Bits*, Bourdain wrote a piece honoring Mexican kitchen staff after he hosted the James Beard Awards (a prestigious U.S. culinary awards event). Despite the fact that many restaurant kitchens around the United States employ and are even run by Latinos, none was in attendance at the awards ceremony, a situation Bourdain found offensive. He suggested that the United States open up immigration to Mexico and Central and South America, if only to keep the United States full of hard-working, talented chefs.

Bourdain had another landmark year in 2007. His *No Reservations* Beirut episode was nominated for an Emmy Award. Then in April, he married his Italian girlfriend, Ottavia Busia, and did what he vowed only a year before, in an article in *The Observer*, that he would never do: He had a child. A daughter, Ariane, was born on April 9, 2007. Her birth inspired him to stop smoking (mostly), and, as one reporter noted, he attempted to refrain from using profanity. Bourdain has also made an effort to have his family travel with him in safe, family-friendly locations such as Italy and London. He published his eighth book, *Anthony Bourdain No Reservations: Around the World on an Empty Stomach*, in 2007. This latest work is more of a photo essay than travel memoir of his *No Reservations* experiences, interspersed with some of his writing.

But the year 2007 again brought negative publicity for Bourdain. That year a revealing photo of Bourdain surfaced in the book *My Last Supper: 50 Great Chefs and Their Final Meals* by Melanie Dunea. Dunea wanted to capture the spirit of the chefs she photographed, so when it came time for Bourdain, she suggested a photo where he was completely nude, smoking a cigarette and holding nothing but a massive beef bone in front of his private parts. Bourdain wrote the introduction to the book and noted therein that this photo was created because he had yet to learn an important lesson, which is to never make an important career decision after a few drinks.

Over the years, Bourdain has been a guest on several television shows, including *Late Night with David Letterman, Late Night with Conan O'Brien, Nova*, and several episodes of *Top Chef*. Bourdain also wrote a blog based on his experiences on *Top Chef* and in 2008 was nominated for a Webby Award for "Best Blog Cultural/Personal." In 2009, Bourdain continued his work on *No Reservations*, as it entered its sixth season, and wrote for various publications. His writing occasionally appeared on food writer and friend Michael Ruhlman's blog. In 2009, Bourdain's show *No Reservations* was nominated for three Emmy awards for Outstanding Cinematography for Nonfiction Programming and Outstanding Picture Editing for Nonfiction Programming for the Laos episode, as well as for Outstanding Nonfiction Program.

CONCLUSION

Bourdain started as a disgruntled chef with a nasty drug habit, but over the years he has transformed himself into a respected food writer and television show host. In the cooking world, he went from working at failing restaurants to running and writing the cookbook for Les Halles, a well-known French brasserie in Manhattan. Bourdain's food writing has also matured over the years, starting off with entertaining and frightening stories from a professional kitchen and ending with insights into ancient and modern cultures around the globe. Thanks to his blunt and forward manner, Bourdain's television shows have evolved from cookie-cutter Food Network shows to gutsy accounts of eating and cooking around the world. Bourdain has truly become an icon of the modern American food world.

NOTES

1. Anthony Bourdain, *Kitchen Confidential: Adventures in the Culinary Underbelly* (New York: HarperCollins, 2000), 19.

2. Bourdain, *Kitchen Confidential*, xv.

3. Anthony Bourdain, *Anthony Bourdain's Les Halles Cookbook* (New York: Bloomsbury, 2004).

FURTHER READING

"Anthony Bourdain Clarifies Criticism of Alice Waters," Eat Me Daily Blog (January 23, 2009) http://www.eatmedaily.com/2009/01/anthony-bourdain-clarifies-criticism-of-alice-waters/

Bourdain, Anthony. *A Cook's Tour: Global Adventures in Extreme Cuisines*. New York: HarperCollins, 2001.

Bourdain, Anthony. *Anthony Bourdain No Reservations: Around the World on an Empty Stomach*. New York: Bloomsbury, 2007.

Bourdain, Anthony. *Anthony Bourdain's Les Halles Cookbook*. New York: Bloomsbury, 2004.

Bourdain, Anthony. Anthony Bourdain's Web site. http://www.anthonybourdain.net/

Bourdain, Anthony. *Kitchen Confidential: Adventures in the Culinary Underbelly*. New York: HarperCollins, 2000.

Bourdain, Anthony. *The Nasty Bits: Collected Varietal Cuts, Usable Trim, Scraps and Bones*. New York: Bloomsbury, 2006.

Bourdain, Anthony. "Nobody Asked Me, But . . ." Michael Ruhlman: Notes from the Food World Blog (February 8, 2007) http://blog.ruhlman.com/ruhlman com/2007/02/guest_blogging_.html

Constantine, Mary. "Bad Boy Anthony Bourdain Enjoys Good Times as a Dad." *Knox News* Online (March 20, 2009) http://www.knoxnews.com/news/2009/mar/29/bad-boy-bourdain-enjoys-good-times-dad/

Dunea, Melanie. *The Last Supper: 50 Great Chefs and Their Final Meals*. New York: Bloomsbury, 2007.

Federigan, Bret. "Culinary Picks and Pans: A Viewer's Guide to Food TV with Anthony Bourdain." MSN Online (March 2009) http://tv.msn.com/culinary-picks-and-pans/?GT1=28130

Ferguson, Euan. "Regrets? He's Had a Few . . ." *The Observer* Online (April 30, 2006) http://www.guardian.co.uk/lifeandstyle/2006/apr/30/foodanddrink.features8

Miller, J. J. "Anthony Bourdain Braises and Praises." *O, The Oprah Magazine*. March 1, 2004.

O'Neal, Sean. "Anthony Bourdain Interview." The A.V. Club Online (January 8, 2008) http://www.avclub.com/articles/anthony-bourdain,2132/

Travel Channel Anthony Bourdain No Reservations Web site: http://www.travel channel.com/TV_Shows/Anthony_Bourdain/ci.Meet_Anthony_Bourdain.show?vgnextfmt=show&idLink=28eec51a4fdc7110VgnVCM100000698b3a0a

Leena Trivedi-Grenier

Cecilia Chiang poses with Chinese specialties at the Mandarin Restaurant in San Francisco, California, ca. 1982. (Kelly-Mooney Photography/Corbis)

Cecilia Chiang

From the early 1960s to the present, Sun Yun "Cecilia" Chiang has been an American food pioneer who has introduced many food professionals and enthusiasts to some of their first encounters with high-end Chinese Mandarin cuisine. Twice forced to flee her homeland of China, Chiang eventually settled in the San Francisco Bay Area, where she befriended and taught notable chefs such as James Beard, Marion Cunningham, M. F. K. Fisher, Charles Williams, and Gerald Asher. Chiang's Mandarin restaurants and her style of well-cooked, fresh, local, and sustainable foods exposed most Americans, for the first time, to non-Cantonese Chinese cuisine. As Chiang's regional ethnic cuisine and ancient foodways caught on, she became the mentor for many of the 1970s food revolution's stars, including Alice Waters and Jeremiah Tower, and in the 1990s to her own son Philip Chiang when he cofounded the P. F. Chang restaurant chain. She also authored two books and consulted on the establishment of scores of restaurants across the nation. Throughout these years she learned many lessons while confronting common American prejudices against women and Asians, using her talent and her love for the cooking of her homeland to overcome these roadblocks.

For most of human history, the skills of the hearth have belonged to women. Yet this role came under attack in the 20th century, especially after World War II, as powerful business and cultural messages, aimed at women, fostered the adaptation of fast foods. This mixed message forced many women to question what they knew about nurturing their families. Given this scenario, Chiang serves as a model for what has been seen as women's struggle to regain control of their natural foodways.[1] She left her world of second-class female Chinese citizenship and emerged in a postwar America that was struggling for political, gender, and economic equality. Her successful blending of her old Chinese and new American gender roles gave her the opportunity to become a restaurateur, chef, businesswoman, wife, mother, and food pioneer by using her Mandarin food traditions to both cultivate her modern American feminine role and to financially support her family.

BACKGROUND

Mid-nineteenth-century Western traders in China observed a small elite group in northern China with a distinctive high-end lifestyle. They identified this group by the Romanized word "Mandarin," derived from the Chinese word "Manchu," meaning "big shot." People from this group embraced literature and art, filled the ranks of government offices, and enjoyed a distinctive Chinese haute cuisine. Over time, Westerners used the word "Mandarin" to describe anything exquisite, stylish, or exotic that came from China.

Americans were first introduced to Chinese food in the 19th century when Chinese workers began immigrating to the United States as Sino-U.S. maritime trade developed. Their numbers peaked during the 1849 California Gold Rush and the 1860s building of the Central Pacific and Transcontinental Railroads. Since most of the new immigrant workers came from the southern coastal province of Guangdong (Canton), most Americans over the next century believed that Cantonese food represented the entire Chinese foodway.

Large-scale Chinese immigration ended with the 1882 Chinese Exclusion Act, which effectively established a 60-year ban on Chinese immigration, and the Immigration Act of 1924, which excluded all classes of Chinese immigrants. Until 1943, however, there was some limited Chinese immigration through San Francisco Bay's Angel Island Immigration Station. The reopening of the United States to Chinese migrants came with the Immigration Act of 1965, which cleared the way for Chinese from all provinces who were escaping the ravages of the communist regime. It was during this new era of immigration that Chiang introduced Americans to Mandarin cuisine.

This new immigrant surge allowed Americans to experience a "second revolution of Chinese food."[2] Most importantly, the introduction of new Chinese cuisines coincided with the Cold War era "Food Revolution" that had begun with the likes of Julia Child's *Mastering the Art of French Cooking* (1961) and with food literati James Beard, M. F. K. Fisher, Craig Claiborne, and cookbook author Helen Evans Brown, who formally introduced America to the new "West Coast" cuisine in her 1952 *West Coast Cook Book.*

During the 1960s and 1970s, Americans underwent social, cultural, and political changes, many of which were centered in the Bay Area. This counterculture movement took on big business and government by politicizing food and nurturing a movement of what would later be called "foodies."[3] Much of the food movement energy arose in the University of California at Berkeley, where student activist and budding food pioneer Alice Waters opened her Chez Panisse restaurant.

During this time, most believe that Chiang's pioneering culinary style awakened Americans' senses and appreciation for true Chinese regional food. In less than two decades, her restaurant achieved a national reputation and served guests from all over the country. She began teaching Mandarin cooking classes that included students such as Julia Child, James Beard, Alice Waters, Marion Cunningham, Jeremiah Tower, and actor Danny Kaye.

Eating in Japan with Alice Waters

I took Alice [Waters] to Japan. One day we were in Kyoto, I still remember the restaurant called the Tao Tao. Just a small restaurant, with a big counter. So at that time, I don't think Alice really had had sashimi or raw seafood, and Marion [Cunningham] was with us also. So Alice said, "Cecilia, I don't want to travel and get sick." I said, "I understand that." I said, "When you travel, it's no fun to get sick." I said, "I guarantee you, you are not going to get sick." I managed to still speak some Japanese, I said, "I want some really fresh fish." For instance, they call the shrimp ebi. I said, "From the box, with the sawdust." They keep all these live shrimp in a little wood box. They wetted the sawdust, they presented it to us. Alice said, "What is this?" She was looking at fish covered with all the sawdust. I said, "Here is the fresh shrimp, this sweet shrimp, it's moving." So they rinsed the sawdust. The tail is still wiggling. And they said, "You want sashimi or you want sushi?" Sushi they put on the rice, sashimi just serve that. So Alice said, "I want both, I want to try both." So they cut the head off, it's still moving, and they remove the shell. I said, "Alice you wanted fresh, this is real fresh." So they put in their mouths, still wiggling, but the meat is just so sweet, so juicy, so good.

—Cecilia Chiang, interview conducted by Victor Geraci, 2005–2006,
Regional Oral History Office, The Bancroft Library,
University of California, Berkeley, 2007

EARLY YEARS

Childhood in China

Chiang's birth name, Sun Yun, is a derivative of Sun, her family name, and Yun, meaning "flower of the rue." Sun Yun was born in 1920 in Beijing to a wealthy family, the seventh daughter among 12 children who resided in a 52-room Ming era former palace. Her gentle, handsome, and Western-educated father, Sun Lung-kwong ("Bright Dragon"), retired at age 45 to devote his life to the joys of leisure. Chiang's mother, Sun Shueh Yun-hwei ("Hidden Glory"), came from a wealthy traditional family that owned silk, textile, and flour mills in Wu-His. At an early age, Sun Shueh Yun-hwei's parents had moved her to Peking as part of an arranged marriage to Chiang's father. Out of homesickness, she developed an interest in cooking and made sure to teach her new husband's cooks the famous dishes of her home province. In a 2006 interview, Chiang described her mother as a perfectionist who loved food, embroidered, and never allowed her bound feet to get in the way of her managing the family's finances. Her considerable household duties included supervision of staff that included *feng shui* consultants, tailors, 12 *amahs* (nannies), a fireplace keeper, nine dogs, seven cats, assorted birds, gardeners, cooks, and household servants. Typical of their family's status, each of the children had a personal nanny, and the parents made no outward demonstrations of affection. Chiang could not remember ever seeing her parents kissing or showing emotion.[4]

During her first 20 years, Chiang knew little about the workings of her home's kitchen because it was run by the *ta shih-fu* (head chef), and children were forbidden from entering his domain. Because her father was Western-educated and progressive and had witnessed the pain his wife suffered, he forbade the binding of any of his daughters' feet. Most of Chiang's early childhood food experiences came from participating in Chinese holidays and observing her mother's strict supervision of the arts of pickling, preserving meats, preserving fruits and vegetables in the cellar, and cooking whole fish and barbecued spareribs.[5]

What Chiang did learn was that Chinese cooking used seasonal fresh food and that meals helped created a true sense of family. Because of her exposure to these wealthy foodways and her parents' mealtime discussions, she acquired a connoisseur's palate and the ability to evaluate quality food and preparation styles. The family practiced *tsao-fan* ("early rice") or breakfast and the Hunan tradition of three meals a day. Family meals, known as *pien-fan* ("casual rice"), included rice, meats, seafood, vegetables, and fruits for dessert. Normally, her father was served at 6:30 in the evening, and the children sat down at 7:00 to be served by their *amahs* on small plates.

Luckily for Chiang, her father believed in educating his daughters. While her brothers studied with home tutors, she and her sisters attended the Sisters of the Sacred Heart Bridgeman Academy, an American missionary school. Later she attended Fujen University near Pei Hai, where she studied Chinese literature and, at the suggestion of one of her Catholic professors, changed her name to Cecilia. At home, the family enjoyed Western magazines, books, music, and clothing, and many of her cousins traveled to the United States and Europe for their education.

Exiles from China

Twice in the 1930s and 1940s, Chiang faced major shifts in her life and learned to use food as a metaphor to survive and retain her heritage. When she was 20, Japanese forces marched through China between 1937 and 1939, and the family's circumstances rapidly deteriorated as the Japanese ransacked the homes of the wealthy. In 1942 her parents, worried for the fate of their daughters, decided that Chiang and her number five sister, Teresa, would escape to Chongqing, in Free China, to the home of an uncle in the Chinese Air Force. During the six-month, 1,000-mile journey by foot, the girls, dressed in fur-lined cheongsams (body hugging Chinese dresses) with gold stitched into the hems, faced Japanese soldiers who threatened to kill them with bayonets. They encountered a school friend whose father, a general, helped them escape the rest of the way to their uncle. Chiang adapted quickly to her new life and taught Mandarin at the American and Russian embassies, where she met Lian Chiang, a former professor and successful businessman. In 1945, as the war ended, they married and settled in Shanghai, where she gave birth to a daughter, May, and a son, Philip.

The next major disruption to her life occurred in 1949 as Chinese communist reprisals against educated and wealthy citizens forced her immediate family to flee to Tokyo, Japan. As if having to leave the country was not bad enough, the family faced a mix-up in their authorized Chinese communist diplomatic flight out of the country. At the airport they learned that there were only three seats left on the plane and they could only take one of their two children. The decision fell to Chiang's husband, who chose to take their two-year-old daughter May and leave their son Philip in the care of one of Chiang's sisters. It was over a year until she saw her son again. While reflecting on these two forced exiles, Chiang commented that she was grateful to have known the best of that vanished Chinese world. In her words, "That life is gone forever. But if I remember the past with gratitude it is also without regret. If not for the war, I would have never known that I could work, and support two children and carve a career for myself in a new country. My eyes had been opened to other ways and other freedoms."[6]

RESTAURANTS

Rebuilding a Life outside China

Chiang quickly created new opportunities for her family in Tokyo. Always a businesswoman, she opened a 300-seat Chinese restaurant, with the help of relatives and friends, called the Forbidden City. It quickly became a success with Chinese expatriates, Americans, and locals. This is where she discovered that food would be her ticket to a new life.

In 1958, Chiang left Tokyo to spend time with her recently widowed sister in San Francisco. During her visit she frequented the city's Chinatown and one day met two friends from Japan who had plans to open a restaurant on Polk Street. They asked her to help negotiate the deal because of her English skills and experience with her Tokyo restaurant. Chiang liked the idea and as part of the agreement paid the $10,000 deposit due to the landlord. When her friends walked away from the deal and Chiang could not get her deposit back, she decided to open the restaurant herself. This was not an easy decision, considering that her husband and two children, ages 8 and 10, were still in Japan. In her words, "I was really thinking if in the first year, year and a half, if I could not make it, I would just close and go back to Japan. I just wanted to educate the American people and tell them, 'Besides chop suey, there is something else! It tastes better!'"[7]

Opening a Mandarin Chinese restaurant was risky because most Americans believed Asian cuisine to be Cantonese. Adding to the problem was the decline of most American Chinatowns after years of restrictive immigration from Asia. This all changed when the Immigration Act of 1965 helped replenish America's Chinatowns.[8] Increasing numbers of Chinese immigrants now became interested in Chiang's Mandarin ways, and curiosity peaked even more when President Richard M. Nixon visited China. Further fueling the interest in Chiang's new Chinese cuisine was an emerging Bay Area "foodie" culture that was curious about new ethnic foodways. In just over a decade,

Chiang helped revolutionize Chinese cooking in San Francisco with her Mandarin Peking-Shandong and Sichuan-Hunan specialties. She stated, "I think I really did something to the food industry in America. For instance, when I brought the Sichuan food and the Hunan food to my menu many people asked me, 'How [do] you pronounce this?' They said, 'What's all this about?' I said, 'Spicy is Sichuan' and I explained everything to them."[9]

Despite Chiang's passion, the restaurant had marginal profits in the first years, and Johnny Kan, of the famous San Francisco Kan's restaurant, advised her to change the menu to cater to American taste buds, which were familiar with chop suey, and to quit serving dishes like pot stickers. He also advised her to abandon the menu of over 200 dishes that included lamb, eggplant, sizzling rice soup, smoked tea duck, and beggar's chicken. Chiang also had difficulty getting her more exotic ingredients, which she had to import from Taiwan at great expense. Yet her can-do spirit never allowed her to give up on her quest to educate American palates.

Recognition and Expansion

The turning point for the business came when San Francisco food writer Herb Caen reviewed Chiang's restaurant. The next day she received over 100 calls inquiring about her restaurant. Recognition continued when Victor Bergeron of Trader Vic's restaurant, along with Hollywood actor and amateur chef Danny Kaye, visited the restaurant and praised her approach. From that point on, Chiang's restaurant was featured in magazines, and the only downsides were that she was unable to meet the needs of her regular customers and her resident status prevented her from getting a liquor license.

Chiang realized that it was time to expand her business, and she found a suitable location in San Francisco's high-profile Ghirardelli Square. When she approached the real estate agent about leasing the location, he said, "Mrs. Chiang, I don't think there is a chance you're going to get into Ghirardelli Square; the owners do not want any Chinese restaurants." When she asked why, he curtly responded, "Chinese restaurants are too greasy, too dirty, and have a lot of mice and a lot of cockroaches." Undaunted, Chiang invited the agent to her restaurant and quickly converted him to her cause. She then convinced Bank of America to loan her $750,000. Thus began what she described as "the biggest break of my whole life."[10]

Eight years after the first restaurant opened on Polk Street, the new Mandarin restaurant opened with a $250-per-person black-tie benefit that supported the San Francisco Opera Guild. Customers loved the newly remodeled 300-seat restaurant, and over the next few decades it become a Bay Area food landmark. The tough personal decision for Chiang was to stay in the United States. To do so, she amicably split up with her husband, whom she never divorced, and took full custody of her two children, by then teenagers. Her new success gave her the opportunity to purchase a home in the affluent St. Francis Wood community, where she became the first non–European American resident.

For over 23 years, the Mandarin restaurant defined upscale Chinese dining, introducing customers to Sichuan dishes like *kung pao* chicken, twice-cooked pork, minced squab in lettuce cups, and tea-smoked duck. Her signature dish of beggar's chicken, a whole bird stuffed with dried mushrooms, water chestnuts, and ham and baked in clay, became a favorite of Chuck Williams, the founder of the Williams-Sonoma chain, who in turn introduced Chiang to his friend James Beard. As a result, Beard and Chiang became lifelong friends and he an admirer of her pig's feet, pork kidneys, and "Two Crispiness" (chicken gizzards with pork stomach) dishes.[11]

From this point on, the restaurant's and Chiang's fame grew. Jerry di Vecchio, then the food editor at *Sunset Magazine*, called the restaurant glamorous and sophisticated. Playwright Lillian Hellman came to the restaurant quite regularly and assisted Chiang in publishing her first book, cowritten with Allen Carr: *The Mandarin Way* (1980). During those early years, Chiang also began mentoring Bay Area food pioneers Alice Waters, Jeremiah Tower, and Marion Cunningham, who on weekends brunched on the deck of Chiang's new Belvedere, California, home. Many of the 1960s and 1970s Bay Area food revolution pioneers also attended Chiang's cooking school to learn her cooking techniques and recipes and to seek advice on running a restaurant. Chiang remembered, "When I started it was mainly all male students and later women like Jamie Davis (Schramsberg Champagne), Maria Theresa (Herb Caen's wife) and Margarit Mondavi (Mondavi Winery) attended. They were all cooking with me—Marion Cunningham, James Beard and Julia Child. They all came to my cooking school."[12]

During this period, Alice Waters's Chez Panisse Berkeley restaurant began to gather national attention. In Waters's determination to politicize food as a means to counter ever-increasing industrialization, she used her French experiences to bring Americans back to the ideas of local, seasonal, and organic fresh meats, vegetables, and fruits. Waters also turned to her mentor Chiang for advice on Chinese food traditions as they pertained to these issues. Chiang remembered that "the first time Alice Waters came to my restaurant she asked me many questions. She said, 'You know, Cecilia, your food is quite different to me. What is it? Tell me, what is it? Is it the vegetables you serve? They are the same vegetables I get in Chinatown, but yours are a different taste. What is it?' I said, 'In the old days in China, we did not have refrigeration and we had to buy daily from the market and cook it right away. Vegetables, my mother always said, We try to keep the original flavor, the original color, and also the original texture.' The whole thing is just fresh. Nothing else. It is just that simple." Chiang and Waters became close friends and colleagues, and the two traveled together throughout Europe, Japan, and China to gather new techniques, recipes, food ideas, and restaurant management tips.[13]

As Chiang's reputation grew, her list of rich and famous clients expanded to include opera singer Joan Sutherland and her husband Richard, Luciano Pavarotti, Rudolf Nureyev, June Francis, the Kennedy family, the Shah of Iran, Arthur Miller, Norman Mailer, Lillian Hellman, Margaret Truman, Paul

Newman, Joanne Woodward, John McEnroe, and Placido Domingo. One famous music group she recalled in the 1960s was Jefferson Airplane. She remembered serving the group, who "wore the weirdest clothes," and planning great feasts for them. On their third visit, they left her an envelope with a thank-you note and two hand-wrapped cigarettes. Her son Philip later explained that the cigarettes were marijuana.[14]

Chiang's mission to bring high-end Chinese cuisine to Americans continued throughout the 1980s and 1990s, and she expanded her operations by opening a second Mandarin restaurant in Beverly Hills as well as two smaller, more casual Mandarette restaurants. Philip managed the Beverly Hills operation and her daughter May opened a restaurant in San Francisco that did not do as well. Philip later went on to establish the highly successful P. F. Chang restaurant chain.

CONCLUSION

Besides mentoring food pioneers and running restaurants, Chiang has also kept busy as a consultant for new San Francisco restaurants like Betelnut and Shanghai 1930. Her women's network has always been important for providing both personal and professional relationships. On her 70th birthday, friends Waters, Cunningham, and Ruth Reichl—women colleagues who had provided an anchor for her life—organized a party at Joseph Phelps winery. She remembered a conversation with Nancy Oaks of San Francisco's Boulevard Restaurant about the differences between male and female chefs. Chiang firmly believed "that food for women is all about nurturing and that for men it is a way to earn a living." Yet, in a restaurant world dominated by men, Chiang made an impression.[15]

Retired since 1991, Chiang has not slowed her pace and still consults for Chinese restaurants and raises funds for causes like the Chinese American International School in San Francisco, where students from all backgrounds study the Mandarin language. With her help, the school became the nation's first Mandarin immersion K–8 school. She still enjoys entertaining and cooking for friends at home and, according to Bay Area cooking teacher and friend Mary Risley, produces "wonderful, elaborate, hard-worked food."[16] Chiang continues to travel extensively and dines out frequently at restaurants like Quince, Scott Howard, Coco500, and Delfina. As for the newer Bay Area's Chinese restaurants, she complains that "they're getting worse, not better. It makes me sick inside."[17] However, Chiang deserves a lion's share of the credit for educating Bay Area diners in Chinese foodways. She believes that she has "changed what average people know about Chinese food."[18] In 2007, Chiang released her memoir cookbook, *The Seventh Daughter: My Culinary Journey from Beijing to San Francisco,* with cowriter Lisa Weiss. Using an M. F. K. Fisher literary style and food as a metaphor for life, it describes her life in China and the United States and received a James Beard Foundation nomination.

NOTES

1. Catherine Manton, *Fed Up: Women and Food in America* (Westport, CT: Bergin and Garvey, 1999); and Alice P. Julier, Review of "Fed Up: Woman and Food in America; Consuming Geographies: We Are Where We Eat," *Contemporary Sociology* 29:4 (July 2000): 645–647.

2. John D. Keys, *Food for the Emperor: Recipes of Imperial China with a Dictionary of Chinese Cuisine* (San Francisco: Ward Ritchie Press, 1963), xxii.

3. Warren J. Belasco, *Appetite for Change: How the Counterculture Took On the Food Industry* (Ithaca, NY: Cornell University Press, 1989).

4. Cecilia Chiang, "Cecilia Chiang: An Oral History," conducted by Victor Geraci, 2005–2006, Regional Oral History Office, The Bancroft Library, University of California, Berkeley, 2007.

5. Cecilia Sun Yun Chiang, *The Mandarin Way* (San Francisco: California Living Books, 1980); and Cecilia Chiang with Lisa Weiss, *The Seventh Daughter: My Culinary Journey from Beijing to San Francisco* (Berkeley, CA: Ten Speed Press, 2007).

6. "Cecilia Chiang: An Oral History."

7. "Cecilia Chiang: An Oral History."

8. Lawrence K. Hong, "Recent Immigrants in the Chinese-American Community: Issues of Adaptations and Impacts." Paper from the American Sociological Association, 1976.

9. "Cecilia Chiang: An Oral History."

10. "Cecilia Chiang: An Oral History."

11. Charles E. Williams, "Chuck Williams and Howard Lester, Volume II: Williams Sonoma: Mastering the Homeware Marketplace: 1994–2004," interview conducted by Victor W. Geraci, 2004, Regional Oral History Office, The Bancroft Library, University of California, Berkeley, 2004.

12. "Cecilia Chiang: An Oral History."

13. "Cecilia Chiang: An Oral History."

14. "Cecilia Chiang: An Oral History."

15. "Cecilia Chiang: An Oral History."

16. Mary Risley, "Mary Risley: Food Educator and Proprietor of the San Francisco Based Tante Marie's Cooking School," an oral history conducted in 2004 by Victor W. Geraci, Regional Oral History Office, The Bancroft Library, University of California, Berkeley, 2006.

17. "Cecilia Chiang: An Oral History."

18. "Cecilia Chiang: An Oral History."

FURTHER READING

Belasco, Warren J. *Appetite for Change: How the Counterculture Took on the Food Industry*. Ithaca, NY: Cornell University Press, 1989.

Chiang, Cecilia Sun Yun. *The Mandarin Way*. San Francisco: California Living Books, 1980.

Chiang, Cecilia, with Lisa Weiss. *The Seventh Daughter: My Culinary Journey from Beijing to San Francisco*. Berkeley, CA: Ten Speed Press, 2007.

Chiang, Cecilia. "Cecilia Chiang: An Oral History," conducted by Victor W. Geraci, 2005–2006, Regional Oral History Office, The Bancroft Library, University of California, Berkeley, 2007.

Hong, Lawrence K. "Recent Immigrants in the Chinese-American Community: Issues of Adaptations and Impacts." Paper from the American Sociological Association, 1976.

Julier, Alice P. Review of "Fed Up: Women and Food in America; Consuming Geographies: We Are Where We Eat." *Contemporary Sociology* 29:4 (July 2000): 645–647.

Kamp, David. *The United States of Arugula: How We Became a Gourmet Nation.* New York: Broadway Books, 2006.

Keys, John D. *Food for the Emperor: Recipes of Imperial China with a Dictionary of Chinese Cuisine.* San Francisco: Ward Ritchie Press, 1963.

Knickerbocker, Peggy. "Empress of San Francisco." *Saveur Magazine* no. 43 (May/June 2000): 62–72.

Manton, Catherine. *Fed Up: Women and Food in America.* Westport, CT: Bergin and Garvey, 1999.

McNamee, Thomas. *Alice Waters and Chez Panisse; The Romantic, Impractical, Often Eccentric, Ultimately Brilliant Making of a Food Revolution.* New York: Penguin Press, 2007.

Muscatine, Doris. *A Cook's Tour of San Francisco: The Best Restaurants and Their Recipes.* New York: Charles Scribner Sons, 1963.

Muscatine, Doris. "Doris Muscatine: Food and Wine Writer." Interview conducted by Victor W. Geraci, 2004, Regional Oral History Office, The Bancroft Library, University of California, Berkeley, 2006.

Reichl, Ruth. *Tender to the Bone: Growing Up at the Table.* New York: Broadway Books, 1998.

Risley, Mary. "Mary Risley: Food Educator and Proprietor of the San Francisco Based Tante Marie's Cooking School." Oral history interview conducted in 2004 by Victor W. Geraci, Regional Oral History Office, The Bancroft Library, University of California, Berkeley, 2006.

Tower, Jeremiah. *California Dish: What I Saw (and Cooked) at the Culinary Revolution.* New York: Free Press, 2003.

Victor W. Geraci

Julia Child shows a salade nicoise she prepared in the kitchen of her vacation home in Grasse, southern France, on August 21, 1978. Julia Child, who brought the intricacies of French cuisine to Americans through her television series and books, died on August 13, 2004. (AP/Wide World Photos)

Julia Child

Julia Child brought the joys of cooking and entertaining into millions of American homes. Americans grew to love her and tried to emulate her panache in the kitchen, where she was a kind of Lucille Ball—theatrical, funny, physical, with a knack for perfect timing and a message America was ready to hear: Cooking—real, French cooking—was neither intimidating nor out of reach, but accessible to everyone.

Child discovered cooking in midlife and embraced it with all her might. At six feet, two inches tall, Child was an unlikely role model. Her forthright manners, hearty humor, and distinctive warbly voice made her a television phenomenon during the 1960s–1990s. Her books, television series, and magazine articles about sophisticated French cuisine appealed to women trying to reestablish a new sense of feminine roles in an era of populist social movements. Despite her appearances, Child faced challenges, including an unrequited college romance, rejection from publishers, and breast cancer, but with a spirit of adventure, she persevered. Americans watched Child mature into old age with vitality, friends, and intellectual interests.

EARLY YEARS

Childhood and College

Child's start in life was auspicious. John McWilliams Jr. and Caro (Julia Carolyn) Weston met in 1903 and married in 1911. They welcomed the first of their three children, Julia Carolyn McWilliams, into their Pasadena, California, home on August 15, 1912. John McWilliams was a conservative banker known for Scottish thrift and a stubborn streak, while Caro, who was 33 when she married, was athletic and strikingly individualistic with the "Weston twinkle."[1] Child remembered her mother's only ungraceful characteristic as "a voice which wavered in the high ranges, never seeming to emanate from her chest."[2] Child learned to appreciate community from her father, who was active in the Chamber of Commerce and in fund-raising for the local chapter of Community Chest (known today as the United Way). The young, affluent family was social and loved the outdoors. They employed a cook, and Child grew up with "zero interest in the stove."[3]

Child benefited from the best educational opportunities her parents could provide. While her father wanted to prepare her for an advantageous marriage, her mother was more liberal in letting her children develop their own talents and interests. Child attended Polytechnic School from fourth to ninth grade and then transferred to an elite girl's boarding school in Ross, California. After graduating from high school, she enrolled at Smith College in Northampton, Massachusetts, to study history and liberal arts as her mother had done.

Smith College, landscaped by Frederick Law Olmsted, was a beautiful environment where communal ties were made around shared meals rather than through a domestic science curriculum. Child remembered Smith College fondly: "You do not feel as if you're an inferior sex when you are in an all woman school."[4] While at Smith College, Child took four years of French, French literature, and Italian. Although she could read French and Italian, she could not speak either fluently. Vivacious and fun-loving, she was a renowned campus prankster. While studying to become a writer and bohemian, she wrote for Smith's student humor magazine *The Tatler.*

Child followed in her father's footsteps, becoming chairman of the campus chapter of Community Chest and raising money for local charities, which were especially strained during the Great Depression. She left Smith College with the ability to synthesize and classify information, as well as with close personal friends and a moral and intellectual engagement that came from belonging to a small affluent academic community. After college, Child capitalized on her typing skills and worked as a copywriter for the advertising department of the high-end New York City furniture store W. & J. Sloane. She had little direction, and after a disappointing college romance, returned to her family in California.

Accidental Career Woman

With the onset of World War II, Child moved to Washington, D.C., to be where the action was. Too tall for the Navy, in 1941 she volunteered for director William "Wild Bill" Donovan's newly established agency called the Office of Strategic Services (OSS). The forerunner of the Central Intelligence Agency, the OSS was established by President Franklin D. Roosevelt as an umbrella organization for espionage. Child passed confidential documents between the OSS and agents in the field. She held a high-security clearance but found civil service work to be dull.

In 1945 Child was dispatched to the China-Burma-India theater of war, where she met Paul Child, an artist specializing in maps and graphs in Ceylon (now Sri Lanka), who was 10 years her senior. Although they both had rather bohemian mothers, their backgrounds and traditions varied greatly. Paul's Francophile Boston upbringing made him well versed in different cuisines. He also impressed Child with his photographic skills and fluency in French. Child remembered that Paul was "eastern, very impressive, much more sophisticated than I."[5] This made her feel "awkward and hickish" at times.[6] Paul's first impression was that Julia was a "sloppy thinker, a woman who gasped when she talked excitedly."[7] Despite this, their love blossomed as he introduced her to a more sophisticated view of the world.

Child followed Paul to his new assignment in China, where she learned about Chinese literature and fine Chinese cuisine. After the war they returned to the United States and married in September 1946. Before their wedding, Child took a bride-to-be's cooking course to learn basic cooking from two British women in Los Angeles. When she unsuccessfully attempted to cook a very ambitious meal for Paul, she realized that she could not cook and became more determined "to learn to cook well."[8]

Becoming a Cook

In 1948 the Visual Presentation Department for the U.S. Information Service assigned Paul to work at the American Embassy in Paris. There Child studied conversational French, and Paul took her to the restaurant at France's oldest inn, called La Courrone, in Rouen, France. During that excursion, they enjoyed *filet de sole meunière*, and Child remembered, "I didn't know such food existed."[9] Her life had changed forever.

Empowered by her new passion for food, Child enrolled in a six-month course at the Cordon Bleu on October 4, 1949. There, with the guidance of master chef Max Bugnard, she took a course for housewives, but proprietor Madam Elizabeth Brassart did not favor American students. While Europeans struggled to reconstruct their lives after the war, Americans took advantage of the strong dollar to travel en masse to Europe and buy up cultural artifacts with their money. As a result, many Europeans who were confronted with inflation and food rationing began to view Americans as brassy. However, Child had fallen in love with French culture and cuisine and determinedly signed up for a yearlong $450 course for professional chefs, thus becoming the first American woman to attend the Cordon Bleu on the GI Bill.

Hungry to learn, Child wanted to know what to do in the kitchen and why and how to do it. Bugnard taught Child and 11 other former GIs the basics of French cuisine, and she blossomed under his tutelage, discovering that "cooking was a rich and layered and endlessly fascinating subject."[10] Child attended classes between 7:00 and 11:00 A.M. and then rushed home to prepare lunch for Paul. She graduated from the Cordon Bleu on March 15, 1951, as a top-class home cook.

Before her marriage, Child had seen herself as an ordinary woman with unused talents; now she was a fearless student and soon would be a teacher. In 1952, Child and fellow Cordon Bleu students established their own cooking school, called L'Ecole des Gourmettes (School of the Epicures). Their first session commenced in a kitchen located at 81 Rue de l'Universite, and the school quickly developed a loyal following among Americans living in Paris. Later, so as not to offend the staff at the Cordon Bleu, they changed the name to L'Ecole de Trois Gourmandes (School of the Three Hearty Eaters).

In 1956, as Paul's assignment in Paris ended, the couple returned to the United States and resettled in their home in Georgetown. Not one to be idle, Child started teaching cooking classes in the spring of 1957 for women in the Washington, D.C., area. Soon she was commuting to Philadelphia to teach a similar class for eight women. Paul had designed the distinctive L'Ecole de Trois Gourmandes insignia that Child wore when she taught her classes, usually on a simple blouse of blue with a straight skirt. This gave her a clean, professional, yet approachable and distinctly American look.

COOKBOOKS

Mastering the Art of French Cooking

Child's ties to France and French cuisine continued. While in France she had begun to collaborate with two French women, Simone Beck and Louisette Bertholle, on a cookbook project. They sought to create a synthesized yet task-layered manuscript that would teach the basic elements of Cordon Bleu cooking and that could be used by ordinary cooks in home kitchens. Beck and Bertholle had begun the project and recruited Julia to assist them in writing this cookbook for American audiences. Child brought precision and discipline to the project by testing and retesting recipes and rewriting them to get the language perfect. After years of work, the trio signed a contract with publisher Houghton Mifflin, only to have it ultimately reject the 500-page manuscript, saying it would be too formidable for American readers.

However, the manuscript made its way to the desk of Judith Jones at the publishing house of Alfred A. Knopf in the summer of 1959. Jones, an unabashed Francophile, had worked with translations of works by Jean-Paul Sartre and Albert Camus. She had made a name for herself in publishing at Doubleday when, while working in Paris, she retrieved Anne Frank's diary from a rejection pile and advocated for its publication. Jones immediately saw the value of the manuscript before her. She recognized "that the genius in these pages lay not only in explaining all the techniques so meticulously but in the structure, which was based on master recipes and their variations."[11]

While the Childs were living in France, American chefs, including James Beard and Helen Evans Brown, had been nurturing an emerging culinary intelligentsia that challenged home-cooking classics like *Joy of Cooking* (1931) and *Fannie Farmer* (1896). Jones was aware of this trend and saw the value of a French cookbook for American cooks. Unwilling to give up on the three women, she garnered support from knowledgeable colleagues, including food editor for *House Beautiful* magazine, Helen McCully, to convince Alfred A. Knopf to publish the women's work. The first volume of *Mastering the Art of French Cooking* appeared in 1961, when Child was 50 years old. Through this process, Child met a gastronomic community that embraced her approach to cooking. McCully shared a typescript copy of the manuscript with Jacques Pépin and Jean-Claude Szurdak to get their feedback. Pépin, disappointed that he had not thought of the project himself, remembered, "Someone had taken the training and knowledge that Jean-Claude and I had acquired as apprentices and *commis* (French for kitchen apprentice) and codified it, broken it down into simple steps that someone who had never boiled a kettle of water could follow."[12] Child and Pépin met at McCully's home in 1960, and Pépin remembered, "The introductions over, we did what food people always do, talk shop. And in the case of Julia and me, we did so in French because her French was far more fluent than my English."[13]

With precise step-by-step instructions and helpful "cook's eye view" illustrations that clearly delineated the elements for preparing fine French cooking, *Mastering the Art of French Cooking* addressed the fears American women had about preparing French cuisine. Once a reader absorbed the information and tried the recipe, then that know-how could be applied to similar recipes found in other cookbooks. Most importantly, if readers followed their instructions, they could reasonably count on successful outcomes. Child had not only mastered the art of French cooking, she had mastered the art of cookbook writing.

TELEVISION SHOWS

Pioneer Edith Green

While not the first to teach cooking on television, Child became a natural pioneer in moving American food interests forward with educational television during the second half of the 20th century. Before public broadcasting, during the late 1940s and early 1950s, local commercial television stations had hired prominent local cooks to demonstrate food preparation and thereby attract more female viewers. For commercial television, the product was the message. Across the country, dozens of male and female performers, including Breta Griem in Milwaukee, Scoot Kennedy in New Orleans, Kay Middleton in Chicago, and Edith Green in San Francisco, captivated viewers and helped build a sense of community.

In the San Francisco television market, 49-year-old food educator Edith Green was the first to host a locally produced television cooking show, *Your Home Kitchen,* on KRON (NBC). She joined KRON when the station went on the air on November 15, 1949, with one of the first live hourlong daily cooking shows in the United States. Green had coauthored a practical cookbook during the war that taught young housewives how to prepare nutritional meals with homegrown and rationed foods. The book became obsolete in the postwar United States as advertisers encouraged consumers to go to supermarkets and purchase processed and frozen foods. Broadcasters communicated a consistent message that housewives should be efficient home economists with neat kitchens that had tied curtains and the latest white appliances. Network cooking demonstrations rarely provided exact recipes and contained subliminal messages to leave the cooking to professional dietitians and the labor to Chop-o-matics and Wonder Shredders.

Like Child, Green had been a cooking instructor, and *Your Home Kitchen* set the standard for cooking shows, introducing and endorsing products used in the cooking demonstration. The show was an immediate hit. A *San Francisco Chronicle* columnist wrote, "This culinary marathon, set in a model kitchen, rates acknowledgement as one of the better programs of any type on the local air. Authoritative, authentic, easily passed and loaded and useful copy material for the kitchen brigade. Edith Green's carefully prepared and intelligently presented food séance has acquired a wide following through the process of providing solid step-by-step information pleasantly and convincingly presented."[14] Although Green did not have Child's charisma, *Your Home Kitchen* retained the highest ratings for a locally produced NBC program. However, predatory network executives, wanting to profit from advertising for network shows in local markets, axed Green's show in 1953.

Child's Debut on Educational Television

Child's television career began serendipitously in 1961, when an early morning fire destroyed the WGBH facilities and forced the station to go dark. As a result of the fire, local newspapers, theaters, and other groups offered free advertising to WGBH, and local companies volunteered to underwrite production of specific programs, creating a new commercialized model of sponsorship for educational television in which the product sponsors were acknowledged with credits. This approach provided Child with an unprecedented opportunity. Whereas in commercial broadcasting the product has commercial breaks for advertising, in educational broadcasting, Child became a real person with real branding opportunities of her own.

A smart businesswoman, Child had contacted WGBH, the public television station in Boston, to promote *Mastering the Art of French Cooking*. At the time, WGBH did not have demonstration equipment, so Child brought her own hot plate, like the one she used in France, along with a copper bowl and whisk, apron, mushrooms, and a dozen eggs to demonstrate how to prepare an omelet. She remembered that "I demonstrated the proper technique for cutting and chopping, how to 'turn' a mushroom cap, beat egg whites, and make an omelet."[15]

Meanwhile, educational television had begun its transformation into what is today known as the Public Broadcasting Service (PBS). When Child sought to promote *Mastering the Art of French Cooking* at WGBH-Channel 2 in Boston, it was an unexplored format for PBS. In the beginning, Channel 2 aired programming Monday through Friday between 5:30 and 9:00 P.M. Like many other early educational television stations, most of WGBH's programming consisted of televising course lectures that had been taped live. Child brought author E. B. White's observation of public broadcasting's mission to fruition. White said, "Noncommercial television should address itself to the ideal of excellence not the idea of acceptability . . . television should be the visual counterpart of the literary essay, should arouse our dreams, satisfy our hunger for beauty, take us on journeys, enable us to participate in events, present great drama and music, explore the sea and sky and hills."[16] Public broadcasting carried Child's warm personality into American homes so that she became a member of their families. As PBS expanded children's programming, young viewers would tune in to *Sesame Street* and see Big Bird and friends, and then stay tuned to Julia Child for cooking fun that encouraged viewers of all ages to work through spills and kitchen mishaps. It was a very different model from Green's.

"This is Julia Child. Bon Appétit!"

The viewers loved Child's demonstration of preparing omelets, and when she was in front of the cameras, it was like the sun had come out. WGBH received 27 letters asking for more cooking demonstrations. Since the station had never produced a cooking show, it invited Child back to develop three half-hour pilot programs of *The French Chef* for television in 1962. The test series began with a program called "The French Omelets," followed by "Coq au Vin" and "Soufflés." Child and producer Russell Morash had the idea of taping it before a live audience, but instead they decided to shoot the program in "one uninterrupted 30-minute take."[17]

The program's sponsor, the Boston Gas Company, provided a demonstration kitchen in its facility in downtown Boston with a freestanding stove and a work counter, and it was credited at the end of the program. The Childs went to the site to sketch the demonstration kitchen and then went home to block out and choreograph logical sequences for demonstrating the recipes.

The French Chef pilot was taped in black-and-white film with an uninterrupted 30-minute take on June 18, 1962, and the "The French Omelet" program aired on July 25, 1962. Child remembered, "There I was in black and white, a large woman sloshing eggs too quickly here, too slowly there, gasping, looking at the wrong camera while talking too loudly, and so on. Paul said I looked and sounded just like myself, but it was hard for me to be objective."[18] Viewers wanted more, and Child and the crew produced a series of 26 more cooking programs.

Child smartly started her television cooking program with a hearty beef stew: good ordinary fare in line with the philosophy of L'Ecole de Trois Gourmandes and not a Cordon Bleu high-end masterpiece. She opened the show with a concise summary of exactly what she was going to demonstrate and started with the fundamentals, explaining the different cuts of beef and the amount of beef needed for a single portion. She instructed the viewer that excess moisture from the beef should be removed before browning and which type of spatula was best for the task at hand. Preparing the stew was quick and well rehearsed; pans appeared and then disappeared behind the camera's view.

The production used three cameras: front on, angled, and a "giraffe" for the bird's eye overhead view over the stove. Child sometimes looked into the wrong camera, but she would catch herself and turn to the right camera. She demonstrated how to peel onions before braising them; how to wash and prepare mushrooms prior to sautéing; and then recommended that the stew be served with a classic boiled-potato-with-parsley dish, a green salad of romaine, French bread, and a young full-bodied wine. Her pace was a little too fast, so she had to fill in time at the end by reviewing what she had just done and suggesting more tips. Child informed her viewers that the next program would be about making French onion soup and closed her first show with "This is Julia Child. Welcome to *The French Chef*, and see you next time. *Bon Appétit!"*

In the second program, "Making Your Own French Onion Soup," Child was more polished in her use of the demonstration kitchen. Even though the camera picked up glare from utensils and swayed off the mark on occasion, Child was learning about broadcasting while her viewers learned about French cooking. The viewer saw the proper way to cut onions beneath the titles as Child deftly demonstrated more basic cooking techniques, including how to select and care for knives. She advised her viewers on how to "get in the habit of using the tool correctly," then explained that using sharp knives to cut onions helped to prevent tears. Child taught that communicating directly with the people in the marketplace, including butchers, was the best way to learn about products. Gone was the schoolmarm; the viewer was transported to Child's kitchen. She removed the steamy concoction from the broiler to the kitchen table and recommended an appropriate wine, green salad, and fruit for dessert. Child concluded with what would become one of her trademark quips: "This is really the soup that made the onion famous." She signed off, "That is it for today on *The French Chef*. This is Julia Child! Bon Appetit!" The credits appeared over more shots of the steamy soup. Child's recipe for success was complete.

Another more subtle innovation came with Child's interaction with her set. Viewers had the feeling that they were not observing a cook in a demonstration kitchen, but rather, they were friends in Child's kitchen. Each program culminated with Child sweeping up a beautifully prepared meal and freely moving from the kitchen to a dining area, where the viewer expected a guest to join her as soon as the cameras faded to black. This format influenced the way architects designed new homes; following Child, housewives began displaying cookware within easy reach instead of hiding them in cabinets. Moreover, Child's sparkle and energy quickly established her as a local celebrity. But despite her carefree manner, Child was hardworking and purposeful in her campaign to empower Americans in the kitchen. She shot four episodes a week while also writing a weekly food column for *The Boston Globe*.

"The Courage of Your Convictions"

WGBH's new studios were completed at 125 Western Avenue in Allston on August 29, 1963. That same year, the National Association of Educational Broadcasters created a new division of educational stations to represent stations before the government, to compile data about fund-raising activities, to hold regional conferences, and to establish an educational television program library service. The original series *The French Chef* ran nationally on public television between 1962 and 1972, with 119 episodes in black and white and 72 in color, and as an early component of the educational television program library, many early episodes of *The French Chef* were rebroadcasted so many times that they simply wore out.

The 50-year-old homey and unpretentious Child and her *French Chef* series established a loyal marketable audience for cooking programs. The earliest programs were crude and illustrated a "technical clunkiness" present in many live shows of the era. While the earlier television chefs on commercial television bowed down to the needs of sponsors, or were shown the door for demonstrating, Child first appeared on television at a time when Madison Avenue advertising agencies marketed processed foods and prepackaged mixes without challenge from television cooks, along with the message that housewives should get out of the kitchen. Women were not necessarily encouraged to go out and pursue careers, but rather to get out of the house to consume.

Like her father, Child had a kind of golden power that swept away obstacles in front of the cameras and in life. Her charm was like a wave that did not ask for permission of ships and shells before moving forward. Like her mother, she was fiercely independent and held strong opinions. This was apparent in her later television repartee with other chefs, including close friend Pépin as they debated the merits of different cooking techniques.

Child credited her success with *The French Chef* to her life in France and to the presence of a French chef in the Kennedy White House during the early 1960s. Judith Jones observed that Child "was empowered by her husband Paul, who had a highly analytical mind and a fine, educated palette."[19] Both women believed that cheap airfares and cultural exchanges had changed the American palette in the postwar years. Child believed that the Kennedy administration, particularly with Jacqueline's French heritage and their French chef, had created an atmosphere conducive for introducing French cuisine to Americans. But Child also had something other television cooks lacked: impeccable timing and the ability to ad-lib. Pépin stated, "Julia was expert at playing to the camera, and even though she sometimes said something that sounded as though she had just thought of it at the last moment, she had planned it in advance."[20]

Child also appeared to be the master of kitchen improvisation, explaining to viewers how experimentation can lead to success. In "The Potato Show," she demonstrated how to sauté potatoes and set out to flip the mixture, asserting, "This is a daring thing to do . . . you have to have the courage of your convictions with a loose mash like this."[21] As she flipped the mixture, some of the potatoes landed on the stovetop. "That did not go so well," she lamented. "You can always pick it up . . . if you are alone in your kitchen." Dumping it back in the skillet without skipping a beat, she concluded, "Who is to know? The only way you can learn is to just flip it." Child added, "You haven't lost anything. . . . You can always turn it into something else." She patted the mixture down, topped it off with cheese and more cream, and exclaimed: "This is awfully good!" Later in the program, Child demonstrated a recipe for potato pancakes, stating, "I am going to flip it—by gum." After executing a perfect flip, she signed off: "Courage, and Bon Appetit. This is Julia Child."

OTHER ENDEAVORS

With her unique style, Child provided consumer information on PBS that encouraged viewers to think critically and to ask informed questions on food and nutrition. She created awareness on public television that gave her tremendous clout, allowing her to became a reliable voice promoting the culinary arts, as well as promoting food safety and more variety in the marketplace. When Child demonstrated a recipe with a certain cut of meat, she created a demand. For example, beginning in 1964, Child bought meat, poultry, and fish for her WGBH productions at Savenor's Market located in Harvard Square. Beyond developing a long friendship, proprietor Jack Savenor generated publicity for the market when he appeared on *The French Chef*.

In 1965, Child received the George Foster Peabody Award for "distinguished achievement in television" for *The French Chef*. Then in 1966 she became the first educational television personality to receive an Emmy Award. By 1965 *The French Chef* was being carried by 100 PBS stations in the United States. In 1966, Child collaborated with Paul to produce *The French Chef Cookbook* (1968), based upon the television show. Paul also provided photographs and editorial assistance when Julia collaborated again with Simone Beck on the second volume of *Mastering the Art of French Cooking* (1970).

Had Child stopped with *Mastering the Art of French Cooking* and *The French Chef*, she would have held an important place in culinary history, since these works were substantive and groundbreaking. But she went on. By 1970, PBS had started its first season with a network of 198 television stations. The Polaroid Corporation provided a grant for color film to use for the regular demonstration programs as well as shoots taped on location. This enabled the Childs to travel to locations in France to show viewers food sources and basic preparation within cultural and geographical contexts. It was only the beginning. On a more profound level, Child began to be involved in multiculturalism, exploring cuisines from different regions, and in the counterculture, exploring the implications of macrobiotics for Americans.

Child encouraged consumers to rely less on processed foods and more on their creativeness in the kitchen. A new book, *From Julia Child's Kitchen* (1975), marked a turning point for Child as she began to integrate more American food into her repertoire. She asserted, "I have always looked at French cuisine from an American point of view."[22] With this book, she included recipes for beginners and fast and economic home consumption, offering readers the following advice: "Learn how to cook—that's the way to save money."[23] For her pioneering work, Child received numerous honors both in France and the United States. In 1980, she became the first woman to be inducted into La Commanderie de Cordons Bleus de France.

In 1989, Child published another book, *The Way to Cook*, which had accompanying video books produced in collaboration between WGBH and Knopf. In television, she transitioned from public to commercial broadcasting, appearing on the Dick Cavett and Phil Donahue shows before regularly appearing on

---

Pastry Dough—Pâte Brisée

B.T.F.P.—Before The Food Processor—it was only the practiced cook who produced decent pastry dough. And what a to-do it was: first the making of a fountain of flour on a clean board, the clearing of a space in its center for the butter and liquids, and the working of them together with cool, deft fingers—all done by that practiced cook with an infuriatingly calm smile of superiority. Now, in less than 5 minutes, that wonderful F.P. machine enables any one of us to make perfect pastry dough every time. We are thus, with our own triumphant smiles, instantly masters of the quiche, the tart, the turnover, countless hors d'ouevre niblets, to say nothing of the chicken pot pie.

—Julia Child, *The Way to Cook*. New York: Knopf, 1989, p. 380

ABC's morning show *Good Morning America* in short two-and-a-half-minute segments in 1980. When Pépin's *La Méthode* (1979) was published, he was asked to appear with Child on Tom Snyder's *Tomorrow Show*. Child cut her finger during her customary cooking preparation moments before they were to go on air, but she carried on with the interview, and the event became a legendary anecdote to be used in other interviews and for Dan Aykroyd's famous spoof on *Saturday Night Live*.[24]

Child continued to be featured in more WGBH series for PBS: *Julia Child & More Company* (1980), *Dinner at Julia's* (1983), and *The Way to Cook* (1989). She continued spotlighting American recipes, ingredients, and wines with her on-location shoots and helped establish the American Institute of Wine and Food in Napa, California. This 1981 venture with vintners Robert Mondavi and Richard Graff provided an educational venue to "advance the understanding, appreciation and quality of wine and food." As the matriarch of the PBS cooking show family, Child's role as teacher expanded, and she began to mentor younger chefs. Pépin appeared on Martin Yan's *Yan Can Cook* show for KQED in 1988 and was asked to tape his own series for the station.[25]

Child's roles as student and teacher blurred as she used her tremendous name recognition to propel new culinary trends into the spotlight. When she was no longer able to maintain a rigorous television schedule, she worked with A La Carte Production on *Cooking with Master Chefs* (1993), *In Julia's Kitchen with Master Chefs* (1995), and *Baking with Julia* (1996). In these series, she cooked alongside a variety of master chefs, including Marcus Farbinger of the Culinary Institute of America, Leah Chase (The Queen of Creole Cuisine), French-born proponent of French and California fusion cuisine Michel Richard, Italian-born Roberto Donna, and master pastry chef Jacques Torres.

Comedians such as Dan Aykroyd, Fannie Flagg, Carol Burnett, John Cleese, and others parodied Child's penchant for kitchen mishaps and cover-ups. However, beyond being a master teacher who did not discriminate by age, Child was also an entertainer who appealed to multiple generations of possible cooks. Many people think of Child whenever they hear the distinctive breezy theme for *The French Chef,* written by John Morris and recorded by Arthur Fiedler and the Boston Pops in 1972. In 1975, Child mentored American-born Chef Brocket (played by actor Don Brockett) on *Mister Rogers' Neighborhood.* In this program, Mister Rogers visits Brocket Bakery, where he finds Child preparing Spaghetti Marco Polo, which the three eat using chopsticks.

CONCLUSION

Child retained a unique presence on the world stage as a woman excelling in a field traditionally dominated by men. By her later years, her experiences, friends, and great love Paul had evolved her soul far beyond the sheltered girl from Pasadena, California. Child was not the first television cook, but she developed the largest audience for a PBS series during the 1960s and established herself as a formidable consumer advocate. In 1993, she was the first woman to be inducted into the Culinary Institute Hall of Fame and received France's Legion d'Honneur, its highest honor, in November 2002. She was the first television cooking show icon to use educational television to create awareness about food preparation of haute cuisine, reminding viewers that cooking is an art form and that kitchens were places of individual discovery and innovation. In 2002, the Smithsonian's National Museum of American History opened an exhibit of the turquoise-colored kitchen in which three of her cooking shows were filmed. Child died in Santa Barbara, California, at the age of 91 on August 13, 2004.

NOTES

1. Noel Riley Fitch, *Appetite for Life: The Biography of Julia Child* (New York: Doubleday, 1996), 9.

2. Fitch, *Appetite for Life,* 9.

3. Julia Child and Alex Prud'homme, *My Life in France* (New York: Alfred A. Knopf, 2006), 3.

4. Alice Julier, "Julia at Smith," *Gastronomica: The Journal of Food and Culture* 5:3 (Summer 2005): 44.

5. Charlotte Painter, *Gifts of Age: Portraits and Essays of 32 Remarkable Women* (San Francisco: Chronicle Books, 1985), 75.

6. Painter, *Gifts of Age,* 75.

7. Painter, *Gifts of Age,* 7.

8. Child and Prud'homme, *My Life in France,* 5.

9. "Julia Child: America's Favorite Chef," *American Masters,* written and produced by Marilyn Mellowes (Boston: WGBH Educational Foundation, 2004), DVD, 58 min.

10. Child and Prud'homme, *My Life in France,* 58.

11. Judith Jones, *The Tenth Muse: My Life in Food* (New York: Knopf, 2007), 60.

12. Jacques Pépin, *The Apprentice: My Life in the Kitchen* (Boston: Houghton Mifflin, 2003), 182.

13. Pépin, *The Apprentice,* 196.

14. Child and Prud'homme, *My Life in France,* 236.

15. Terrence O'Flaherty, *Variety,* September 12, 1951.

16. *It's Been a Great 30 Years* (Boston: WGBH Educational Foundation, May 1985).

17. Child and Prud'homme, *My Life in France,* 120.

18. Child and Prud'homme, *My Life in France,* 242.

19. Judith Jones, "Julia: The Ever-Curious Cook." *Gastronomica: The Journal of Food and Culture* 5:3 (Summer 2005): 26.

20. Jacques Pépin, "My Friend Julia Child," *Gastronomica: The Journal of Food and Culture* 5:3 (Summer 2005): 12.

21. "The Potato Show," *The French Chef,* DVD, disk 1, no. 2.

22. Julia Child, *From Julia Child's Kitchen* (New York: Alfred A. Knopf, 1975), ix.

23. Child, *From Julia Child's Kitchen,* xi.

24. Pépin, *The Apprentice,* 267.

25. Pépin, *The Apprentice,* 258, 265.

FURTHER READING

Fitch, Noel Riley. *Appetite for Life: The Biography of Julia Child.* New York: Doubleday, 1996.

Jones, Judith. "Julia: The Ever-Curious Cook." *Gastronomica: The Journal of Food and Culture* 5:3 (Summer 2005): 26–28.

Jones, Judith. *The Tenth Muse: My Life in Food.* New York: Knopf, 2007.

Julier, Alice. "Julia at Smith." *Gastronomica: The Journal of Food and Culture* 5:3 (Summer 2005): 44–53.

Painter, Charlotte. *Gifts of Age: Portraits and Essays of 32 Remarkable Women.* San Francisco: Chronicle Books, 1985.

Pépin, Jacques. *The Apprentice: My Life in the Kitchen.* Boston: Houghton Mifflin, 2003.

Pépin, Jacques. "My Friend Julia Child." *Gastronomica: The Journal of Food and Culture* 5:3 (Summer 2005): 9–14.

Reardon, Joan. *M. F. K. Fisher, Julia Child, and Alice Waters: Celebrating the Pleasures of the Table.* New York: Harmony Books, 1994.

Stumpf, Bill, with Nicholas Polites and Dick Swift. *Julia's Kitchen: A Design Anatomy.* Minneapolis, MN: Walker Art Center, 1977.

WGBH. *It's Been a Great 30 Years.* Boston: WGBH Educational Foundation, May 1985.

Publications by Julia Child

Beck, Simone, with Louisette Bertholle and Julia Child. *Mastering the Art of French Cooking.* New York: Alfred A. Knopf, 1961.

Tour of Dining Décor 1965: Recipes. San Francisco: Women's Board of the San Francisco Museum of Art, 1965.

The French Chef Cookbook. New York: Alfred A. Knopf, 1968.

Beck, Simone, with Julia Child. *Mastering the Art of French Cooking*. Vol. 2. New York: Alfred A. Knopf, 1970.

Complete Dinners from the French Chef Cookbook (advertising promotion for Dove Soap). New York: Bantam, 1972.

Lunch & Party Dishes from the French Chef Cookbook (advertising promotion for Dove Soap). New York: Bantam, 1972.

From Julia Child's Kitchen. New York: Knopf, 1975.

Los Angeles Planned Parenthood Presents Julia Child: Luncheon Spectaculars. Los Angeles: Planned Parenthood, 1976.

Julia Child: A Benefit for the UCSD Medical Center: Tuesday, February 7 and Wednesday, February 8, 1978, Mandevill Center, University of California. San Diego, CA: ECSD Medical Center Auxiliary, 1978.

Julia Child's Menu Cookbook. New York: Random House, 1978.

The Way to Cook. New York: Alfred A. Knopf, 1978.

A Culinary Collection: Julia Child at the Denver Art Museum. Denver: Denver Art Museum, 1979.

With E. S. Yntema. *Julia Child & More Company*. New York: Alfred A. Knopf, 1979.

Cooking Demonstration, the Schlesinger Library, Radcliffe College by Julia Child, Tuesday March 27 at 8:00 pm; Wednesday, March 28 at 8:00 pm; Thursday, March 29 at 2:00 pm, Harvard University Science Center. Boston: Abbott Printers, 1984.

With Mary Mapes Dunn. *Recipes from the Inauguration of Mary Mapes Dunn as the Eighth President of Smith College, September, 1985, Northampton, Massachusetts*. Northampton, MA: Marilyn Nelson and the Committee for the Inauguration, 1985.

With E. S. Yntema. *Julia Child & Company*. New York: Alfred A. Knopf, 1989.

With music by Lee Hoiby. *Bon Appetit! A Musical Monolog for Mezzo-Soprano and Chamber Ensemble*. New York: G. Schirmer, 1989.

With Nancy Verde Barr. *In Julia Child's Kitchen with Master Chefs*. New York: Alfred A. Knopf, 1991.

What's in It? The Busy Cook's Diet and Nutrition Guide to The Way to Cook *Cookbook*. Norwood, MA: Nutriinfo, 1991.

Cooking with Master Chefs. New York: Alfred A. Knopf, 1993.

The Way to Cook: Fear of Food, Indulgences & Small Helpings (broadside). Berkeley, CA: Okeanos Press, 1993.

With Dorie Greenspan. *Baking with Julia Based upon the PBS Series by Julia Child*. New York: Morrow, 1996.

Julia's Delicious Little Dinners. New York: Alfred A. Knopf, 1998.

With Burton Wolf. *An American Feast: A Celebration of Cooking on Public Television*. San Francisco: Bay Books, 1999.

With E. S. Yntema. *Julia's Casual Dinners*. New York: Alfred A. Knopf, 1999.

Julia's Menus for Special Occasions. New York: Alfred A. Knopf, 1999.

With Jacques Pépin and David Nussbaum. *Cooking at Home*. New York: Alfred A. Knopf, 1999.

Julia's Kitchen Wisdom: Essential Techniques and Recipes from a Lifetime of Cooking featuring Martin Yan, Lidia Matticchio Bastianich, Paul Prudhomme, Jacques Pépin, and Nathalie Dupree. New York: Alfred A. Knopf, 2000.

With Alex Prud'homme. *My Life in France*. New York: Alfred A. Knopf, 2006.

ARCHIVAL COLLECTIONS

Julia McWilliams Child Papers, The Arthur and Elizabeth Schlesinger Library, Radcliffe College, Cambridge, MA.

Television Series

The French Chef with Julia Child (Boston: WGBH Educational Foundation, 1962–1972), video recording.

Julia Child & Company (Boston: WGBH Educational Foundation, 1978), video recording.

Kitchen Cocktail Party (Washington, DC: PBS Video, 1978), video recording.

Julia Child & More Company (Boston: WGBH Educational Foundation, 1980), video recording.

Dinner at Julia's (Boston: WGBH Educational Foundation, 1983), video recording.

The Way to Cook (Boston: WGBH Educational Foundation/Knopf Video Books, 1984), video recording.

Television and the Cook (Louisville, KY: International Association of Cooking Schools, 1985), video recording.

A Taste for Norway (Boston: WGBH Educational Foundation, 1992), video recording.

Dinner at Julia's (Guilford, CT: A La Carte Productions/Maryland Public Television, 1993), video recording.

Cooking with Master Chefs (Guilford, CT: A La Carte Productions/Maryland Public Television, 1993–1994), video recording.

With Graham Kerr. *Cooking in Concert* (Guilford, CT: A La Carte Productions, 1994), video recording.

The Best of Food and Wine: A Worldwide Culinary Tour Featuring Video Tips from Six of the World's Greatest Chefs (Seattle, WA: Multicom, 1995), computer file.

In Julia's Kitchen with Master Chefs (Guilford, CT: A La Carte Productions/Maryland Public Television, 1995), video recording.

With Jacques Pépin. *Julia Child and Jacques Pépin: Cooking in Concert* (Guilford, CT: A La Carte Productions, 1995), video recording.

Baking with Julia (Guilford, CT: A La Carte Productions/Maryland Public Television, 1996), video recording.

Julia Child: Home Cooking with Master Chefs (Guilford, CT: A La Carte Productions/ Maryland Public Television, 1996), CD-ROM.

With Jacques Pépin. *Julia Child and Jacques Pépin: More Cooking in Concert taped at the TSAI Performance Center at Boston University in Association with Boston University's Culinary Arts Program* (Guilford, CT: A La Carte Productions, 1996), video recording.

Selected Appearances and Articles

"Julia Child Writes for *The Epicure* about the Pleasures of Cooking." *The Epicure* (Fall/Winter 1963): 19–24, 73–78.

Fiedler, Arthur. *Evening at the Pops* (Polydor, 1972), sound recording, 35 min.

Mister Rogers' Neighborhood. Program 1354 (Pittsburgh: WQED / Family Communications, 1975), video recording, 30 min.

"La 'Nouvelle Cuise': A Skeptic's View." *New York* (July 4, 1977): 32–34.

Primordial Soup (Washington, DC: National Air and Space Museum, 1981), video recording, 10 min.

Television and the Cook (Louisville, KY: International Association of Cooking Schools, 1985), video recording, 90 min.

NOVA: How to Create a Junk Food (Northbrook, IL: Coronet Film & Video, 1988), video recording, 58 min.

"On Writing a Cookbook: 1988 Versus 1960." *Radcliff Quarterly* (December 1988): 6–7.

Reading Rainbow (No. 069). "Florence and Eric Take the Cake" (Baltimore, MD: GPN Educational Media, 1990), video recording, 30 min.

Julia's Homecoming: An Evening with Julia Child at the Valley Hunt Club (Pasadena, CA: Pasadena Valley Hunt Club, November 7, 1990), video recording.

Krainin, Julian (with Michael R. Lawrence). *Memory & Imagination: New Pathways to the Library of Congress* (San Francisco: KQED, 1990), video recording, 58 min., 35 sec.

With Tim White. *Julia Child, Seafood Safety* (Washington, DC: U.S. Department of Commerce, 1991), aired on Fox Morning News and Fox 10 O'Clock News, WTTG-Fox Channel 5, on October 14, 1991), video recording, 7 min., 49 sec.

Some Thoughts on American Foods in the 90's (Chicago, IL: National Restaurant Association, 1992), sound recording, 46 min.

With Robert Mondavi; read by Eric Brotman. *The Sound of Wine* (Berkeley, CA: Audio Literature, 1992), audio recording.

With C. Wayne Calloway. *Resetting the American Table: Creating a New Alliance of Taste & Health* (San Diego: Nuffer, Smith, Tucker, 1992), video recording, 6 min., 28 sec.

American Conservatory Theater. *Bon Appetit: Two Musical Monologues*; music by Lee Hoiby; words by Ruth Draper and Julia Child, dir. Carey Perloff, musical dir. Todd Sisley, Jean Stapleton (as Julia Child); pianist Todd Sisley, presented December 14, 1992–January 9, 1993.

Wornum, Barbara (with Maria Tucci). *M. F. K.: American Writer Mary Frances Kennedy Fisher* (Santa Monica, CA: Direct Cinema, 1993), video recording, 43 min.

We're Back! A Dinosaur's Story (Universal City, CA: MCA Universal Home Video, 1993), animated video recording, 71 min.

"How I Learned to Love Cooking." *Parade* (November 13, 1994): 13.

Inside Hunger (Atlanta, GA: Georgia Public Television Production, 1995), video recording, 56 min.

With Maya Angelou. *City Arts of San Francisco Presents Julia Child Recorded Live at the Herbst Theatre, May 1, 1995* (Petaluma, CA: Pacific Vista Productions, 1995), audiocassette tape, 59 min.

Robert & Margrit Mondavi: Visions and Reflections. Napa, CA: Janssens; San Francisco: Arion Press, 1996.

Jewish Cooking in America with Joan Nathan: What Is Kosher? (Owings Mills, MD: Maryland Public Television/Frappe, 1998), video recording, 58 min.

American Masters, "Julia Child: America's Favorite Chef" (Boston: WGBH Educational Foundation/Thirteen/WNET New York, 2004), DVD, 60 min.

Meredith Eliassen

BETTY CROCKER MAKEOVER

| 1936 | 1955 | 1965 | 1968 |

| 1972 | 1980 | 1986 | 1996 |

Minneapolis-based General Mills created a new image for Betty Crocker from 75 computer-fed photos of real women, for a new facelift on the 75th anniversary of Betty Crocker products in 1996. (AP/Wide World Photos)

Betty Crocker

Betty Crocker is one of the oldest, and perhaps the most successful, trade characters in U.S. food advertising. Since her "birth" in 1921, she has been a continual presence in U.S. popular culture, and, more recently, she has also had an active international life. Although many Americans may not be able to provide a physical description of Betty Crocker, an astonishingly large number of American men, women, and children recognize her name and have ideas about what she stands for. Over her long life as a brand icon, Betty Crocker has had a number of distinct images and meanings. She began as a food and cooking expert who represented the difficult skills needed to cook "from scratch," but today she represents convenient and time-saving food.

Betty Crocker first emerged following a significant shift in food culture in the United States. In the early 20th century, a variety of cultural trends created a situation in which many women believed they did not have the skills they needed to cook good meals for their families. As the practice of hiring in-home cooks declined, some women from middle- and upper-class families found themselves cooking for the first time. At all economic levels, families were becoming smaller, women were starting to marry at younger ages than their own mothers had, and physical distances between relatives were growing larger. As a result, many women had fewer opportunities to learn how to cook from their mothers, grandmothers, or aunts. These new and largely untaught cooks had numerous questions and concerns, and in the search for answers many turned to the companies that supplied the raw ingredients for cooking. This was especially true of companies that sold flour, because homemade baked goods were an important part of most family diets. Baking, however, is one of the more difficult cooking skills to learn.

The Washburn Crosby Company of Minneapolis, Minnesota, became acutely aware of its customers' concerns when, in response to an ad campaign that included a customer mail-in component, it received hundreds of letters seeking help and information about how to cook. Recognizing that it would be good for business to answer these questions, the company hired a number of food economists to write replies to customer letters. After a short time during which one of the senior male managers signed the response letter, the company chose to invent a female trade character, who might resonate better with the women who were its primary customers. The character was given the name "Betty Crocker" in 1921. The company history recounts that the name "Betty" was chosen because it sounded wholesome and cheery to Samuel Gale and James Quint, the executives in charge of developing the response plan. They chose "Crocker" to honor a recently retired company director.

Betty Crocker first existed as a signature rather than as a complete character, and today that signature remains her most widely recognized feature. At first, the company's secretaries each provided a sample signature for Betty Crocker, and the handwriting of Florence Linderberg was considered the best match to the character's developing persona. Over time, variations of the signature were devised, but today elements of the original can still be seen in the bold signature of Betty Crocker on many products and in much company advertising, often written within the bowl of a stylized red spoon.

In creating Betty Crocker, Washburn Crosby followed a model that had already proved useful to a number of U.S. food companies. As these companies became larger and as regional and national brands replaced local firms, it was important to find ways to connect with the customers. Identifying a spokesperson or developing a trade character was a technique that many food companies used to create a direct personal relationship with their customers. In some cases, real individuals were asked to be spokespeople. However, these individuals brought their own separate personality to the companies, and they could not be totally and exclusively connected to a company or even controlled. Most companies found that a real spokesperson worked best in shorter, focused campaigns for specific products. For long-term representation of an entire company, it was usually more efficient to craft a fictional trade character. When a company created such a character, it could ensure that that character would represent the product in a way that would symbolize the company exactly as desired and also could be molded over time to create continuing emotional ties between the customers, the products, and the company.

Although many changes have occurred in U.S. advertising, trade characters continue to be successful components of advertising campaigns. Sometimes, companies create a trade character that is anthropomorphic but not human, like Mr. Peanut (created in 1901), the Jolly Green Giant (1958), Charlie the Tuna (1961), and the Pillsbury Doughboy (1965). Sometimes, companies have chosen to create trade characters like Uncle Ben (created after World War II) and Aunt Jemima (one of the very first trade characters, who first appeared in the late 19th century) who are closely or distantly based on a real person. But the most successful trade characters have tended to be those who, like Betty Crocker, are wholly invented but seemingly real individuals, who have been specifically designed to embody key components of the products and companies they represent.

EARLY YEARS

The 1920s

In addition to responding to customer letters, Betty Crocker helped Washburn Crosby actively reach out to the public. Almost as soon as the company created "Miss Betty Crocker," the brand character offered a box of recipe cards to those who purchased Washburn and Crosby flour. Significantly, the company chose to make Betty Crocker an unmarried woman, even though most of her initial audience was married women. Her singlehood underlined Betty Crocker's professional life as a food expert, one who, like many professional women at the time, had chosen not to marry. Betty Crocker was presented a back story as a home economist, and she was made the titular manager of the company's test kitchens. By providing Betty Crocker with this professional resume, the company ensured that her audience would see Betty Crocker as someone with the experience and authority to provide trustworthy answers to women's cooking questions and whose recipes women could follow with confidence. Indeed, Betty Crocker's initial recipe offer was extremely popular and was followed by many recipe booklets, most focused on baking and all of which underlined the connection between Betty Crocker and Washburn Crosby by specifying that Washburn Crosby brands of flour were essential to the recipes' success.

Not only did the company have Betty Crocker interact with individual women by answering their letters and sending them recipes, but it also had her speaking to large general audiences over the radio. Like Betty Crocker herself, radio stations and regular radio shows developed early in the 1920s. In October 1924, Washburn Crosby, which had acquired a radio station of its own, began a program featuring Betty Crocker that provided cooking information and other advice to homemakers. The company's effort was not the first of its kind; in many ways the Washburn Crosby show copied a Chicago program that had been developed by the People's Gas Company. By 1924 the Betty Crocker radio program was airing every Monday, Wednesday, and Friday, and just a year later, in 1925, a second program was added, doubling the opportunities to hear Betty Crocker talk about food and homemaking.

The first of the on-air Betty Crockers was Blanche Ingersoll, and she was joined by 12 other women who broadcast as Betty Crocker on different regional stations, resulting in somewhat different voices and messages in the different radio markets. However, the company provided the scripts that were to be used in every region, and in 1927, when a national broadcasting network became available, every market heard the same Betty Crocker, voiced by Marjorie Child Husted, a trained home economist. Husted remained in the role until she retired in 1950, creating techniques for developing and testing recipes and writing scripts for the shows. She often represented Betty Crocker in public events as well.

On the *Gold Medal Flour Radio Cooking School,* Betty Crocker taught new cooks many different cooking skills. In the 27 years that the school was broadcast over the radio, more than a million listeners asked for a certificate of completion for their participation, and undoubtedly many more listened and learned from some or all of the shows. During the radio shows, Betty Crocker often read letters from listeners, sometimes using a listener question as a springboard to a discussion, sometimes simply sharing praise for company products. The company did not, however, broadcast the letters from the several men who wrote in to ask Betty Crocker to consider marrying them. As might be expected on a program sponsored by a flour company, baking, especially cake baking, was a frequent topic for the Betty Crocker radio programs. Betty Crocker's emphasis on homemade cakes as perfect for every occasion—including her repeated claim that men, especially husbands, love cake—has been identified as one of the reasons for the continuing emphasis in American cuisine on cakes as an ideal dessert for special occasions.

Washburn Crosby merged with many small regional milling companies in 1928 to form a new company called General Mills. Betty Crocker remained an integral part of the new company's advertising and helped customers make an easy transition from the old company to the new, both on the radio and in the grocery aisles. Soon after the consolidation, in 1929, Betty Crocker became associated with another traditional method of strengthening customer connections to a company. General Mills began a box-top redemption program in which individuals and, later, groups could collect box tops to use in exchange for merchandise that was selected and endorsed by Betty Crocker. The redemption program, which began with the offer of a spoon and other silverware but grew to include a whole catalog of different products, was very successful and lasted until 2006, long after many similar programs had ended.

The Great Depression and World War II

Throughout the 1930s and 1940s, Husted was quite active as Betty Crocker's public face. On several occasions she was sent to Hollywood, where Betty Crocker did cross-promotions with a number of Hollywood stars. Betty Crocker also appeared with movie stars in fan magazines and put together booklets of the stars' favorite recipes and homemaking tips, which were eagerly purchased by listeners of the radio shows.

At the same time that Husted was representing Betty Crocker on the radio and in person, General Mills decided it needed a specific advertising image of Betty Crocker that was not a photograph or representation of Husted herself. The company tried out a number of different images, most of youthful women with short hair. None of these were completely satisfactory, and in 1936 General Mills hired Neysa McMein, a well-known illustrator who often worked for *McCall's Magazine*, to create a portrait of Betty Crocker. McMein had to work for some time to create an image that satisfied General Mills. Her final, successful image was of a slightly older woman with streaks of gray in her hair and eyes that were described as "slate blue." Although it was not a full-length portrait, one could see in the picture that Betty Crocker was a professional woman, with tailored clothing just visible. She was a bit older than many of the women in her audience (the company's press release called her "an ageless 32"), which helped to create her authority. General Mills offered reproductions of the portrait to the public and used it in company advertising and sometimes in product packaging.

Throughout the Great Depression and during World War II, Betty Crocker's radio programs provided a reassuring voice that helped women to cope with food rationing and economic fears as well as their cooking dilemmas. Soon after it was formed, leadership from the National Recovery Administration (NRA), one of the central organizations in President Franklin D. Roosevelt's "New Deal," approached General Mills to ask that Betty Crocker help

Americans who were facing reduced incomes to change their menu choices and cooking practices to save money. Together with the NRA, General Mills produced and distributed recipes and menus that focused on lowering the cost of feeding the American family. Betty Crocker's radio show, as well as public nutrition classes and cooking demonstrations sponsored by General Mills, provided opportunities for interested cooks to learn more about how to put the printed materials into action.

When the United States entered World War II in 1941, Betty Crocker became even more active. It was clear that wartime listeners to the Betty Crocker radio shows often felt overwhelmed by the economic downturn and the war fears that intruded into their kitchens. The company received 4,000 to 5,000 letters every day with questions and concerns. In addition to staff-written replies to those letters, General Mills sent out over 7 million copies of a free Betty Crocker recipe booklet called *Your Share* to help women whose cooking responsibilities were becoming even more arduous as they tried to cope with shortages, rationing, and, in many cases, their own long hours of employment outside the home. In 1942, General Mills, which had published many recipe booklets, produced its first true cookbook, a small paperback titled *Betty Crocker Cook Book of All-Purpose Baking*, which included 220 recipes and was sold for 25 cents. More than 800,000 copies were distributed, but because many were completely worn out or discarded, they are not easily available today. In 1944, as another way to help women feel better about themselves and especially their role as chief cooks in their homes, Husted created the Betty Crocker Home Legion Program, which focused on recognizing the role of the homemaker in the war effort. More than 70,000 women enrolled. In 1945, General Mills and Betty Crocker worked with the Office of War Information on a four-month-long series of special programs to help women use their family ration coupons efficiently.

All of these activities combined to increase awareness of and appreciation for Betty Crocker in the public mind. Many Americans believed that Betty Crocker was a real person, and the company made it easy to continue to believe this, doing little to point out that she was only a trade character. In 1945, a *Fortune* magazine survey found that more than 90 percent of Americans recognized and admired Betty Crocker, and in 1949 *Business Week* called her one of the most successful advertising icons ever developed.

The 1950s and Beyond

The various Betty Crocker radio programs continued throughout the 1950s, but as televisions became more available to average Americans, radio became a less popular form of entertainment and source of information. From the time of the earliest TV transmissions, Betty Crocker was present, exploring how this new medium could be used. General Mills hired a new Betty Crocker for its television efforts, Adelaide Hawley (later, Adelaide Hawley Cumming). Unlike Husted, Hawley was not a professional home economist and had little experience of any kind with cooking, but she did have a wealth of experience in broadcasting. However, although General Mills sponsored two different Betty Crocker television programs, neither was able to attract audience interest. The company then gave up on the idea of offering a show but continued to buy advertising time that featured Betty Crocker. The commercials' small doses of Betty Crocker proved very effective, and the campaigns included a long series of advertisements on *The George Burns and Gracie Allen Show* in which Betty Crocker helped Gracie Allen make cakes and other items. Hawley remained the television Betty Crocker until 1964, though after 1960 most General Mills television commercials for Betty Crocker products did not actually show Betty Crocker herself. Most, however, included a shot of Betty Crocker's famous signature.

Although Cumming provided a living image of Betty Crocker in the 1950s and 1960s, until 1955 General Mills continued to use the visual image of Betty Crocker created by Neysa McMein as her official portrait. In 1955, General Mills retired the McMein image in favor of one in which Betty Crocker appears a little older, with additional amounts of gray in her hair. This image was used until 1965, when a new, younger Betty Crocker was created who wore a three-strand pearl necklace and whose hair showed no traces of gray. Over the next 18 years, four additional visual images (one each in 1969, 1972, 1980, and 1986) of Betty Crocker were developed, used for a while, and then replaced.

In 1972, the Minneapolis-St. Paul chapter of the National Organization of Women filed a class-action complaint against General Mills arguing that the image of Betty Crocker in use at the time was both sexist and racist. Although the complaint received some national and local attention, it was dropped and the company was not seriously disturbed, though it did update Betty Crocker's image that year. Indeed, Mercedes Bates, who oversaw the image changes between 1969 and 1986, said that, to her, Betty Crocker was always a "career woman" and "a *professional*, first and last."[1]

Attention to Betty Crocker declined in the 1980s and 1990s, though she was never completely absent from General Mills advertising or American popular culture. In 1996, General Mills took the opportunity of Betty Crocker's 75th anniversary to "relaunch" her as a symbol of the company's food products. During the first nine months of 1996, there were 45 individual newspaper stories, many more published as the result of wire service offerings, and at least 71 other print and electronic media stories, in all totaling more than 58,000 words about Betty Crocker. Although ordinarily General Mills did not announce the changes it made in Betty Crocker's image to the public at large, as part of the relaunch the company decided to focus an advertising campaign on the creation of a new portrait of Betty Crocker. The company held a contest to find 75 women of diverse ages and backgrounds who in their own lives represented ideals that they shared with Betty Crocker. A composite portrait was developed from the images of these individual women. The resulting Betty Crocker is no longer a blue- or green-eyed woman of white heritage, but someone with brown hair and eyes and a warm brown skin tone. This image may remain the official Betty Crocker, or the company may decide to create a new Betty Crocker as cultural changes occur.

In addition to the official images of Betty Crocker, which are available on a company Web site, other images of Betty Crocker can be found, especially from her earliest years. Many of these are variations on the McMein portrait. For example, the 1948 *Picture Cooky Book* includes an image of Betty Crocker that is recognizable as based on the McMein portrait, but in this image Betty Crocker is wearing a green jacket. In all of her official portraits she wears red. But images of Betty Crocker have never been the most important part of her persona. Advertising copy from General Mills sometimes included a small image of Betty Crocker, and Betty Crocker cookbooks sometimes include a small image of Betty Crocker on the spine, front, or back cover, but Betty Crocker's voice, whether over the air on the radio or in print, has been much more important than her physical image in her development as a trusted trade character and icon of American cooking. Many of the more than 200 Betty Crocker cookbooks have been published without her image, but almost every one has a title that begins "Betty Crocker. . . ." And most have included an opening letter to the reader, usually identified as "Dear Friend" or "Dear Friends," and signed "Betty Crocker" or sometimes "Cordially, Betty Crocker."

COOKBOOKS

In 1950, General Mills published *Betty Crocker's Picture Cookbook*. Though many Betty Crocker recipe booklets and at least one small cookbook had been published earlier, this was a comprehensive and innovative book, unlike any other that Betty Crocker, or other publishers, had produced up to that time. The book had 16 chapters and 2,161 recipes, as well as copious numbers of photographs and drawings to illustrate cooking techniques and show what foods should look like, not just at the end of cooking, but throughout the process of preparation. In some ways, the *Picture Cookbook* had taken the best of what the new medium of television offered—the ability to show cooking in action—and moved this to print. *Betty Crocker's Picture Cookbook* was an immediate success, selling more than 1 million copies in the first year, an astonishing record for cookbooks at the time.

Despite having hundreds of pictures, the first edition of the *Picture Cookbook* does not include an image of Betty Crocker. However, Betty Crocker is a vibrant presence in the *Picture Cookbook*, which, like the majority of Betty Crocker cookbooks, begins with a letter to readers that begins "Dear Friends" and is signed by Betty Crocker. She also signs the introductory notes that begin each of the book's sections, and her voice is directly present in some of the recipe notes, where she might, for example, refer to "my radio talks." This pattern is repeated in many of the cookbooks that followed, though over time there were some subtle shifts in the language used, as it became less important, and perhaps less possible, to pretend that there was a real Betty Crocker.

An example of how the prose voice of Betty Crocker changed over time can be seen among the introductions to the recipe for chocolate chip cookies in early and later cookbooks. In the 1948 *Betty Crocker's Picture Cooky Book,* a note printed before the chocolate chip cookie recipe tells the reader that it was first introduced on "my series of radio talks on Famous Foods from Famous Eating Places." Readers of the 1948 cookbook might have heard Betty Crocker on the radio, and for many of them she was a very real person. By 1958, a more sophisticated audience better understood that Betty Crocker was a symbol, and in *Betty Crocker's Cooky Carnival* the same recipe begins with a reference to "our series of radio talks." This corporate plural was retained in the 1963 *Betty Crocker's Cooky Book.*

Another example of Betty Crocker's changing voice can be seen in the introductory letters to "Dear Friend" from Betty Crocker. Whereas the introductions in the cookbooks of the early 1950s are all signed by Betty Crocker, the "Dear Friends" introduction in the 1956 edition of *Betty Crocker's Picture Cookbook* is signed not by Betty Crocker but by "McGraw-Hill Book Company," the publisher. A 1981 cookbook, *Betty Crocker's Mexican Cooking,* has a foreword signed by "The Betty Crocker Editors." But the power of Betty Crocker as a symbol remains strong, and some later cookbooks, including the 2001 edition of the *Betty Crocker Picture Cookbook*, have returned to the format of a "Dear Friends" introduction signed by Betty Crocker herself.

Betty Crocker's voice in the early booklets and cookbooks focuses on the difficult but rewarding work of learning to cook dishes that require precise techniques and careful construction. Cooking is presented as a serious and important activity. For example, in the 1942 *All Purpose Baking* recipe booklet, the introduction tells readers that "daily, Betty Crocker and her staff critically test Gold Medal Flour . . . in the General Mills kitchens," and later in the section of cake recipes, Betty Crocker tells her readers that "cakes have become the very symbol of home life in our country." In this booklet, cake recipes call for General Mills flour varieties by name, and cakes are cooked "from scratch." Betty Crocker is, as she was on the radio, an authority and a helpful teacher. In the 1950 edition of *Betty Crocker's Picture Cookbook*, cakes are still, readers are told by Betty Crocker herself, "a symbol of home life," and more than 50 recipes are offered for home baking, along with two different standard methods for mixing cake batters. Only at the very back of the book are cake mixes mentioned, in a section on "shortcuts." Betty Crocker is still encouraging women to cook from scratch.

But in the 1958 edition of the *Picture Cookbook,* the use of cake mixes is encouraged on a par with scratch cooking. Indeed, Betty Crocker here has become a cheerleader for convenience who encourages women to use mixes and other prepared elements as the foundation for their cooking. A similar progression takes place in the *Betty Crocker Good and Easy Cookbook.* In the first two editions (a small-format book in 1954 and a large-format version in 1962), cake recipes are included as well as information on how to modify Betty Crocker cake mixes for individual personal taste. But the 1996 edition has no recipes for homemade cakes or even a mention of using a modified boxed cake mix.

CONCLUSION

Betty Crocker Today

Just as she quickly entered radio and then television, Betty Crocker was launched into the Internet with numerous Web pages, including separate sites for U.S., British, and other audiences. Millions of recipes have been downloaded from these sites, where visitors can also join a "community," purchase cookbooks or general merchandise from the Betty Crocker store, and learn about new General Mills products. In addition to the company's Web sites, there is a Betty Crocker Facebook page, a MySpace page, a Betty Crocker Twitter feed, and an iPhone app with Betty Crocker recipes available for downloading.

Betty Crocker as Icon

Betty Crocker's brand meaning has changed over time, and the character's persona has become more complicated. Initially the message of Betty Crocker encouraged women to focus on learning traditional cooking techniques and represented a level of expertise and knowledge, and concern for homemaking, to which women were invited to aspire. Betty Crocker was almost a modern version of the Roman goddess of hearth and home, Vesta, who was an exemplar of wholesomeness and the patron goddess of bakers. However, as General Mills added more and more prepared and "convenience" food items to its product list, Betty Crocker became an enthusiast for "the easy way" and came to represent the idea that housework and cooking were chores to be reduced and avoided. Cooks interested in learning traditional techniques might ignore or abandon Betty Crocker in favor of cooks like Julia Child or magazines like *Gourmet*. Today, both aspects of Betty Crocker are active in popular culture.

Sometimes Betty Crocker continues to represent the consummate homemaker, as she did in her early radio shows. For example, a Canadian novelist, Francois Gravel, titled one book in a multivolume family saga *Adieu, Betty Crocker*. In this novel, the central "farewell" is to the idea of a "perfect" homemaker. A blogger calls her site "Not Quite Betty Crocker," in self-deprecation, and in other online commentary women use "Betty Crocker" as shorthand when describing how they are not living up to a traditional model of homemaking or cooking. Similarly, the Minnesota Historical Society sells a kitchen towel with an embroidered message "So I'm not Betty Crocker, deal with it," and an online book review refers to "Betty Crockerland" as a world of "1950s traditionalism."

At the same time, a number of references in popular culture use "Betty Crocker" to represent what is shoddy, even fake—to imply convenience at the expense of excellence. For example, to underline his distaste for a theory he disdains, the economist Thomas Leonard coined the term "Betty Crocker historiography." To mock the errors that he saw in a negative review of a book of philosophy, the philosopher Paul Churchland used the term "Betty Crocker's Theory of Consciousness" and discussed at length the factual errors in a Betty Crocker microwave cookbook. Matthew Crawford, another philosopher who is also a motorcycle mechanic, was quoted in *The New Yorker* as ridiculing a faux-custom motorcycle as a "Betty Crocker cruiser."

Like many other cultural artifacts, Betty Crocker continues to grow and to become not only what she is but also what the culture brings to her, filled with the multiple meanings that her different users project onto her, just as her portrait is now composed of a multiplicity of women's images. As long as she continues to appear as a trade character for General Mills, as long as Betty Crocker cookbooks continue to be published, and as long as Betty Crocker cake mixes are sold, Betty Crocker will continue to be an icon of U.S. cooking culture.

NOTE

1. George P. Edmonston, Jr., and Chuck Boice, "Up Close and Personal: OSU's Connection to 'Betty Crocker,'" *Oregon Stater*, OSU Alumni Association, http://www.osualum.com/s/359/index.aspx?sid=359&gid=1&pgid=508

FURTHER READING

Edmonston, George P., and Chuck Boice. Up Close and Personal: OSU's Connection to "Betty Crocker." http://www.osualum.com/s/359/index.aspx?sid=359&gid=1&pgid=508 (accessed August 2009).

General Mills, Betty Crocker http://www.generalmills.com/en/Brands/Baking_Products/Betty_Crocker.aspx

Mandese, Joe. "Sorry Jolly: The Media Love Betty; Spindex Special: Elsie Lags the Pack as Parade of Ad Icons Are Relaunched." *Advertising Age* 70:37 (September 6, 1999): 6.

Marks, Susan. *Finding Betty Crocker: The Secret Life of America's First Lady of Food.* New York: Simon and Schuster, 2005.

Marling, Karal Ann. *As Seen on TV.* Cambridge, MA: Harvard University Press, 1994.

Parkin, Katherine J. *Food Is Love: Advertising and Gender Roles in Modern America.* Philadelphia: University of Pennsylvania Press, 2006.

Shapiro, Laura. "'I Guarantee': Betty Crocker and the Woman in the Kitchen." In *From Betty Crocker to Feminist Food Studies: Critical Perspectives on Women and Food,* ed. Arlene Voski Avakian and Barbara Haber. Boston: University of Massachusetts Press, 2005, 29–40.

Shapiro, Laura. *Something from the Oven.* New York: Viking Press, 2004.

Stuart, Bonnye. *More Than Petticoats: Remarkable Minnesota Women.* Guilford, CT: TwoDot Press, 2004.

JoAnn E. Castagna

Chef Phillip Crispo, right, leads a cooking class comprised of mostly Marines at the Culinary Institute of America (CIA) in Hyde Park, New York, January 15, 2008. The Marine Corps wants better cooks, so for more than a year they have sent select Marine cooks to immersion courses at CIA. (AP/Wide World Photos)

Culinary Institute of America

The Culinary Institute of America (CIA) in Hyde Park, New York, is considered a leader in culinary education. Founded in 1946, it established the concept and the curriculum for professional courses of study in the culinary arts in the United States. Before the CIA, chefs were typically expected to learn their craft through apprenticeship. The CIA also published the first comprehensive professional culinary textbook: *The Professional Chef*. Now in its eighth edition, this publication became the gold standard for culinary instruction.

The CIA pioneered sequential education in which each student builds knowledge and skills in the most logical progression, moving from product knowledge, to skills, to the preparation of cuisines, to actual restaurant practice. CIA programs evolved to offer both associate's and bachelor's degrees, and this pattern has been copied across culinary schools, many based on CIA content and teaching principles. Maintaining its quality leadership, CIA education continues to emphasize an extraordinary number of hours of "laboratory" (hands-on cooking) classes with controlled student-faculty ratios.

The CIA leadership is furthered by the college's exceptional chef faculty. Among the chefs who instruct and lead the school are 24 American Culinary Federation Certified Master Chefs (CMCs) and Retail Bakers of America Certified Master Bakers (CMBs), prestigious designations earned through a rigorous testing process, giving the CIA the largest concentration of CMCs and CMBs anywhere. Chefs from CIA have also been involved in the International Culinary Competition (*Internationale Kochkunst Ausstellung*, familiarly known as the "Culinary Olympics") for many years and have brought home numerous medals. The faculty have come from the best-known restaurants and hotels throughout the world. The CIA faculty are also noted for their publishing, and several of the CIA's cookbooks have won awards, such as the James Beard Foundation Awards, which *Time* magazine has called the "Oscars of the food world."[1]

The CIA has the largest single campus for culinary arts education, with extensive kitchen laboratories and restaurants. These are constantly updated to allow students to work with the most up-to-date equipment possible. The CIA's on-campus restaurants in both New York and California, staffed by students, have won numerous national awards, including *Restaurants and Institutions* magazine's prestigious Ivy Award. As a reflection of the college's reputation, over 100,000 people visit its Hyde Park campus yearly.

CIA graduates have excelled in all fields of the culinary arts; they can be found at leading restaurants, corporations, food magazines, and on television. Some graduates who educate and entertain on television and in magazines include Anthony Bourdain, Michael Chiarello, Cat Cora, Rocco DiSpirito, Duff Goldman, and Sara Moulton. Some CIA graduates who are leading chefs and restaurateurs include Grant Achatz, Marcel Desaulniers, Todd English, Susan Feniger, Melissa Kelly, Michael Mina, Cameron Mitchell, Bradley Ogden, Charlie Palmer, Alfred Portale, Waldy Malouf, and Roy Yamaguchi. In addition to the world of fine dining, CIA graduates impact what millions of Americans eat every day by serving other segments of the foodservice and hospitality industry. These graduates include Dan Coudreaut, director of

A Pastry Chef Reflects on Her CIA Experience

[Chef] Sara Moulton claimed that the best time in her life was while she was at the Culinary Institute of America, much to the consternation of her husband. Unfortunately, for my husband, I would have to agree. It's not only that you are attending the best culinary school in the country, or that you are living in one of the prettiest areas in the world. It's that you are surrounded by people who want to be there just as much as you do. The teachers, the students, every one of them I hope, is pursuing the idea that if you do what you love, you'll never work a day in your life.

But, that's not to say that this is the be-all, end-all of life at the CIA. The relationships that form are some of the closest you'll ever have in your life. Not only do you go to school with these people, but you live with them as well. All the intensity and emotion you pour into your love of the craft spills over into the rest of your life during your time there. Cooks work hard and play hard. While at the CIA, I cliff jumped into a river in the Catskills, got a tattoo, had one of the best meals in my life at Gramercy Tavern in New York City, and waded through an inch of water on the second floor of my dorm from someone pulling the fire hose out at 6am, among other things. It is stories like these that make those of us who attended the CIA oblivious to anyone else whenever we meet, as we compare notes about our times there. And it is all of those experiences that will always keep my time at the CIA at the top of my list.

—Sarah Steele, pastry chef and CIA graduate,
email with Elizabeth Demers March 1, 2010

culinary innovation for McDonald's; Steve Ells, who founded Chipotle Mexican Grill; and Christopher Martone, executive chef at Subway Restaurants.

When 50 students met in 1946 for the first session of an eight-month cooking course, held in an ill-suited building in New Haven, Connecticut, no one thought the school would last five years, let alone that it would grow and thrive, and that 60-some years later it would have evolved into an accredited four-year college with over 2,500 students and over 40,000 graduates. But thanks to several dynamic leaders and two opportune real estate purchases, that is exactly what happened.

EARLY YEARS

New Haven

In 1945, the New Haven Restaurant Association identified two problems: For reasons related to World War II, trained chefs and cooks were scarce, and people leaving the military needed a marketable skill. Richard H. Dargan, the association's president, and Charles Rovetti, executive secretary, resolved to open a first-class restaurant trade school and train chefs. Their decision to ask Connecticut attorney and mover and shaker Frances Roth to start the school was one of two pivotal events in the school's early history.

Roth had skipped college and gone directly from high school to New York University law school. At 21, she became the first woman admitted to the Connecticut State Bar Association. She was obviously someone who, if she knew what she wanted, would be aggressive in surmounting any obstacle. During World War II, Roth headed the Connecticut War Council's Vice Control Committee, identifying places that should be off-limits to military personnel. As a result, she met many restaurateurs in the area. This energetic woman had a reputation for being able to "get things done."[2]

On May 22, 1946, the New Haven Restaurant Institute's first class met in a former bar at 169 State Street. The Connecticut State Board of Education had accredited it, so its students qualified for benefits under the GI Bill, and all 50 students were former military people. Roth credited James Rowland Angell, a former Yale president, with much useful advice on starting the school. In June 1946, the New Haven Restaurant Association's newsletter, *The Tribune*, announced a second crucial event: Katharine Angell, his wife, a leader in New Haven society, had joined the board of governors. She had already founded a library for the school and had established a loan fund for students whose GI Bill payments were delayed. Angell knew many influential people, and she also had money, which she used to help the school at some key times.

In February 1947, the board changed the school's name to the Restaurant Institute of Connecticut, because it favored applicants from Connecticut. Besides giving preference in admissions first to handicapped veterans who could handle the work, and second to general veterans, the school showed no bias against students either by sex or race. A photo often identified as the school's first graduating class (actually the second class) includes four women and an African American man among the graduates. The African American, Jefferson Evans, would later return to the school as a faculty member.

The school's reputation drew many applicants, and the former bar was too small to house the program. In September 1947, the school bought a mansion at 393 Prospect Street. This house bordered Yale University, and the university held the first mortgage on the property with Angell's guarantee on the loan. In 1948, Angell became chair of the board, a post she would hold until 1966. She and Roth made a formidable team, creating the foundation for the world-class culinary college. Later, the school named the building Angell Hall to honor James Rowland Angell, who died in 1949.

Although the school had already received much exposure as the only one of its kind, this photogenic mansion helped generate even more publicity. The school did not have to pay for advertising because of the coverage it received from sources such as *The New York Times* and *Look* magazine. Glowing articles described the curriculum, the excellent job offers its graduates received, and the imposing mansion.

Almost all early students at the school paid for their education with GI Bill funds. Because of problems with the interpretation of regulations as applied to the institute, Roth contacted her congressman, and in December 1950, she was invited to testify at hearings of the House Select Committee to Investigate Educational and Training Programs under the GI Bill. Roth's testimony about the school educated the representatives about some financial realities of running a school and the many frustrations of dealing with the GI Bill administrators. These included policies such as the Veterans Administration (VA) holding back all payments to the school because of a dispute over a relatively small amount of money; slowness in VA response to questions; difficulty in getting a direct answer to many questions; and her belief that the VA considered trade schools inferior to "real" colleges. One charge was that the "school made excessive charges to the Veterans' Administration for food used in the course of its instruction, which food was in turn served daily to the students and teachers at a teaching meal . . . and in effect gave free meals to the students."[3] Roth justified the students' seven-course lunch—often of gourmet food—by arguing, "Many a boy has come in here who has never seen a lobster, and yet he must be competent to prepare a lobster thermidor." She justified their actually eating the lunch: "You can't very well throw it out. They have to criticize it. They have to know what they have produced."[4]

By 1951, in addition to course work, the school expanded students' learning opportunities by preparing meals at Yale's athletic training tables, catering buffets for Yale football games, baking breads and desserts for local orphanages and the New Haven school system, and baking and decorating birthday cakes for Yale students. As a result of the national attention the school attracted, in May of 1951, former first lady Eleanor Roosevelt welcomed Roth to her radio program. Roth discussed her efforts to improve U.S. culinary education and to raise chefs to the prestigious status that they held in Europe. She bragged that the school had students from 38 states and that virtually every student had three or four job offers upon graduation.

In 1950 and 1951, the school experimented with names to reflect the fact that it attracted students from all over the country. It shortened the name to the Restaurant Institute and then changed it to the Culinary Institute. Finally, in June 1951, the board adopted the name the school has used ever since: the Culinary Institute of America.

The program's reputation continued to grow, and in the fall of 1951 CIA students exhibited eight specialty dishes at the Société Culinaire Philosophique's Chef Salon in New York—the first nonprofessional group to exhibit at this annual event. When First Lady Mamie Eisenhower christened the world's first nuclear-powered submarine, the USS *Nautilus*, in Groton, Connecticut, in January 1954, 150 CIA students catered the luncheon for 1,000 people and created a 54-inch-long sugar scale model of the submarine as a centerpiece.

As the school's fame grew, more and more aspiring students applied, and again, space grew tight. Around 1958, the institute purchased a mansion next to Angell Hall, called Taft House because President William Howard Taft had owned it when he taught at Yale. Later, the school purchased a third property on the block, ending up with 10 acres of land. In 1959, the institute constructed an auditorium, later named Roth Auditorium, for cooking demonstrations and in 1963 added two dormitories for the ever-increasing student population.

In May 1962, CIA students prepared a luncheon for the launch of the nuclear submarine the USS *Lafayette*, which First Lady Jacqueline Kennedy christened. She was reported to be completely "captivated" by the meal that the culinary students prepared.[5]

In 1964, Roth decided to retire, and the board chose Jacob ("Jack") Rosenthal, vice president and marketing director for the Chock Full o' Nuts Corporation, as codirector with Roth from July 1965 through June 1966, when he assumed full directorship of the institute (the board instituted the title of president in 1973). As an ardent gastronome and active member of several gastronomic and wine societies, with degrees in education and business, Rosenthal was an ideal person to take over as the CIA's leader.

New York

Rosenthal made a major change to deal with the CIA's space problem: In 1969, he instituted morning and evening classes, allowing the school to double its enrollment. He also sought more opportunities for students to practice cooking in real-life situations. He had students cook sumptuous dinners for the food and wine societies to which he belonged, allowing them to prepare elaborate dishes that were beyond the CIA's budget. Eventually, despite double shifts, the school needed more space, and the board began searching for a new home. In 1970, Herman Zaccarelli, a monk involved in foodservice management and a member of the institute's board, alerted Rosenthal to the campus of St. Andrew-on-Hudson, a Jesuit novitiate in Hyde Park, New York. The novitiate was closing, and its spacious building and grounds were for sale.

Rosenthal liked the possibility of the new space and worked with board members to secure their approval. In December 1970, the CIA purchased the site. The building must have seemed large enough to fill all future needs of the school, but the sizeable campus surrounding it (then around 70 acres, now 172 acres) also provided room for expansion.

It would be almost two years before the CIA moved from New Haven to Hyde Park. Rosenthal spent most of this time in Hyde Park supervising renovations to the building and made Joseph Amendola the acting New Haven director. Amendola had begun his baking career at age nine as an apprentice in his uncle's pastry shop in New Haven. At 19, he moved on to a series of other jobs, striving to learn as much as he could about all kinds of baking. During World War II, he joined the U.S. Army Air Corps and became a pastry chef in the General Officers' Mess in Europe. He began teaching baking classes at the CIA in 1948. Upon becoming director, he was also promoted to vice president. Amendola stayed with the CIA for 39 years, until 1987, and then continued as an active "CIA Ambassador" until his death in 2008. Baking and Pastry students at the institute still use his textbook, *Understanding Baking.*

The red brick and limestone Georgian-style building in Hyde Park, four stories plus attic and basement, was even more impressive than the New Haven mansion. The CIA built 20 kitchens and bake shops on the ground floor and basement, and rooms on the upper floors became classrooms, administrative offices, and temporary dormitory rooms. Rosenthal borrowed funds from the New York State Dormitory Authority to build three dormitories, which opened in September 1974. They were later named Katharine Angell, Pick/Herndon, and Jacob Rosenthal Residence Halls.

With the move, Rosenthal obtained a charter from the New York State Board of Regents. The school could now award a college degree (an Associates degree in Occupational Studies, AOS), rather than just a certificate. Classes began in Hyde Park in September 1972, with a formal dedication ceremony in October 1972. To give students practical experience, Rosenthal opened a coffee shop in an old diner he had brought to the campus. A second restaurant, the Epicurean Room and Rabelais Bar-Café, soon renamed the Escoffier Restaurant, opened in June 1973. Students prepared the food and served customers as part of their classes. Working in the restaurants for outside patrons allowed them to experience the pleasures and pressures of an actual restaurant. Having overseen the move and the main building's renovation, Rosenthal decided to retire. The new school he left behind would have been almost completely unrecognizable to New Haven Restaurant Institute graduates, with its imposing building, double shifts of classes, and emphasis on gourmet food.

Henry Ogden Barbour succeeded Rosenthal as president in July 1974 and served until September 1977. Barbour had previously been vice president of Manpower Development for Intercontinental Hotels and had also been president of the CIA's board from 1970 through 1974. He had ambitious ideas of building on the CIA's brand name by opening satellite campuses in several major U.S. cities.

Barbour made another major change in class scheduling. Previously, the school had scheduled classes in semesters. In September 1976, Barbour instituted the Progressive Learning Year (PLY) system, which organized courses in three-week blocks. During a block, students would take only a few classes. Many classes would meet for six or seven hours, allowing students to learn processes that take several hours, such as baking bread. The PLY system proved so workable that the CIA still uses it today, but implementing it was costly. Barbour also built a President's House that came in greatly over budget, and he moved ahead on plans for a satellite campus in Denver. The board worried about all these expenses and thought that it was not a good time to expand, so in October 1977 the board terminated Barbour's contract.

The three years following Barbour's departure were tumultuous. Amendola became acting president while the board searched for a new president. They chose J. Joseph Meng, who arrived in September 1978. Meng had previously been vice chancellor for the Executive Office at the City University of New York. However, he was not a good fit for the CIA position. As an academic administrator, he did not have the necessary mindset for running a culinary college, and he resigned after 13 months. After his departure in November 1979, Charles A. LaForge Jr., a board member and owner of the Beekman Arms restaurant in nearby Rhinebeck, served as acting president until a permanent president could be found. LaForge had a degree from Cornell's School of Hotel Administration and 25 years of experience in the hospitality industry.

Finally, the board convinced one of its members, Ferdinand Metz, to become president. His term began in June 1980 and lasted for over 20 years. Metz had learned to cook during apprenticeships in his native Germany and had also earned an MBA from the University of Pittsburgh. His experience ranged from being a chef at famous restaurants such as Le Pavillon to 10 years as senior manager in charge of new product development at Heinz U.S.A. When he became the CIA's president, he was the president of the American Culinary Federation and manager of the U.S. team for the 1980 International Culinary Competition (the "Culinary Olympics"), the first year that the United States won a gold medal. Like Roth, he was clearly a person who could get things done, and following three years of stagnation while the school searched for direction, he became a major force in the school's development.

With a new president and new directions, the program again began to thrive. In 1981, the CIA became and remains the only approved site to administer the prestigious American Culinary Federation Master Chef Certification exam. This challenging test involves proving that the applicant has fulfilled certain educational requirements, has worked as a chef de cuisine, working pastry chef, or executive sous-chef for at least two years, and has "supervised at least three fulltime people in the preparation of food."[6] Candidates take a grueling eight-day sequence of tests, both written and cooking, including a "mystery basket" test. They receive a group of foods, and within half an hour they must design a five-course menu using all of the foods and then prepare that menu within the next five hours. This test is so rigorous that there are currently only 61 CMCs.

Metz's term included many achievements. He added four restaurants to the campus: the American Bounty (1982; American food); the Caterina de' Medici Room (1984; Italian food; it became the Ristorante Caterina de' Medici and moved into the new Colavita Center for Italian Food and Wine in 2001); St. Andrew's Café (1985; "flavorful fare in a family-friendly setting"; it moved into the new General Foods Nutrition Center in 1989); and the Apple Pie Bakery Café (2000; baked goods and café cuisine).

Many people who visit the Hyde Park campus are surprised at the large number of buildings on the grounds, and Metz was responsible for many of them. When he took over the presidency, the major buildings were the Jesuit novitiate (named Roth Hall in honor of Roth, who had died in June 1971) and the three original dormitories. Metz also added the McCann Student Center (1981; now used for classes, offices, and a tutoring center); the Continuing Education Center (1984; originally dedicated as the "East Wing"; rededicated in 1994 as the J. Willard Marriott Continuing Education Center); Hudson Hall (1986; a dormitory); the Shunsuke Takaki School of Baking and Pastry (1990); the Conrad N. Hilton Library (1993; it includes the Danny Kaye Theater); and the Student Recreation Center (1998).

On the education front, Metz presided over several significant changes. Since its move to Hyde Park, the CIA had offered an AOS degree in Culinary Arts. In November 1990, the first students entered classes for a second degree track, the AOS in Baking and Pastry Arts. In 1994, an even more momentous event was the admission of the first candidates for the bachelor's degree in Professional Studies (BPS), with tracks in Culinary Arts Management and Baking and Pastry Arts Management.

OTHER ENDEAVORS

Expansion

In the meantime, the CIA began a search for a second home on the West Coast. In 1992, it acquired Greystone, a former Christian Brothers monastery and winery in St. Helena, California. In August 1995, the CIA began offering continuing education courses and a 30-week Baking and Pastry Certificate at the new center (Greystone now offers both tracks of the AOS degree, as well). The CIA opened the Wine Spectator Restaurant and the Ken and Grace DeBaun Bakery Café there to give students venues to obtain practical restaurant experience.

During Metz's presidency, the CIA produced several seasons of a TV show, *Cooking Secrets of the CIA*. These programs were filmed on campus and included food demonstrations by CIA faculty members with help from CIA students. During this time two events epitomized the institute's reputation. In 1989, renowned French chef Paul Bocuse declared it "the best [culinary] school in the world," and sent his son, Jerome, to study at the CIA.[7] And in October 1995, the CIA had the honor of preparing and serving a four-course lunch for U.S. president Bill Clinton and Russian president Boris Yeltsin when they met at the nearby Franklin D. Roosevelt Home and Museum.

Leaving a solid legacy, Metz retired in November 2001. His successor was L. Timothy Ryan. On the CIA's staff since 1982, Ryan was the first alumnus (1977) to become its president. He had led planning and development of the American Bounty Restaurant. Ryan was named director of culinary education in 1986, vice president of education in 1988, senior vice president in 1994, and executive vice president in 1998. He worked closely with Metz in all these positions.

Under Ryan, in March 2002, the school earned accreditation from the prestigious Middle States Association of Colleges and Schools, which accredits the CIA's neighbors Vassar, Bard, and Marist Colleges, as well as regional universities, including the CIA's former neighbor, Yale University. This involved a major effort from faculty and staff committees that produced reports on numerous aspects of the college, plus visits from Middle States review teams.

To map out future development in an orderly fashion, Ryan commissioned an outside company to create a campus master plan to examine current buildings, potential sites for future buildings, traffic patterns, and the overall appearance of the campus. Following this plan, the school constructed six lodge-style dormitories (2004–2006), an Admissions Building (2006), and the elegant Anton Plaza in front of Roth Hall, which covers a two-story parking garage (2005).

Promoting Diversity

Another noteworthy project was the opening in 2007 of the CIA's San Antonio branch campus, the Center for Foods of the Americas, in a former Pearl Brewery building. The 30-week culinary arts certificate program, continuing education courses, and conferences there focus on Latin American cuisines and cultures, and one of the goals of the program, called "El Sueño" (The Dream), is "to promote Latino diversity in the U.S. foodservice industry."[8]

There is much confusion about the history of women students at the CIA. In the early years, most classes had few or no women, which led some people to believe that women were not admitted at all. However, the first class included one woman, the second class included four, and from 1946 through 1965, the school's catalog included admission requirements such as "Who May Enroll: Any young man or woman who has completed a high school course or its equivalent."

Despite an effort to admit women, from 1966 through 1970, the school did not admit women to general classes (those who had started before then were allowed to finish their studies), although it did admit women for the summer courses. The school did not address the change until a note appeared in the 1969–1970 catalog stating, "Girls are not accepted for the regular course— but are welcome in the special summer courses. The reason for this is that with so few girls applying it is uneconomical for the Institute to provide the special facilities, washrooms, etc. required."[9] The 1970–1971 catalog elaborated, "It is a matter of regret to all concerned at the Culinary Institute that existing facilities do not permit admission of women. However, the admission of women is under consideration by the Board and the final decision will depend on the number of women who apply. Women who are interested in attending the Culinary Institute are asked to write for an application form and if the number is sufficient, it is possible that the Institute Board may be able to work out early admission plans."[10]

Finally, in 1971, the catalog stated, "Anyone between the ages of 17 and 35 is eligible for admissions if he or she is a high school graduate or can furnish a high school equivalency certificate." From that time on, women have again been included in the student body; currently over 40 percent of students are women. The school removed the age limit in 1974.

The school has also encouraged applications from students of all races and nationalities. In the 1960s, the Arabian American Oil Company (Aramco, now Saudi Aramco) in Saudi Arabia sent some Arab foodservice employees to the school, and students from other countries attended, as well. The CIA actively recruits in several foreign countries, and the current student body includes around 175 students from 37 countries. Korea sends the most students of any foreign country.

AOS Degree

Originally, the school offered an eight-month program in which cooking was the main course of study. According to the initial institute brochure, "Seventy-eight complete menus or daily bills of fare will be composed, discussed, and prepared in the presence of the student body,"[11] who would then have an opportunity to prepare the meals themselves. However, from the beginning, the school also taught other skills that a restaurant owner or manager would need, including nutrition, special diets, bacteriology, sanitation, food inspection, safety, restaurant accounting, cost control, and government regulations affecting restaurant and hotel operation. After a period of experimentation and growing pains, around 1954, the school firmed up a curriculum that remained relatively stable for the remainder of Roth's tenure as director.

Currently, all AOS students take courses in Introduction to Gastronomy, Mathematics, Writing, Product Knowledge, Food Safety, Nutrition, Management, Menu Development, Controlling Costs and Purchasing Food, and Restaurant Law.

In their freshman year, Culinary Arts AOS students study Meat and Seafood Identification and Fabrication (cutting whole or partial animals into individual or multiserving pieces); Skill Development; Cuisines of Asia and of the Americas; Quantity Food Production; and *Garde Manger* (the "cold kitchen": appetizers, buffets, and reception foods). In their sophomore year they study Cuisines of the Mediterranean; Baking and Pastry; Wines; and Catering. In their last 12 weeks, affectionately known as "Restaurant Row," they work in St. Andrew's Café or the Ristorante Caterina de' Medici, spending a block cooking and then a block studying and practicing table service, beverage service, guest relations, and professional communications. They then choose either the Escoffier Restaurant or the American Bounty, where they spend their next-to-last block cooking and their last block in Advanced Hospitality and Service Management (waiting tables, but also studying customer service, wine and spirits, restaurant trends, merchandising, reservation and point-of-sale systems, inventory control, and cost management).

Baking and Pastry Arts AOS students take courses in Ingredients and Equipment, various types of breads, rolls, cakes, cookies, pastries, tarts, chocolates and confections, Design Principles, Cake Decoration, and Culinary Skills for Bakers. They spend their penultimate block in the Apple Pie Bakery Café preparing food and practicing inventory control, sales analysis, and overall operations, and their last block there studying in-depth beverage preparation and serving.

Between their freshman and sophomore years, AOS students do an externship in which they gain supervised real-life experience in an approved foodservice site.

BPS Degree

The BPS degree candidates take the freshman and sophomore courses for their preferred track and graduate with their AOS. The BPS-specific courses begin in the junior year with Composition and Communication, Computers in the Food Business, History and Cultures of Europe, Economics, Accounting, a choice from three languages (French, Italian, or Spanish), Marketing and Promoting Food, Organizational Behavior, and Psychology. Seniors continue courses in the language they studied in their junior year, and also take Financial Management, History and Cultures of the Americas and of Asia, Human Resources Management, Restaurant Operations, Leadership and Ethics, and a few choices of electives in their last semester. In addition, Culinary Arts students take Advanced Cooking, and Baking and Pastry Arts students take Advanced Pastry.

In the Food, Wine, and (Agri)Culture Seminar, BPS students choose one of the trips to California, the Pacific Northwest, Spain, or Italy, where they visit food production sites, agricultural sites, vineyards and wineries, famous and innovative restaurants, and cultural and historical sites.

The CIA only closes for five weeks a year. Taken without interruption, the AOS courses run for 21 months, and the BPS courses (junior and senior years) run for 17 months.

Continuing Education and Food Enthusiast Courses

The Culinary Institute of America offered continuing education (CE) courses for food professionals as early as 1960. Originally, these took place in the summer, when certificate students were off. Now a CE building with classrooms and kitchens serves 3,000 to 4,000 students per year. In addition to open-access courses, the CIA designs courses for specific customers, usually a corporation or a military group.

The CIA also offers courses at all of its campuses for food enthusiasts, people who are not foodservice professionals but want to learn professional techniques. They range from one-day programs to weeklong programs such as the various Boot Camps. Over 2,500 people a year attend these classes.

Conrad N. Hilton Library

The CIA's library is one of the largest private culinary libraries in the United States. In addition to its culinary and gastronomic volumes, it has a well-rounded collection, including books about management, business, psychology, history, and literature, that support nonculinary classes. Special collections include the CIA's archives, approximately 1,000 rare books, cookery pamphlets dating back to the late 1800s, and approximately 30,000 menus from all over the world. The library is open to the public for research.

COOKBOOKS

The CIA has a long history of publishing culinary textbooks and popular cookbooks. The original faculty members discovered that no adequate textbook existed, and students received mimeographed pages of recipes and other materials. In 1962, the CIA published the first edition of its enduring textbook, *The Professional Chef*. This publication changed its title for its fifth and sixth editions to *The New Professional Chef*, then changed back to *The Professional Chef* for the seventh and later editions. It has been the bible for many thousands of culinary students, both at the CIA and at other schools.

In 1995, the CIA published its first two cookbooks aimed at the food enthusiast audience: *An American Bounty* and *Cooking Secrets of the CIA*, the first companion book to its television program. Subsequent popular cookbooks have included *Cooking at Home with the CIA* (2003), *Baking at Home with the CIA* (2004), books of recipes from CIA restaurants, and subject-specific books (such as *Soups, Chocolates and Confections, Breakfasts and Brunches, Gluten-Free Baking,* and *Cake Art*).

The CIA also develops books related to specific aspects of its course work to supplement *The Professional Chef*. These include *Garde Manger: The Art and Craft of the Cold Kitchen; The Professional Chef's Techniques of Healthy Cooking; At Your Service: A Hands-on Guide to the Professional Dining Room; Baking and Pastry: Mastering the Art and Craft; The Kitchen Pro Series; Exploring Wine; WineWise*; and others. Many of these books have come out in one or more updated editions. Although published by outside publishing companies, these books are written by CIA employees and edited by the in-house publishing department.

Drawing on faculty and staff expertise, the CIA's cleverly named Food & Beverage Institute (FBI) produces and distributes instructional videos and DVDs about all aspects of culinary arts and restaurant management, plus series (for example, *Great Chefs, Tastefully Speaking, Zagat Lecture Series on Hospitality and Service*) of interviews with and speeches by people famous in the food, restaurant, and hospitality arenas.

CONCLUSION

From a small cooking school created to serve returning World War II veterans, the CIA has grown into a mature four-year college with a student body exceeding 2,500 and two branch campuses. While the New Haven Restaurant Institute had at most one or two competitors in the United States, the CIA now has hundreds. Many of these have modeled their courses on the CIA's and employ CIA graduates as teachers and administrators. Faculty committees revise course content and structure on a regular basis. Throughout the year, employees work to update kitchens, classrooms, computer systems, and more. The goal of everything that people do at the CIA is to fulfill its mission: "To provide the world's best professional culinary education."

NOTES

1. Lisa McLaughlin, "From Martinis to Mojitos," *Time*, 27 (Jan. 2003), 61.
2. Craig Claiborne, "Food News: From Court to Kitchen," *New York Times* (25 Jan. 1950), 20C.
3. United States Congress House Select Committee to Investigate Educational Programs under GI Bill. *Investigation of GI Schools: Hearings Before the House Select Committee to Investigate Educational and Training Programs under GI Bill, Eighty-first Congress, second session, created pursuant to H. Res. 474. Dec. 11 and 12 1950, Dec. 14 and 15, 1950, and Dec. 18–20, 1950.* Washington: U.S. GPO, (1951), 508.
4. United States Congress House Select Committee to Investigate Educational Programs under GI Bill. *Investigation of GI Schools: Hearings Before the House Select Committee to Investigate Educational and Training Programs under GI Bill, Eighty-first Congress, second session, created pursuant to H. Res. 474. Dec. 11 and 12 1950, Dec. 14 and 15, 1950, and Dec. 18–20, 1950.* Washington: U.S. GPO, (1951), 512–513.
5. "School for Chefs: Aromas of Finest Cuisine Waft across an Unusual 10-acre Campus," *National Observer* (24 Feb. 1964), 12.
6. American Culinary Federation, "Initial CEC® Certification Examination. Certified Executive Chef® (28 October 2009), http://www.acfchefs.org/download/documents/certify/certification/Initial_Application_CEC.pdf
American Culinary Federation, "Initial CCE® Certification Examination, Certified Culinary Educator™ (28 October 2009), http://www.acfchefs.org/download/documents/certify/certification/Initial_Application_CCE.pdf CEC or CCE certification is a prerequisite for Master Chef certification.
7. "Renowned Chef Paul Bocuse Visits Institute," *Taste,* a CIA publication (Jan 1990), 35.
8. The Culinary Institute of America, *The Culinary Institute of America announces a bold new dream – El Sueño – to promote Latino diversity in the foodservice industry*, Hyde Park: The Culinary Institute of America (16 May 2007), http://www.ciachef.edu/admissions/news/news_story_univ.asp?iNewsID=562&strBack=%2Fadmissions%2Fnews%2Fnews%5Farchive%5Funiv%2Easp&strlocationname=Media+Room
9. The Culinary Institute of America, *Catalogue 1969–1970* (New Haven: The Institute, 1969), 36.

10. The Culinary Institute of America, *Catalogue 1970–1971* (New Haven: The Institute, 1970), 36.

11. The New Haven Restaurant Institute, *Announcing an opportunity to learn the restaurant and hotel trades at the New Haven Restaurant Institute,* brochure for the school (New Haven: The Institute, 1946), Unpaginated.

FURTHER READING

Culinary Institute of America. *Baking and Pastry: Mastering the Art and Craft.* 2nd ed. Hoboken, NJ: Wiley, 2009.

Culinary Institute of America. *The Professional Chef.* 8th ed. Hoboken, NJ: Wiley, 2006.

Goldstein, Darra. *Baking Boot Camp: Five Days of Basic Training at the Culinary Institute of America.* Hoboken, NJ: Wiley, 2007.

Ruhlman, Michael. *The Making of a Chef: Mastering Heat at the Culinary Institute of America.* New York: Henry Holt, 1997.

Ryan, L. Timothy. "The Culinary Institute of America: A History." PhD Diss., University of Pennsylvania, 2003. Ann Arbor: UMI, 2003.

Shulman, Martha Rose. *Culinary Boot Camp: Five Days of Basic Training at the Culinary Institute of America.* Hoboken, NJ: Wiley, 2006.

The Conrad N. Hilton Library. http://library.culinary.edu

The Culinary Institute of America. http://www.culinary.edu

Christine Crawford-Oppenheimer

Marion Cunningham, 82, a venerated figure in the food world, is shown at home in Walnut Creek, California, May 27, 2004. Cunningham revised *The Fannie Farmer Cookbook* and in 2003 received a lifetime achievement award from the James Beard Foundation. Her latest book is *Lost Recipes*, intended to encourage families to go back to cooking and eating at home. (AP/Wide World Photos)

Fannie Farmer and Marion Cunningham

Fannie Farmer was a New England culinary instructor and author who became one of the most influential food figures of her day. Her most famous work, *The Boston Cooking-School Cook Book*, was the first to standardize recipe measurements for home cooks. Millions of cooks all over the world still use that title's revised editions.

Marion Cunningham, a late-blooming champion of the family meal who worked with food great James Beard, became one of the most recognizable home cooks in America thanks in part to her testing and editorship of three editions of Fannie Farmer cookbooks in the latter half of the 20th century.

It is fitting that Farmer and Cunningham will be forever linked as pioneers of practical cookery in the United States. Although Farmer died seven years before Cunningham was born, the two women likely would have respected each other's work and found friendship through their commonsense approaches to food. They each overcame infirmity to achieve positive and long-lasting culinary legacies, and they found fulfillment in careers dedicated to better cooking in the home.

FANNIE FARMER

EARLY YEARS

Growing Up

Fannie Merritt Farmer, the oldest of four daughters, was born to John Franklin Farmer and Mary Watson Merritt in Boston, Massachusetts, on March 23, 1857. The family moved to Medford, Oregon, when she was young, and she did not grow up learning how to cook.

In the last half of the 19th century, women faced a mass-market flurry of newfangled kitchen appliances, utensils, and manufactured ingredients. As greater numbers of Americans moved to cities, away from proximity to their own vegetable gardens and livestock, many urbanites lost basic cooking skills or needed help learning to navigate the rapid technological changes that took place in the kitchen, resulting in a wholesale change in how people cooked. In response, cooking schools opened in the Northeast to teach cookery as a profession and to help women cope with challenges at home. Moreover, there was no standardization of recipes or measurement, and wood or coal stoves did not always heat to consistent temperatures. During this era, directions for making food were imprecise at best, such as calling for "lumps the size of walnuts" with no mention of what temperature or which pans to use.[1]

Around the time of her graduation from high school, Farmer suffered a stroke that left her partially paralyzed. She recuperated at home over the course of several long years and subsequently regained her ability to walk, albeit with a limp. The stroke derailed her academic prospects, and she was unable to attend college as her parents had hoped. This brush with physical limitations gave Farmer a special empathy for invalids and the sick population at large, especially regarding how and what they ate.

Farmer's first real foray into cooking for others came when she began to cook meals for the boarders her parents took into their home. As her food was favorably received, she gained the confidence to work as a domestic outside the home in her mid-twenties. Soon her family and the family who employed her formally recognized her talents and interest in the culinary arts, and together they enrolled Farmer at the Boston Cooking School. Cooking was then considered an acceptable means for a single woman to earn a living. Farmer would never marry.

At the school, the 28-year-old student was drawn to the areas of domestic science, nutrition, kitchen hygiene, and cooking for those who were ill. Farmer did so well that she was invited to join the faculty upon her graduation in 1889. Two short years later she became principal of the school, and by 1902, Farmer had opened her own academy, Miss Farmer's School of Cookery. Her courses, designed for gentlewomen and housewives, emphasized plain family cooking. She had found her calling.

Professional Years

At an early point in her career, Fannie received an invitation from a flour company to judge a recipe contest. This experience convinced her that uniformity was the missing ingredient in home cooking.[2] Only 5 percent of the entries contained specific measurements, partly because even cutlery and utensils of the era were not standardized. Ever mindful of the ingredient problem and food health issues, Farmer compiled fastidious notes and studied physicians' research about nutrition. At the top of her list was the development of exact portioning, achieved by using level measures.

COOKBOOKS

Her attention to such detail paid off when she was asked by the *Woman's Home Companion* magazine to write a biweekly cooking column. Farmer's sage food and cooking advice encouraged many readers to trust her as an authority, and she continued her column until two weeks before she died. Regular writing also helped her to put together her first cookbook. It contained hundreds of recipes, lists of menus, tips for the kitchen, and a chapter on cooking for the sick. The first chapter starts with a passage that underscores Farmer's views: "Statistics prove that two-thirds of all disease is brought about by error in diet. . . . Physicians agree, with but few exceptions, that the proper preparation of food for the sick is of as great importance to the restoration of health as administration of drugs."[3]

The Book That Changed Home Cooking

In 1896 Farmer released her seminal book, *The Boston Cooking-School Cook Book*. Her publisher, Little, Brown and Company, did not predict strong sales, so Farmer had to cover the cost of the first run of 3,000 copies with her own money. Luckily for her, she retained future copyrights, since the book was an immediate and perennial bestseller.

Farmer's goal was to simplify and demystify home cooking. Oddly enough, some chapter introductions had enough scientific information to make Farmer's work more akin to that of modern food geek Alton Brown than, say, a latter-day Irma S. Rombauer, author of *The Joy of Cooking*, whose interests lay in entertaining and home cooking rather than food science or nutrition. Farmer's chapter on eggs, for example, first lists their physical composition: protein, 14.9 percent; fat, 10.6 percent; mineral matter, 1 percent; water, 73.5 percent.

Farmer's recipes specified the sizes of pans to use, gave serving suggestions, noted the length of time needed, and gave visual cues of cooking. It is hard to overstate how revelatory, or even revolutionary, this was for the average home cook. Over time, Farmer saw her influence grow. When she judged a gelatin recipe contest some 18 years after that first stint as a flour recipe contest judge, she noted that 90 percent of the entries called for level measures.[4]

Other Cookbooks

As women's magazines began to provide more content on matters of house-keeping, Farmer dropped some of this context from the subsequent editions of her book. However, her interest in convalescent cooking intensified, and in 1904 she published *Food and Cookery for the Sick and Convalescent*. The book was well received by the medical community, and she was invited to lecture on the topic at the Harvard University Medical School.

At age 50, Farmer suffered a second stroke that confined her to a wheelchair for the next seven years. But she had come too far to revert to becoming a shut-in. During her convalescence she published *A New Book of Cookery* (1912), the last of the six cookbooks she authored. In addition to her biweekly magazine column, Farmer continued to develop recipes and give talks, the texts of which were printed by the *Boston Evening Transcript*. In fact, Farmer delivered a lecture 10 days before she died in Boston on January 15, 1915, at age 57.

CONCLUSION

Farmer's "Boston" cookbook was reprinted and revised a number of times before her death, accounting for sales of more than 360,000 copies. Her sister, Cora Perkins, edited subsequent editions of the cookbook until 1951, at which point Farmer's niece, Wilma Perkins, took over the editing and republishing process. By then, more than 2.5 million copies had been sold. The era of numerous revisions by family members ended when *Fannie Farmer*'s new publisher asked a little-known California home cook named Marion Cunningham to step in. Cunningham helped keep Farmer's advice current and in the consciousness of modern cooks.

MARION CUNNINGHAM

EARLY YEARS

One could make the case that Marion Cunningham's life story has two discrete chapters: before and after food. Details about the octogenarian's early life are incomplete. In newspaper interviews, Cunningham generally did not provide much information about those years. The stories seem disconnected to the woman beloved and sought after for what her friend and mentor, the late James Beard, called "a critical palate."[5]

Cunningham was born in Los Angeles on February 7, 1922, an only child of an Italian mother (née Spelta) and an Irish father. Her parents were immigrants who made enough money in New York to move to California. Cunningham's mother had tuberculosis in her youth and always seemed frail to the young Marion. After World War I, her father developed Reynaud's phenomenon, which caused him to lose a leg, as well as some fingers and toes. Although her father had something of a temper and was an alcoholic, Cunningham was a devoted daughter who remembered both him and her mother as being kind and good. The family's main source of income was the monthly disability payment her father received.

After a time the family moved to the small, less expensive community of Glendale, where, in kindergarten, Cunningham would meet her future husband. Her Italian grandmother lived with the family for a few years, so for a while the women and the girl spoke only Italian at home. That was until the thoughtful daughter realized how isolating it was for her father not to understand conversations in his own home. Cunningham's grandmother loved to cook and spent all day in the kitchen, and Cunningham watched and learned.

Cunningham did not like to study in school, however, perhaps because she found it hard to concentrate. She graduated from Glendale High School with no intention of going to college. For the next few years she worked at a variety of jobs, but nothing seemed to hold her interest.

In 1943, Cunningham married Robert Cunningham in a small, simple ceremony. She was 21 and he was just six months older. She has described him as a keen student and an idealistic patriot who didn't like food the same way she did. He joined the Marines and went to serve in World War II. While he was away, Marion had the first job she really liked: running a Union Oil service station. She learned to fix tires, changed oil, and kept the place operating after the owner was unable to do so. She was genuinely motivated enough to dream of buying her own station someday, but Robert would have none of that.

Cunningham did not hold a grudge against him, and she led a somewhat carefree life in her first few years of marriage. Robert served in the Corps for more than four years; the last of these he spent in Santa Ana, and the couple rented a house in Laguna Beach. Here Cunningham learned to body-surf and earned money waxing cars. Friends from her high school days came to stay with her, and the couple went to Mexico several times a year. She enjoyed the food, the lazy days of vacation, and watching Mexican families as they ate together.

After the war, Robert finished law school and the couple moved to Beverly Glen Canyon in Los Angeles, where Robert began to practice law. Cunningham entertained at home and did not work. During that time, she became a member of the American Institute of Wine and Food, where her thoughts on modern isolation and the need for community and family meals began to take shape. At age 36, Marion gave birth to Mark and, 19 months later, to Katherine. While Robert worked long hours, Cunningham focused on being a wife and mother. She checked out cookbooks from the library and tried many recipes, especially from author James Beard, and she enjoyed producing meals for her children and her friends. As the children grew older, however, Cunningham developed unhealthy addictions to smoking and drinking wine. She was also a self-described agoraphobic, plagued by anxieties that had increased since she was a girl. One of her greatest apprehensions was driving over the San Francisco Bay Bridge.

Cunningham resolved to stop both smoking and drinking and had the will to make it happen, but she has also credited her success to a *Life Magazine* story about a Sausalito man who had similar symptoms. This man met his fears head-on, which is what Cunningham eventually did as well. After the birth of her daughter, she developed a hand tremor and consulted a doctor, who diagnosed and treated her for hyperthyroidism and a goiter. Six weeks into the successful treatment she felt her physical and mental symptoms begin to subside.

Cunningham took up swimming, which suited her tall, athletic frame and restored her health and vigor. It was an activity she continued into her eighties. Because of Robert's new job at a law firm in Oakland, the family moved close to Walnut Creek. Marion fell in love with the area, named for its towering trees. She taught drawing to elementary school students, and the Cunninghams built a comfortable house, kept quarter horses, and spent time outdoors. She always liked having cats and dogs about.

The Cunninghams designed their new home for entertaining, especially in Marion's kitchen. She began to teach cooking classes in her home for $6 a person, and the classes became popular after the *Contra Costa Times* wrote a story about her courses. To improve her own skills, she also took cooking classes from cooks who would later populate the ranks of restaurateurs in the Bay Area.

COOKBOOKS

Discovery and Reinvention

When Cunningham was 50, a friend suggested a trip to Seaside, Oregon, to take a cooking class taught by James Beard. This was no small feat considering that Cunningham had never traveled outside of California. At the time, Beard, the East Coast cookbook author, was trying to extend his market reach across the United States and supplement the income from his cookbooks. Over the course of the two-week-long class, he was drawn to Cunningham and asked her to be his assistant as he toured and taught.

This was a big step for Cunningham. As a result of this working relationship and mentorship, she and Beard became close friends and colleagues and were referred to as "the perfect couple" by many observers. (Robert Cunningham had no reason to be threatened, since Beard was gay.) Cunningham spent 11 years working with Beard. That meant traveling by air. Cunningham had never been on a plane, but she summoned the courage to fly, first from San Francisco to Los Angeles as a test.

When Beard and Cunningham were not together, they corresponded by mail. Her letters impressed him so much that when Beard's editor, Judith Jones, told him she was looking for someone "nonprofessional" to update the *Fannie Farmer* cookbook, he suggested Cunningham. The hesitant Cunningham flew to New York to meet with Jones, who was impressed enough to give her the job. Over the next five years, Cunningham tested every one of the hundreds of *Fannie Farmer* recipes, often giving away the results to her neighbors. She had the fortitude to reject some dishes that were too outdated and later figured that, with all the money she spent on testing, she probably only broke even on the $30,000 she received.

Nearly 2,000 recipes made the cut for the 1979 edition of the *Fannie Farmer Cookbook* (12th edition).[6] Many people believed that the 57-year-old Cunningham was responsible for returning Farmer's original book to its rightful place as the premier American home cookbook, and she reestablished Farmer as an American culinary icon. Book reviews called the new edition "brilliant."

Cunningham hoped to have the chance to work again with legendary Knopf editor Jones, who was known for her clarity, honesty, sense of humor, and down-to-earth personality. Jones encouraged those who shared her passion about the magic of cooking, particularly her fascination with baking. Cunningham learned so much from her that she pitched a *Fannie Farmer Baking Book* to Jones. The editor approved the project, and the book included 800 of Cunningham's own recipes, which were much more detailed than Farmer's. The Farmer name brought the book and Cunningham a built-in audience that responded enthusiastically to the new work.

As Cunningham befriended women who were professional bakers and cookbook authors, she would ask them to explain things, like the mysteries of meringues and salt-rising bread. In 1989 these women formed a group called the Baker's Dozen, which included Flo Braker, Amy Pressman, and Alice Medrich as part of the group's inner circle. They would meet once a month, sometimes to tour a bakery facility and always to share and compare techniques. Cunningham wanted the costs involved, such as lunch, kept to a minimum. The San Francisco chapter of the Baker's Dozen prompted the initiation of chapters in southern California, Chicago, and New York, and the original group grew to more than 400 strong. After a painstaking two years, the group published a cookbook called, appropriately enough, *The Baker's Dozen Cookbook,* although Cunningham was not directly involved in producing it.

During this time, Cunningham's individual fame grew and she blossomed into a guru for foodies nationwide. Her newfound popularity increased with the 13th edition of the *Fannie Farmer Cookbook,* where she made further refinements to the text, such as eliminating box-top recipes. Since microwave ovens had come into vogue, Jones pushed her to test new recipes with them. Cunningham told Jones that this method was "ruining good food," but in the end, she worked out sound advice for microwave cooking.

OTHER ENDEAVORS

After the deaths of her husband in 1983 and her dear friend Jim Beard in 1985, Cunningham further reinvented her life. She widened her circle of friends to include food icons such as Alice Waters of Chez Panisse, Chuck Williams of Williams-Sonoma (a guest at her Thanksgiving table each year), winemaker Robert Mondavi, Mandarin food pioneer Cecilia Chiang, food critic and later *Gourmet* magazine editor Ruth Reichl, Michael Bauer of *The San Francisco Chronicle,* and vegetarian cookbook author Deborah Madison. Cunningham had originally introduced Beard to Waters, and later she would go on food-focused trips abroad with Waters, Chiang, and Reichl. Waters later hired "Great Chefs of France" producer Billy Cross to tape-record the story of Cunningham's life. As a result, she and Cross became traveling pals and longtime friends.

Cunningham, who loved to drive fast cars, used proceeds from the *Fannie Farmer* books to buy a Jaguar, the first of several elegant cars. Her weekly dinners out with friends netted her an impressive number of speeding tickets, and she put about 2,500 miles per month on her odometer. Cunningham lived the kind of social life she had long desired: visiting friends and feeling free enough to travel, including over the previously dreaded Bay Bridge. She stayed at the Vermont home of Christopher Kimball of *Cook's Illustrated* for a week and made maple sugar for the first time. She watched him prepare all the family meals and proclaimed him a topnotch cook.

Perhaps because she and Julia Child were of similar stature and presence, people thought that they should be friends. Cunningham had great admiration for Child, but the two women were not especially close. They both empowered home cooks, but Cunningham had a taste for simpler food and considered the family meal at home to be a crucial element of everyday life. Her *Breakfast Book* in 1988 clicked with audiences during an era when breakfast as a meal was enjoying a revival.

AWARDS AND HONORS

Cunningham's waffle recipe became legendary, and fellow food professionals and friends counted themselves lucky when they received invitations to enjoy waffles at her house on Sundays. In 1992, she followed her popular *Breakfast*

Book with a *Supper Book*. Cunningham turned 70 that year, and her friend Alice Waters put on a grand birthday dinner with 120 guests. Cunningham appreciated the way Waters used organic, seasonal ingredients, yet she herself shopped at the grocery store instead of the farmers' market and harbored a not-so-secret affection for iceberg lettuce, as did her friend James Beard.

More formal honors came her way. In 1993, she hosted a cooking show on television called *Cunningham & Company* that was both fun and collegial. That same year, Les Dames d'Escoffier bestowed upon her its Grande Dame Award "in recognition and appreciation of her extraordinary achievement and contribution to the culinary arts." In 1994, she was named scholar-in-residence by the International Association of Culinary Professionals. She also wrote biweekly columns that appeared in *The Minneapolis Star, The San Francisco Chronicle*, and *The Los Angeles Times*, plus articles for *Gourmet, Bon Appetit,* and *Food & Wine* magazines. She even became a paid, short-term spokeswoman for the Iceberg Lettuce Commission.

CONCLUSION

As celebrity chefdom arose in America, Cunningham liked to call herself "the last living home cook," with some 2,500 cookbooks in her collection. Her concern about the decline of cooking and community only increased with time. She believed in the humanity of food, that it created bonds and connections lost in modern life. In her mid-eighties, Cunningham gradually fell victim to Alzheimer's disease. She limited time spent with friends and eventually moved to a nursing home near her home, where she further restricted visitors. A quotation from her in 2002 sums up her life's work succinctly: "Anyone can cook. I just wish more people did."[7]

NOTES

1. Kathleen Ann Smallzried, *The Everlasting Pleasure: Influences on America's Kitchens, Cooks, and Cookery from 1565 to the Year 2000* (New York: Appleton-Century-Crofts, 1956).

2. Smallzried, *The Everlasting Pleasure.*

3. Fannie Merritt Farmer, *The Original Boston Cooking-School Cook Book* (Boston: Little, Brown and Company, 1896).

4. Kathleen M. Poplawski, "Fannie Farmer: The Woman behind the Cookbook," *Milwaukee* (WI) *Journal* (December 28, 1973).

5. Marion Burros, "At Lunch with Marion Cunningham: A Grande Dame of Home Cooking Is Still at the Stove," *The New York Times* (December 3, 2003).

6. Greg Atkinson, "America's Cook: In Word and Spirit, Marion Cunningham Keeps Us at the Table," *Pacific Northwest Magazine* (January 23, 2004).

7. Michelle R. Smith, "Fannie Farmer Writer Marion Cunningham: Anyone Can Cook!" *The New York Times* (July 8, 2002).

FURTHER READING

Cunningham, Marion. *The Fannie Farmer Baking Book*. New York: Alfred A. Knopf, 1984.

Cunningham, Marion. *The Fannie Farmer Cookbook*. New York: Alfred A. Knopf, 1996.

Dougherty, Robin. "Between the Lines with Marion Cunningham: Remedies for a Takeout World." Boston Globe/Boston.com. www.boston.com/bostonglobe/

Farmer, Fannie Merritt. *The 1896 Boston Cooking-School Cookbook*. New York: Gramercy, 1997.

Jones, Judith. *The Tenth Muse: My Life in Food*. New York: Alfred A. Knopf, 2007.

Severson, Kim. "A Cooking Kinship: Marion Cunningham and Alice Waters on Friendship and Lettuce." San Francisco Chronicle. http://articles.sfgate.com/2001-05-27/living/17600314_1_alice-waters-lettuce-cookbooks

Bonnie S. Benwick

Cookbook author and food critic Mary Frances Kennedy Fisher at her home in Sonoma, California, April 28, 1971. (AP/Wide World Photos)

M. F. K. Fisher

Food writer Mary Frances Kennedy Fisher delighted her readers with stories about the pleasures of food and eating. Her lively and often sensuous prose evolved from her belief that writing about food meant writing about life. It meant writing about hunger and love, not just food. She wrote 31 books and countless articles, and her extensive journals and letters also provide insight into her life and her thoughts about food. She was more than a food writer, however. Fisher "was an icon, a person you read because she understood your dreams," according to another noted food writer and editor, Ruth Reichl.[1] Poet W. H. Auden said her writing was "unsurpassed by any other American author."[2] Fisher received many such accolades, particularly in the final decades of her life when writing about food was more accepted.

EARLY YEARS

Childhood and Family

Fisher related a story her father told her about her birth on July 3, 1908. She claimed he told her mother, "'Edith . . . it's nine minutes to midnight, if you don't hurry I'm going to call this child Independencia,' and she was so horrified, you know, probably thinking what will the nicknames be, or something, that she gave a great heave and there I was."[3] Fisher, the firstborn, was named for her maternal grandmother and began her life in Albion, Michigan, where her father, Rex, a fourth-generation newspaperman, ran the *Albion Evening Recorder* with his older brother, Walter. Fisher described her mother as "a strange combination of prairie princess . . . and a Daisy Miller type . . . seemingly sophisticated but inwardly naïve."[4] The next child, Edith Anne, was born two years later and was known as Anne. Two more children, Norah (1917) and David (1919), were born after the family moved to California.

After Anne's birth, the Kennedys began thinking about moving to a warmer climate. Rex took his family and followed family members to the West Coast, where brother Ted and his parents lived. In 1911, Rex sold his part of the newspaper to Walter, packed up the family, and headed for Spokane, Washington. They spent the summer on Maury Island in the Puget Sound area. It took a little over a year for the family to finally settle in the Los Angeles Quaker community of Whittier, California, where Rex purchased *The Whittier News*, one of three newspapers in the town. The Episcopalian Kennedys were among the minority who were not Quakers. Fisher's maternal grandmother, Mary Frances Holbrook, joined the family in Whittier and lived with them in a house that Fisher described as "a veritable palace."[5] Shortly after the move to Whittier, her father also purchased a cottage at Laguna Beach, where the family escaped to on Saturday afternoons after the paper was printed.

Fisher's transformative experiences with food began in Whittier. Early memories included spending time in the kitchen with the family cooks. She observed what they did, listened to them, and sampled the food they prepared.

Grandmother Holbrook dictated the family diet. She was a proponent of John Harvey Kellogg's diet, which favored whole grains and little meat. She also favored root vegetables, even though fresh vegetables were bountiful in California. When the grandmother traveled, the family consumed tastier meals. Fisher noted the difference in what the family ate during these periods. Gwendolyn Nettleship, her mother's friend, also influenced how Fisher preferred to dine throughout her life. The girls spent time in "Aunt Gwen's" kitchen eating and talking quietly. They also spent summers at the cottage in Laguna Beach with Nettleship, eating simple meals and seafood.

Additional influences included favorite family cookbooks and Grandmother Holbrook's recipes. *The Settlement Cookbook* (1901) and Fannie Farmer's *The Boston Cooking-School Cookbook* (1896), both American icons, contained tried and true recipes. *The Settlement Cookbook* included non-kosher recipes from the German Jewish Community in Milwaukee, while Farmer's cookbook featured recipes such as Parker House rolls, lobster bisque, and Boston baked beans. Cooks loved the latter book because recipes were written as if Farmer were teaching the cook how to create the dishes. *The Miriam Cookbook* (1903), published by the Miriam Circle Ladies' Aid Society of the M. E. Church in Albion, was also a family favorite.

Writing came naturally to Fisher's whole family, and she began writing at an early age. She started her first novel at age nine but stopped when she realized her parents found her stories amusing. In a later interview, she recalled filling in at her father's newspaper when the writers took vacation: "Sometimes I would write 14 or 15 stories a day on an old stubborn Remington standard. It was hard work, but I learned a lot."[6] Despite how naturally writing seemed, she did not consider a future as a writer for many years.

The family moved to the Ranch in 1919, a house on Painter Avenue complete with an orchard and bountiful gardens covering 13 acres just outside the city limits of Whittier, California. There Fisher learned to revel in what she created in the kitchen. After Grandmother Holbrook's death in 1921, the "family's diet became absolutely heathenish,"[7] featuring milk, cream, butter, and baked goods. Fisher worked with her mother in the kitchen and learned how to bake and prepare tea trays for her mother's friends who visited in the afternoons.

Education

Fisher claimed she realized the power of language as early as age three. Formal education took place in a number of different schools, but her real education took place at home, where she learned the power of creative language through the books she read and the conversations she heard and participated in with her family. Fisher attended several schools during her grade school years because the family moved from town to the Ranch. She learned about the dynamics between Quakers and Protestants at school and how to deal with being different from the majority. As a teen she attended the Bishop's School in La Jolla and Miss Harker's School in Palo Alto along with Anne. During this time she began to develop her palate. While at Miss Harker's School, the sisters spent many weekends in San Francisco, especially in Chinatown. Their mother entertained them at her favorite restaurants when she visited her daughters. Writing continued to be an important part of Fisher's life in high school, and she honed her skills by composing poetry and stories.

The choice of colleges became a contest between mother and daughter. Fisher wanted to attend Vassar, but her mother preferred finishing schools for young women. Fisher wanted to move away from home but did not want to go somewhere where she did not know anyone else. The family eventually decided that she would join her cousin Nancy at Illinois College in Jacksonville, Illinois. Fisher did not enjoy the institutional food served on campus, so she and her cousin would go to stores and restaurants in town to eat. She ended her freshman year short of credits and so attended summer classes at Whittier College and UCLA.

While attending UCLA, the 20-year-old met Alfred Young Fisher, a Princeton graduate spending his summer in Los Angeles. The son of a Presbyterian minister, he attended Princeton on a full scholarship and studied humanities and English. Following his graduation, he moved to Wyoming to teach English at a boarding school to earn money so he could study overseas. In the fall, Fisher chose to remain in California and attended Occidental College in Eagle Rock, California, along with Anne. Alfred Fisher reminded her of Percy Bysshe Shelley, and he courted her with sonnets and love letters for the next year when he returned to Wyoming. They were married on September 5, 1929.

Dijon, France

Shortly after marrying, the Fishers moved to Dijon, France, where Al pursued his doctoral work in literature and where they spent three years. This was the first of many overseas trips that influenced and shaped her taste and provided opportunities for observing habits at the table and procedures in the kitchen. While her husband studied and composed his epic poem, *The Ghost of the Underblows,* Fisher studied French and art, observed life, and soaked up the experience of living abroad. Lawrence Powell, a lively and fun-loving friend of Fisher's from Occidental, also came to Dijon to study for a Ph.D. in literature.

The Fishers first lived in a pension owned by Madame Ollangnier. Her hearty meals taught Fisher about thrift and shopping at the specialty shops available in France. Fisher explored Dijon, wandering through the shops and writing letters to family and friends, gathering material for her early books. She later wrote that Dijon was the place where "I started to grow up, to study, to make love, to eat and drink, to be me and not what I was expected to be."[8] It was here that she read Jean Anthelme Brillat-Savarin's *Physiology of Taste* (1825). Her culinary style began to emerge as she distinguished the American palate from the French palate. She also continued to develop her awareness of the pleasure that fresh ingredients provided in simple meals.

In 1930, a Madame Rigoulot bought the pension from the Ollangniers. She was a much more elaborate cook, in Fisher's opinion to make up for her lack of attention to her appearance. Rigoulot offered to teach Fisher to cook, but she declined because she did not want to spend her time cooking while living in Dijon.

After two years, Fisher traveled to California to visit while Al remained in France. Her parents desired her presence at home, hoping she could persuade Anne not to rush into a marriage. Norah returned with her to France and attended convent schools until the Fishers returned to California in 1932. Meanwhile, the Fishers moved into an apartment with a small kitchen, where Fisher was able finally to learn how to prepare food on her own.

The Great Depression

The Depression began the year the Fishers married, but it did not truly affect their lives until they returned to California. Al could not find a teaching position in a university, so the young couple lived at the Ranch with her parents as well as at the family cottage in Laguna Beach. Al eventually found a position as an English instructor at Occidental College. The couple met Gigi and Dillwyn Parrish during this time. Dillwyn, known as Timmy, and Fisher became close friends. While Al taught, Fisher spent her time at the Los Angeles Public Library writing the essays that would eventually become her first book, *Serve It Forth* (1937).

FOOD BOOKS

Switzerland, 1937–1939

In 1936 Dilwyn Parrish, who had separated from his wife, invited Fisher to accompany him and his mother to their home in Switzerland. On the surface Fisher served as a companion for Parrish's mother. Al did not object to being separated from her, which puzzled her. In 1937 Al and the Fishers traveled to Switzerland together to join an artistic community that Dilwyn and his sister Anne hoped to create. As Al and Fisher became more distant, she drew closer to Dilwyn. The months they spent at Le Paquis were the happiest ones of her life. She returned to California in 1937 to inform her family that she planned to divorce Al. He had accepted a position at Smith College in Massachusetts, where he would spend the rest of his career. Her family unexpectedly supported her decision. She returned to Switzerland to be with Parrish and to continue working on her second book. She married Parrish in 1938.

Viking published *Serve It Forth* in 1937. It would start Fisher on the path to becoming one of the most respected food writers of the 20th century. The book established her style with essays about her philosophies on eating and food. She drew upon her experiences in France and described eating as a sensual experience. This was her first volume based on her memories of food. Parrish assisted Fisher with this book by sending the essays to his sister, Anne Parrish, a novelist. Parrish's editor, Gene Saxton, shared the manuscript with editors in London. Excerpts of the book appeared in *Harper's Monthly* prior to its publication. Reviews were favorable for the most part. A review in the June 20, 1937, *New York Times* stated, "This is a delightful book. It is erudite and witty and experienced and young."[9] A few weeks later another reviewer was not so kind. The reviewer noted, "What redeems the book is Mrs. Fisher's hearty masculine gusto" but "it is rather a collection of rambling essays, historical and personal, dealing with food and feeders in general."[10] A few dismissed her book, but Fisher did not pay attention to these critics. She did not think of herself as a "writer" merely because she had published a book and was uneasy with that label throughout her life. In her family, writing was just something one did.

Fisher was, however, carving out a niche. In the introduction to *Serve It Forth*, she noted that some books on writing tried to imitate Brillat-Savarin's, some were about what to eat and full of recipes, and some were memoirs of famous gourmets. She wrote, "Now I am going to write a book. It will be about eating and about what to eat and about people who eat. And I shall do gymnastics by trying to fall between these three fires, or by straddling them all."[11] The theme of this first volume was hunger, in all its various forms. How does one satisfy hunger? Is it merely physical or is it deeper?

Parrish and Fisher visited Bern, Switzerland, before returning to the United States. While they were there, Parrish suffered an embolism that caused him constant pain the rest of his life. The couple traveled around Switzerland to try to find a cure.

California

In January 1939 the Parrishes moved back to California and in the San Jacinto Hills purchased land and a cabin, which they named Bareacres. Parrish's illness was finally diagnosed as Buerger's disease. The chronic and unbearable pain would eventually lead to amputation of his leg, and they spent the majority of their time at Bareacres caring for his needs. They completed part of the renovations, and Fisher returned to writing while Parrish painted. She provided for the family by turning again to writing about food, placing essays in magazines and completing the manuscript for her second book, *Consider the Oyster* (1941). She also wrote fiction, which she had attempted before. Her novel, *The Theoretical Foot*, was never published, and in fact caused friction between her and her sister-in-law, Anne, because of the way she portrayed characters based on real people. Parrish, with no hope of recovery from his illness, committed suicide in August 1941.

Consider the Oyster, published a few weeks after Parrish's death, felt like a bittersweet event. Fisher interspersed recipes with the essays to present a comic history of the oyster and the ways in which people reacted to oysters, both physically and emotionally. The thin volume contained 12 essays and showcased Fisher's storytelling ability as she created tall tales, including some of the recipes, memories of eating oysters, and memories of stories told to her. The first essay in the book, "Love and Death among the Mollusks," is a spoof of Virginia Woolf's *Orlando* (1928).

After Parrish's death, Fisher spent time at the Ranch and in Mexico before she moved to Hollywood, where she took a job as a writer at Paramount Pictures. She also continued writing about food. The United States had entered World War II, and times were difficult. Fisher wrote *How to Cook a Wolf* (1942), which concentrated on how to cook during times of scarcity. This book included recipes and philosophies about food and about living and was

---

From How to Cook a Wolf

Fisher wrote How to Cook a Wolf *(1942) to help people get through World War II when they had no food and no money. She revisited the book some 40-plus years later to update it and make it more generally about how to eat well and nutritiously, even while flat broke. The gist is, when the wolf is at the door, one can cook him.*

There are many ways to make a little seem like more. They have been followed and changed and reinvented for ten thousand years, with small loss of dignity to mankind. Indeed, sometimes their very following is a thing of admiration, because of the people who are poor and who refuse to be obsessed by that fact until it becomes "repulsive and disturbing."

Of course, it takes a certain amount of native wit to cope gracefully with the problem of having the wolf camp with apparent permanency on your doorstep. That can be a wearing thing, and even the pretense of ignoring his presence has a kind of dangerous monotony about it.

For the average wolf-dodger, good health is probably one of the most important foils. Nothing seems particularly grim if your head is clear and your teeth are clean and your bowels function properly.

Another thing that makes daily, hourly thought about wherewithals endurable is to be able to share it with someone else. That does not mean, and I say it emphatically, sharing the fuss and bother and fretting. It means being companionable with another human being who understands, perhaps without any talking at all, what problems of basic nourishment confront you. Once such a relationship is established, your black thoughts vanish, and how to make a pot of stew last three more meals seems less a nightmare than a form of sensual entertainment.

—M. F. K. Fisher, "How to Be Cheerful Though Starving," in
How to Cook a Wolf. New York: North Point Press, 1942/1988, pp. 80–81

the vehicle that introduced her to many new readers. She offered simple recipes and nutritional information that included eating whole grains, vegetables, and organic meat, well before this style of eating became popular. The book featured recipes for a basic soufflé omelet, bread, and prune roast along with those for soap and mouth wash. Again, her advice drew on her experiences in France, shopping in the markets, and being able to obtain fresh food.

In December of 1942 Fisher discovered she was pregnant. Instead of telling her family and friends about her pregnancy, she told them she had accepted a government job that forced her to be out of touch. She spent the months until her daughter Anne Kennedy Parrish (later called Anna) was born, writing articles about food for magazines and writing her autobiography, *The Gastronomical Me* (1943). In her letters she talked about adopting a child, rather than giving birth to her daughter. After Anne's birth, she returned to Bareacres. Fisher never revealed the name of the father of her first child.

Fisher continued to write about food and work as a writer for Paramount Pictures. She did not return to fiction, as some urged her to do. *The Gastronomical Me* begins with a foreword that explains why she writes about food: "It seems to me that our three basic needs, for food and security and love, are so mixed and mingled and entwined that we cannot straightly think of one without the others."[12] The book begins with her earliest memories regarding food and continues through her youth and life in France and Switzerland. Her essays include her philosophy about preparing and serving food. She wrote about love for the people in her life as well as the sadness. It was her most personal book to date. She talked about how her hunger for life changed as she grew and experienced new things.

New York

Fisher took Anna and a nursemaid to New York for the summer of 1945. Shortly after she arrived, she met Donald Friede, an editor and publisher. He asked her to marry him, and on an impulse, she did on May 19, 1945. They spent the rest of the summer in the apartment she had sublet in Greenwich Village. Fisher spent much of the summer researching at the New York Public Library for a new anthology on banquets and feasting in literature and history. In the fall, she was pregnant again, and the family returned to Bareacres.

Here Let Us Feast (1946), the book she wrote in New York, draws on her knowledge and the literature of gastronomy. Her personal voice and vignettes add to the volume. Following this volume, she once again turned to fiction, but her novel *Not Now but Now* (1947) failed to capture readers' attention as her culinary writing did. Friede's publishing contacts helped her expand her magazine work, and she began writing for *Atlantic Monthly, Vogue, Town & Country,* and *Today's Woman.* She also had a new editor, Pat Covici at Viking. Friede worked on a memoir at Bareacres and tried to establish contacts on the West Coast.

Fisher's second daughter, Kennedy Friede, was born March 12, 1946. While Friede looked for employment in Hollywood and worked on his memoir, Fisher supported the family again with her magazine writing and book projects. She wrote columns for magazines such as *Gourmet* and *House Beautiful* about seasonal celebrations and special events. One of her regular columns in *Gourmet* became *Alphabet for Gourmets,* published in 1949. The essays that made up the book were reflections on her life during the 1940s in Hollywood and later in Bareacres. One commentator referred to the book as "witty, pungent and highly civilized, but also it has a special charm."[13]

Rather than being how-to columns or collections of recipes, Fisher's essays and books demonstrated an intellectual side of the kitchen and were more literary than readers were used to. She thought about her guests' needs and their preferences in food and drink when she entertained. She considered the role of the cook, not as merely as a preparer of meals, but as an artist or a craftsman. Her book *With a Bold Knife and Fork* (1969) reflected on this role and on the various identities a cook passed through. She knew that menus changed and evolved, as did tastes and interests.

In 1946 Fisher accepted an opportunity to prepare a new translation of Brillat-Savarin's *Physiology of Taste,* which had influenced her books and writing. This was to be published as a deluxe edition for the Limited Editions Club. It was one of her most scholarly works, and her translation continues to be considered the best. Her notes and glosses react to Brillat-Savarin's writing and do not merely explain it.

Whittier

Fisher eventually realized the she and Friede were not compatible; they were opposites. She divorced him and returned to live at the Ranch after her mother died in 1948. She cared for her father and raised her daughters there from 1949 to1953. Due to her father's illness, she took over *The Whittier News* during these years. Because she also took care of all the household chores, she had little time for culinary writing. However, she did revise *How to Cook a Wolf,* which became a book about how to live economically in any age, not just wartime.

When her father died in June 1953, Fisher moved to St. Helena, California. Her next book, *The Art of Eating,* was a compilation of her best writing about food and life over 15 years. Clifton Fadiman, the noted critic, wrote the introduction to the first edition, praising her writing as he had in reviews of her previous books. This volume has been republished several times, including as a 50th anniversary edition with additional introductions by James Beard and Joan Reardon.

The family sold *The Whittier News* after her father died. The inheritance from the sale helped Fisher financially. In 1954 she took her daughters and went to Provence. The trip was supposed to be only for a few months, but they stayed in France for two years. The girls attended convent schools while

Fisher observed life in France once again and gathered material for future writing projects. She compared the prewar France with the France of the 1950s. Near the end of their trip, they rented a house where Fisher once more had a kitchen to work in. The house gave her an opportunity to cook with the fresh foods she found in the markets and small shops she loved in France. *The Art of Eating* appeared in 1954 and received high praise by critics. One compared the book to "a refreshing breeze flowing from twin sources of sense and sensibility," and another noted that it was "a book on the verge of being a novel."[14]

The family returned to Napa, California, in 1955 and Fisher became more interested in wines. Her writing was slow during this period, however, as she tried to reshape her prose based on what she had experienced in life. She also sold Bareacres during this period.

In 1959 the family once again ventured to Europe, this time to Switzerland. They also returned to Provence in 1960, where Fisher worked on the book *A Cordiall Water: A Garland of Odd & Old Receipts to Assuage the Ills of Man and Beast* (1961). This book drew on many sources, personal and scholarly, presenting folk cures, healing recipes, and other advice for good living.

Wine in Napa Valley

For the next decade Fisher concentrated on the wine industry of the Napa Valley. She wrote and spoke about wine and was one of the founders of the Napa Valley Wine Association. In 1964 she published *Map of Another Town: A Memoir of Provence*, a guide to her favorite places in Provence. This work was well received and was somewhat different from previous works.

Other food writers had entered the public scene in America by this time. Julia Child, who became one of Fisher's friends, published *Mastering the Art of French Cooking* (1961), and James Beard and Craig Claiborne were becoming widely known as writers and chefs. Fisher's popularity continued to grow through her articles in *The New Yorker*, where new pieces of writing as well as excerpts appeared. Time Life selected her to write the first volume of their series titled *Foods of the World*. She authored the volume *The Cooking of Provincial France* (1968), which afforded her an opportunity to return to France, live with a family, and study their habits. Controversy surrounded the book upon publication, however, because it incited journalistic wars about the food establishment: who was in and who was out. Craig Claiborne and Robert Courtine, a French gastronomic critic, both dismissed the book. Although Claiborne eventually did compliment Fisher in his review. Overall, Fisher and Child found these battles amusing.

After this venture Fisher wanted to do something different, so she accepted a teaching position in Piney Woods, Mississippi. Teaching provided a way to earn money while she studied Southern cuisine, one of her reasons for moving to Mississippi. The administrators of the school did not entirely approve of Fisher's methods, which were not as formal as they would have liked. She surmised that gaining the trust of her students did not sit well with them. She was not invited to return.

Putnam published a number of chapters in *The New Yorker* prior to releasing *With a Bold Knife and Fork* (1969). The book included many recipes as well as memories of childhood, feasts, and special events throughout her life. The memories of comfort foods drew letters from many fans who related to Fisher's experiences. Her friendships with Child, Claiborne, and Beard deepened during this period.

OTHER ENDEAVORS

During the final decades of her life, Fisher turned to autobiography. Her stories were not always as others remembered them. *Among Friends* (1971) relates stories about her childhood in Whittier and the cultural differences between the Episcopalian home she grew up in and the larger Quaker community.

Fisher lived in Glen Ellen, California, in the Sonoma Valley in "Last House," the home built for her by her friend David Bouverie. A descendant of William Bouverie, the Fifth Earl of Radnor, Bouverie moved to California in the 1930s. He purchased 500 acres, where he built eight country-style buildings that drew the attention of architectural, home and garden, and society magazines.[15] Bouverie and Fisher met when he accompanied an interviewer to her home.

Although Fisher's health began to limit travel, she ventured to France one more time with Norah and visited her friends Julia and Paul Child in Provence. She also embarked on a trip to Japan to learn about native cuisine before writing an introduction to her friend Shizuo Tsuji's book, *Japanese Cooking: A Simple Art* (1981). Norah accompanied her on the trip as well. They visited several cities, attended private classes, and explored markets that were different from any Fisher had seen. She also went to her beloved Marseilles, where she had spent many holidays. She wanted to write a book about this place, and in 1973 she returned there to work on *A Considerable Town*, published in 1978.

Fisher's health began to decline in the 1970s. It worsened as she aged, with failing eyesight, arthritis, and Parkinson's disease. She remained in demand, however, and was asked to write introductions to other people's books and to speak and lecture. North Point Press in Berkeley reprinted her books, and the paperback editions brought her out-of-print books to a new generation of readers. *As They Were,* issued in 1982, presented previously published and written essays.

Once again Fisher annotated a cookbook from her collection. This time it was Catherine Plagemann's *Fine Preserving*. Her own copy contained detailed annotations and was the basis for the reprinted version in 1986.

Several more volumes were published before Fisher's death, including a more successful volume of fiction titled *The Boss Dog* (1990). She also worked on her journals and letters during her final years. These were published posthumously.

CONCLUSION

In one of her journals Fisher wrote that "by now people sometimes refer to me as a stylist, or they talk about my style, and I think this is because of my habit of putting words onto paper as much as possible as I say them in talking or telling. I have always tried to speak clearly—that is, to make what I am saying clear and logical to the listener or reader . . . and, of course, to make it interesting if the story itself is interesting. But I do try to tell it in *my* way."[16] Throughout her life, she never thought of herself as a writer but rather as someone who wrote because that was just what people in her family did for a living. She also wrote that she never really liked being known as "M. F. K. Fisher"; her name was Mary Frances. But because the first editor used her initials, they remained her moniker throughout her writing career.

Before her death Fisher placed her papers at the Schlesinger Library at Radcliffe College, Harvard University. Her career was recognized with awards toward the end of her life. She was elected to the Dames d'Escoffier in New York (1978) and to the American Academy and National Institute of Arts and Letters (1991). The Dames d'Escoffier continues to provide an award in M. F. K. Fisher's name for culinary writing.

Fisher died in 1992 shortly before her 84th birthday. Although she never considered herself a food writer, she is remembered as one of the greatest food writers of the 20th century. Betty Fussell, food historian, wrote, "Reading M. F. K. Fisher never made me as hungry for food as it made me hungry for the company of one who was so tartly witty and wise, so provocative and persuasive, so artful and contradictory that, like Shakespeare's Cleopatra, 'she makes hungry where most she satisfies.'"[17] Others remembered Fisher with similar praise, recalling her sensuous prose, her wit, and her charm. She captured textures and senses in her cooking and in her writing about cooking and the places she loved. Fisher's works endure the test of time and communicate her love for the kitchen and the written word.

NOTES

1. Dominique Gioia, ed., *The Measure of Her Powers: An M. F. K. Fisher Reader* (Washington, DC: Counterpoint, 1999), ix.

2. Susan Stanberg, "M. F. K. Fisher Is More Than a Cookbook Author," in *Conversations with M. F. K. Fisher*, ed. David Lazar (Jackson: University Press of Mississippi, 1992), 122.

3. Stanberg, "M. F. K. Fisher Is More Than a Cookbook Author," 123.

4. Dominique Gioia, compiler, *A Welcoming Life: The M.F.K. Fisher Scrapbook* (Washington, DC: Counterpoint, 1997), 4.

5. Joan Reardon, *Poet of the Appetites: The Lives and Loves of M. F. K. Fisher* (New York: North Point Press, 2004), 10.

6. Bert Greene, "America's Finest Food Writer—M. F. K. Fisher: An Intimate Portrait," in *Conversations with M. F. K. Fisher*, ed. David Lazar (Jackson: University Press of Mississippi, 1992), 110.

7. Joan Reardon, *M. F. K. Fisher among the Pots and Pans: Celebrating Her Kitchens* (Berkeley: University of California Press, 2008), 22.

8. M. F. K. Fisher, *Long Ago in France: The Years in Dijon* (New York: Prentice Hall, 1991), xiv.

9. K. W., "About the Various Pleasures of Eating," *The New York Times* (June 20, 1937).

10. Ralph Thompson, "Books of the Times," *The New York Times* (July 13, 1937).

11. M. F. K. Fisher, *The Art of Eating* (New York: Wiley, 2004), 6.

12. Fisher, *The Art of Eating*, 353.

13. Rex Stout, "Suggestions for the Sensitive Palate," *The New York Times* (October 9, 1949).

14. Reardon, *Poet*, 241.

15. Reardon, *Poet*, 362.

16. M. F. K. Fisher, *From the Journals of M. F. K. Fisher* (New York: Pantheon Books, 1999), 3.

17. Fisher, *The Art of Eating*, xvii.

FURTHER READING

Fisher, M. F. K. *The Art of Eating. 50th Anniversary Edition.* New York: Wiley, 2004.

Gioia, Dominique, compiler. *A Welcoming Life: The M. F. K. Fisher Scrapbook.* Washington, DC: Counterpoint, 1997.

Gioia, Dominique, ed. *The Measure of Her Powers: An M. F. K. Fisher Reader.* Washington, DC: Counterpoint, 1999.

Lazar, David, ed. *Conversations with M. F. K. Fisher.* Jackson: University Press of Mississippi, 1992.

Reardon, Joan. *M. F. K. Fisher among the Pots and Pans: Celebrating Her Kitchens.* Berkeley: University of California Press, 2008.

Reardon, Joan. *Poet of the Appetites: The Lives and Loves of M. F. K. Fisher.* New York: North Point Press, 2004.

Mildred Jackson

Cookbook author and columnist known for bringing healthy vegeterian cooking into the mainstream, Mollie Katzen. (Mollie Katzen, 2009)

Mollie Katzen

Mollie Katzen's *Moosewood Cookbook* (1977) and its sisters, *The Enchanted Broccoli Forest* (1982) and *Still Life with Menu* (1988), popularized vegetarian cooking, not only bringing it out of the "hippie fringe" but also helping make the vegetarian craze a mainstream part of the American palate. As *The New York Times* has noted, these three books "have captured the spirit of a generation of epicures who brought their idealism and global awareness to food."[1] Mollie Katzen has over 6 million copies of books in print, including the many books for adults and children written after her departure from the Moosewood Collective and Restaurant in Ithaca, New York, with which she is still, in the popular imagination, intrinsically connected.

In 2007, *The Moosewood Cookbook* was elected to the James Beard Award hall of fame. Katzen has also created and hosted several television series around her works and has partnered with Walter Willett and the Harvard School of Public Health Nutrition Roundtable to promote healthy eating and to fight obesity. An artist, writer, cook, and musician, married, with two adult children, Katzen lives in Berkeley, California, where she runs Mollie Katzen Designs with her husband and continues to write cookbooks.

EARLY YEARS

Katzen was born in 1950 in Rochester, New York. Her parents, Betty and Leon Katzen, were Jewish, though they did not keep strict kosher in their home. Katzen learned to cook from her grandmother, whom she describes as "a wonderful, intuitive cook who never measured a thing, . . . [who] made her own phyllo dough, and beautiful challahs."[2] Her mother, conversely, cooked convenience foods. Her only childhood experience in cooking was making mud pies, and Katzen, whose first job was flipping burgers, apparently was not exposed to fresh produce until her teen years.[3] Yet, Katzen was always interested in food and the kitchen. She remembers that she "started make-believe cooking when I was a toddler, using invisible ingredients, plus grass, flowers, and mud. I started cooking with real food when I was about 8 or 9. My mother and grandmother let me follow them around the kitchen, and I was entranced. I tested and wrote my first recipe when I was 9. It was for a chocolate dessert that leaked out of the oven door and across the floor. My wonderful, patient mother, instead of yelling at me, said, 'Well this is certainly original. Let's give it a name.' We called it 'Creeping Australian BooBoo.'"[4]

Katzen attended Cornell University but thought it was not the right fit for her and decided to attend the San Francisco Art Institute instead, where she put herself through the bachelor's program by working in restaurants. Upon returning to Ithaca, she attended the Eastman School of Music in Rochester, New York, but soon left to help found the Moosewood Restaurant, drawing on her college experiences working in one of San Francisco's most popular vegetarian bistros. She and her brother Joshua were two of Moosewood's original seven founders and owners.

Moosewood's Mission

There is no specific dogma attached to the Moosewood cuisine. It bases itself on wholesomeness, and tries to present itself artfully. With the exception of fresh fish (served on weekends) we are a vegetarian restaurant. The reasons are various, ranging from simplicity of one sort (health, lightness, purity) to simplicity of another (convenience, economy). We also want to spread the notion that protein and aesthetics need not be sacrificed when you leave meat out of a meal. Most of these recipes, including soups, salads and even some desserts are protein-minded, and meals can be built without even including an entrée. Cheese, eggs, nuts, grains, beans and bean curd are the staples upon which this cuisine is designed, and most of the recipes here, in addition to glorifying the vegetable, take these basics into account.

—Mollie Katzen, *The Moosewood Cookbook: Recipes from Moosewood Restaurant.*
Berkeley, CA: Ten Speed Press, 1977, p. viii

In 1972, seven friends got together to found a vegetarian collective dedicated to sustainability. Moosewood was a local maple tree, and the collective "was begun . . . by a group of friends who enjoyed getting together to cook and eat, and who wanted to engage in a community project."[5] The collective quickly grew to about 20 people, who recycled their profits back into the business and shared it among the staff. In describing the era, one journalist noted that it was "a time of passion and conviction, of high ideals and unconventional ideas: the war against the war was winding down, feminism was gearing up, Watergate was still unfolding, and vegetarianism was the diet of choice for an increasingly small planet. In areas like the Finger Lakes where land was cheap, hippies and others were trying new ways of living together."[6]

The restaurant's philosophy was simple and perfectly reflected the communal zeitgeist of the early 1970s. According to the first edition of *The Moosewood Cookbook*, "There is no fixed chef. Menu-planning is a rotating position, open to anyone experienced, inspired and willing enough to handle it. This sharing of the chef's role helps to keep the menu, which changes constantly, refreshed and various."[7]

COOKBOOKS

Moosewood

The popularity of the recipes served at Moosewood empowered Katzen, in 1974, to compile them, meticulously hand lettered and illustrated, in a spiral-bound book that was for sale at the restaurant. She sold 800 copies of the original 5,000 print run in the first week. Doubleday made an offer for the book, but the iconoclastic and offbeat Ten Speed Press, in Berkeley, California, offered a then astounding $10,000 (five times Doubleday's opening bid) and gave Katzen full creative freedom. In 1977, Ten Speed Press brought out the first hardcover edition. As a *New York Times* reviewer later observed, "The book reeks of Ms. Katzen's own style: funny, warm and intimate. The borders and titles are embellished with simple pen-and-ink sketches of vegetables and fruits, intermingled with dancing cherubs, winged pears and talking animals. Under a Chinese duck sauce recipe, a duck offers a caveat: 'No duck in there.'"[8]

The recipes in *The Moosewood Cookbook* are rich and filling, resplendent in dairy, cheese, and eggs. They represent the best of vegetarian comfort food and include creamy soups and chowders, hearty stews, stroganoffs, quiches, and curries. The book further harks back to its midcentury roots with the inclusion of variants on cottage cheese plates, waldorf salads, casseroles, and chilled soups. At the same time, it is forward-thinking, introducing foods that are commonplace now but in the 1970s were unfamiliar to many Americans, such as falafel, tofu (which Katzen describes as "an excellent protein food, and very charming"), tempura, and tortillas.[9] She even includes a full-page diagram on how to eat a tostada: "Take a tortilla. Put it on your plate. Cover it with refried beans, spreading them imaginatively into place. Sprinkle on some grated cheese. It will melt onto your beans. Yum yum. Arrange handsful of olives, pickled peppers, shredded cabbage, chopped eggs and tomatoes in a pile the height of which considers the dimensions of your mouth. Ladle on some hot sauce and a hunk of sour cream. Eat it sitting down, holding the plate under your chin to pick up what drops as you progress from one end of the tostada to the other. If you need two hands to eat it, find a trusted friend to hold up your plate for you."[10]

After Moosewood

In 1978, Katzen left Moosewood, and a legal battle later ensued between herself and the Moosewood collective over the rights to the name. Katzen eventually won the rights to the *Cookbook* and to her royalties, while the collective retained the rights to the Moosewood name in reference to all other matters.

Sales of the book were slow at first. *The Moosewood Cookbook* did not earn out its advance for three years. Yet the book had begun to develop a devoted following. Its unique style and presentation won it thousands of fans, drawn not only to the quirky style and the offbeat recipes, but to its aesthetics as well. As Katzen remembers, "I hand lettered my earlier books because that was how I wrote everything. I didn't own a typewriter or a computer. In a way these books were similar to, and extensions of, my personal journals."[11] Double-day, still evidently wishing to have Katzen in its stable, offered her the chance to write a sequel to *Moosewood*, but the author was seriously considering a return to music. Then, during an interview in 1997, Katzen admitted that she had a "kind of a depressed epiphany, an epiphany that I hate performing the piano. I can barely play with my friends in the room. I can't stand performing; I'm very shy about it. Am I crazy? Why don't I write the cookbook? So I took the contract and never played the audition."[12]

The Enchanted Broccoli Forest came out in 1982, but not with Doubleday. Katzen canceled the contract and took the book back to Ten Speed Press, which again gave her free rein. In many ways, *The Enchanted Broccoli Forest* is an extension of *Moosewood*, featuring the same distinctive and artistic hand lettering and illustrations and commitment to meatless meals. Yet, if *Moosewood* is an introduction to vegetarian cooking and eating, *Forest* is its older sister—grown up enough to wear stockings, go to dances, and taste its first champagne. The book has a stronger focus on ethnic foods and includes more Jewish recipes, such as tsimmes, kugels, blintzes, and challah. If tofu was charming in *Moosewood,* in *Forest* it is downright brazen. In addition to several Asian interpretations, Katzen includes Tofu-Nut Balls, Tofu, Spinach, and Walnut Loaf, and even a page of suggestions for Tofu for Children. Curries abound, and the baking section is much expanded. A section of menu planning also appears. Katzen is clearly much more self-confident about the possibilities for meatless eating in *The Enchanted Broccoli Forest*, exploring the culinary creativity she chose at the expense of a career as a musician. Moreover, this book firmly plants Katzen on the side of the home cook rather than the chef. Katzen notes in the afterword that "the bulk of humanity feels quite excluded from 'haute cuisine.' If more people can feel welcome in the world of careful, expressive and healthful (not to mention delicious) food preparation, we won't need to turn to junk food."[13]

Katzen followed up *The Enchanted Broccoli Forest* with *Still Life with Menu* (1988). The title reflects Katzen's passions for art and food, and the book features the author's original full-color artwork juxtaposed against the recipes. A still life of peaches and watercolors sets off a recipe for peach-filled spice cake, while a row of apples in a moonlit windowsill complements a menu featuring an applesauce cocoa cake. Organized entirely around menus, *Still Life* is the first of Katzen's cookbooks that does not feature the distinctive hand lettering of the earlier titles. As Katzen notes, "I stopped hand lettering when working on *Still Life with Menu*, as I started illustrating my books with full-color, full-composition pictures. The handlettering no longer fit the design, and by that time I had acquired a computer and learned to type."[14]

Like Katzen herself, her books changed with and reflected the times. "In 1972, when I began work on my first cookbook, I didn't know anyone who worked a 9–5 full-time job. Most of my contemporaries were either in graduate school (indefinitely) or following creative, self-motivated, very flexible styles of living," she wrote. Yet, "those days have evolved into these days, and now everyone I know has made serious commitments to life and work, and is very, very busy. Many of us who once paid careful attention to everything we ate—and could afford the time to be conscientious about healthy 'natural' eating—frequently find ourselves grabbing food on the run."[15] The earthy seventies seemingly morphed overnight into the more-is-better nineties. Katzen, too, followed the trend, leaving the collective, divorcing her first husband, and remarrying and moving to Berkeley. As she later remembered, "I was always in conflict with the counterculture, and I never fit into a collective. My heart was in the idea of sharing, but I found that a creative impulse was best. And that's a very auto-cratic impulse, which is not about sharing."[16]

In addition to her vegetarian books for adults, Katzen has written several cookbooks for children, most notably *Pretend Soup and Other Real Recipes: A Cookbook for Preschoolers and Up* (1994), which *The New York Times* calls "the gold standard for children's cookbooks."[17] More recently, *Salad People and More Real Recipes: A New Cookbook for Preschoolers and Up* (2005) targets the youngest chefs, while *Honest Pretzels: And 64 Other Amazing Recipes for Cooks Ages 8 & Up* (2009) is for older children.

In 2000, Katzen, concerned with the high fat content of the recipes in *The Moosewood Cookbook* and buoyed by the trend in low-fat, healthier eating, revised the classic cookbook to tone down the fat and make the recipes both healthier and more varied in flavor. For example, a recipe in the original for "Cheese-Beans," which called for two cups of grated cheese, was replaced in the revision with "Tart and Tangy Baked Beans," making the two cups of cheese "optional" and including a grocery list of spices and other ingredients not included in the 1977 recipe, such as cumin, cider vinegar, and molasses. Additionally, in the new introduction, Katzen wrote, "I found that my cooking had changed over the years, becoming more streamlined in preparation—and lighter in 'weight,' while richer in flavor."[18] She also revised *The Enchanted Broccoli Forest* (2000). The reaction to the revisions was mixed. Some readers felt betrayed by the changes, while others embraced the healthier style. Even her publisher was initially unsure about the revisions, because the original titles were still selling.

OTHER ENDEAVORS

The Moosewood Collective

Though Katzen left Moosewood in 1978, shortly after the publication of *The Moosewood Cookbook*, the collective itself kept busy running the restaurant and publishing a series of cookbooks of its own. The split with Katzen had been less than amicable, resulting in a lawsuit that gave her the rights to "Moosewood Cookbook" but allowed the collective to continue to use the term "Moosewood." That bothered Katzen. She noted, "One of the reasons I wanted to come out more is because there were all these other books being written with the name Moosewood on them. I wanted people to know, 'I'm Mollie and I did these books. I'm a person, not a collective.'"[19]

The collective is still a collective, however, and proud to be so. One must pay one's dues to become a member: "All collective members begin as employees of the restaurant, waiting on tables, busing, helping in the kitchen. Since the collective is legally restricted to 18 members, employees become members only when someone leaves."[20] Just as described in the 1977 *Moosewood Cookbook,* the members continue to take turns planning menus and working, and they make decisions as a group. They have published over a dozen cookbooks, most using the Moosewood name. The popularity of the Moosewood cookbooks has resulted in what long-term collective member Joan Adler has called the "enshrinement" of the restaurant. She notes, "People come here as if they're on a pilgrimage."[21]

Katzen Today

Katzen has published 16 books, with millions of copies in print. In addition to cookbooks and children's books, she has written several books for adults, most focused not just on vegetarian cooking but on the preparation of vegetables themselves. More broadly, *Mollie Katzen's Sunlight Café* (2002) explores the delights of breakfast. As Katzen notes, "Breakfast is the Camelot of foods: It's illusory. People love it, and it's not really there."[22] Her most recent title, *Get Cooking: 101 Simple Recipes to Get You Started in the Kitchen* (2009), is geared toward beginners, making easy such potentially daunting dishes as stuffed squash, curry, and cherry clafouti.

In 1998, Katzen's track record with healthy eating and her identification with vegetarianism led her to join the Harvard School of Public Health Nutrition Roundtable. She also consults with Harvard Dining Services to help create healthier alternatives for students and faculty at campus dining functions. With Walter Willett of the Harvard School of Public Health, she co-wrote a diet book, *Eat, Drink, & Weigh Less: A Flexible and Delicious Way to Shrink Your Waist without Going Hungry* (2006).

It may surprise readers to find out that Katzen herself is not a vegetarian, but she is committed to ethical, sustainable, and organic eating. In a 2007 interview, Katzen said, "For about 30 years I didn't eat meat at all, just a bite of fish every once in a while, and always some dairy. . . . Lately I've been eating a little meat. People say, 'Ha, ha, Mollie Katzen is eating steak.' But now that cleaner, naturally fed meat is available, it's a great option for anyone who's looking to complete his diet."[23] She has become more political about healthy eating as well, stating in a 2007 interview, "At this point I'm uncomfortable eating things—fruits and vegetables that are not organic. . . . I've had a long career of writing about food and my food is always categorized as healthy or niche. That's fine, although I would like to go mainstream. But in the course of that, even though I have written some of the most basic vegetarian cookbooks, I have never been on a bandwagon about it. But with all the organics legislation that's being discussed, with the free trade, the loosening up of standards around pesticides, I have become very opinionated about organics. I am becoming more of an activist about it."[24]

Katzen was not the first vegetarian cookbook author or even arguably the best, but her influence is undeniable. Since *The Moosewood Cookbook* first appeared in 1973, both vegetarianism and its guidebooks have exploded on the culinary scene. Once a kooky fringe lifestyle, vegetarianism and its variants have truly become a widely accepted alternative to what food writer Michael Pollan has called "the omnivore's dilemma" of ethical eating in a world of factory farms and processed foods. Yet Katzen has her detractors. One writer in a *New York Times* review of vegetarian cookbooks wrote, "Unfortunately, *The Moosewood Cookbook* looks like the kind of book that used to turn off nonvegetarians. Its hand-printed recipes are hard to read, and good recipes like mushroom strudel and zucchini-crusted pizza are hidden by the rustic drawings."[25] Ironically, the same publication hailed *The Moosewood Cookbook* as one of the top 10 best-selling cookbooks of all time.

CONCLUSION

Katzen's commitment to healthy eating, deliciousness, and home cooking in lieu of fast food and junk food remains unshaken. She creates recipes and books that are geared not for the professional chef but for all who venture into the kitchen. Katzen believes that everyone—even children and beginners—can cook wholesome, wonderful food in their own homes, and in the space of their own lives. As organic food maven Alice Waters has observed, Katzen "helped make vegetarian cooking accessible to everyone. She's unpretentious and homespun."[26] Katzen herself said, "My attitude in writing 'Moosewood' was to assume the reader knew little or nothing about vegetarian cooking, . . . to make it as user-friendly as possible and to address the reader as though I were talking to a friend."[27]

NOTES

1. Peggy Garfinkel, "Beyond Moosewood: Vegetarian Food for the Committed Eighties," *The New York Times* (January 4, 1989) http://www.nytimes.com/1989/01/04/garden/beyond-moosewood-vegetarian-food-for-the-committed-80-s.html?scp=5&sq=mollie%20katzen&st=cse

2. Alex Witchel, "Breakfast as the New Cure-all," *The New York Times* (October 9, 2002) http://www.nytimes.com/2002/10/09/dining/breakfast-as-the-new-cure-all.html?scp=1&sq=mollie%20katzen&st=cse

3. Garfinkel, "Beyond Moosewood."

4. "About Mollie," MollieKatzen.com, http://www.molliekatzen.com/faq.php

5. Mollie Katzen, *The Moosewood Cookbook* (Berkeley, CA: Ten Speed Press, 1977), vii.

6. Nancy Harmon Jenkins, "A Seventies Restaurant of Ideas and Ideals," *The New York Times* (October 24, 1990) http://www.nytimes.com/1990/10/24/garden/a-70-s-restaurant-of-ideas-and-ideals.html?scp=9&sq=moosewood&st=cse

7. Katzen, *Moosewood Cookbook*, viii.

8. Garfinkel, "Beyond Moosewood."

9. Katzen, *Moosewood Cookbook*, xiii.

10. Katzen, *Moosewood Cookbook*, 145.

11. Mollie Katzen Online, "About Mollie," MollieKatzen.com, http://www
.molliekatzen.com/faq.php

12. Janet Fletcher, "The Enchanted Mollie Katzen: Her 'Crunchy' Cookbooks
Endear Her to Legions of Fans," *The San Francisco Chronicle* (September 17, 1997)
http://www.sfgate.com/c/a/1997/09/17/FD50506.DTL

13. Mollie Katzen, *The Enchanted Broccoli Forest* (Berkeley, CA: Ten Speed Press,
1982), 290.

14. "About Mollie," MollieKatzen.com.

15. Mollie Katzen, *Still Life with Menu* (Berkeley, CA: Ten Speed Press, 1988), 15.

16. Witchel, "Breakfast as the New Cure-all."

17. Kim Severson, "Cookbook Publishers Try to Think Small," *The New York
Times* (May 14, 2008) http://www.nytimes.com/2008/05/14/dining/14kids.html?_r=2
&scp=3&sq=mollie%20katzen&st=cse

18. Mollie Katzen, *The New Moosewood Cookbook* (Berkeley, CA: Ten Speed
Press, 2000), ix.

19. Fletcher, "The Enchanted Mollie Katzen."

20. Jenkins, "A Seventies Restaurant of Ideas and Ideals."

21. Jenkins, "A Seventies Restaurant of Ideas and Ideals."

22. Witchel, "Breakfast as the New Cure-all."

23. Christine Lennon, "Why Vegetarians Are Eating Meat," *Food & Wine* (August
2007) http://www.molliekatzen.com/presskit/MK_food_wine.pdf

24. Cheri Sicard, "An Interview with Mollie Katzen," August 6, 2007, Fabulous
Foods.com, http://www.fabulousfoods.com/index.php?option=com_resource&
controller=article&category_id=231&article=21167

25. Marian Burros, "Not Just for Vegetarians," *The New York Times* (April 1,
1987) http://www.nytimes.com/1987/04/01/garden/not-just-for-vegetarians.html?scp
=10&sq=mollie%20katzen&st=cse

26. Garfinkel, "Beyond Moosewood."

27. Garfinkel, "Beyond Moosewood."

FURTHER READING

Books by Mollie Katzen

The Moosewood Cookbook. Berkeley, CA: Ten Speed Press, 1977.
The Enchanted Broccoli Forest. Berkeley, CA: Ten Speed Press, 1982.
Still Life with Menu. Berkeley, CA: Ten Speed Press, 1988.
Pretend Soup and Other Real Recipes: A Cookbook for Preschoolers and Up. Berkeley,
     CA: Tricycle Press, 1994.
Mollie Katzen's Vegetable Heaven. New York: Hyperion, 1997.
The New Moosewood Cookbook. Berkeley, CA: Ten Speed Press, 2000.
The New Enchanted Broccoli Forest. Berkeley, CA: Ten Speed Press, 2000.
Mollie Katzen's Sunlight Café. New York: Hyperion, 2002.
Salad People and More Real Recipes: A New Cookbook for Preschoolers and Up.
     Berkeley, CA: Tricycle Press, 2005.

The Vegetable Dishes I Can't Live Without. New York: Hyperion, 2007.
Coauthored with Walter Willett. *Eat, Drink, & Weigh Less: A Flexible and Delicious Way to Shrink Your Waist without Going Hungry.* New York: Hyperion, 2007.
Honest Pretzels: And 64 Other Amazing Recipes for Cooks Ages 8 & Up. Berkeley, CA: Tricycle Press, 2009.
Get Cooking: 150 Simple Recipes to Get You Started in the Kitchen. New York: Harper Studio, 2009.

Elizabeth S. Demers

Author Diana Kennedy, a leading expert on Mexican cuisine, tends to her garden at her home in Zitácuaro, Mexico, May 25, 2010. (AP/Wide World Photos)

Diana Kennedy

Through persistence and grueling work, Diana Southwood Kennedy, born and raised in the outskirts of London, England, elevated herself to become one of the world's most respected and knowledgeable authorities on Mexican food and cooking. In 1981, the Mexican government awarded her the highest honor for foreigners, the coveted Order of the Aztec Eagle, and in 2002 the British government awarded her the prestigious MBE (Member of the British Empire). Such was the esteem for her work in preserving and documenting indigenous Mexican culture.

Kennedy began teaching Mexican cooking in New York City in 1969 at the behest of Craig Claiborne, then *The New York Times*'s food-news editor and restaurant critic. From that start she wrote eight detailed, groundbreaking books on Mexican cuisine. When she began her work, with a few exceptions like Jane Butel and Elena Zelayeta, no one else was writing seriously in English on the cuisine of the United States's neighbor to the south.

Kennedy often found her recipes under extreme hardships, during long trips along backcountry roads with many flea-bitten nights spent on hard beds. Like an anthropologist, she gathered oral testimonies to reclaim knowledge that might otherwise have disappeared as cooks died, the climate changed, and agribusiness took over private and communal land. What drove Kennedy was her concern for the land and its people.

Early on, Kennedy embodied the environmental ideals of the late 20th and early 21st century. The last place she envisioned herself living was on an eight-acre ecological compound outside of Zitácuaro called Quinta Diana. This property provided an early opportunity for her to practice a form of chemical-free agriculture later embraced by Michael Pollan, Alice Waters, and other environmentally conscious writers and chefs. Kennedy's awareness of natural foods appeared in comments strewn throughout her books.

Although the burgeoning immigration of Mexican nationals into the United States over the last several decades has accounted in part for the greater availability of authentic Mexican ingredients (chilies, fruits, cilantro, tomatillos), by the end of the 20th century Kennedy's insistence on culinary authenticity had made more of those ingredients available to American cooks in just about every grocery store in the United States.

EARLY YEARS

"The Making of a Palate"

Kennedy grew up in Essex, England, in a solid middle-class English family.[1] During her childhood, various experiences sowed the roots of her food-loving life. Her mother, in particular, seems to have passed on to Kennedy a certain *savoir faire* tempered with frugality in regard to food. In her book *Nothing Fancy: Recipes and Recollections of Soul-Satisfying Food* (1998), Kennedy remarked, "There was never much money around for luxuries, but because my mother was so versatile in the kitchen, despite her full-time teaching job, we ate extremely well from a variety of foods of such good quality that it would be difficult to match them today."[2] Some of her mother's dishes stuck in her memory, such as jams and other preserves, meat rolls, bread sauce, the "parson's nose" (turkey's tail), stews, Shrove Tuesday pancakes, beef or pork tongue, and fish.

However, Kennedy did not like the thick, strong-flavored soups served in her childhood. Nor did she favor the ubiquitous English white sauce. The manner of cooking vegetables common in her childhood caused her to say, "I shudder when I think of how vegetables were cooked when I was young. You could smell the cabbage or Brussels sprouts boiling before you got to the kitchen, and the smell lingered until the next day."[3] Yet Kennedy dedicated *The Essential Cuisines of Mexico* (2000) to several people who influenced her, one being her mother, of whom she wrote, "To My Mother, Who just expected me to cook everything she did."[4]

While she attended a "fancy" girls' school in Hampstead, thanks to the generosity of her rich godmother, Kennedy reveled in the facility's gloriously equipped kitchen. In cooking classes she learned the fundamentals of pastry making, as well as tapioca pudding, and her "bête noire" (flourless chocolate cake). She applied her newfound culinary knowledge at home, where she and her sister cooked regularly as a part of growing up.

Other people and events also influenced Kennedy's culinary journey. Trips to Sainsbury's gourmet counter in Edgware, just outside London, thrilled her, especially the ingredients from all over the world. Kennedy's Aunt Maud, who lived in Jamaica, provided another source for her culinary wanderlust, inspiring her to recreate Maud's Spiced Pressed Beef with a shot of Jamaican rum. World War II and Kennedy's service with the Women's Land Army Timber Corps presented further opportunities to develop her palate for her later work in Mexican cuisine. Of that experience, Kennedy said, "In the Forest of Dean we would toast our very dull sandwiches over the smoldering wood fires and roast potatoes and onions in the ashes to help eke out our rations on those raw, frosty mornings. . . . we would stop for the farmhouse teas: thick cream and fresh scones, wedges of homemade bread spread thickly with freshly churned butter, wild damson jam, buttery cakes that had been beaten with the bare hand."[5] She tolerated meatless days and she "began to appreciate the freshness of local country foods."[6]

After the war, Kennedy spent time in Dumfriesshire, Scotland, as a housing manager. She worked with mining families in small villages, who shared superb homemade shortbread—and their recipes—with her. She would later adopt this methodology in her studies of Mexican cuisine. While working in Scotland, she also traveled on a "shoestring budget" to Spain, France, and Austria, where she thought that she really began to learn to cook.

Traveling to different regions of the world helped build her culinary skills. Wanderlust then called Kennedy to Canada, where to keep food on the table she labored at a number of jobs, ranging from "running a library to selling Wedgwood china."[7] And then in the 1950s came her fateful Caribbean travels. First she went to Puerto Rico to attend the first Casals Festival, where she stayed with a Puerto Rican family and learned to enjoy traditional local food. Then she visited Jamaica with its "callaloo, lambie stew, and soursop ices," and finally spent time in Haiti. She was on her way back to England when, in her hotel, she met Paul Kennedy, a correspondent for *The New York Times* who was in Haiti covering the 1956 revolution. At the same time, another revolution occurred, albeit quietly, as Diana and Paul fell in love.

Mexican Adventure

In 1957, Kennedy boarded a cargo ship out of Antwerp and headed toward Veracruz, Mexico, where she rejoined Paul and married him. Their marriage lasted only 10 years, as Paul died of cancer in 1967 in New York, where the Kennedys moved in 1965 seeking treatment for the cancer. In the intervening eight years, however, Kennedy lived in Mexico City in an apartment near Chapultepec Park, where she cooked and learned Spanish. Cooking from her "bibles for French and Italian food," Elizabeth David's *French Provincial Cooking* (1960) and *Italian Food* (1954), Kennedy later realized that David had provided a sort of impetus for her work in Mexican cuisine. Certainly Kennedy's image-evoking writing style owes something to David, as the following passage suggests: "Even the sea was hot to swim in, but the beer was very cold and the metallic freshness of the oysters and the lime juice with our food refreshed us."[8]

Kennedy soon began her extensive forays into Mexican cooking. Her expertise did not happen overnight: She admitted that the enormity and complexity of the ingredients in Mexican cuisine overwhelmed her in the beginning.[9] With the help of her first maids, Luz, Rufina, and especially Godileva, to whom she felt the greatest debt, Kennedy mastered techniques and gained deeper awareness and knowledge of the ingredients available to regional Mexican cooks.

Other influences worked on Kennedy at the time, too. Paul supported her growing interest: "He would collect recipes for me when I couldn't accompany him on his travels through Central America and the Caribbean."[10] Paul, because of his *New York Times* contacts and credentials, enabled Kennedy to meet interesting and powerful people. A case in point occurred in 1963 when Paul and Diana drove to Puerto Vallarta so that Paul could interview film director John Huston during the filming of *The Night of the Iguana*, featuring stars Richard Burton and Elizabeth Taylor. Many years afterward, Grayson Hall, a member of the *Iguana* cast, attended Kennedy's first cooking classes in New York.

A number of Mexican cookbook authors and scholars also assisted Kennedy in her search for authenticity at this point of her studies. Kennedy found inspiration in the work and friendship of Agustín Aragón y Leyva,

Tortillas

The simplest food is always the most difficult to prepare, for there are no predominant flavors to mask bad or indifferent ingredients or the careless handling of those ingredients. The corn tortilla *provides the best example of this idea that I know. The ideal* tortilla *is made of carefully selected dried corn; just the right amount of lime (calcium oxide) should be added to the cooking water—too much will make for a dull yellowish, bitter-tasting* tortilla *with an acrid smell. If the corn is left too long over the heat, the dough will be sticky and impossible to make into* tortillas. . . .*

A superbly made tortilla *almost melts as you bite into it and when properly stored lasts some time without drying out. But the perfect* tortilla *is hard to come by nowadays, even in Mexico City, let alone in the United States. . . .*

—Diana Kennedy, *The Art of Mexican Cooking.*
New York: Clarkson Potter, 2008, p. 5

a Mexican filmmaker and gastronome, and especially appreciated having access to his vast library of cookery books. She started collecting her own antique Mexican cookbooks, including another of her "bibles," *Nuevo Cocinero Mejicano: Diccionario de Cocina*, published in Paris in 1878. She paid about US$16 for it in the Lagunilla flea market in Mexico City. In particular, Kennedy began to rely on the work of Josefina Velázquez de Léon (whose work later provided many recipes for Kennedy's second book, *The Tortilla Book*, 1975). Velázquez de Léon was one of the first women to travel around Mexico and focus on regional cookery. Her influence on Kennedy became more obvious with every book that Kennedy published because of her increasing focus on regionalism, especially in the last book on Oaxaca, published in 2009.[11]

Kennedy continued to entertain and cook for a wide range of visitors who came to the Calle Puebla apartment in Mexico City, including Craig Claiborne, at the time the food-news editor and restaurant critic for *The New York Times*. After eating an opulent feast of Mexican dishes cooked by Kennedy, Claiborne reminisced: "But the thing that I most vividly recall about our first meeting was her offer to buy me a Mexican cookbook. 'No,' I demurred, 'I'll wait for the genuine article. The day you publish one.'"[12]

Paul Kennedy fought a two-year battle with cancer, and he and Diana finally made the decision to move to New York City in 1965 so that Paul could receive more treatment. He died in 1967, and Kennedy stayed on in New York. Claiborne encouraged her to teach Mexican cooking classes, but she could not work up the enthusiasm. In her words; "I suppose I wasn't ready to start a new venture; I was too saddened and worn by the previous three years. But the idea had planted itself, and in January 1969, on Sunday afternoons, I did start a series of Mexican cooking classes—the first in New York."[13]

COOKBOOKS

The Real Work Starts

With the support of Claiborne and editor Frances McCullough, who attended one of Kennedy's first cooking classes, Kennedy began writing her first cookbook, *The Cuisines of Mexico* (1972). McCullough said, "When we did this book, nobody had any idea of what we were talking about, . . . American cooks were ready for a fascinating new cuisine and also Diana's personality in part made her books."[14]

Prior to *The Cuisines of Mexico*, no books resembling this had appeared in English. Southwestern cookery expert Jane Butel wrote about New Mexican cookery, and *Sunset* magazine released the ninth printing of its *Mexican Cookbook* (originally published in 1969), but aside from a few community/charity cookbooks and books by Elena Zelayeta, that was about it for Mexican cookbooks in English.

Beginning with *The Cuisines of Mexico*, Kennedy wrote and published a total of eight cookbooks in a little over 37 years: an average of about five years per book. She told an interviewer that she "thoroughly distrust[s] authors who come out with a new book every two years."[15] Her other books include *The Tortilla Book* (1975), *Recipes from the Regional Cooks of Mexico* (1978), *Nothing Fancy: Recipes and Recollections of Soul-Satisfying Food* (1984), *Mexican Regional Cooking* (1985, a reprint of *Recipes from the Regional Cooks of Mexico*), *The Art of Mexican Cooking* (1989), *My Mexico* (1998), *The Essential Cuisines of Mexico* (a compilation from Kennedy's first three books, plus 30 new recipes, 2000), *From My Mexican Kitchen: Techniques and Ingredients* (2003), and *Oaxaca al Gusto* (2008).

In *The Cuisines of Mexico*, as in *The Tortilla Book*, Kennedy wrote the recipes in a long, rather convoluted format similar to that used by Julia Child in *Mastering the Art of French Cooking* (1961).[16] This approach served her well in all her future books. For content she relied on traveling across Mexico and interviewing large numbers of people, some of whom shared antique and family cookbook manuscripts with her. Besides local informants, including bus drivers and farmers, she talked with chefs, restaurateurs, and botanists. Until she bought her land near Zitácuaro in 1980, she spent her summers traveling throughout Mexico and then returned to New York City in the fall, where she continued to teach cooking classes.

Kennedy wrote of seeking *sacahuil*, a giant *tamal* (tamale or masa dish wrapped in corn husks) only found in Pánuco in Veracruz state: "The day before I went I stood in line to reserve my ticket on the early bus. Then the next day I got up at the crack of dawn and braved torrential rains and hurricane winds to get to the bus station on time. . . . The town [Pánuco] itself was almost dead, and the air hot and heavy as I made my way from one little restaurant shack to another. . . . and then it finally dawned on me that Sunday was the only day for the *sacahuiles*—and this was only Friday." Upon her return on Sunday, the taxi's mechanical problems threatened to sabotage her quest to find *sacahuiles*. "I swear that the driver was so scared by my ranting and raving that he coaxed the car to the edge of Pánuco, where it finally stopped dead." But she got her *sacahuil* when someone slaughtered the necessary pig.[17] Later, she traveled, usually alone, in her white Nissan extended-bed pickup truck along winding back roads to isolated enclaves in search of recipes and knowledge that might otherwise be lost as people died, industrial agricultural expanded, and precious farmland turned into housing developments.

Kennedy gleaned recipes and ideas from antique cookbooks, such as the recipe for *Pescado en Cilantro* (Fish in Cilantro) in *The Cuisines of Mexico*. The bibliographies of her books include many Spanish-language cookbooks. Typical of her sources is one listed in *Recipes from the Regional Cooks of Mexico*. A cook named Leticia Castro let Kennedy use recipes from a family manuscript cookbook that had been handed down for several generations. In Zacatecas and San Luis Potosí, she found recipes that came from *Manual de Cocinero y Cocinera* (published in the Puebla in 1849), stemming from a literary magazine of the time called *La Risa* (The Laugh), and another cookbook she examined was a charity cookbook published in Durango in 1898 for the sisters of St. Vincent de Paul.[18]

While Kennedy's chief goal in her work was to collect and document recipes and techniques that were in danger of disappearing, she periodically observed historical and social influences on recipes and foodstuffs. Archaeological evidence appears in the headnotes of some of her recipes. For instance, in *The Cuisines of Mexico*, Kennedy mentions that bones of the Robalo (a type of fish) were found in kitchen hearths at the Olmec site of San Lorenzo in Veracruz, dating to 1200–1000 B.C.[19]

But always, Kennedy's major sources remained people, with knowledge often never recorded in written form. Time after time in interviews, Kennedy spoke of her pride in attributing recipes and information to the proper sources. In *Recipes from the Regional Cooks of Mexico*, she dedicated the book to the Mexicans who most influenced her and her work: Agustín Aragón y Leyva; Salvador Novo; Jaime Saldívar; Josefina Velázquez de Léon; Victoriano, from Tlacotalpan; Chanita, from Pánuco; and Fidel Loredo.

During all the time Kennedy spent writing and researching her books, she continued to teach, sometimes hired by the Mexican government and other times by various businesses, such as Williams-Sonoma, for classes in large U.S. cities like New York, Atlanta, and San Diego. Her earnings from her books and teaching supported her travel and maintenance costs for Quinta Diana. There she set about creating a center for the study of Mexican cuisine and a place to experiment with growing different plants and resurrecting land that had been badly damaged by mismanagement. Except for bug spray for wasps,

Kennedy did not allow any chemicals to be used on her land, and she practiced strict recycling and water conservation practices.[20] But all was not paradise. Kennedy wrote, "Building and adapting an ecological house of adobe to suit my needs took years of time and patience . . . in fact, in 1980 I moved into what I now realize was an incomplete shell, and even some of that shell had to be altered and rebuilt. There is no main water supply to the house. . . . For the first two and a half years of living in my house I had no refrigerator and no car to go and get last-minute supplies."[21]

In the books following *The Cuisines of Mexico*, the headnotes became less personal, not so much about her as about the cooks and the foods. *The Tortilla Book*, called derivative by one reviewer, came about because of a fall sustained by Kennedy in Riverside Park in New York City.[22] While she was recuperating, unable to follow her usual energetic routine, Kennedy compiled recipes for *The Tortilla Book*, most derived from the work of Josefina Velázquez de Léon. Except for *Nothing Fancy*, a collection of recipes encouraged by her editor, Frances McCullough, Kennedy's writing tended not to dwell much on her personal life aside from her ecological house.

Another trend that became apparent with each new book was Kennedy's emphasis on ingredients, both common and esoteric. This preoccupation culminated in *From My Mexican Kitchen: Techniques and Ingredients* (2003), an encyclopedic, lavishly illustrated book showing what many ingredients unknown to the general reader look like. In 2000, she published *The Essential Cuisines of Mexico*, a compendium of her first three books, *The Cuisines of Mexico*, *The Tortilla Book*, and *Recipes from the Regional Cooks of Mexico*, along with 30 new recipes, bringing her work in a fresh format to a new generation of readers and cooks.

More and more, Kennedy's books showed people how to maneuver in the kitchen. The reader learns to process a freshly killed chicken in *The Art of Mexican Cooking* and can follow step-by-step photos for making *Pan de Muerto* (Bread for the Day of the Dead) in *From My Mexican Kitchen*. Kennedy served an apprenticeship in a Mexican bakery, and her step-by-step account of the Mexican baking process was truly unique.[23]

Oaxaca al Gusto, published in Spanish in 2008 and in English in 2010, took Kennedy's work to the ultimate point by giving detailed attention to 10 regions within the state of Oaxaca. This same love had also permeated her other books, filling them with wistful, wishful comments about the beauty of the area and the lusciousness of the food. In this, probably her last book, the text is studded with gemlike photos of Oaxaca.

In addition to her books, Kennedy wrote a number of articles for magazines such as *Food & Wine* and *Mexico Desconocido*, in which she expounded on recipes for "insects, wild plants, including dried *cuitlacoche* and mushrooms, the influence of medieval Spain in the Matanzas of Puebla, and finally delving into old cookbooks, to find recipes that are still viable today and to learn of their attitudes toward food and their advice to the cooks."[24]

Because Kennedy chose to live so close to the earth at Quinta Diana, gaining firsthand knowledge of farming, food preservation, and cooking, her concern for the future of Mexican cuisine and for the health of the planet came through very clearly in her books, articles, and comments in interviews:

> Everyone has got to become much "greener" in the kitchen. Caterers in particular should reduce their use of foil and plastic wrap which they use in excess. We should refuse to accept ingredients from suppliers that are overly-packed with Styrofoam in particular. Cut out waste in the kitchen and insist on composting or finding someone to compost. And energy: just for (that silly) style's sake every recipe starts with pre-heat oven. Then the preparation may take an hour or so and that oven is supposedly still on. And the magazine (I won't say which) that says: "heat oven to 350. Place 1 tomato on a tray and roast until slightly charred!!!!!!!!!!!!!!!!!!!!!" ONE TOMATO IN A LARGE OVEN even if you don't have to pay the bill. And how about the instruction to rinse your greens under a running (cold) tap!!! Never get the grit out that way. And washing dishes under running hot water, or rather boiling water that has had cold added.
>
> NOBODY wants to talk about these things . . . they are not "sexy" subjects. And to hell with the stupidities of the health department inspectors like insisting on those dead, white plastic chopping boards! These are things that I worry about in this careless age.[25]

AWARDS AND HONORS

Accolades

Over the years Kennedy won a number of awards, in particular the coveted Order of the Aztec Eagle by the Mexican government in 1981, which was similar to being knighted by the queen of England, and the Member of the British Empire (MBE) in 2002 from the British government for furthering cultural relations between the United Kingdom and Mexico. Other awards and recognition included a Silver Medal from the Tourism Secretariat for the promotion of Mexican culture through its foods (1971), an Amando Farga Font special award from the Mexican Food Writers Association (1980), a Jade Molcajete from the Tourism Secretariat and Holiday Inn hotel chain (1984), and an Amando Farga Font special award from the Mexican Restaurant Association (1991). She was also named Academic Researcher by the Mexican Society of Gastronomy (1992), was recognized by the Domecq Cultural Institute (1995) and the Mexican Restaurant Association (1999), and was named La Feria de Puebla by the Mexican Cultural Secretariat and the Tourism Secretariat (2001). She won a Special Gold Medal Award from the Mexican Restaurant Association (2000); a Silver medal from CANIRAC, the Mexican Food and Beverage Industry (2001); and a Lifetime Achievement Award from the International Association of Cooking Professionals (IACP) (2003). Her work in sustainable foods was recognized by the Monterey Bay Aquarium.

Criticisms

Generally, most authors contend only with critics who pick apart the written work and leave the writer unscathed. But sometimes the personality of the author looms so large that critics bring that persona into the critiques as well. Such was the case with Kennedy.

Despite the stories abounded about her legendary temper and preoccupation with precision, many food critics like Kennedy. As McCullough once stated, "She is such an amazing person, with so much passion, knowledge and energy, and she is so funny. People sometimes miss that about Diana. They think she is prickly or difficult."[26] For some reviewers, that part of Kennedy was hard to ignore. Noted critic Mimi Sheraton, reviewing *Recipes from the Regional Cooks of Mexico*, wrote that Kennedy was a "precise and no-nonsense teacher."[27]

Other critics questioned whether there could actually be many cuisines in Mexico: "The book has great personal warmth, which is very nice indeed, but the author has not quite convinced me that there are cuisines in Mexico rather than one cuisine. I imagine that cookery which flavors practically everything with chili peppers, albeit different ones, would produce variations on a theme rather different themes. I may be wrong, but I was not told how the cuisines differ." This comment, made on her first book, could well have propelled Kennedy to move forward into the regionalism that marked all of her ensuing work.[28]

Other reviewers, like Raymond Sokolov, recognized the immense contribution that Kennedy was making. He called *The Cuisines of Mexico* "a long-awaited work, the product of years of exploration south of the border by a meticulous cook whose discoveries show once and for all how impoverished Mexican restaurant menus in this country are."[29] However, even in reviews of her later books, critics such as Florence Fabricant, in her review of Kennedy's *My Mexico*, seemed to pick out only the exotic, like fried ants, wasps, and black iguana mole, ignoring the painstaking work Kennedy did in compiling the recipes and information about ingredients.[30]

CONCLUSION

After years of writing and teaching, Kennedy's contribution to the world of gastronomy loomed large. Eight cookbooks, awards and acclaim from around the world, and legions of former students all ensure that Kennedy's work will continue to influence scores of people in the future. Her work came at a time when most Americans knew Mexican food only as tacos, burritos, tortillas, and chili à la Taco Bell or as street food best not eaten in polite company.

Kennedy's work enables future scholars to examine the recipes she recorded—always attributed by name to the women or men who generously shared them with her—and compare them with other recipes, pondering their historical significances and origins. Spanish-language versions of her books will widen her audience and raise awareness within Mexico itself of what its culinary legacy entails. As Kennedy said, "I love to teach, I can learn all the time. The day we've stopped learning, our minds are closed, and we become very dull, our food becomes dull."[31]

From an average of 10 to 15 Mexican cookbooks per year prior to the publication of *The Cuisines of Mexico* in 1972, the publishing world produced almost twice as many each year afterward, in part because of Kennedy's pioneering work. Her work inspired, and still inspires, numerous authors and chefs, such as Rick Bayless of Frontera Grill and Topolobampo in Chicago and Tom Gilliland of Fonda San Miguel in Austin, Texas. Books began to come from Mexican chefs like Ricardo Muñoz and Roberto Santibañez. Kennedy and her work also influenced countless numbers of people, such as Marilyn Tausend, author of *Savoring Mexico*, and Betsy McNair, author of *Mexicocina: The Spirit and Style of the Mexican Kitchen* (2006), who helped raise awareness about Mexico and its cuisines by writing books and leading travel tours of the country.

But Kennedy herself summed up the most profound impact of her work by saying, "Perhaps I am surprised and very happy that the Mexicans themselves use my books and are so generous in acknowledging, as they say, . . . 'what I have done for their regional cuisines.'"[32]

NOTES

1. Kennedy's date of birth is not in the public record.
2. Diana Kennedy, *Nothing Fancy: Recipes and Recollections of Soul-Satisfying Food* (Garden City, NY: Doubleday, 1984), 6.
3. Kennedy, *Nothing Fancy*, 49.
4. Kennedy, *Nothing Fancy*, Dedication.
5. Diana Kennedy, *The Cuisines of Mexico* (New York: Harper & Row, 1972), xvii.
6. Kennedy, *Nothing Fancy*, 7.
7. Joan Nathan, "The Keeper of the Chilies: Part Hermit, Part Crowd Pleaser," *The New York Times* (July 24, 1996), C4.
8. Kennedy, *Cuisines of Mexico*, 219.
9. Kennedy, *Nothing Fancy*, 8.
10. Kennedy, *Nothing Fancy*, 3.
11. Diana Kennedy, *The Tortilla Book* (New York: Harper & Row, 1975), 7; and Diana Kennedy, *My Mexico: A Culinary Odyssey with More Than 300 Recipes* (New York: Clarkson Potter, 1998), 121–122.
12. Kennedy, *Cuisines of Mexico*, xv.
13. Kennedy, *Cuisines of Mexico*, xix.
14. Nathan, "Keeper of the Chilies," C4.
15. Interview with Christina Waters, *Metroactive Santa Cruz* (May 28, 2008) http://www.metroactive.com/metro-santa-cruz/05.28.08/dining-0822.html

16. But by the time Kennedy published *Recipes from the Regional Cooks of Mexico*, she wrote recipes in a format more commonly used in cookbooks.

17. Kennedy, *Cuisines of Mexico*, 85.

18. Kennedy, *Cuisines of Mexico*, 224–225; recipe for *Pescado en Cilantro* taken from Diana Kennedy, *Herbs for Pot and Body*; *Recipes from the Regional Cooks of Mexico* (New York: Harper & Row, 1978), 85; Kennedy, *My Mexico*, 136.

19. Kennedy, *Cuisines of Mexico*, 227.

20. Kennedy, *My Mexico*, 8.

21. Kennedy, *Nothing Fancy*, 4, 108.

22. Barbara Hansen, "More Than a Translation," *The Los Angeles Times* (January 22, 1976), G11.

23. Kennedy, *Regional Recipes*, 182–205.

24. Kennedy, *My Mexico*, viii.

25. Email between Cynthia Bertelsen and Diana Kennedy, July 11, 2009.

26. Kennedy, *Nothing Fancy*, 2.

27. Mimi Sheraton, "Cookbooks," *The New York Times* (December 3, 1978), BR8.

28. Nika Hazelton, "Cooking by the Book," *The New York Times* (December 3, 1972), BR96.

29. Raymond Sokolov, "Cultures of the World Depicted in Ounces, Cups and Spoonfuls," *The New York Times* (October 5, 1972), 58.

30. Florence Fabricant, "Memories of Mexico, Seasoned by Time," *The New York Times* (December 2, 1998), F5.

31. JeanMarie Brownson, "Straight-talking Diana Kennedy: Maven of Mexico's Culture, Food," *Chicago Tribune* (May 19, 1983), NW-A1.

32. Email between Cynthia Bertelsen and Diana Kennedy, July 11, 2009.

FURTHER READING

Guillermoprieto, Alma. "Disappearing Dishes: How Diana Kennedy Is Rescuing Everyday Food." (Letter from Mexico.) *The New Yorker*. August 19 and 26, 2002, 98–101.

Kennedy, Diana. *The Cuisines of Mexico*. New York: Harper & Row, 1972.

Kennedy, Diana. *The Tortilla Book*. New York: Harper & Row, 1975.

Kennedy, Diana. *Recipes from the Regional Cooks of Mexico*. New York: Harper & Row, 1978.

Kennedy, Diana. *Nothing Fancy: Recipes and Recollections of Soul-Satisfying Food*. New York: The Dial Press, 1984.

Kennedy, Diana. *Mexican Regional Cooking*. New York: HarperCollins, 1985.

Kennedy, Diana. *The Art of Mexican Cooking: Traditional Mexican Cooking for Aficionados*. New York: Bantam Books, 1989.

Kennedy, Diana. *My Mexico: A Culinary Odyssey with More Than 300 Recipes*. New York: Clarkson Potter, 1998.

Kennedy, Diana. *The Essential Cuisines of Mexico*. New York: Clarkson Potter, 2000.

Kennedy, Diana. *From My Mexican Kitchen: Techniques and Ingredients*. New York: Clarkson Potter, 2003.

Kennedy, Diana. *Oaxaca al Gusto*. San Pedro Garza Garcia, Mexico: Plenus, 2008.

Kennedy, Diana. *Oaxaca al Gusto: An Infinite Gastronomy*. The William and Bettye Nowlin Series in Art, History, and Culture of the Western Hemisphere. Austin: The University of Texas Press, 2010.

O'Neil, L. Peat. "Organic in Mexico: A Conversation with Diana Kennedy." *Gastronomica* 6:1 (2006): 25–34.

Cynthia D. Bertelsen

The famous Southern chef Edna Lewis stands in the dining room of the Gage & Tollner restaurant, 1989. (James Marshall/Corbis)

Edna Lewis

From the start of American cookery, women of African descent have stirred many pots, created some of its beloved delicacies, and in particular shaped its most towering regional cuisine—Southern foodways. These women acted both as ambassadors of traditions brought from West and Central Africa and as culinary mediators—fusing their heritage with traditions brought from Western Europe and those contributed by Native Americans. Through several hundred years under the shadow of the institution of slavery, black women— some enslaved, some free—cooked in homes across the nation, learning and mastering the cooking styles of kitchens high and low, and passed those skills on to their sons and daughters, who in turn became master cooks, caterers, and multitalented domestic laborers renowned for their talents. After slavery, many of those black women would continue that tradition working as cooks and domestics, but most would leave history unknown and unremarked upon, faceless and without a name. However, just before that era finally came to a close amid social and cultural change and turmoil, a chef emerged from a small black community in Virginia and lived an extraordinary life that gave a name, a face, and a voice to the history that produced her and the history she made. That chef was Edna M. Lewis.

EARLY YEARS

Freetown

Immediately after the Civil War, formerly enslaved blacks across the South set about the task of reorganizing their lives and creating communities where they could enjoy their new lives as free people. In northeastern Orange County, nestled in the Piedmont region of Virginia, eight families settled near the town of Lahore in a village they called Freetown. Among the settlers were Chester and Lucindy Lewis, the grandparents of Lewis. Chester was a community leader. He and his wife helped found Bethel Baptist Church, the site of many communal church dinners and a place to which Lewis would return on her many visits home. He also organized Freetown's first school in their living room, staffed by teachers brought all the way from the West Indies and Oberlin College and Hampton Institute (now Hampton University).

Orange County and north-central Virginia hold a special place in American food history as the seats of the Madisons, the Monroes, the Jeffersons, and the Randolphs: founding families with gourmet tastes and an appreciation for the fertility and bounty of the land. The influence of these families, their enslaved communities, and the dishes for which their plantation kitchens were lauded could be felt in the tastes and flavors of local cooking. Whether it was the fine tables of Montpelier or closeby Monticello, the legacy of Mary Randolph (cousin to the Jeffersons and author of *The Virginia Housewife*, the first Southern cookbook), or the cooking of the black women who formed the "waiter-carriers" of Gordonsville, famous for their fried chicken and hot rolls served at train side, this county was a crossroads of culinary influences that would make a significant mark on American cuisine. Even after years of intensive cultivation in tobacco, wheat, and corn, the rolling hills and fields of Lewis's home produced excellent produce, wild plant foods, orchard fruit, richly flavored wild game, and grass- and corn-fed livestock.

On April 13, 1916, coincidentally the birthday of another Virginia icon, Thomas Jefferson, Edna M. Lewis was born in the hamlet of Freetown. One of six children, Lewis grew up on one of the many small farms that produced wheat and corn. Raised in a loving home and a solid, self-sufficient community that treasured education, faith, and good food, she was surrounded by a world where everybody played a role in provisioning the table. Lewis noted that "the farm was demanding but everyone shared in the work—tending the animals, gardening, harvesting, preserving the harvest, and every day, preparing delicious foods that seemed to celebrate the good things of each season. As well, there was the bounty yielded up by the woods, fields and steams."[1]

The Lewis farm produced corn, wheat, beans, melons, peanuts, black-eyed peas, and sweet potatoes. The gardens were rich with cymlings or white pattypan squash; pole beans; rape, turnip, and mustard greens; tomatoes; onions; eggplants; potatoes; and cabbages. In the yards rambled cows, pigs, chickens, turkeys, and guineas. Each homestead had patches of fresh herbs—usually sage, purple basil, chervil, mint, tarragon, and thyme. The streams gave up shad and turtles, and the forests and fields provided deer, rabbits, and other game. Lewis fondly recalled gathering wild foods like sassafras roots, hickory nuts, persimmons, watercress, dandelions, and lamb's quarters. Albemarle pippins, Kieffer pears, Muscatine grapes, peaches, and blackberries were made into beverages, desserts, and refreshing fresh snacks.

As Lewis matured, she took note of several key aspects of food and made them the hallmarks of her cooking. As during her childhood, each food was homegrown or locally obtained and enjoyed in its peak season. "The main thing about Southern cooking was that the food was homegrown, fresh and not hybridized . . . [y]ou picked the food from the garden each day, and nothing was store bought. You had your own meat or you bought it from your neighbor. The food had a better taste when it wasn't injected with something, like everything is today."[2] The food of her childhood was not overly seasoned; herbs and spices were used solely to enhance the taste of naturally fresh food. Certain ingredients—lard, sugar, butter, smoked meat—were what she considered to be indispensable to Southern foodways: "The secret is in the ingredients, if you don't put Southern ingredients in, it's not Southern cooking. . . . Some think the ingredients are too heavy or out of date, but I don't think we should throw away our culture because of some fad or new ideas."[3]

Just as important to the components of home cooking were the events around which the food was enjoyed. In Lewis's childhood, each season brought meals prepared at their peak, and Sunday dinners were as sacred as the time spent at church. The laying-by time of August brought the homecoming and Revival Week. Race day, Emancipation Day, hog butchering, Easter, and Christmas punctuated the year, bringing familiar sights, sounds, and tastes. On Emancipation Day, celebrated April 16, 1862, formerly enslaved men and women would tell stories of slavery and freedom, a thanksgiving service would be held, and the community would have dinner on the grounds with game, roast chicken, pork and fall greens, sweet potatoes, pickles, preserves, yeast bread, and deep dish pies made from apples or damson plums.

Each of the women in Lewis's family seemed to contribute a different skill to the table. Lewis remembered, "My first memory of who I was, it was food. I didn't cook but I lived among a group of women who were all good cooks; because a man was taught if you didn't choose a woman who was a good cook, he was embarrassed. No one taught me to cook, I just saw it."[4]

Lewis's mother ("Mama Daisy") was the star of the kitchen on Revival Day, and her masterful cakes and pies were famous throughout Freetown. Mama Daisy made sweet potato pies in the summer kitchen in an old wood stove and ash cakes in cabbage leaves on the open hearth. Lewis's aunt Jennie Hailstalk was an expert at making perfect lye hominy. Her measurements were done on top of coins and in pinches and handfuls. Lewis's grandmother, cousins, sisters, and women at the church were all role models in the kitchen. The men, for their part, were experts at bringing meat products to table like wild game, hams cured with salt and brown sugar over hickory, and long-roasted meats.

Of course, life in Freetown was not perfect. It was still the segregated South with the threat of violence and hatred hanging in the air. Freetown may have provided for the education of its young, but the community had to sacrifice money and send its sons and daughters away for them to come close to having an education equal to that of Orange's white youth. Most blacks were not in the professions, farming was central to making a living, and stories of lynchings, violence, destruction of property, and other emblems of white supremacy surrounded the safe bubble in which Lewis grew up. In the documentary film *Fried Chicken and Sweet Potato Pie* (2005), Lewis recalled, "When I was a girl they used to hang black men. You couldn't do anything about it because they'd kill you. It scared the life out of us." As the Great Depression closed in, Lewis recalled an incident in which a white man rode up to their home and the apprehensive children hid and watched as the man politely asked her mother for food. "I realized how bad things had become, for a white man to ask us for something to eat."[5]

Moving North

Upon the death of Lewis's father, when she was 16, Lewis decided to join the Great Migration of millions of blacks to the North in search of better jobs, more opportunities, and lives that were, at least by law, desegregated. At first she went to Washington, D.C., a common stop for migrants out of Virginia. Lewis remembered, "I didn't have any feelings about leaving, none at all, that was the Depression, what kind of work was I going to do on the farm?"[6]

Washington was a step above rural Virginia, but segregation was still legal, and despite its growing importance as an international political city, it was a southern town with limitations for blacks. After a brief stint as a cook at the Brazilian embassy, Lewis moved on to New York City. After she got off the bus in Manhattan, a friend found her a job at a Brooklyn laundry. Bewildered by her first ironing job—she had never ironed before—she was fired within hours. She did odd jobs to support herself around the city, including a stint as a live-in housekeeper. She also became a typist for *The Daily Worker*, a premier Communist Party publication. Her association with the Communist Party was an empowering experience; it gave her a lifelong concern for workers' rights and social justice, and as a result she tirelessly campaigned for the Scottsboro boys, a group of black youth sentenced to death for the supposed crime of assaulting two white women on a train car. "When I first came to New York I joined the Communist Party, they were the only ones who were encouraging Blacks to be aggressive and encouraged them to participate," Lewis noted.[7]

Lewis became an expert seamstress and became involved in the New York fashion scene, and she often boasted that during that time she made a dress for Marilyn Monroe. She found work dressing windows at Bonwit Teller, at which time she came into contact with another window dresser and antiques dealer, John Nicholson, as well as fashion photographer Karl Bissinger. Her newfound circle of friends was diverse, politically active, and centered in the arts community. The country girl from Virginia had become a bohemian. Their small apartments became an independent social network where political dissidents and people from the fashion world, the visual arts, literature, and journalism all came together for spirited dinner parties. Although Lewis did not know it then, association with this mélange of creative individuals and their connections would help her find her voice in the larger world.

Initially the round-robin dinner parties allowed each person the opportunity to share his or her meager larder with the others in the group. However, as these potluck affairs continued, the handsome, wide-eyed black woman from Virginia introduced her friends to a cuisine that was as familiar as the home cooking they had all grown up with but exotic enough to get them talking and asking questions. Lewis recalled, "It was a nice group of young people. We used to cook for each other on the weekends. I was the only one cooking Southern food. It was at these parties I started to get my reputation for my cooking."[8] Lewis stuffed her friends with the very things that Mama Daisy and Aunt Jennie had made for her in Freetown. At a time when Americans turned inward, out of economic and emotional necessity, to investigate the regionalisms and opportunities that existed in indigenous American culture, Lewis's culinary tour of her childhood was irresistible.

In that first decade or so in New York, it was more than Lewis's cooking that set her apart. Her friend Karl Bissinger recalled, "She looked like an African queen. Five foot eight or nine. She was tall, she was handsome. She was not beautiful she was handsome. There was no denying when you looked at her that she was not just anybody's chef, this was a personage. Particularly the gracious manner that went with it."[9] She began to wear the colorful clothing and the shawls that became her signature dress. She avoided stereotyping with her soft-spoken but loudly eloquent conversations, and she affirmed her cultural heritage while becoming an international, cultured, classic beauty. These qualities attracted Steven Kingston, a former merchant seaman, politically active lawyer, and fellow member of the Communist Party, and they married.

RESTAURANTS

Café Nicholson

On a trip to Europe, Lewis's friend John Nicholson frequented a wonderful restaurant in Rome named Café Greco. He was so impressed with the eatery that he wanted to move its design to New York, where it would serve as a novelty restaurant. Nicholson found a spot on East 57th street and decorated it like no other establishment in New York. A reviewer described the café as "a turn-of-the century Parisian pleasure palace." Its decorative tiles, bronze statues, marble-top tables, and eclectic mix of décor made it a natural place to eat as well as to be photographed. Shortly before the café opened, Nicholson gave Lewis an opportunity: "Edna was about to take a job as a domestic. She looked at the cafe and said it would make a wonderful restaurant. I said to her, 'Edna, if you want to, I'll give you half of this, no money down.'"[10]

In 1949, Lewis became head—and only chef—and equal partner at Café Nicholson. With a small kitchen and only 30 seats, the café had a ready clientele made up of Nicholson, Bissinger, and Lewis's friends with a network that extended to the avant-garde artists, actors, and literati of the time, and it soon became a place where "high society loves to meet high bohemia."[11] There was no menu because Lewis and Nicholson preferred that the food be fresh and as seasonal as possible, and they used the best things available at hand. The first night they ran out of food by 6 P.M. and Nicholson had to run to purchase more ingredients.

Café Nicholson was first and foremost distinguished by Lewis's cooking. Her persona and her cuisine were the draw. A rare Southern black cook in uptown New York City with no formal training, she turned out roast chicken with herbs "brown as autumn chestnuts," according to *The New York Daily Tribune*, caramel cake, fruit cobblers, filet mignon, broiled oysters, and a chocolate soufflé one had to taste in order to believe it ever existed. All of the food was simple and elegantly served, and on occasion Lewis would intersperse her menu with the treats of her youth. It was a fancy culinary refuge for bohemians and expatriate Southerners alike, who could get this kind of high-style, simple, and flavorful food nowhere else.

The clientele of Café Nicholson were among the most cosmopolitan and urbane in all of New York. Guests included Ira Gershwin, Muriel Draper, Jean Renoir, Gloria Vanderbilt, Marlene Dietrich, Marlon Brando, Dean Martin, and Jerry Lewis—the who's who of the early 1950s. Lewis noted, "All the famous Southerners would come. We always had Tennessee Williams, William Faulkner, Truman Capote. He was one of my favorites. He would come to my kitchen looking for biscuits. 'Oh don't you have any biscuits?' We didn't make biscuits. He had real wide lapels and penny loafers. He was cute! Everybody went gaga when he came."[12] Although Southern food was no doubt being made in the restaurants, rent parties, and church kitchens of Harlem, Café Nicholson was a safe, mostly white establishment that provided a way for Southern expatriates to enjoy authentic home cooking by an authentic black Southern cook.

COOKBOOKS

Six years later, Lewis left Café Nicholson because she and her husband argued frequently over what he thought was its "bourgeois" nature. Lewis did private catering, cooked as a private chef, and gathered more knowledge and experience as she tried her hand at raising pheasants in New Jersey, teaching cooking classes, and visiting the farmers' markets of New York City. She would often recharge herself in Freetown, visiting each year for family events and the annual homecoming week at Bethel Baptist Church. Though she was a New Yorker now, she never lost touch with the soil from which she sprang. One article published in the *Fredericksburg Free-Lance Star* noted that she would bring hams, preserves, pickles, country sausage, and cracklins back to New York. This constant connection, including relatives sending her special fruits and wild game from home, would prove vital to helping Lewis introduce blacks and Southerners to American cooking.

The Edna Lewis Cookbook

It was an accident that led to the creation of *The Edna Lewis Cookbook* (1972). Lewis noted, "I fell and broke my leg and wound up in the hospital bored to death. I got the nurse to bring me a pad and pencil and I started writing. That's exactly how it happened."[13] The hospital time and recovery allowed her to contemplate writing down her first collection of recipes, aptly entitled *The Edna Lewis Cookbook*. She worked with Evangeline Peterson, and her first cookbook honored her experiences at Café Nicholson. The food included was elegant and international and spoke to her appreciation for simple, fresh food and a refined palette. With its publication in 1972, Lewis began to catch the attention of culinary writers and experts the nation over, and yet the voice of her childhood had not yet emerged to bring the world a vision of Southern cooking and the Southern palette.

The Taste of Country Cooking

In 1972, Lewis worked as a museum educator in the African exhibit in New York's Museum of Natural History near Central Park West. At the suggestion of Robert Bernstein, the CEO of Random House, she was able to meet Judith Jones, the cookbook editor at Alfred A. Knopf who had worked with Julia Child. Lewis was accompanied by Evangeline Peterson, with whom she had collaborated on her first cookbook. Lewis and Peterson wanted to bring a cookbook to life that would celebrate Lewis's Southern roots. Disappointed by what she saw as the loss of real Southern cooking in the country inns of the region, Jones was impressed with the beautiful word pictures that Lewis began to weave about her experiences growing up in Freetown and the wonders of the Piedmont countryside of Virginia. The process of bringing food to table, the memories of the people who were its masters, and the memories and tactile sensations only a child can know made Lewis's narrative irresistible. After looking at a few sample pages, Jones was unimpressed. Peterson left the writing to Lewis, and every Thursday afternoon when Lewis was off from her work at the museum, they began to write out Lewis's memories longhand on yellow legal pads.

Across a three-year period Lewis wrote her masterpiece. The 1976 edition of *The Taste of Country Cooking* earned her the respect and notice of food greats James Beard, M. F. K. Fisher, and Craig Claiborne, who opined in 1979, "It may well be the most entertaining regional cookbook in America." Beard's famous quote made it onto the book's jacket: "Edna Lewis makes me want to go right into the kitchen and start cooking. Rarely does a book transmit such a feeling of warmth and friendliness, as well as a knowledge of good food and good cooking." Upon reading the book, M. F. K. Fisher wrote Jones, telling her that Lewis's "book is fresh and pure the way clean air can be. . . . It is in the best sense American, with an innate dignity, and freedom from prejudice and hatred, and it is reassuring to be told again that although we may have lost some of all of this simplicity, it still exists here."[14] Though the publisher may not have intended it to happen, the book came out at the same time as Alex Haley's *Roots*, the celebration of the Bicentennial, and a renaissance of interest in black culture. It established Lewis as a sort of a "culinary Phillis Wheatley," comparing her to the first black poet.[15]

Breaking from the traditional organizational themes like categories of foods or ingredients, *The Taste of Country Cooking* took readers on a culinary tour of Lewis's youth, leading them season by season through her sensual memories and most vivid recollections of what made the food of her childhood so delectable. The menus were lifted straight from memory—late spring lunches, early summer dinners, Sunday Revival dinners, wheat-harvesting meals, and cool evening suppers. The key markers were the events around which food played a pivotal role. Lewis introduced readers to foods that had grown exotic in the American palette—Jerusalem artichokes, wild persimmons, lamb's quarters, and poke salad greens. Most of all, her anecdotes about elders drinking coffee ("java") from bowls, keeping baby chicks warm behind the cook stove in winter, and making blanc mange (an influence from the kitchens of Jefferson and Madison) from fresh spring milk made readers feel they had settled down for a long talk around a kitchen table with a pot of something good sputtering in the background.

The Taste of Country Cooking also laid the groundwork for Lewis's life-long legacy of preserving the foods and culture presented in the cookbook. To her, Southern cooking was not a deep-fried, gloppy, greasy mess of over seasoned truck-stop chow; it was an art, a process, time-honored and tied to the land from which the food came. Long before the first decade of the 21st century made superior eating an organic, locally centered, natural, folk experience, Lewis championed all of these virtues as the themes of the cookbook became her platform for the rest of her life. Her introduction makes it clear: "I am happy to see how many young people are going back to the land and to the South. They are interested in natural farming and they seem to want to know how we did things in the past. . . . I hope this book will be helpful to them." *The Taste of Country Cooking* was a guide for capturing some of the simple blessings that had brought her "thus far along the way."[16]

In Pursuit of Flavor

In Pursuit of Flavor, published in 1988, followed *The Taste of Country Cooking*. The cookbook, also published by Alfred A. Knopf, reflected Lewis's roots as well as her wings—Virginia, New York, and all spots in between. The reader got to know Lewis the maturing cook and food expert by walking with her through New York's Union Square Greenmarket as she talked to farmers and meat and produce vendors. Instead of being organized by the seasons and events of her youth, each chapter reflected food at its source and aimed to show cooks that cooking with the seasons and making dishes in their own best time were paramount to the gustatory experience. She emphasized actively selecting the best foods for each recipe, how to cut them or let them ripen to bring out the greatest amount of flavor, and the proper combinations that allowed dishes to accentuate each other at the table.

In Pursuit of Flavor also brought forth her experiences in the Carolinas and with other cooks from across the African Diaspora. Foods like benne (sesame seeds), okra, red rice, Brunswick stew, and she-crab soup, which she perfected at the historic Middleton Place plantation, an 18th-century mansion outside Charleston, South Carolina, now entered the Lewis culinary palette. In honor of Lewis's recently adopted son, an Eritrean student named Afeworki Paulos, the cookbook included a recipe for Ethiopian bread.

OTHER ENDEAVORS

Collaboration with Scott Peacock

Although their relationship would engender some controversy, the key event in Lewis's later years was her chance meeting with Scott Peacock, a young chef from Alabama. As a gay, white, young man and a trained chef, Peacock was everything that Lewis was not. They met at a Southern foods festival in Atlanta. Lewis had hundreds of pies to make, and Scott volunteered to help. In an interview, Peacock recalled, "The first time I met Miss Lewis was at a gala celebration of Southern cooks in Atlanta in 1988. At the time, I was the chef at the governor's mansion here in Atlanta, and she was at Gage & Tollner in Brooklyn."[17] In Lewis's memory, Peacock stepped in to help her make the fried pies, but she was skeptical. "I thought oh my God, all my pies are going to be ruined. He didn't ask me anything, he made the dough and rolled it out and cooked it. I thought, oh my God, he can cook!"[18]

The friendship bloomed when Peacock kept calling Lewis for hints, ideas, tips, and treasures of her wisdom. Before this, Peacock did not really have an interest in Southern cooking as a gourmet pursuit. He noted, "We spent countless nights talking about cooking, about her experiences working for Franklin Roosevelt's presidential campaigns, and about her grandfather, who was a freed slave. We picked wild blackberries, cooked turtle soup and shad roe and listened to Bessie Smith."[19] He also said, "Part of that light bulb going off was realizing just how different was Lewis's experience and the cooking she had grown up with, although simple country cooking, too, was so different from what I'd grown up with, and yet some of the things were very similar." He met her at a crucial stage in his career, as he was contemplating moving from Georgia to Italy to "reinvent" himself as a chef. His friendship with Lewis became a mission of personal self-awareness: "Over time Miss Lewis helped me see the value of myself—as a Southerner, a cook, a gay man, and a human being (not necessarily in that order). She never passed judgment, celebrating me for exactly who I was, yet her unconditional love inspired me to always strive toward being a better person."

Lewis moved in with Peacock in 1992, finally leaving New York and returning to the South, albeit Atlanta and retired in the mid-1990s. By this time, she had traveled back and forth across the South and had broadened her own Southern repertoire, having cooked and directed kitchens at the Fearrington House in Pittsboro, North Carolina, and at Middleton Place. Lewis came out of retirement to found an organization to preserve Southern foods and food traditions. One of the efforts she helped seed became, in part, the current Southern Foodways Alliance. Peacock's cooking benefited from her tutelage at the Horseradish Grill, where her philosophy influenced his practice, and once again, under Lewis's hand, his business prospered. Peacock liked to joke that they became widely known as "the odd couple of Southern cooking." Inspired by "youth and alcohol," Peacock helped make the occasion of Lewis's eightieth birthday particularly special for her, cooking a meal for 75 guests on an open hearth of an old plantation kitchen. Turtle soup, baked shad, roasted chicken, buttermilk biscuits and seasonal, organic vegetables brought Lewis back to the milestones of her life.

The Gift of Southern Cooking

In 2003, Lewis and Peacock published a joint work based on 10 years of living together and sharing secrets and knowledge as chefs who had both researched the past and used the historical and folk spectrum of Southern cooking to innovate dishes that would fit in the tradition. That year, *The Gift of Southern Cooking*, published by Alfred A. Knopf, became a landmark in the career of Peacock and a seal on that of Lewis. Large and encyclopedic, the work signified the older generation of Southern cooks meeting the new. The work further benefited from beautiful pictures of traditional southern dishes and their preparation, not the least of which documented the final years of Lewis as a professional chef and home cook. The brand-name quality Lewis and Peacock both brought to *The Gift of Southern Cooking* made it a landmark book and a fitting collective project honoring their unique friendship.

Poet Nikki Giovanni on Edna Lewis

When I read in Food and Wine *that [Edna Lewis] would be cooking at Middleton [Middleton Place in Charleston, South Carolina], I immediately booked myself in for the week so that I could run the menu. After a day and an evening I had the pleasure of Ms. Lewis joining me at my table. I had come to Middleton alone so I had read and sort of meandered. She came over and much to my amazement knew that I write poetry. She talked about meeting Langston Hughes and her days in Harlem. Then she asked if I cooked. I do and I am proud to say so. What is your favorite dish? You should try my quail I said. I then explained how I sautéed it. How I split the back, put a half-stick of unsalted butter and a bit of thyme and garlic, then browned on one side at medium heat then turned. I noticed a strained look coming over her face but I dismissed it as I raved about my dish. . . . That look on her face stayed with me until I got back home. I was living with my mother then . . . and asked her where did we get our quail recipe. In one of those magazines she said. Mother is a pack rat so I started digging old* Food and Wines *out. And there it was. Edna Lewis's Quail. My letter started: Dear Ms. Lewis: You must think I am an idiot. I've been cooking your quail recipe for so long that I think it's mine. Will you ever forgive me????? And she has. And I still make great quail. I just give credit where credit is due.*

—Nikki Giovanni, "To Edna Lewis," in *Cornbread Nation: The Best of Southern Food Writing.* Chapel Hill: University of North Carolina Press, 2002, p. 31

AWARDS AND HONORS

Lewis passed away in her sleep on February 13, 2006. Peacock gave her a quiet, private memorial in Atlanta before she was taken to Unionville, Virginia, to be buried among her siblings and ancestors. Lewis took with her not only memories of her own experience and centuries gone by but also a host of awards and culinary recognitions that set her apart as an African American chef. She was inducted into the Taste of Heritage Foundation African American Chefs Hall of Fame in 1997. She received a Lifetime Achievement Award from the International Association of Culinary Professionals in 1990, the James Beard Living Legend Award in 1995, the title of Grand Dame by Les Dames d'Escoffier, and a Lifetime Achievement Award in 1999 from the Southern Foodways Alliance. In 2009, her story was further immortalized by a children's book based on her childhood memories, *Bring Me Some Apples and I'll Make You a Pie: A Story about Edna Lewis,* authored by Robbin Gourley. In 2009, Lewis was posthumously recognized by the Library of Virginia as an African American Trailblazer.

Yet, more important than all of her awards and accolades were her wisdom and her intellectual legacy, her views on what it meant to be an American, a Southerner, and a black cook looking backward and forward to save her dear and precious legacy. Perhaps no words are more fitting that those quoted in her award-winning posthumously published essay (2008), "What Is Southern?": "So many great souls have passed off the scene. The world has changed. We are now faced with picking up the pieces and trying to put them into shape, documenting them so the present-day young generation can see what southern food was like. The foundation on which it rested was pure ingredients, open-pollinated seed—planted and replanted for generations— natural fertilizers. We grew the seeds of what we ate, we worked with love and care."

CONCLUSION

In an interview with National Public Radio, John T. Edge from the Southern Foodways Alliance eulogized that Lewis's great accomplishment in an extraordinary life was that she said, "Look here, look to the South, and Ms. Lewis in some ways helped us see the value in our food. She gave us the pride to hold our cast iron skillets high."

NOTES

1. Edna Lewis, *The Taste of Country Cooking* (New York: Alfred A. Knopf, 2003), xiv.

2. *Fried Chicken and Sweet Potato Pie,* DVD, directed by Bailey Barash (Atlanta, GA: Barash Productions, 2008).

3. Gwendolyn Glenn, "Southern Secrets from Edna Lewis," *American Visions* (Feb-March 1997) http://findarticles.com/p/articles/mi_m1546/is_n1_v12/ai_1925 7630/

4. Glenn, "Southern Secrets from Edna Lewis."

5. Glenn, "Southern Secrets from Edna Lewis."

6. Chang-Rae Lee, "The Quiet Cook," *Gourmet* (November 2001).

7. *Fried Chicken and Sweet Potato Pie.*

8. Lee, "The Quiet Cook."

9. *Fried Chicken and Sweet Potato Pie.*

10. *Fried Chicken and Sweet Potato Pie.*

11. Susan Scott Neal, "Country Girl Has the Best of Two Worlds," *Fredericksburg Free-Lance Star* (September 17, 1978), 17.

12. *Fried Chicken and Sweet Potato Pie.*

13. Neal, "Country Girl Has the Best of Two Worlds," 17.

14. Judith Jones, *The Tenth Muse* (New York: Alfred A. Knopf, 2007), 119.

15. Personal conversation with Psyche Williams-Forson, August 30, 2009.

16. Edna Lewis, *The Taste of Country Cooking* (New York: Alfred A. Knopf, 1976), xv.

17. *Fried Chicken and Sweet Potato Pie.*

18. *Fried Chicken and Sweet Potato Pie.*

19. Larry Buhl, "First Person: Scott Peacock—Food and Friendship," *The Advocate* (March 28, 2006), 29.

FURTHER READING

Buhl, Larry. "First Person: Scott Peacock—Food and Friendship." *The Advocate.* March 28, 2006, 29.

Edge, John T. Interview by Debbie Elliott. February 18, 2006. National Public Radio. http://www.npr.org/templates/transcript/transcript.php?storyId=5222253

Fried Chicken and Sweet Potato Pie, DVD. Directed by Bailey Barash. Atlanta, GA: Barash Productions, 2008.

Glenn, Gwendolyn. "Southern Secrets from Edna Lewis." *American Visions* (February/ March 1997).

Gourley, Robbin. *Bring Me Some Apples and I'll Make You a Pie: A Story about Edna Lewis.* New York: Clarion Books, 2009.

Jones, Judith. *The Tenth Muse: My Life in Food.* New York: Alfred A. Knopf, 2008.

Lee, Chang-Rae. "The Quiet Cook." *Gourmet* (November 2001).

Lewis, Edna. *The Taste of Country Cooking.* New York: Alfred A. Knopf, 1976.

Lewis, Edna. "What Is Southern?" *Gourmet* (January 2008) http://www.gourmet .com/magazine/2000s/2008/01/whatissouthern_lewis

Lewis, Edna, and Mary Goodbody. *In Pursuit of Flavor.* New York: Alfred A. Knopf, 1988.

Lewis, Edna, and Evangeline Peterson. *The Edna Lewis Cookbook.* Indianapolis: Bobbs-Merrill, 1972.

Lewis, Edna, and Scott Peacock. *The Gift of Southern Cooking: Recipes and Revelations from Two Great Southern Cooks.* New York: Alfred A. Knopf, 2003.

Randall, Joseph. "Chef Hall of Fame" and "An Interview with Edna Lewis." http://www.chefjoerandall.com/edna-lewis.htm#EdnaLewisInterview

Scott Neal, Susan. "Country Girl Has the Best of Two Worlds." *Fredericksburg Free-Lance Star.* September 17, 1978, 17.

Wells, Gully. "Praise the Lard and Edna Lewis." *Conde Nast-Traveler.* October 2003, http://www.concierge.com/cntraveler/articles/5670?pageNumber=3

Michael Twitty

Chef Joan Nathan, right, and Alice Waters, left, the executive chef and owner of Chez Panisse in Berkeley, California, look over the produce at a farmer's market in Washington, January 18, 2009. (AP/Wide World Photos)

Joan Nathan

Joan Nathan has done more than any other cookbook author to bring Jewish and Israeli cooking to mainstream America. The author of 10 books, Nathan has won the prestigious James Beard Award three times and Julia Child/International Association of Cooking Professionals (IACP) Awards twice—an unusual achievement for even the most accomplished chefs and food writers. Producer and host of two award-winning PBS documentaries, she also contributes to *The New York Times* and other national publications. Yet, while she is "the preeminent authority on Jewish cooking in America," Nathan also focuses more broadly on the immigrant experience as reflected in its richest incarnation—the preparation and eating of food.[1] With an ethnographic eye, Nathan has tracked down the vanishing foodways of immigrants both in America and in Israel to show not just how people have preserved the culinary traditions of their cultures, but how those traditions shift and adapt, borrowing from each other and their host countries to produce new, vibrant dishes that simultaneously capture an immediacy and historic resonance.

EARLY YEARS

Childhood

Nathan grew up in Providence, Rhode Island. Although her family was Jewish, she was not raised in a strictly observant household and did not keep kosher.[2] Her mother had grown up on the lower East Side of Manhattan, "and has always celebrated holidays quietly. 'Jewish events didn't have such a display of showiness then as they have today,' [her mother] said. 'Maybe it was because we had a small family, but you ate and went to synagogue, that's it. No one made such a gantse [big] business about food.'"[3]

Cooking, Nathan notes, was "not a family tradition."[4] Her grandmother had been a milliner and hired a housekeeper to clean and cook. Nathan's mother, Pearl Gluck, went to Barnard College and then, in 1937, married her father Ernest Nathan, a German immigrant, and moved to Providence, where "all the other young wives . . . cooked."[5] War rationing, and later her father's faltering business, caused Nathan's mother not only to enter the workforce as a teacher, but also to give up her own housekeeper and learn to cook. In the mid-20th century, Providence was a manufacturing and port city, peopled by Anglo Americans, French Canadians, Swedes, Portuguese, Irish, and, perhaps most famously, Italians. Nathan remembers, "As a child, I looked on a trip to Federal Hill [Little Italy] as some children would a visit to a candy store. . . . My father and I would return with our arms loaded with fresh pasta, crusty bread, fennel, chestnuts, prosciutto, and provolone cheese. My father would try out his schoolboy Italian on the merchants, and I drank in the atmosphere, which started me on my way to loving foreign languages, ethnic cultures, and good home cooking."[6]

Israel

Although Nathan has always liked cooking and "even loved home economics," she did not pursue a path into cooking right away.[7] After graduation from high school, she attended the University of Michigan in Ann Arbor, a town that, before the foodie revolution, featured "grubby health food stores."[8] She pursued a degree in French literature and then earned a master's in public administration from the John F. Kennedy School of Government at Harvard University.

In 1970, at the age of 26, Nathan decided to go to Israel to "see what it was all about."[9] She landed a job as foreign press attaché with Jerusalem mayor Teddy Kollek—an enduring relationship that also changed her life. Kollek, who was mayor of Jerusalem from 1965 to 1993, is a towering figure in Israeli history. He had come to Palestine in 1934 and worked tirelessly on Zionist and, later, Israeli causes, spying for the British agency MI5 under the code name "the Scorpion" and helping to unify the city of Jerusalem after the 1967 Six-Day War, turning it "from a parochial hilltop town . . . to a modern metropolis."[10] He was also passionate about the unification of Jerusalem, and as Nathan says, "I learned through him about the power of food as a bridge to people."[11]

COOKBOOKS

The Flavor of Jerusalem

As part of her job, Nathan had to explain Israel and Jerusalem to foreign visitors and dignitaries. The experience took her all over the city, where she and the mayor met and dined with Jews, Arabs, and immigrants from the far reaches of the world. Along with fellow mayoral staffer Judy Stacey Goldman, Nathan, "almost as a joke," decided to write a book that would capture the unique character of Jerusalem through the culinary lives of its diverse residents. "I never thought of it as a career, but it sold 25,000 copies in the States and suddenly I was a food writer."[12]

The Flavor of Jerusalem reflects the sense of optimism, inclusiveness, and wonder found in Jerusalem and Israel in the early 1970s, following the chaos and uncertainty of Israel's early years as a state and the tumultuous Six-Day War that changed the borders of the modern Middle East and for the first time in decades put all of Jerusalem under Israeli control. With the tagline "International recipes from the many recipes of the sacred city," *The Flavor of Jerusalem* gives an immediate sense of what the city must have been like for its residents, most of whom were immigrants or children of immigrants, and many of whom had been unable to visit relatives or friends in parts of the city on the other side of the Jordanian-Israeli border. The Jerusalem that comes off the pages is dynamic, welcoming, and diverse, soaked in religious tradition. As Nathan and Goldman write in their introduction, "A typical gastronomic tour of the city might begin with Turkish coffee in a café, followed by ten o'clock caviar and vodka at one of the two Russian churches or perhaps at a new immigrant's home, lunch at a Hungarian Jewish or a Moslem restaurant, tea and crumpets at the Anglican archbishop's and dinner at an Oriental bar mitzvah or a wedding in Mea Shearim, the very Orthodox section, where females must dress modestly, with long sleeves and skirts that cover the knees."[13]

The Flavor of Jerusalem contains elements that would become the hallmarks of Nathan's later books: oral histories and interviews with home cooks and professionals alike, many of them elderly; portraits and historical photographs and other images, such as a photograph of Itzhak Rabin visiting the Church of the Holy Sepulchre in 1967, or a Russian immigrant speaking to her children in Moscow on the telephone; and recipes that run the gamut from complex and fancy to simple and ordinary. The book captures the zeitgeist of the city in the early 1970s and reveals the diversity not only among the city's religious populations, but within them as well. Moroccan, British, Greek, Russian, German, and other recipes elbow against each other and in the process reveal Jerusalem's rich and turbulent past.

The Jewish Holiday Kitchen

Upon her return to the United States, Nathan built on her municipal experience and took a job with New York's mayor Abraham Beame as the director of public information. In that capacity, she helped create the first Ninth Avenue Food Festival in 1974, a highly popular event that showcases the cultural diversity of Hell's Kitchen and continues as a major tourist attraction to this day.

In 1979 Nathan published her second cookbook, *The Jewish Holiday Kitchen*. In their review of the expanded edition in 2004, *Publishers Weekly* called the book "a landmark work that juxtaposed recipes with oral histories."[14] As in *The Flavor of Jerusalem*, Nathan used food as the vehicle to discover life stories. In her books, the recipes and the biographies are indistinguishable from each other. This time, Nathan focused on the Jewish holiday cycle, beginning with one of the most important, the Sabbath. With its origins in the Fourth Commandment (to keep the seventh day of the week as a day of rest, dedicated to God), the Sabbath is celebrated worldwide, usually with special, festive foods. Nathan considers various Sabbath menus: Seattle Sephardic, Old New York Sephardic, Hungarian, Minsk, and Baltimore. The recipes—all kosher—feature common elements of the Sabbath dinner, such as fish, chicken, and salads, but the resemblance stops there. The cook can choose from Greek Fish with Plum Sauce, Sephardic Cold Spicy Fish, Zamosc Gefilte Fish, or Stewed Fish with Lemon Sauce. The one constant is challah, the making of which is a mitzvah (a good deed or commandment) for Jewish women. As Nathan says, "When my daughters turned 13, I asked Manfred Loeb, a baker, to come over and teach them how, and he and they together would make enough challah for their bat mitzvahs. Now when friends' children are getting bar or bat mitzvahed I'll go over and do a session with them."[15]

The book similarly celebrates Rosh Hashanah, Yom Kippur, Passover, Hannukah, and other holidays and led to Nathan's involvement in the award-winning 1994 PBS/Maryland Public Television series *Passover: Traditions of Freedom*, in which Nathan visited six families to explore how people in Israel and the United States celebrate this most visible Jewish holiday. Originally, Nathan was not supposed to be an on-air talent, but the producers quickly realized that she would be the centerpiece of the show, which featured Jewish food experts as well as the families.[16]

An American Folklife Cookbook

Nathan was now officially a food writer and cookbook author. For her next project, she combined her dual interests in cultural diversity and food but moved away from the Jewish focus and overlay of her previous books. In *An American Folklife Cookbook*, Nathan traveled around the United States and often tracked down elderly people whose recipes were representative of local food cultures. The book celebrates American regional cuisine and the roles immigrants and local ingredients have played in shaping the distinctive culinary traditions of such diverse American landscapes as Louisiana, Minnesota, the Eastern Seaboard, the West Coast, and the Deep South. But unlike other regional cookbooks, *An American Folklife Cookbook* is organized not geographically, but rather by where and how one gathers ingredients, and by what the cooking accomplishes. The first chapter, "Our Early Traditions," ranges widely. It discusses the gastronomic proclivities of "gourmet president" Thomas Jefferson and includes adaptations of dishes he enjoyed. Nathan then visits a Virginia nonagenarian named Mattie Ball Fletcher, whose house and garden sit in the shadow of acclaimed restaurant, The Inn at Little Washington. Nathan neatly juxtaposes Fletcher's cozy home and kitchen with the elegance of the restaurant, drawing the comparison further as she contrasts the breads, candies, and other dishes Fletcher turns out of her kitchen, often for barter or profit, with the inn's nouvelle cuisine. As Fletcher notes, the inn's "food's quite pretty, but it's not cooked long enough, don't you think?"[17] Nathan highlights both aspects of Southern cookery, placing Fletcher's recipes for green beans (slow-cooked) next to the inn's "nouvelle-cuisine green beans." Recipes for rhubarb desserts, baked goods, and salad dressing appear in counterpoint, showing off possible variations for local ingredients prepared by traditional and modern cooks.

Nathan then leaves Virginia and travels to New England to visit the kitchen of Marian Green Whipple, born in 1891, who makes such dishes as apple pie, doughnuts, baked beans, and boiled dinner. From there she moves to New Mexico, where she explores Mexican and Indian cooking with the Suina and Lovato families, and winds up the chapter in Appalachia, in the kitchen of an octogenarian African American woman named Eddie Washington, who works all night as an attendant for another elderly woman and spends her days in her own kitchen, baking. Nathan writes that, after returning from work in the morning, "Eddie heads straight to the green-and-white Kalamazoo wood-burning stove in her kitchen. She pulls a lid off the top of the stove, inserts two blocks of hardwood, one discarded corncob, and a piece of crumpled newspaper. Then she walks outside, splits four more pieces of wood, and piles them in the woodbox behind the stove."[18] The dishes Washington turns out on her wood stove are varied and impressive: pound cake, lemon meringue and peach pies, coconut and Lady Baltimore cakes, cooked cabbage, deer steak, and apple dumplings.

In the next chapter, Nathan turns her attention away from traditional American cooking to the way people cook on the farm. She visits a beekeeper in Vermont, a Pennsylvania farm family, a Texas ranch, and a California couple who cook from the huge garden at their Malibu home. Nathan then focuses on seafood, with trips to Louisiana, Martha's Vineyard, and Maryland. She explores ethnic cuisines that meld together, such as those of Vietnamese in Maryland, Armenians in Massachusetts, Norwegians in Minnesota, Jews in South Carolina, and Italians in Providence. In her most unusual chapter, Nathan shows the culture of vocational cooking—not in restaurants or diners, but in logging camps, fire houses, boarding houses, vineyards, and a tiny Manhattan apartment, yielding such unexpected recipes as firehouse chili, barbecued salmon (loggers), fig preserves (boarding house), and chilies rellenos (California vineyard). A reviewer in *The New York Times* observed that "Joan Nathan is fast becoming a chronicler of America's ethnic traditions. . . . Some of the recipes she has uncovered are delightful. . . . Some are dull, reflecting cooking in this country that seldom makes its way to the pages of slick culinary magazines. But the people about whom Miss Nathan writes do not, she says, 'need food writers to define for them what is American food.'"[19]

Ultimately, in *An American Folklife Cookbook*, the stories of the people Nathan interviews are as compelling as her recipes. This mix of oral history, culinary reclamation, celebration, and preservation had by this time become Nathan's trademark cookbook style. The pictures in all of her books reflect this orientation—they are often family snapshots, or candid images of people cooking in their own kitchens, rather than gourmet dishes presented and shot by food stylists and photographers. When food is shown in the pictures, it is almost never on its own, but as a part of the larger room and family life of Nathan's subjects. In 1985, the R. T. French Tastemaker Award went to *An American Folklife Cookbook*.[20]

Jewish Cooking in America

Nathan followed up the success of *An American Folklife Cookbook* with a return to Jewish cooking. *The Children's Jewish Holiday Kitchen* is a slim volume, designed for children and their parents who want to cook easy and child-friendly recipes for the Jewish holiday cycle. It harkened back to her earlier work on Jewish cooking traditions and was inspired by her own kids' adventures in the kitchen. Nathan was now also writing for *The New York*

Times on immigrant and Jewish culinary traditions. But she was also on the lookout for a new project. Her agent told her that she "should only write a book on a subject about which I feel passionate."[21]

After *The Flavor of Jerusalem*, Nathan had published her next three books with Schocken Books, a Jewish press that was part of the Random House family, as was Alfred A. Knopf. After the success of *An American Folklife Cookbook*, Nathan had the opportunity to work with legendary Knopf editor Judith Jones, whom she credits as coming up with the idea for *Jewish Cooking in America*. Jones had also been Julia Child's editor and had worked with such luminaries as Marcella Hazan and Marion Cunningham. Jones not only had her finger on the pulse of cookbook publishing, but to some extent defined the field.

During the late 1980s and early 1990s, Nathan was in the middle of researching and writing the book that would solidify her place in the pantheon of American food icons. *Jewish Cooking in America* was released in 1994. It took five years to write, and unlike her previous books, where she relied primarily on interviews and oral histories, was based on copious amounts of historical research. She traced not only the diversity of American Jewish cooking, but its history and chronology, paying homage to the long line of Jewish cookbooks in America, including the legendary *Settlement Cook Book* from Milwaukee. Her introduction briefly reviews the history of Jewish migration to America, from the earliest Jewish fur traders in the 18th century, through 19th-century German migrations and the "rise of Eastern European Jewry," to the political upheavals of the 20th century. Throughout, Nathan emphasizes the ways Jewish food evolved in America, from its earliest inceptions to mass production and advertising. The combination of regional ingredients in the New World, regional migration streams from the Old, and the ways in which cooks adapted their recipes to their new lives created a uniquely American Jewish cuisine. This cuisine has been shaped both by generations and new immigrants, by Ashkenazi Jews from Eastern Europe, Sephardic Jews from North Africa and the Middle East, and Jews from Latin America, Russia, Turkey, and Italy.

As in all her books, Nathan discusses the rules of kashrut, or keeping kosher, and the Jewish holiday cycle. However, *Jewish Cooking in America* is organized along the lines of a traditional cookbook, with chapters on appetizers, main courses, breads, soups, meats, and desserts, among others. This structure emphasizes the diversity of Jewish communities in America, but, more remarkably, it shows the way Jewish cooks interpret the same or similar dishes with wildly divergent results. In the section on cholents, a heavy, hearty stew that is slow-cooked under low heat for Saturday dinner, one can find chili rubbing elbows with Boston baked beans and Moroccan stew. Nathan presents an 18th-century recipe for haricot stew with beans, "surely one of the oldest recipes for this dish [cholent] in this country," a few pages away from her mother's meatloaf recipe, and then briskets served Texas style, Kansas City style, and Cleveland style braised in Coke.[22] She sprinkles the chapters with quotations from Jewish American writers, historical episodes, and ads for kosher products like Crisco, for which "the Hebrew Race Has Been Waiting 4,000 Years."[23] In addition to historical recipes and oral histories, Nathan pays homage to famous restaurants, cafes, delicatessens, and food manufacturers. The religious aspects of food come through as much as the ethnic, family, and community facets of meals and dining. Nathan manages to convey the entire spectrum of Jewish culinary history in America in 300 kosher recipes and over 450 pages.

Matzah Balls

Baton Rouge Jews like their food spicy, even at the seder table. Journalist Carol Anne Blitzer offended the Southern sensibilities of 102-year-old Celina Aaron Maas when she showed up to photograph her preparing matzah balls for a Passover story. To help the elderly lady, Mrs. Blitzer brought with her some mixed Manischewitz matzah balls for the picture. Mrs. Maas took one look at them and cried, "Yankee matzah balls!" She then got out a butcher knife and started cutting up green onions and sprinkling on red pepper to stud the dumplings, then molded them into smaller balls for the photograph. Like Mrs. Maas, the two hundred Baton Rouge "old time" Jewish families, most of whom have German and Alsatian roots, prefer their food hot, and they like their matzah balls with some bite. In Baton Rouge there is much discussion over which is the correct and the best-tasting matzah ball. Some make these ecumenical dumplings with matzah meal only, while others use a combination of matzah and matzah meal, following recipes brought to this country over one hundred years ago. Most disdain the mild nutmeg and ginger, which were typically German and are found as spices in matzah-ball recipes in Charleston and elsewhere. All scorn Yankee matzah balls, which are too big and too soft.

—Joan Nathan, *Jewish Cooking in America.*
New York: Knopf, 1995, p. 399

Two Passover Menus from Jewish Cooking in America

Nineteenth-Century German Dinner

Stewed Fish à la Juive

Chicken Soup with Marrow Balls

Turkey with Chestnut Stuffing

Lemon Pecan Torte and Mississippi Praline Macaroons

Southern Seder

New Orleans or Charleston Chicken Soup

Cajun Matzah Balls

Georgian Fried Chicken

Greens

Sponge Cake with Strawberries

Jewish Cooking in America won not only the 1995 James Beard "Food of the Americas" Award but also the Julia Child Award for Best Cookbook of the Year from the IACP. Knopf published an expanded edition in 1998, and in 2001, the James Beard Foundation elected Nathan to its prestigious Who's Who list.

The book also helped Nathan land another PBS show, *Jewish Cooking in America with Joan Nathan*, which ran for 26 episodes during 1998–1999. Produced by Maryland Public Television and shown nationally, the show featured Nathan traveling across the country, cooking selected dishes from the book alongside celebrity Jewish chefs and cooks, including Daniel Boulud and Sheila Lukin, and Wolfgang Puck, who is a fan of Jewish cooking, as well as extraordinary home cooks. Nathan writes, "I think my favorite was 95-year-old Dora Falganik from Cleveland, Ohio, who had never been on TV before, was born in Russia, spoke English with a Yiddish accent and was an absolute natural. . . . There was also another woman named Eva Young who was a Holocaust survivor. She was in five different camps. We got all of her survivor friends, who weren't so old, together in the Catskills, and she cooked for them. So that was a good one. And there was a woman in Vermont who I thought was pretty good, too. She's 97 and still cooking a lot."[24]

America's Preeminent Jewish Food Expert

In 1997, Nathan revisited the Jewish holiday theme and published *The Jewish Holiday Baker*, with Schocken Books. Again, kosher and organized by holiday, the book features rich variants on traditional holiday breads and pastries—nine kinds of challah, honey and fruit cakes for Rosh Hashanah, hamentashen for Purim, as well as meringues and matzah cookies for Passover. Nathan writes of "challah-hopping" Jerusalem, visiting bakery after bakery to find ever more interesting varieties of the braided Sabbath bread. Her recipe for "Ultimate Challah" reveals the depth of tradition in Jewish baking, as well as its mutability: "Adapted from Brizel's Bakery in Jerusalem, the bread was perfected with the help of Jack Wayne of West Bloomfield Hills, Michigan, who comes from a long line of bakers in Lodz, Poland, once a center of Jewish customs and traditions."[25] Nathan's success with *Jewish Cooking in America*, the holiday cookbooks, her articles and TV appearances, and her two PBS series had made her truly the preeminent expert on Jewish food in America.

But Nathan also was interested in returning to the subject of Israeli cuisine. Two decades had passed since she had worked for Mayor Kollek. "The night of November 4, 1995," she writes, "when I learned of the assassination of Israel's prime minister, Itzhak Rabin, I felt compelled to write a book about the foods of modern Israel." For Nathan, Rabin was "an emblem of the vibrant, dynamic spirit of Israel, a blending of many cultures and ethnic and religious diversity. I wanted to capture that spirit through the medium I knew best—food and culinary traditions. I wanted to show the richness of Israel's past and present through its many cuisines."[26]

Israel had changed since Nathan first lived there in the early 1970s. *The Flavor of Jerusalem* focused specifically on the culinary and ethnic traditions of the holy city, but it also showed how politics and geography affected peoples' lives, and their food. *The Foods of Israel Today*, conversely, features cuisines from the entire country and all of its ethnic groups. Like the United States, Israel is a country of immigrants with an imperial past. The Turkish and British regimes left their stamp on Palestine, as did the Arabs and Jews who lived there before the creation of the state of Israel. In her introduction, Nathan provides a short history of Palestine and Israel from the mid-19th century, focusing primarily on its foodways, diets, and agriculture. The land of Israel has seen many changes. Once a desert with a few native crops such as dates and olives, it now plants grapes and apples in the Golan Heights and creates arable land through drainage and reclamation projects. Overcoming poverty, the environment, and political strife, Israelis have managed to create a nation with a diverse and exciting palate of flavors. As Nathan writes, "Through culinary haunts one can uncover the enormously exciting story of how these pioneers transformed a harsh land to one bursting with new produce and culture."[27]

As in her previous Jewish cookbooks, all the recipes in *The Foods of Israel Today* are kosher. The book follows Nathan's successful formula of recipes combined with biographical profiles, historical anecdotes, and quotations. Under her pen, Israel comes alive as a land where immigrants brought the best of their traditions and shared them with other newcomers. One of Nathan's themes is that foodways are not stagnant—they evolve over time and geography. Thus, the cuisines of the United States and Israel—both heavily influenced by some of the same immigrant groups (Jews and Germans, for example)—are completely different. Indeed, even some of the recipes from *The Flavor of Jerusalem*, like peppery Jerusalem kugel and citrus roast chicken, make a reappearance here, but have been tweaked and changed over the course of 30 years in Nathan's kitchen. Although many of the cooks she interviewed in her first book are long dead, Nathan finds plenty of cooks, politicians, and restaurateurs of surprisingly diverse backgrounds. The book received excellent critical attention and endorsements from major food personalities, including Sara Moulton, Daniel Boulud, Lynne Rossetto Kaspar, and Paula Wolfert, who called it a "major work."[28]

Nathan followed up *The Foods of Israel Today* with an expanded edition of *The Jewish Holiday Kitchen*. Now called *Joan Nathan's Jewish Holiday*

Cookbook, it capitalizes on her fame as America's preeminent Jewish cooking expert and combines the original book with *The Jewish Holiday Baker* in one integrated volume.

The New American Cooking

Yet, as acclaimed as *The Foods of Israel Today* was, it did not receive the same recognition as *Jewish Cooking in America*. For her next major project, Nathan shifted her focus again to the variety of American cooking. Like *Foods of Israel, The New American Cooking* (2005) functions as a kind of temporal update to her earlier work, *An American Folklife Cookbook*. Nathan traveled around the country, talking and eating with chefs and cooks about their work. Yet, instead of focusing on octogenarian home cooks, as she had previously in her study of regional American food, in her new book she reflected the shift in American culture toward a "foodie mentality," slow food, localism, and the organic movement. Instead of farmwives and firehouses, Nathan visited organic farms, small restaurants, suppliers, growers, and chefs who are at the leading edge of the organic movement. In this sense, *The New American Cooking* truly represents the way American cooking has changed in the 10 to 15 years since her last exploration of American ethnic and occupational cooking. The recipes are not kosher. They feature ingredients most Americans did not cook with 20 years ago, like cilantro, lemongrass, and free-range meats and poultry. They reflect new immigrant streams, the ingenuity and creativity of chefs and food producers, and, above all, the changing American palate in response to these sweeping cultural changes. Again organized by course and guided by Judith Jones of Knopf, *The New American Cooking* juxtaposes biographies, stories, and anecdotes with recipes. The book presents contemporary American cooking at its very best and most inclusive.

The New American Cooking was a runaway success and netted Nathan her third James Beard Award in 2006 (winning in the Food of the Americas, the same category she won for *Jewish Cooking in America*) and the IACP Award for Best Cookbook of the Year for 2005.

When one of Nathan's daughters saw a copy of *Jewish Cooking in America* featured on an episode of the hit television show, *Sex and the City*, she remarked, "Mom, you've arrived!"[29] But Nathan had arrived long before that. She worked with legendary editor Jones. She once threw a birthday party for Julia Child. And, in 2009, Nathan famously nearly choked to death on a piece of chicken at a party she was hosting for celebrity chefs at her home in Washington, D.C. As she wryly observes, "You would think that a house full of chefs would be the safest place if you were choking. But, unfortunately, more people have heard of the Heimlich maneuver than actually know how to administer it."[30] With Alice Waters frantically searching for someone who could perform the maneuver, and Nathan convinced she was about to die, "ruining her own party," she was saved by timely intervention, and a proper Heimlich, from superstar chef and host of Bravo TV's hit show *Top Chef*, Tom Colicchio.

CONCLUSION

Today, Nathan lives and works in Washington, D.C., with her husband and three children. She is researching and writing a book on the culinary lives of the Jews of France. If the hallmark of her body of work is the marriage of oral history, biography, history, and food, it is also the ways in which these foods change over time, even in her own books. Nathan is more than an ethnographer of Jewish and immigrant food in America and Israel. She is more than a food writer. With her fascination for the flavor of human life, she is a true icon of American cooking.

NOTES

1. Library of Congress Webcast, Book Fest 2007, National Book Festival in Washington, DC. "Joan Nathan" http://www.loc.gov/today/cyberlc/feature_wdesc.php?rec=4190

2. Irene Sax, "A Chat with Joan Nathan," Epicurious.com, http://www.epicurious.com/articlesguides/chefsexperts/interviews/joannathaninterview

3. Joan Nathan, "For a Daughter, Rosh Hashanah Is a Holiday Frozen in Time," *The New York Times* (September 24, 2003) http://www.nytimes.com/2003/09/24/dining/for-a-daughter-rosh-hashana-is-a-holiday-frozen-in-time.html?scp=1&sq=%22joan%20nathan%22%20%22for%20a%20daughter%22&st=cse

4. Nathan, "For a Daughter."

5. Nathan, "For a Daughter."

6. Joan Nathan, "An Italian Christmas Eve in Providence," in *An American Folklife Cookbook* (New York: Schocken Books, 1984), 279.

7. Sax, "A Chat with Joan Nathan."

8. Library of Congress Webcast.

9. Joan Nathan and Judy Stacey Goldman, *The Flavor of Jerusalem* (Boston: Little, Brown and Company, 1974), author bio.

10. Scott Wilson, "Longtime Mayor of Jerusalem Dies at 95," *The Washington Post* (January 2, 2007) http://www.washingtonpost.com/wp-dyn/content/article/2007/01/02/AR2007010200139.html; Ronen Bergman, YNet News.com, March 29, 2007 http://www.ynetnews.com/articles/0,7340,L-3382779,00.html

11. Joan Nathan, *The Foods of Israel Today* (New York: Alfred A. Knopf, 2001), 3.

12. Sax, "A Chat with Joan Nathan."

13. Nathan and Goldman, *The Flavor of Jerusalem*, 3.

14. Review in *Publishers Weekly,* cited on Amazon.com.

15. Sax, "A Chat with Joan Nathan."

16. Melissa Denchak, "Interview with TV Chef Joan Nathan," FoodandWine.com, n.d. http://www.foodandwine.com/articles/tv-chef-interview-joan-nathan

17. Joan Nathan, *An American Folklife Cookbook* (New York: Schocken Books, 1984), 15.

18. Nathan, *An American Folklife Cookbook*, 58.

19. Marian Burros, "Cooking," *The New York Times* (December 2, 1984) http://www.nytimes.com/1984/12/02/books/cooking.html?scp=13&sq=joan+nathan&st=nyt

20. In 1990 the R. T. French Tastemaker Award became the James Beard Awards, administered by the James Beard Foundation. http://www.jamesbeard.org/index .php?q=james_beard_awards_policies_procedures

21. Joan Nathan, *Jewish Cooking in America* (New York: Alfred A. Knopf, 1994), xii.

22. Nathan, *Jewish Cooking in America*, 163–179.

23. Nathan, *Jewish Cooking in America*, 256.

24. Denchak, "Interview with TV Chef Joan Nathan," http://www.foodandwine .com/articles/tv-chef-interview-joan-nathan

25. Joan Nathan, *The Jewish Holiday Baker* (New York: Schocken Books, 1997), 20.

26. Nathan, *The Foods of Israel Today*, 3.

27. Nathan, *The Foods of Israel Today*, 6.

28. Nathan, *The Foods of Israel Today*, jacket copy.

29. Library of Congress Webcast.

30. Joan Nathan, "A Heimlich in Every Pot," *The New York Times* (February 3, 2009) http://www.nytimes.com/2009/02/04/opinion/04nathan.html?_r=1

FURTHER READING

Jones, Judith. *The Tenth Muse: My Life in Food*. New York: Anchor, 2008.

Nathan, Joan. *An American Folklife Cookbook*. New York: Schocken Books, 1984.

Nathan, Joan. *The Foods of Israel Today*. New York: Knopf, 2001.

Nathan, Joan. *Jewish Cooking in America*. New York: Alfred A. Knopf, 1994.

Nathan, Joan. *Joan Nathan's Jewish Holiday Cookbook*. Rev. ed. New York: Schocken Books, 2004.

Nathan, Joan. *The New American Cooking*. New York: Alfred A. Knopf, 2005.

Nathan, Joan, and Judy Stacey Goldman. *The Flavor of Jerusalem*. Boston: Little, Brown and Company, 1974.

Elizabeth S. Demers

World-renowned chef Jacques Pépin signs a copy of his book *Jacques Pépin: Fast Food My Way*, at a dinner in his honor at Bistro 110 in Chicago, October 5, 2004. (AP/Wide World Photos)

Jacques Pépin

Jacques Pépin, one of America's best-known and most gifted chefs, has been a culinary icon since the mid-1970s, both in the United States and abroad. He has hosted more than 10 highly popular PBS cooking shows and authored more than 20 books, including a best-selling autobiography, *The Apprentice: My Life in the Kitchen* (2003). Known for his passion for culinary technique and the use of fresh ingredients, Pépin has enjoyed a successful career as a professional chef in France and the United States. A former columnist for *The New York Times*, he writes a quarterly column for *Food & Wine* magazine, serves as Dean of Special Programs at the French Culinary Institute in New York City, and is an adjunct faculty member in the Culinary Arts Program at Boston University.

EARLY YEARS

Childhood

Pépin was born on December 18, 1935, in Bourg-en-Bresse, near Lyon, France, where his father, Jean-Victor, a cabinetmaker, and mother Jeanne raised three sons during and after World War II. While his father was away in the military, his young mother did her best to provide and care for their young children. To make ends meet, she worked as a waitress in a nearby hotel restaurant during the day and spent the evenings cooking and sewing clothing for her family.

Pépin's father returned to his family when his tour of duty ended, but shortly afterward, the Nazis arrived in Bourg-en-Bresse in search of local men to work in the German labor camps. One morning Pépin's father was stopped on the street and accused of being a member of *le maquis*, the French Resistance. He and several other men were detained and held at gunpoint for most of the day. Two of the men were taken away and killed; the remaining men were sent home, Pépin's father among them. Realizing that he could not remain in Bourg, he joined the Resistance and moved to the mountains with other *maquis* fighters. Once again, Pépin was without his father for an extended period of time.

With food scarce during the war, particularly in cities and towns, Pépin's mother sent him and his older brother Roland to do summer work on a farm in the Alps. The boys helped with chores and experienced the wonders of country living, which included exposure to foods they had never known in their hometown. Two of the local mountain communities regularly came together for a "bread-baking day," to use the large, common oven and to socialize with neighbors and friends. Young Pépin remembered it as being as exciting as a carnival, and that wood-fired oven would leave a lasting impression on him as he began to develop his passion for food.

School Days

Pépin's first formal schooling came in the form of a Jesuit-run boarding school, Lycée St. Louis, where corporal punishment was the norm. He eventually got used to the strict discipline, but he never got used to the terrible food served at the school. To compensate for and supplement the meager meals, he quickly became adept at bartering for the food that his fellow students received from home.

When the war ended, most Frenchmen still endured food rationing. Despite the food shortages, Pépin's mother decided to open a restaurant. Though not an experienced cook, when business was slow she had watched the chef at L'Hôtel de Bourgogne where she worked. The Pépins could not afford to purchase a successful business, so she chose a struggling restaurant that was on the verge of closing. The family packed up and moved into the rundown building and began the task of putting Hôtel L'Amour into livable condition.

Pépin and his brothers helped in the restaurant kitchen before and after school, peeling vegetables and overseeing the hens that provided fresh eggs. Pépin also learned the importance of "having respect for ingredients."[1] Other chores included tending his mother's garden, where he learned about the variety of herbs and flowers that could be used in cooking. As the restaurant flourished, Pépin became more experienced in the kitchen, but the hotel was sold and the Pépins were forced to find another location. Their new restaurant, Chez Pépin, opened in 1947 in Lyon. Now 12 years of age, Pépin attended the local school during the day and worked in the restaurant kitchen during his free time.

Within a few years the restaurant turned into a profitable business. Having improved and refined her culinary skills, Pépin's mother decided that it was time to move on to the next challenge. She sold Chez Pépin and moved the family to a more upscale neighborhood in Lyon. Their new restaurant, Le Pélican, soon opened, and Pépin began spending more time working and learning in the restaurant kitchen. It was during this time that Pépin began to consider pursuing a career as a chef. At age 14, he began a three-year apprenticeship at Le Grand Hôtel de l'Europe in Bourg-en-Bresse, France.

Training

Pépin and his fellow apprentices worked from 8:30 in the morning until 10:30 at night, seven days a week. They received no pay but earned four days off at the end of each month. Though the days were long, Pépin applied himself and was gradually promoted through the various stations of the kitchen. His culinary education consisted of watching the chef prepare and cook the restaurant's meals. No recipes, books, or other types of formal instruction were used. Pépin's culinary skills improved solely through observation and practice, and finally, after one full year, he was deemed ready to begin working at the stove. Several months later, Pépin was promoted to senior apprentice and given responsibility of the kitchen. Gradually, he began to be treated as a colleague rather than a child, and his confidence grew.

In the spring of 1952, Pépin officially completed his apprenticeship and was ready to begin as a chef trainee. He obtained his first position that summer, at L'Hôtel d'Albion, located in the hills above Aix-les-Bains between Italy and France. There he shared a room in the hotel with four other chef trainees, working 14-hour days and feeding 400 people daily, seven days a week. The pace was much more intense than Pépin had experienced as an apprentice, and he was exposed to foods from other regions of France as well as different techniques and dishes under the tutelage of the chef.

When the hotel closed for the season, Pépin obtained a job at L'Hôtel Restaurant de la Paix, located near Geneva. He was in charge of his own kitchen and could finally cook using his own ideas. His confidence grew, and by age 17, Pépin had grown restless, realizing that he was at a crossroads in his career as a chef. After much deliberation, he returned to Lyon to work briefly in his mother's restaurant until he could locate a position in Paris.

Over the course of 10 years, Pépin worked in restaurants in Normandy and Paris, honing his skills and gaining valuable experience. One opportunity that provided him with a wealth of knowledge and experience presented itself in the form of Le Plaza Athenée, where he worked under the tutelage of Lucien Diat. Chef Diat was a perfectionist and ran a kitchen in the "traditional French *brigade de cuisine*"; once again, Pépin had to master each station before he was allowed to cook.[2]

All was well in Pépin's world at Le Plaza Athenée until the day he received a draft notice for the Algerian War. Pépin was assigned to work as a military chef. During his tour of duty, he worked as a chef to three prime ministers of France: Felix Gaillard, Pierre Pfimlin, and Charles de Gaulle. It was during this time that he met his future best friend, Jean-Claude Szurdak, a gifted pastry chef and cook. Upon discharge from the military, Pépin returned to Le Plaza Athenée, where he began to consider the next steps in his career as a chef. In the end, he decided to obtain a sponsor and immigrate to the United States. Not long afterward, the wheels were set in motion.

THE UNITED STATES

In 1959, Pépin obtained his green card in preparation for a short-term move to New York City. Though his plan was to experience the American culinary world for a year or so, Pépin remained in the United States and never lived in France again. He arrived in September of 1959 and moved into the spare room provided for him by his sponsor, Ernest Lutringhauser.

In a short time, Pépin began his job as chef at Le Pavillon, run by executive chef Pierre Franey and long considered the best French restaurant in the United States. Anxious to make a good impression at his interview, Pépin gave Chef Franey the certificates from each restaurant he had been employed in as well as his official papers from the Gaillard and de Gaulle governments. However, Franey did not care about the certificates and credentials. The fact that

Pépin was French and was a chef was enough for him, and he hired Jacques on the spot.

Pépin soon found that the restaurant world in America differed significantly from that in France. Work arrangements were less structured and the restaurant was far less sophisticated. Fewer chefs were employed there, and they often worked at more than one station in the kitchen. For the first time in his culinary career, Pépin was paid a living wage, earning $86 per week compared with the $140 he had received monthly in Paris. He was soon able to move into his own apartment and return to school to further his education and improve his English-language skills.

Pépin enrolled in the English for Foreign Students program at Columbia University, and although it was not an accredited course of study, it helped him improve his English. On days off, he often went to the Paramount Theatre in Times Square, sitting through several movies at a time to listen to and learn his newly adopted language.

Several months after arriving in the United States, Pépin received news that his best friend and cooking partner from the Charles de Gaulle days, Jean-Claude Szurdak, had been discharged from duty in the Algerian War and was coming to New York. His ship arrived in late June of 1960 and Pépin was there to meet him at the dock.

Szurdak quickly obtained a chef position at La Toque Blanche, which was located on the first floor of their apartment building. The roommates shared household chores and took turns cooking meals. However, having grown up shopping for food in specialty shops and open-air markets, the local A&P supermarket came as a surprise. Many of the vegetables and herbs they were used to buying in France were difficult to find or nonexistent and were sold in containers, not fresh.

In 1960, six months after his arrival in the United States, a friend of Pépin's, Helen McCully, who lived nearby and was the food editor of *House Beautiful* and *McCall's* magazines, asked him to come over to her apartment. When he arrived, she gave him a box filled with typed pages, which turned out to be a cookbook transcript. McCully told him that the manuscript had been written by a woman living in Cambridge, Massachusetts. She asked Pépin if he would read it and give her his opinion.

As soon as Pépin returned to his apartment, he and his roommate began reading the manuscript. When they had finished, they realized that it contained the training and knowledge they had received as apprentices but was broken into simple, understandable language and instruction that any novice cook could follow. The title of the manuscript was *Mastering the Art of French Cooking* (1961), and its author was Julia Child.

McCully believed the manuscript was a work of art and later informed Pépin that "the author is a Californian, and she's a very big woman with a terrible voice." She said, "She will come here and you'll cook for her."[3] That was how Pépin and Child met and became friends, and they remained close friends until her death in 2004.

RESTAURANTS

Howard Johnson's

Less than a year after arriving in the United States, Pépin's career at Le Pavillon ended. The restaurant closed after the staff walked out in protest of years without salary increases and unpaid overtime. Pépin's services as a French chef were still in demand, and he was approached by Howard D. Johnson and Joseph P. Kennedy, both former customers of Le Pavillon. His options came down to helping to improve the food served at Johnson's chain of restaurants or work as a future White House chef. In the end, Pépin decided to join Howard Johnson, where he could experience a truly American work environment.

At Howard Johnson's, Pépin was given free rein to test recipes and experiment with new ideas. Johnson attended every test kitchen tasting and provided feedback on all the dishes he was served. His goal was to improve the food being served at Hojo restaurants and also introduce new menu items that would please the American palate. Pépin's experiments began with smaller quantities of food and gradually increased through trial and error so that each recipe could feed thousands of customers. He was also given the opportunity to test the latest kitchen equipment and technology that might help to provide consistent food quality.

After completing two years of study at Columbia University, Pépin had finished his English for Foreign Students program. However, he still had no high school diploma, so he decided to take the entrance examination to Columbia's School of General Studies. After successfully passing the exam, he went on to complete a series of preparatory classes and eventually gained admittance to the school. He completed his B.A. in philosophy in 1970 and went on to obtain an M.A. in 18th-century French literature at Columbia University in 1972.

Pépin remained at Howard Johnson's throughout the 1960s, an experience that taught him about American culture and eating habits. He found that in the United States, chefs could experiment and introduce new foods to their customers without criticism. If customers liked the taste of the food, they were satisfied.

While employed at Howard Johnson's, Pépin began to spend some of his winter weekends skiing with friends in the Catskill Mountains of New York, where he met his future wife, Gloria. An accomplished skier herself and member of the Ski Patrol, she pretended to be inexperienced on the slopes in order to obtain personal skiing lessons from Pépin. Five months after they began dating, Pépin proposed. They were married in September of 1966 and welcomed daughter Claudine into their lives on December 15, 1967.

La Potagerie

Pépin ended his career at Howard Johnson's in 1970 to open his own restaurant, La Potagerie, in New York City. His modest-priced soup restaurant became a great success, and Pépin felt he was on top of the world. However, a serious accident occurred on the evening of July 21, 1974. While Pépin was driving home after work one night, a deer suddenly appeared on the highway, and as he slammed on the brakes to avoid hitting the animal, his car spun out of control and crashed. His injuries included numerous broken bones: back, pelvis, arm, leg, and both hips. His prognosis was poor, and it was doubtful that he would ever walk again. Pépin was hospitalized for more than three months, where he endured pain, surgery, and physical therapy. Remarkably, he left the hospital in December of that year and was back at home for the Christmas holidays.

OTHER ENDEAVORS

A Teaching Career

After the accident, Pépin was anxious to return to his duties at La Potagerie. However, he found that the restaurant was running efficiently and his daily presence there was no longer critical. He also realized that as a result of his injuries from the accident, he was no longer able to withstand the routine 14-hour workdays of a chef.

At about that same time, Pépin received a phone call from a man who had been referred to him by Julia Child. His wife wanted to learn French cooking and he was hoping that Pépin would agree to fly to Michigan to tutor his wife for $400 a day. Thus began Pépin's teaching career, which ultimately took him all over the world and gave him an opportunity to experience many different foreign cuisines. Over time, one teaching opportunity led to another, and in 1988 he joined the faculty of the French Culinary Institute in New York City, where he now serves as Dean of Special Programs.

Several years later, still frustrated that the culinary arts continued to be considered a trade school education rather than an academic discipline, Pépin and Child approached the president of Boston University with an idea to create a program that would approach food from social, historical, and anthropological perspectives. Their efforts paid off, and in 1992 Boston University established the Master of Liberal Arts Program in Gastronomy. Pépin was immediately hired as an adjunct faculty member, and he continues to teach in the program.

COOKBOOKS

In 1975, Pépin published his first cookbook, *Jacques Pépin: A French Chef Cooks at Home.* As an instructor, he observed the difficulties that many of his students struggled with as they attempted to learn basic culinary techniques, so he made numerous notations that he kept filed away. These would become useful as he continued his writing career.

Not long afterward, Pépin decided that the time had come to write his next book, *La Technique* (1978), which would include basic cooking techniques gleaned from his copious teaching notes. Initially, Simon and Schuster was not interested in publishing it. Pépin's book was unique for its time, and publishers did not believe that readers would be interested in a step-by-step instructional guide on French culinary technique. They eventually issued the book in paperback format. It became a huge success and remained in print for over 20 years.

Pépin has always been passionate in his belief that "simple principles, once mastered, enable you to cook well every day and to improvise using common sense and whatever ingredients are on hand to develop your own delicious creations."[4] Because he had so many notes and ideas left over from *La Technique*, Pépin wrote a second volume titled *La Méthode* (1979). Both titles were later compiled into one volume and reorganized for ease of use under the title *Jacques Pépin's Complete Techniques* (2001). Child pronounced it "a standard kitchen item the world over . . . there has never been anything like it anywhere."[5] Pépin's *Complete Techniques* includes more than 1,000 preparations and recipes, which are demonstrated in thousands of step-by-step photographs. It continues to be used as a textbook in culinary programs all over the United States.

At about this same time, Time/Life Books began publishing a culinary series entitled *Foods of the World* and wanted to include a volume on classic French cooking. Pépin and his friend Chef Pierre Franey were asked to choose the dishes for the book and then write the recipes. But there was one major problem: Neither Pépin nor Franey had learned their trade through written instruction or recipes. The problem was eventually solved by having Pépin cook each of the chosen dishes in the studio kitchen while editorial assistants shadowed him and painstakingly wrote down every step, measurement, and technique. As each dish was completed, photographers came in to shoot pictures from various vantage points. Though Pépin did not know it at the time, this experience would serve him well later in his culinary career.

TELEVISION SHOWS

The success of *Jacques Pépin's Complete Techniques* resulted in an opportunity to turn the book into a television show. The cooking series, *The Complete Pépin*, debuted on public television (PBS) in 1997 to critical acclaim. It led to a number of additional TV shows, including the 1999 PBS series that he cohosted with Child—*Julia and Jacques Cooking at Home*—which garnered them a Daytime Emmy Award in 2001. What made it unique from Pépin's previous cooking shows was its basic approach. No recipes were completed before taping, there was no script, and no rehearsals were held. Instead, he and Child approached the show with their individual ideas on what to cook given the thematic ingredients provided during each episode. They cooked, bantered, disagreed, and improvised on the show, creating a unique experience for the hosts as well as their audience.

Reflecting on the early years of their collaboration during a recent interview, Pépin said that "people loved Julia because she was very straightforward, and she didn't put on any airs, or have any pretension. The first times I did TV with her she'd tell me that I had to lighten up, that I tried to do too many things, and she was right, certainly. We wanted a series that was entertaining and to have a good time, but at the end of each show she would ask, 'What did they learn?' She taught confidence. And she was inspired by all kinds of people."[6]

Among Pépin's other TV shows are *Jacques Pépin's Kitchen*, which included his daughter Claudine as cohost; *Fast Food My Way*; and *More Fast Food My Way* (2008), which has generated much interest and discussion regarding the subject of fast food. To Pépin it means cooking that is easy and fast to prepare, as opposed to the conventional definition of it being processed food. "I use fresh and, occasionally, canned ingredients but certainly never processed food full of all kinds of chemicals. I try to use organic ingredients whenever possible. A simple tomato salad with fresh basil and red onion, for example, is a fast-food recipe as I define the term."[7]

Homemade versus Store Bought

Although I commend anyone who will take hours preparing a dish from scratch, I'm not a snob about cooking—I know that "homemade" doesn't necessarily translate into superlative food. Most French people would not think of baking their own bread or croissants or making their own paté, because these items are readily available and of good quality at local markets.

—Jacques Pépin, *Fast Food My Way*.
New York: Houghton Mifflin, 2004, p. 2

Pépin's television cooking series have been tremendously successful and, along with his many cookbooks, have garnered him fans from around the world. Pépin's vast experience, French influences, and superb technique have created a modern American cuisine based on the best ingredients and the love and sharing of good food.

AWARDS AND HONORS

Over the years, Pépin has been recognized for his many contributions to the culinary arts as a chef, teacher, and writer. When asked whether he enjoyed being a culinary instructor as much as cooking alone, Pépin replied, "Yes, certainly. Food by definition is about sharing. The sharing of knowledge is like the sharing of food. I get a great deal of gratification by passing my knowledge of food on to others."[8] He continued, "I have hundreds of memories of Julia Child, but they're all related to having drinks together, drinking, eating, and sharing food and having fun with other friends, you know? She was great for that."[9]

Pépin has received two of the French government's highest honors: Chevalier de L'Ordre des Arts et des Lettres in 1997 and Chevalier de L'Ordre de Mérite Agricole in 1992; and in 2004, he received France's ultimate civilian recognition, the Legion d'Honneur. The Culinary Trust created the Jacques Pépin Scholarship Fund, which provides an opportunity for high school minority students to study professional culinary techniques, and in 2008, Pépin received a Lifetime Achievement Award from the James Beard Foundation.

CONCLUSION

In his spare time Pépin enjoys cooking and painting. He lives in Madison, Connecticut, with his wife. When asked recently what advice he would give a beginning cook, Pépin replied, "Have a glass of wine before you start cooking."[10]

NOTES

1. Jacques Pépin, *The Apprentice: My Life in the Kitchen* (New York: Houghton Mifflin, 2003), 24–25.

2. Pépin, *The Apprentice*, 138.

3. Pépin, *The Apprentice*, 145.

4. Pépin, *The Apprentice*, 253–254.

5. Pépin, *The Apprentice*, 250–251.

6. Jacques Pépin, "More Fast Food My Way: About Jacques Pépin," *KQED*, http://jacquespepin.com/ 2009

7. Jacques Pépin, "Jacques Pépin: Fast Food My Way," *KQED*, http://www.kqed .org/w/jpfastfood/jacquespepin.html 2004

8. Jacques Pépin, "Jacques Pépin Celebrates! Conversation with Jacques," *KQED*, http://www.kqed.org/w/jacquespepin/conversationjacques.html 2002

9. "Chef Jacques Pépin on Food and the Power of Memory," ABC News *Nightline*, http://abcnews.go.com/Nightline/chef-jacques-pepin-tells-story-dazzling-career/story?id=8461562 2009

10. Jacques Pépin, "One on One with Jacques Pépin" (Interview) http://www.kqed .org/support/membership/guide/webexclusives/article-jpepin.jsp 2008

FURTHER READING

Child, Julia, and Jacques Pépin. *Julia and Jacques: Cooking at Home*. New York: Alfred A. Knopf, 1999.

Hamilton, Dorothy, and Patric Kuh. "Jacques Pépin." In *Chef's Story: 27 Chefs Talk about What Got Them into the Kitchen*. New York: Harper Perennial, 2008, 175–183.

PBS. Julia Child: "Lessons with Master Chefs." *Meet the Chefs*. http://www.pbs.org/juliachild/meet/pepin.html# 2001

Pépin, Jacques. *Jacques Pépin's Complete Techniques*. New York: Black Dog and Leventhal, 2001.

Pépin, Jacques. *The Apprentice: My Life in the Kitchen*. New York: Houghton Mifflin, 2003.

Pépin, Jacques. *Chez Jacques: Traditions and Rituals of a Cook*. New York: Stewart, Tabori & Chang, 2007.

Pépin, Jacques. "More Fast Food My Way." *KQED*. http://jacquespepin.com/ 2009

Lenora Berendt

American chef Paul Prudhomme poses in the kitchen of Jerusalem's convention center, March 18, 1996. Prudhomme and 12 other of the world's greatest chefs prepared a 12-course kosher feast as part of the celebration of Jerusalem's 3,000th anniversary. Prudhomme, known for his Cajun dishes, prepared medallions of veal "Hazrey," specially created for the dinner. (AP/Wide World Photos)

Paul Prudhomme

For those who follow celebrity chefs and cooking television, "Bam!" and "Kick it up a notch!" are expressions that connote a fiery, flavorful, and fun kind of food experience, evoking images perhaps of alligators and swamps and heavy Cajun accents. Cajun food is so ubiquitous today that many people are unaware of its origins or that it is much more than the Cajun popcorn shrimp or spicy Cajun chicken sandwiches offered at many fast-food outlets. However, without Chef Paul Prudhomme, it is unlikely that so many would enjoy the rich, complex, and spicy flavors that are the hallmarks of Louisiana Cajun cuisine. Chef Prudhomme was also one of the first chefs in the United States, along with Alice Waters, to champion the use of fresh, local, seasonal ingredients.

EARLY YEARS

Birthplace in Cajun Country

Chef Prudhomme's rise to fame, fortune, and role as king of Louisiana cuisine is an unlikely, but quintessentially American, success story. Born July 13, 1940, in Opelousas, Louisiana, in the heart of Cajun country, Prudhomme was the youngest of 13 children. Opelousas is the third oldest city in Louisiana, founded by French settlers in 1720. It is the seat of St. Landry Parish, with a population of approximately 25,000 people. It is also the hometown of Tony Chachere, maker of the eponymous seasoning mix that sits in most Louisiana kitchens. Opelousas was named the zydeco capital of the world in 2000 and was also home to Cajun zydeco music king Clifton Chenier.

The Prudhommes were one of the oldest settler families in the area, arriving from France to what was then Spanish territory in 1763 and settling on a Spanish land grant of 50,000 acres. France had ceded the territory to Spain just one year earlier, and it is likely that the Prudhomme land grant was part of an original program of immigration promoted by the French. Prudhomme's maternal ancestors came from Canada, some of the original Acadians, or Cajuns, who were forced to migrate to Louisiana after the British conquered Acadia. The early Prudhommes helped establish the Catholic church and school in Opelousas and arranged for a priest to come from France.

A Rocky Beginning

By the time Prudhomme was born, the family had endured hard times for several generations, and Prudhomme's father, Eli Prudhomme Sr., was a share-cropper farming on borrowed land. He paid out a full third of the profits from growing cotton and sweet potatoes to the landlord. To make ends meet, the family raised vegetables and animals for household use. This was no small matter in such a large family; just feeding them took a lot of work. In Prudhomme's earliest memories, the family had nothing. The house he grew up in had no gas or electricity and his mother, Hazel Reed Prudhomme, cooked meals on a wood-burning stove. Everyone in the family helped out on the farm and gathered foodstuffs from around their home. The family ate squirrels, rabbits, and frog legs brought in by Prudhomme's elder brothers, chickens and their eggs raised on the farm, and crayfish from the nearby swamp.

Prudhomme's job was to help his mother out in the garden and the kitchen. By the time he was seven, when his eldest sister married, he was helping his mother cook every meal. He learned firsthand from her about the power of food and feeding people. Standing on a wooden box at the stove, Prudhomme would watch over the pots and pans cooking, calling out to his mother when the steam started to change color or the noise from frying oil changed, things his mother taught him to look out for and that became ingrained in his technique when he later cooked in restaurants. Prudhomme credits his mother with teaching him the importance of fresh, seasonal ingredients, something that chefs today are "rediscovering." The family had no refrigeration, so vegetables, fish, and meats went into the pot within hours of being harvested or caught. In later years, Prudhomme wondered why he could not get his potatoes to taste like those his mother made. He then realized that it was not his technique but the freshness of the potato. He carried this lesson into all of his cooking.

The Prudhommes farmed a large amount of land, and eventually family fortunes improved. They were able to put in a propane tank and electricity, which allowed his mother to abandon the wood-fired stove. The family could also afford to eat the occasional meal out, and drive-in restaurants both fit the budget and became treasured family outings. They also laid the foundation for Prudhomme's first restaurant. When he finished high school in 1957 at age 17, he opened Big Daddy O's Patio in Opelousas. Big Daddy O's was not his only new commitment; he also married his high school sweetheart that same year.

Nine months after opening Big Daddy O's Patio, Prudhomme's first business venture, and his first marriage, had failed. The restaurant failure was a critical event that would influence him for the rest of his life. Prudhomme recalls, "My mom and dad had these old-time, really high-back rockers. I sat in one of those rockers for a day and a half, just rocking and thinking. My conclusion was, 'I can't handle all this at one time, so let's make some choices.' And the choice was to be in the restaurant business."[1] Prudhomme was $1,500 in debt and heartbroken, but he remained determined to stay in the restaurant business and make a success of it. He paid off his debts and opened another restaurant. That one also failed. His next two restaurants failed. Prudhomme had opened four unsuccessful restaurants in a row, at a very young age, and yet he was not ready to throw in the towel.

With the easy enthusiasm of someone so young, Prudhomme decided that moving to the "big city" might bring more opportunities. He moved to New Orleans, where he worked as a busboy, cook, and magazine salesman. His magazine sales job took him out West, where he eventually landed behind a restaurant stove. He cooked all sorts of food, everything except his native Louisiana cuisine, for almost 10 years. Most of that time was spent in Colorado, but his cooking jobs took him everywhere from truck stops to resorts to an Indian reservation. He worked with chefs of every professional and ethnic background, learning their techniques while also sharing his own food heritage by cooking Cajun and Creole dishes for them, sometimes getting the chance to serve a dish to customers.

During this time Prudhomme took to making his own spice mixes and adding them surreptitiously to whatever he was cooking. People liked it, asking what he had added to the dish to make it so alive. He began to give away little baggies filled with seasonings to his favorite customers, a practice he would continue later at K-Paul's, his first spectacularly successful restaurant. Eventually K-Paul's customer requests for his spice mixes became so numerous that Prudhomme started a new company, Magic Seasonings, to produce and market his seasoning mixes commercially.

With those early positive reactions to his food and flavors from people across the country, Prudhomme began to realize how unique Louisiana cuisine was. He came to see that he found joy not only in cooking the Cajun and Creole dishes he grew up eating, but also in watching other people eat and love these dishes. Twelve years after leaving Louisiana, he decided that his home state was the place to cook, not only because he wanted to help keep Cajun food culture alive but also because he thought that food and cooking were most appreciated in his home state.

RESTAURANTS

Commander's Palace

Returning to Louisiana set the stage for Prudhomme's rise to culinary stardom. He arrived back in New Orleans in 1970 and took a job as a sous-chef in the restaurant of Le Pavillon Hotel. Soon after, a city councilman, Clarence Dupuy, convinced Prudhomme to help him open his new restaurant, Maison du Puy. While chef at the Maison du Puy, Prudhomme met K Hinrichs, a slim blond who worked in the front as a waitress and they started dating, and fell in love. K was to play a vital role in his future success. In 1975 Prudhomme became chef at the famous New Orleans eatery Commander's Palace and K followed, again working the front of house. Owned and operated by Adelaide, Dottie, Ella, Dick, and John Brennan, Commander's Palace was known for its white tablecloth service and impeccable and refined Creole cuisine.

Prudhomme's rural Cajun roots and the refined Creole traditions of the Brennan family made for true culinary electricity. Chef Prudhomme and the Brennans began to experiment and introduced twists on the old classics. Ella Brennan called it "Haute Creole"; patrons at Commander's Palace called it delicious. Prudhomme reinterpreted and refined classic Creole cuisine for contemporary tastes, adding in his special Cajun flavors and techniques. Combining these two culinary traditions was a revolutionary idea.[2]

For people outside of Louisiana, the difference between Creole and Cajun foods is often a source of confusion. Prudhomme calls Cajun cuisine simple, hearty cooking, originally brought from southern France by settlers to Nova Scotia and then to Louisiana with the Acadians. Along the way the Acadians learned from Native Americans how to use a variety of wild ingredients—such as bay laurel leaves, filé powder from the sassafras tree, and a wild variety of different peppers like cayenne and bird's eye—and incorporated those flavors into their cuisine. Creole cuisine, on the other hand, began in New Orleans and is a mixture of French, Spanish, Italian, American Indian, and African tastes. Creole cuisine developed in the kitchens of the wealthy as cooks changed their styles of cooking to fit the tastes of whoever employed them. Creole cooking is often described as more sophisticated and complex than Cajun cooking, as city cooking versus down-home country cooking.

When Prudhomme successfully combined Creole and Cajun at the upscale Creole restaurant, it was something no one had ever done before. Only the freshest ingredients were used, from quails raised on nearby country farms to fish caught the night before they were served. Salads featuring traditional Cajun ingredients such as duck or crawfish were added to the menu.[3] Native pecans and homegrown vegetables became the standard at Commander's Palace. Prudhomme brought incredible creativity to the kitchen, and diners sat up and took notice. According to Ella Brennan, in the 1950s everything in the kitchen had been frozen and prepackaged. Even 20 years later, Prudhomme was one of the few chefs going directly to farmers and producers to get his ingredients. Prudhomme remembers meeting organic food maven Alice Waters when she came to dine at Commander's Palace and the excitement at finding a kindred spirit. "I had never heard anybody be fanatical like I was," he said.[4] Both he and Waters were raising their own chickens, growing their own vegetables, and going directly to the farms to get the freshest ingredients possible.

K-Paul's Kitchen

In 1979, Prudhomme and K opened K-Paul's Louisiana Kitchen, the name a combination of both their first names and a testimony to their partnership. Prudhomme continued to work at Commander's Palace. He was making a good salary, but the couple were not sure their small restaurant could support them financially. Prudhomme and Frank Brigtsen, the chef he and K had hired to man K-Paul's stoves, would work on daily menus first thing in the morning, trying out new dishes to see what would work. Prudhomme would then go off to do lunch at Commander's Palace. According to Brigtsen, Prudhomme opened K-Paul's for K "because they had fallen in love and he wanted to do something with her, [and because] he wanted a place his family could come to town and eat at and feel comfortable."[5]

Prudhomme and talented young chef Brigtsen turned out innovative Louisiana cuisine. K worked the front of house, creating a welcoming atmosphere infused with her personality. She was known to place gold stars on the cheeks of diners who finished their plates and chide those who did not. Located at 416 Chartres Street in New Orleans's famed French Quarter, K-Paul's quickly generated a buzz throughout New Orleans, a city known for its love affair with food. Word spread that the chef at Commander's Palace had his own place where one could buy dinner for $5 to $6.

In his own restaurant, Prudhomme had more freedom than ever before to experiment with flavors and techniques. Shrimp and crabmeat au gratin served in eggplant pirogues (shaped like the Cajun fishing boats of the same name) and panéed (breaded) rabbit with tasso (smoked Cajun ham) sauce greeted diners perusing the menu. Prudhomme also introduced the dish that was to make him famous across the United States: blackened redfish. Rather than fish cooked until it was black, the black color came from a complex blend of spices coating the outside of the tender fish, which was cooked at extremely high heat to sear in the flavors.

The successful combination of K in the front of the house and Prudhomme and Brigtsen in the kitchen brought lines of diners from New Orleans and farther afield to sample Prudhomme's culinary creations. The small, 64-seat restaurant took no reservations, was cash only, and was open only Monday through Friday, but that did not stop hundreds of people, including then Chrysler CEO Lee Iacocca and actor Vincent Price, from lining up at the door. Soon K called on Prudhomme for more help and he quit his job at Commander's Palace. He also hired another promising young chef, Emeril Lagasse, to work in K-Paul's kitchen. After Prudhomme's move full-time to K-Paul's, he and K were married in a small ceremony at the restaurant, taking their vows in front of about 10 guests, mostly K's family from Montana.

COOKBOOKS

Not only diners were recognizing Prudhomme's prodigious culinary talents. In 1980 he became the first American-born chef to receive the coveted Mérite Agricole award from the French government in recognition of his cooking talents and his enrichment of the Cajun and Creole culinary traditions.

But it was with the release of Prudhomme's first cookbook, *Chef Paul Prudhomme's Louisiana Kitchen,* in 1984 that Prudhomme became a household name. On a promotional tour in 1985, Prudhomme drew crowds of thousands, with lines stretching several city blocks, everyone clamoring to taste samples of his creations. He served up jalapeño cheese bread, flounder stuffed with seafood, crawfish "popcorn," and, of course, his signature blackened redfish. Within months, imitators were cropping up across the country, with Cajun-themed restaurants opening in Los Angeles, New York, Washington, D.C., and Houston. McDonald's introduced a Cajun Chicken Sandwich, and Pizza Hut started selling a "Traditional New Orleans-Style Cajun Pizza." Indeed, blackened redfish became so popular and was reproduced in so many restaurants across the country at such frequency that the Louisiana legislature had to restrict commercial redfish catches to save the species from extinction in the Gulf of Mexico. While redfish stocks in both the Atlantic and Gulf Coast have recovered in recent years, an assessment of the Gulf Coast stocks showed that stocks were once again declining and the fishery needs to be more aggressively managed to protect the species.

The cookbook and its new recipes took the nation by storm, and in 1986 it made *The New York Times* bestseller list. Prudhomme had become a bona fide celebrity chef, with profiles in both *Time* and *People* magazines and appearances on national television. He served as the head chef for the Louisiana delegation to President Ronald Reagan's inaugural dinner, turning out over 30 unique dishes for almost 1,000 guests. The nation's leading food magazines, *Bon Appétit*, *Food & Wine*, and *Gourmet*, were writing about K-Paul's, and diners were coming in even larger numbers. Prudhomme was somewhat ambivalent about all this praise, thinking that perhaps it might not be fair to his regular customers to have to wait in long lines to dine at his restaurant. He even went so far as to ask *Food & Wine*, the first national publication to do a write-up on the restaurant, not to print the article. The magazine said it would print the article whether he liked it or not. In Prudhomme's typically generous fashion, the chef then offered to help, sitting for photographs and providing recipes for the publication.

Loss of a Partner

Not much is written about K, but it is clear that she was an essential partner in her husband's success. Serving as the face at the front of the house at K-Paul's, K brought personality, warmth, and a ready smile to the restaurant's clientele and staff. While Chef Prudhomme was gaining accolades and an international reputation, he was also facing something personally devastating. In 1986, the same year Chef Paul Prudhomme's Louisiana Kitchen *reached* The New York Times *bestseller list, K had a rare, incurable form of lung cancer diagnosed. She lived for another seven years but finally succumbed to her illness and died on New Year's Eve 1993 at the age of 48. She spent her final days planning the event that would celebrate her life. The wake was held on a Monday night, when many restaurants are closed, so that all who loved her could attend. Over 1,000 people from Louisiana and across the country came to mourn K's passing. After the ceremony, Prudhomme stood for five hours greeting mourners while K-Paul's staff served up K's favorite foods, including blackened ribs, macaroni and cheese with tomatoes, jambalaya, and chicken and dumplings.*

OTHER ENDEAVORS

From Restaurant to Empire

Although Prudhomme does not have the series of restaurants in hot dining spots like Las Vegas, New York, Chicago, and Los Angeles that seem to be required of today's celebrity chefs, he has nonetheless created a culinary empire. In addition to K-Paul's restaurant in New Orleans's French Quarter, K-Paul's Catering Expedition brings Prudhomme's distinctive food to events across the country, even across the globe at the request of clients. Chef Paul's Smoked Meats produces andouille (a classic Louisiana seasoned, smoked sausage made with pork and potatoes that can be spicy or mild) and tasso (seasoned and smoked pork shoulder used in a wide variety of Cajun recipes). These meat products are sold through an online store and through national distributors.

And then there is Prudhomme's line of Magic Seasoning Blends. After numerous requests from restaurant patrons for the secret to his spice mixes, Prudhomme saw a perfect opportunity to expand on his personal brand. In 1983, he introduced a line of premixed seasoning blends. His Magic Seasoning Blends company now fills a 125,000-square-foot plant, blending and shipping dry spice mixes, rubs, bottled sauces, and marinades to 50 states and over 25 countries. The product consulting arm of the Prudhomme brand also works in a state-of-the-art research and development kitchen to create complete menus or specific food products for other commercial food providers.

In addition to his first blockbuster cookbook, *Chef Paul Prudhomme's Louisiana Kitchen*, Prudhomme has authored eight other cookbooks to date, several of them companion books to his various television series. Prudhomme regularly appeared on local New Orleans television even when he was chef at Commander's Palace, but, with his success with K-Paul's and his first book, his television appearances went national. In the mid-1990s, PBS produced a series called *Chef Paul Prudhomme's Fiery Foods*. His latest television venture was a 26-episode series that first aired in 2007 on PBS titled *Chef Paul Prudhomme's Always Cooking!*

Continuing Largess of Spirit

Known not only for his cooking but also his extremely large size (he weighed 525 pounds when he was only 15), Prudhomme remains one of the United States's premier chefs. Although he has lost well over 300 pounds in recent years through diet and exercise and now appears almost "pleasantly plump," his largeness of spirit only seems to grow. He has a reputation for generosity and kindness, helping his employees to learn and become successful in their own right. Chef Emeril Lagasse got his start with Prudhomme, and Prudhomme and K helped Frank Brigtsen open his award-winning restaurant in New Orleans. Seven years after Brigtsen came to K-Paul's, Prudhomme and K decided he was ready to branch out on his own, and they did everything they could to help him fulfill his dream. They loaned him start-up money, found him a real estate agent, accountant, and lawyer, and even let him take some of K-Paul's staff to his new Eponymous restaurant. Prudhomme also volunteers his time with celebrity appearances for the March of Dimes and other charity organizations.

When New Orleans was truly in need after Hurricane Katrina, Prudhomme was one of the first to return to the city. Three weeks after the storm struck, he and his crew cooked for 3,200 military personnel—first responders and rescuers who had been living off MREs (meals ready to eat) and canned goods. To have food cooked by a chef of Prudhomme's caliber must have truly seemed like manna to the military personnel who were working nonstop in the harrowing conditions after Katrina. He and his team went on to provide over 30,000 meals for police, firefighters, soldiers, and other people who had come to help. Prudhomme continued to provide meals for service workers through his Chefs Cook for Katrina Foundation. In addition to providing much-needed food and comfort, he actively lobbied the business community to invest in rebuilding and revitalizing New Orleans. He wrote positive editorials about New Orleans and her rich food culture and her resiliency, promising that the city would come back and soon be ready for visitors. *Bon Appétit* magazine awarded Prudhomme its Humanitarian Award in 2006 for his relief efforts.

CONCLUSION

Prudhomme's great love of his Louisiana culinary heritage has not diminished in the almost 60 years since he began cooking for a living. K-Paul's celebrated its 30th anniversary in 2009, with the quality of its food and the spirit of its revolutionary chef undiminished. Prudhomme helped to ignite a revolution in American cuisine by bringing the foods, flavors, and cooking philosophy he learned at his mother's side to the world. Today it is *de rigueur* for any highly regarded chef or restaurant to use fresh, local ingredients, but that was not the case even in 1990. Prudhomme championed regional cuisine made with the best, freshest ingredients from the very beginning of his career, and with his great success he was able to share that philosophy with food lovers everywhere. Prudhomme brought Louisiana, and particularly New Orleans, to the world map of culinary destinations. Both in and out of the kitchen, generosity has marked his career.

NOTES

1. Brett Thorn, "Fine Dining Legend Paul Prudhomme," *Nation's Restaurant News* 34:21 (May 22, 2000): 142.

2. Marcelle Bienvenu, Carl A. Brasseaux, and Ryan A. Brasseaux, *Stir the Pot: The History of Cajun Cuisine* (New York: Hippocrene Books), 2005.

3. Bienvenu et al., *Stir the Pot*.

4. Brett Anderson, "The Natural," in *Cornbread Nation 4: The Best of Southern Food Writing*, Dale Volberg Reed, John Shelton Reed, and John T. Edge, Eds. (Athens, GA: University of Georgia Press, 2008) 53–66.

5. Anderson, "The Natural," 56.

FURTHER READING

Bernard, Shane K. *The Cajuns: Americanization of a People*. Jackson: University of Mississippi Press, 2003.

Bienvenu, Marcelle, Carl A. Brasseaux, and Ryan A. Brasseaux. *Stir the Pot: The History of Cajun Cuisine*. New York: Hippocrene Books, 2005.

Carmichael, Judy. Radio interview with Chef Prudhomme from Carmichael's show *Jazz Inspired*. http://www.jazzinspired.com/archive_n-r.shtml

Feibleman, Peter S. *American Cooking: Creole and Acadian*. New York: Time-Life Books, 1971.

Gutierrez, C. Paige. *Cajun Foodways*. Jackson: University of Mississippi Press, 1992.

Prudhomme, Paul. *Chef Paul Prudhomme's Louisiana Kitchen*. New York: Morrow Cookbooks, 1984.

Tabitha Y. Steager

Rachael Ray hosts her "Feedback Festival" party at Stubb's BBQ during the South By Southwest music festival in Austin, Texas, on March 20, 2010. (Getty Images)

Rachael Ray

Rachael Domenica Ray, or "Rach" to her fans, is a celebrity chef and an icon in contemporary American food and television despite having no professional training. Ray is the host of numerous Food Network cooking shows, as well as her own syndicated talk show, *Rachael Ray*. Beyond television, her brand includes cookbooks, a magazine, a line of cookware and bakeware, knives, pantry items (olive oil, vinegar, and stocks), chefs' apparel, and a line of pet foods. Like many celebrity chefs whose popularity and net worth combine to make them powerful marketing tools, Ray also endorses other brands and supports a number of charities. She is also the founder of Yum-O!, "a non-profit organization that empowers kids and their families to develop healthy relationships with food and cooking by teaching families to cook, feeding hungry kids and funding cooking education and scholarships."

EARLY LIFE

Born on August 25, 1968, to Jim Ray, a publisher, and Elsa Scuderi, a restaura-teur, Ray describes herself and her siblings, brother Emmanuel, also known as Manny, and sister Maria, as having grown up in food. The family owned a number of restaurants in Cape Cod, Massachusetts, before her parents divorced and Ray moved to Lake George in upstate New York with her mother, who went on to supervise a chain of restaurants. Ray graduated from Lake George High School in 1986.

Ray moved to New York City in her early twenties, where she worked at the candy counter at Macy's Marketplace before being promoted to manager of their Fresh Foods Department. Two years later, Ray moved on to the new gourmet food market Agata & Valentina as store manager and buyer. But after a series of incidents, including two muggings by gunpoint outside her apartment in 1997, both by the same perpetrator, she packed up and moved back to Lake George, where she worked at Sagamore Resort before being recruited as a buyer for the gourmet food store Cowan & Lobel in Albany, New York.

TELEVISION SHOWS

Thirty-Minute Meals

At Cowan & Lobel, Ray developed the idea for her now-iconic "30-minute meals." Later the title of her first Food Network show, "30-minute meals" was the theme of a series of cooking classes Ray gave in the store to boost holiday sales. The classes proved so popular that soon Ray was asked to prepare a weekly segment for the evening news on WRGB-TV, Albany-Schenectady's CBS station. Her show was nominated for two regional Emmy Awards within a year, and the accompanying cookbook, only available in grocery stores, apparently sold 10,000 copies in 10 days.

The next set of events launched the celebrity chef that millions of people know today. The first event was Ray's appearance on *The Today Show*, followed shortly by a contract with the Food Network. *30-Minute Meals with Rachael Ray* aired on the cable channel for the first time in 2002. By 2006, it was the Food Network's highest rated show, and in that year it won a Daytime Emmy Award for Outstanding Service Show. Ray was nominated for Outstanding Service Show Host.

Economizing on time, money, and cooking skills would remain central to her brand, from shows like *$40 a Day* (2002) to *Rachael Ray's Tasty Travels* (2005), designed to "turn your next vacation into a delicious, affordable feast," to her magazine, *Everyday with Rachael Ray*, launched in 2005 by *Reader's Digest*, which in addition to 30-minute recipes includes various "101" sections (parties, supermarket) and directions for how to create off-the-shelf "fake-out" desserts. Admitting that she is "completely unqualified for every job I've ever had," Ray is one of few celebrity chefs who famously—infamously, to some—encourages her audience to use store-bought convenience products. Her recipes commonly include directions for where to find possibly unusual ingredients in the supermarket. Her "Chicken, Chorizo and Tortilla Stoup (Stew-Like Soup)," for example, requires "3/4 pound chorizo sausage, in packaged meats case near kielbasa," while for her "Why-the-Chicken-Crossed-the-Road Santa Fe-Tastic Tortilla Soup," one will need 3 cups of chicken stock, "available in re-sealable paper containers on soup aisle."

The convenience theme similarly dominates Ray's more than a dozen cookbooks, most of which carry the 30-Minute Meal marker, such as *Cooking Rocks! Rachael Ray 30-Minute Meals for Kids* (2004), *Comfort Foods (2001)*, *Rachael Ray's Top 30 30-Minute Meals* (2005), *2-4-6-8: Great Meals for Couples or Crowds—A 30-Minute Meal Cookbook* (2006), and *Rachael Ray 365: No Repeats—A Year of Deliciously Different Dinners—A 30-Minute Meal Cookbook* (2005). The last one was also "the stupidest idea I ever had," according to Ray. "That many recipes nearly killed me."[1] Her 2007 *Just in Time!* includes "All New 30-Minute Meals, Plus Superfast 15-Minute Meals," and, less characteristically, "Slow-It-Down 60-Minute Meals." Pulling off "the unthinkable," as the Food Network puts it, Ray has also presented a two-part *Thanksgiving in 60* special, featuring "a quick, easy, affordable and delicious holiday meal that you can whip up in just an hour's time." The *Yum-O! Family Cookbook* (2008) is likewise designed to help families "get the very most out of their food-budget dollars," but with added emphasis on "healthy" foods that "are as good for you as they are delish, and they're all quintessential Rachael—fun and creative." Ray's books have frequently been listed as *New York Times* bestsellers.

In 2009, Ray became the producer of a new Food Network show, *Viva Daisy!* Hosted by Daisy Martinez, previously of public television's *Daisy Cooks*, the program focuses on the so-called Latino kitchen and is the first product of Ray's Watch Entertainment production company that is not hosted by Ray herself.

Rachael Ray's Way

Don't measure with instruments, use your hands. You're not baking or conducting experiments for the government—just feel your way through.

Smell and taste the ingredients as you go. Learning about food and flavor is what this book is about. By tasting and sniffing your way through many different types of recipes, your palate will play matchmaker and you will learn how to associate flavors and textures that complement one another.

Commit yourself to not buying take-out food more than twice this week. Cook the other five nights. Get the hang of it. Change the recipes to reflect your own tastes. It is the sincere hope of the author that you will never have to buy another cookbook, including one of her own, again. Cooking quick and easy recipes night after night will build you a pantry and the confidence to learn to live on your own recipes for the rest of your life.

Measuring Rachael's Way:

Handful = about 3 tablespoons
Palmful = about 2 tablespoons
Half a Palmful = you do the math
A Pinch = about ¼ teaspoon
A Few Good Pinches = about 1 teaspoon
Once Around the Pan = about 1 tablespoon of liquid
Twice Around the Pan = more math: about 2 tablespoons, 3 or 4 would be ¼ cup

—Rachael Ray, *30-Minute Meals*. New York:
Lake Isle Press, 1998, pp. 21–22

Beyond the Food Network

In 2006, Ray launched her daily talk show, *Rachael Ray*, which is co-syndicated by Oprah Winfrey's Harpo Productions. Within a month of its debut, Ray was voted "Q" queen, or "most likeable U.S. television host," and the show also recorded the highest premiere ratings for a talk show since the launch of *Dr. Phil* in 2002. Not confined to cooking, *Rachael Ray* regularly features celebrity guests, stories from fans, and fashion and beauty advice. The "Saw It? Want It? Get It!" insert features shopping tips as Ray and her "buddies" inform viewers about "great buys, new products, delicious snacks, cool gadgets," and, as they put it, "anything that gives you value, value, value!" Also typical are sponsored segments, such as

"Rach to the Rescue" (featuring Sears Kenmore Elite appliances), "Hey, Can You Cook?" (Uncle Ben's Rice), and home makeovers (Staples). Other advertising partnerships have included the Egg Board, Wal-mart, and Sara Lee. As of 2009, fans can follow "Rachael Ray Show" on Twitter, and friend "The Rachael Ray Show" on Facebook. Her "Facecook" section also regularly features a different "behind-the-scenes video from Rachael's prep kitchen exclusively for our Facebook fans!" Like the show's website, its Facebook page includes information on how to get tickets to become an audience member. Almost 200,000 people were reportedly on the waiting list for tickets in 2009.

Close and regular interaction between Ray and her fans has been central to her success. Her accessibility helps to explain *Newsweek*'s description of Ray as the "most down-to earth TV star on the planet,"[2] while *Time* magazine has called her "the most accessible celebrity ever."[3] *Rachael Ray* won Daytime Emmy Awards in 2007, 2008, and 2009 in the category Outstanding Talk Show, and she has repeatedly been nominated as Outstanding Talk Show Host. In 2009, despite trying economic times for the entertainment business, *Rachael Ray*, now syndicated by CBS Television Distribution, was renewed up until the 2011–2012 season, with ABC-owned stations identified as key markets.

AWARDS AND HONORS

In addition to her Emmy awards and nominations, Ray's popularity and influence have been recognized by a number of distinctions, both commercial and popular. The men's magazine *FHM* listed her as one of the US's Sexiest Women of 2004, after Ray did a spread for the magazine that consisted of a series of provocative images of the scantily clad celebrity in a kitchen, licking chocolate off a wooden spoon, sucking a strawberry, taking a roast turkey out of the oven, and so on. Ray claims to have thought FHM stood for "Food and Home" when they originally contacted her. After she realized who they really were, she decided to do the shoot anyway, in the name of "everywoman—here she is. . . . And I did it and it was the most scared I've ever been and I wouldn't change a thing. I'd do it again tomorrow," she told ABC's *Nightline* in 2009.[4] *FHM* again ranked Ray as one of US's Sexiest Women in 2006.

In other media, *Business Week* named Ray one of the "Best Leaders of 2006," and she was voted "Television Syndication Personality of the Year" by *Television Week* in 2007. Her magazine, *Everyday with Rachael Ray*, was chosen by *Advertising Age* as "Launch of the Year" in 2006 and was included on their "A-List" in 2008 and "Start Up of the Year" by *AdWeek* in 2007, also the year that a wax figure of the celebrity chef in a replica of her studio kitchen was installed at Madame Tussaud's in New York. Together with Emeril Lagasse, Ray holds the distinction of being the first celebrity chef to cook for NASA astronauts, when they were both asked to devise recipes for the crew of the

Discovery space shuttle in 2006. A selection of their recipes is included in *The Astronaut's Cookbook* (2009).

Ray has been listed on *Forbes's* The Celebrity 100 each year since her first appearance on the list in 2006 (then at number 81, with her top attributes cataloged as "Cute" and "Talented"). At *Forbes's* 2008 count, Ray's annual salary was $18 million. She was listed by *Time* as one of the 100 People Who Shape Our World in 2006, when her colleague Mario Batali credited her in that magazine with having "radically changed the way America cooks dinner" in her less than five years as a food media personality. "At book signings and public appearances," Batali continued, "I have seen her fans faint, tremble, mumble, moan and ultimately hit the front of the line and embrace their food hero, repeating her mantras such as 'let's run a knife through it' and 'easy peasy' like Catholics at Sunday Mass."[5]

In October 2007, Ray appeared on the cover of *Newsweek* magazine for their special edition on Women in Leadership. At the conference of the same name, hosted by the Museum of Natural History in New York, Ray shared a panel with actress Kyra Sedgwick, president and CEO of Lifetime Entertainment Services Andrea Wong, and Mara Brock Aki, executive producer of TV shows *Girlfriends* and *The Game*. Explaining "what is so easy about my job," Ray described her work as "sharing the idea that just learning how to make a few simple dishes for yourself or your cousin or your neighbor not only improves the quality of your life, it improves the quality of the lives of those you choose to share this food with. It just does. It's one of the easiest ways for a poor person to feel rich. Make good food."[6] In 2009, Ray was chosen to receive the Tribute Award for American Women in Radio and Television (also known as the Gracie Awards). The Tribute Award is "bestowed upon an individual who truly makes a difference in the media and beyond."

Beyond media awards, Ray's impact can be measured by the inclusion of EVOO—her shorthand for extra virgin olive oil—in the 2007 edition of the *Oxford American College Dictionary*. The abbreviation summarizes the Ray ethos well: "I first coined 'EVOO,'" she explained, "because saying 'extra virgin olive oil' over and over was wordy, and I'm an impatient girl—that's why I make 30-minute meals!" Despite the fact that food professionals have been using shorthand like EVOO long before Ray, as well as the existence of a restaurant of the same name in Boston since 1998, when the editor-in-chief of *American Dictionaries* appeared on *Rachael Ray* in December 2006 to hand the star a certificate, she explained to Ray that "for a word to go into the dictionary, it has to be useful to people. It's not enough to be a fabulous celebrity. . . . You have to make a word that people like to use." Fans who like to use Ray's language can also use her branded "All-Italian EVOO" in their kitchens, available for purchase through her website.

In keeping with her themes of ease and convenience, Ray is well known for a number of other linguistic shortcuts, such as "sammie" for sandwiches, "stoup" for stewlike soups, "motz" for mozzarella cheese, "delish" for delicious, and her signature "yum-o."

OTHER ENDEAVORS

Promoting Healthy Eating

Boasting illustrious affiliations from its beginnings, Ray's Yum-O! charity was launched in 2006 in partnership with the National Restaurant Educational Foundation and the Alliance for a Healthier Generation, a joint venture by the American Heart Association and the William J. Clinton Foundation. Drawing attention to the fact that hunger and obesity are two problems on opposite ends of the same spectrum, Ray introduced the charity on the set of her talk show with President Bill Clinton as her studio guest. She proclaimed that together they "are going to get rid of hunger in America forever!"

Her Yum-O! venture has seen Ray involved in a number of other projects that focus on the issue of childhood obesity, among them the 2008 South Beach Food and Wine Festival, where Ray, together with Alice Waters of California's Chez Panisse restaurant and British celebrity chef Jamie Oliver, acted as a copanelist at the "Childhood Obesity Initiative Luncheon." Ray has credited Oliver and Waters with inspiring her own program in the fight against obesity. But unlike Oliver, whose *Jamie's School Dinners* campaign famously led the UK government to pledge almost $500,000,000 toward improving school lunches, Ray is less interested in the politics of the food system than in simply championing what she calls "good food and leading people to the good life, whether they're haves or have nots."[7] As she once put it in an interview, "I don't want to talk about obesity. I want to talk about how fun healthy food is, period."[8]

Animal Lover

Ray's interest in healthy food extends to her well-publicized love of animals, in particular, her pit bull Isaboo, who is pictured with Ray on her Nutrish brand of pet food with the tagline "Made with love for my Isaboo and your dog too." Uncharacteristically of celebrity chefs, Ray's website boasts a section containing recipes for pets, such as a "Doggie Tuna Casserole," complete with two tablespoons of Parmigiano Reggiano cheese. Ray did briefly engage in animal politics when she publicly objected to a proposed New York City ban on pit bulls in 2007. She also declared her support for the breed by endorsing the "Unexpected Pit Bull Calendar" on her show shortly after the proposal. Founded in 2004, the calendar features pictures of "misunderstood" pit bulls in order to "combat the negative stereotype held against these dogs." All profits from sales of the calendar go to pit bull rescue and advocacy groups.

Since then Ray has established a pet charity called Rach's Rescue, "to highlight organizations that are dedicated to helping animals in need." Proceeds from sales of Ray's Nutrish pet food go to these organizations, which include North Shore Animal League America, America's Vet Dogs, ASPCA, and Bad Rap. Mutt Madness, similarly, is a "fun 'brackets' program" organized by Ray in which a number of organizations that practice "no-kill animal wellness" compete by public votes for a series of cash prizes and $50,000 as the grand prize. Mutt Madness claims to donate more than $200,000 to animal welfare programs.

Endorsements and Branding

Ray has put her name and face to a number of leading brands, including Burger King and Nabisco crackers. In 2007, mobile phone providers AT&T and Limelife launched "Rachael Ray Recipes on the Run," allowing subscribers to access recipes, cooking tips, and meal ideas and to develop shopping lists on their phones. She has collaborated with fabric manufacturers Town and Country to produce a brand of kitchen textiles designed to complement the colors of Ray's existing lines of kitchenware. She also has a range of towels and linens, including her signature "Moppine," an all-in-one oven mitt and kitchen towel manufactured by Westpoint Home. Ray's knives and the Yum-O! Kids' Cooking and Baking Range are made by the Austrian firm Füri.

Arguably her most well known commercial affiliation has been Ray's endorsement of Dunkin' Donuts, thanks in particular to the negative publicity the coffee and baked goods chain received when it claimed it was forced to withdraw a television ad because of Ray's attire. She was wearing a black and white scarf, and some people interpreted its resemblance to a kaffiyeh as Ray's, and Dunkin' Donuts's, support for Islamic fundamentalism and terrorist activity. Media responses were quick to charge Dunkin' Donuts with "caving" to the accusation and thereby confirming it by pulling the ad, despite the fact that, as one *Newsweek* article put it, the scarf in question is "worn by millions, including Middle Eastern men, arty college students, tourists, Kanye West and even U.S. troops, who use it to keep the sand and dust at bay." "Shouldn't we be more offended," the author continued, "that Ray was shilling their weak iced coffee, a beverage that should be criticized for impersonating, well, iced coffee. But cries of 'Bad java!' just don't seem to catch the attention the way racist rhetoric against Arabs and Muslims does."[9]

Criticism

Like many high-profile media personalities, Ray has been the target of public criticism for almost as long as she has been in the limelight, including an online "Rachael Ray Sucks Community," "created for the people who hate the untalented twit known as Rachael Ray." The site is now defunct but ran for almost six years with a membership of close to 2,000. Apart from gratuitous stabs at hcr voice, appearance, and mannerisms, much of the criticism leveled at Ray focuses on the fact that she is not a qualified chef and that—contrary to the aim of many television cooks, among them professionally trained chefs—her use of convenience products and language encourages people to accept, rather than to improve on, their limited cooking skills.

One of her most outspoken critics from the food media world has been fellow celebrity Anthony Bourdain, himself a qualified chef, acclaimed author, and television personality. Having previously referred to her, among other things, as a "bobblehead" and suggesting that she sells nothing more than the "smug reassurance that mediocrity is quite enough," in 2007 Bourdain famously described Ray's affiliation with Dunkin' Donuts as "evil" and "like endorsing crack for kids."[10] At the time, Ray's public relations staff issued a statement begging to "respectfully disagree" with Bourdain's opinion. Yet during her 2009 *Nightline* interview, Ray took the opportunity to respond to the charge, stating first that "I absolutely love Tony Bourdain," and that she has "an enormous amount of respect for him." As for his accusation, she stated that "quite frankly, without me explaining my mindset, I think that's a very fair thing he said, and I have no problem with it." She went on to explain her reasons for agreeing to endorse Dunkin' Donuts's products, among them the fact that the company had agreed to remove transfats from their doughnuts, that they had given financial support to the Yum-O! charity, and that the deal ensured Ray free coffee for life. Soon after the interview, Bourdain published a Facebook note confessing that Ray's kind words about him, combined with his recent discovery that she is a fan of one of his own favorite bands, the New York Dolls, "caused me no small amount of confusion, panic and misery. I don't know whether to go out and shoot a puppy, or send Rachael a fruit basket." According to a thank-you note he later published on his website, Ray was the one who sent Bourdain a fruit basket in the end, together with a note asking him not to hurt any puppies. This example is characteristic of Ray's generally charitable response to media criticism. As she put it in an answer to one of a series of questions sent in by *Time* readers in 2008, "There is very little that isn't true. I'm not a chef, I don't bake, I am loud, I am goofy, and after a while, my voice is annoying."[11]

Another typical criticism levelled at Ray is that many of her recipes require more than 30 minutes, with several journalists having set out to disprove this mainstay of her brand by reporting on how much longer some of the "30-minute meals" have taken them to cook. In Ray's defence is one notably avid fan, host of the blog "Everything Rachael Ray," started in 2006 and tagged "Not an official Rachael Ray site or affiliated with Rachael Ray in any way," in which she reports and comments, true to the blog's name, on everything to do with Ray. Responding to two newspaper articles discrediting the 30-minute theme, the blogger suggests that "30-minutes" is simply another shorthand for "quick and easy," and that anyone who complains about an extra 10 or 15 minutes is missing the point. Ray also personally responded to the allegations on the blog section of her website by giving a number of pointers designed to help minimize time in the kitchen. Her suggestions included having one of her branded "garbage bowls" handy to avoid having to run back and forth from the garbage can, and washing vegetables as soon as one comes home from the store so they are ready to use straight from the fridge.

Rachael Ray received another bout of negative publicity in 2008 when a former employee of the show filed a $1 million lawsuit against CBS for workplace discrimination and wrongful termination because he suffered from anorexia. Ray herself was not named as a defendant, but media headlines continued to report the incident as "Rachael Ray Anorexia Lawsuit."

CONCLUSION

While one index of the growing cult of celebrity chefs in the past decades is an increasingly tabloid atmosphere around food personalities, their personal lives have also come to feature more strongly as an element of their public personas, particularly as much food television has moved to a "reality TV" format compared with the studio-bound instruction familiar to viewers of early shows like Julia Child's *The French Chef*. Ray is no exception and indeed says that there is no real difference between her public and private personalities. As she claimed in one of the advertisements for *Rachael Ray* just before its debut in 2006, "Everybody wants me to keep being me and that's all I know how to do."

In a celebrity culture, and also one in which there exists some anxiety about food and lifestyle, especially in the shadow of a so-called obesity epidemic, sharing—or exposing—private information is one sure way to build the trust of fans. One blogger's glowing description of *Rachael Ray* explains the attraction: "She [Ray] has segments like 'outing' her closet where she shows hideous items from her closet. She even outed her husband as a pretty man by bringing in his dopp bag (men's toiletry kit) and showing us all the creams and such he uses daily. . . . She *is* the girl next door."

Ray married lawyer John Cusimano on September 24, 2005. Despite a spate of media rumors less than two years into their marriage about an imminent divorce due to alleged infidelities on Cusimano's part, the couple remain together, dividing their time between their New York apartment and a house in the Hamptons. Ray also owns the cabin in the Adirondacks where her mother lives. Cusimano plays guitar and sings in a band, The Cringe.

Following ineffective vocal chord therapy to correct a benign cyst, possibly caused by overuse of her voice, Ray underwent minor throat surgery in 2009, after which she was obliged to use paper and pen to communicate with her husband. The operation was successful, so Ray quickly resumed her boisterous place on the stage and, thanks to television, in the homes of all her fans, where she will likely continue to inspire the (r)evoo-lution in American cooking that she has helped to set in motion.

NOTES

1. Kim Severson, "Being Rachael Ray: How Cool Is That?" *The New York Times* (October 19, 2005).
2. Marc Peyser, "The Grill Next Door," *Newsweek* (September 12, 2005).
3. Joel Stein, "Rachael Ray Has a Lot on Her Plate," *Time* (September 5, 2006).
4. Cynthia McFadden and Sarah Rosenberg, "Rachael Ray: 'I Don't Regret a Thing,'" ABC News Nightline, March 2, 2009, http://abcnews.go.com/Nightline/Recipes/rachael-ray-regret-thing/story?id=6976299
5. Mario Batali, "Rachael Ray," *Time* (April 30, 2006).
6. Rachael Ray, "My Journey to the Top," *Newsweek* (October 15, 2007).
7. J. M. Hirsch, "Rachael Ray Teams with Bill Clinton to Fight the Epidemic of Childhood Obesity," *Associated Press* (May 2, 2007).
8. Kim Severson, "A New Alliance in the Fight against Childhood Obesity," *The New York Times* (April 25, 2007).
9. Lorraine Ali, "Not So Sweet: Why Dunkin' Donuts Shouldn't Have Caved in the Controversy over Rachael Ray's 'Kaffiyeh' Scarf," *Newsweek* (May 30, 2008).
10. "Rachael's Dunkin' Gig 'Evil,'" *New York Post* (October 11, 2007).
11. Rachael Ray, "10 Questions for Rachael Ray," *Time* (April 17, 2008).

FURTHER READING

Ray, Rachael. *30-Minute Meals*. New York: Lake Isle Press, 1999.

Ray, Rachael. *Rachael Ray's Open House Cookbook*. Lake Isle Press, 2000.

Ray, Rachael. *Comfort Foods*. Lake Isle Press, 2001.

Ray, Rachael. *Veggie Meals*. Lake Isle Press, 2001.

Ray, Rachael. *30-Minute Meals 2*. Lake Isle Press, 2003.

Ray, Rachael. *Get Togethers: Rachael Ray 30-Minute Meals*. Lake Isle Press, 2003.

Ray, Rachael. *Cooking Rocks!: Rachael Ray 30-Minute Meals for Kids*. Lake Isle Press, 2004.

Ray, Rachael. *Rachael Ray's 30-Minute Meals: Cooking 'Round the Clock*. Lake Isle Press, 2004.

Ray, Rachael. *Rachael Ray's 30-Minute Get Real Meals: Eat Healthy Without Going to Extremes*. New York: Clarkson Potter, 2005.

Ray, Rachael. *Rachael Ray 365: No Repeats: A Year of Deliciously Different Dinners*. New York: Clarkson Potter, 2005.

Ray, Rachael. *Rachael Ray 2, 4, 6, 8: Great Meals for Couples or Crowds*. New York: Clarkson Potter, 2006.

Ray, Rachael. *Rachael Ray's Express Lane Meals*. New York: Clarkson Potter, 2006.

Ray, Rachael. *Rachael Ray: Just in Time*. New York: Clarkson Potter, 2007.

Ray, Rachael. *Yum-O! The Family Cookbook*. New York: Clarkson Potter, 2008.

Ray, Rachael. *Rachael Ray's Big Orange Book*. New York: Clarkson Potter, 2008.

Ray, Rachael. *Rachael Ray's Book of 10: More Than 300 Recipes to Cook Every Day*. New York: Clarkson Potter, 2009.

Signe Rousseau

Ruth Reichl, editor of the legendary and now defunct *Gourmet* magazine, poses for a portrait at the magazine's test kitchen, July 8, 1999. (AP/Wide World Photos)

Ruth Reichl

Ruth Reichl, former editor-in-chief of *Gourmet* magazine and coproducer of public television's *Gourmet's Diary of a Foodie,* is the former restaurant critic for both *The Los Angeles Times* and *The New York Times*. Reichl has worked with virtually every great American food icon, including M. F. K. Fisher and Alice Waters, and has chronicled her life in three wildly successful, critically acclaimed, best-selling memoirs.

Waters, renowned chef and owner of Chez Panisse who spearheaded the organic food revolution in the 1970s, says about Reichl, "Ruth has the bracing authority of one whose palate is never jaded, who loves to share everything she knows, and who never takes herself too seriously. Is there another food writer alive who conveys as much generosity and sheer good will?"[1]

EARLY YEARS

Surviving Childhood

Reichl, born January 16, 1948, was raised by her parents Ernst and Miriam Reichl in Greenwich Village in Manhattan. Reichl's mother had a profound influence on her relationship with food, which she chronicled in her first memoir, *Tender at the Bone* (1999). Her mother introduced her to adventurous ingredients such as cactus fruit, whole suckling pig, sea urchins, and even chocolate-covered grasshoppers. However, her mother also suffered from bipolar disorder and in depressive episodes would take to her bed for weeks at a time, leaving young Reichl to fend for herself, in the kitchen and in life. One year, her mother even forgot to prepare Thanksgiving dinner.

During manic phases, Reichl's mother would cook not only unpalatable meals but also dangerous ones that often resulted in food poisoning. From a very young age, Reichl coped by taking tiny bites of food and chewing slowly. This helped her to avoid spoiled or awful-tasting foods and also developed her palate. "My mother was such a scary cook. She literally couldn't tell when the food was spoiled. When the major adult in your life isn't reacting you have to taste things very slowly to see if you want a second bite. Even at 2 years old, I had to focus on flavor and pay attention to taste in a way most people don't do," says Reichl. "Like a hearing child born to deaf parents, I was shaped by my mother's handicap, discovering that food could be a way of making sense of the world." In deep and profound ways, Reichl shaped her career by her reactions to her mother's illness. She began cooking at a young age and found solace, comfort, and peace in the kitchen and around food. Her father, a sweet but docile book publisher, was so intent on escaping his wife's manic episodes that he did not seem to realize he was abandoning his young daughter to face them alone.

At the age of six, Reichl spent time in the kitchen of her "Aunt" Birdie, actually her father's former mother-in-law. The aunt's housekeeper, Alice, was the first person Reichl encountered who understood the power of cooking.

Reichl lovingly recalls helping Alice roll dough for apple dumplings and making chicken croquettes and creamed onions. Alice taught her the secret to fried oysters, which included carefully draining and drying the oysters and cooking them in very hot Crisco.

In her second memoir, *Comfort Me with Apples* (2001), Reichl recounts, "The year I was seven Mom became so depressed she took to her bed and spent months eating candy bars and thumbing through the same book, reading the pages over and over as the mail piled up in the front of the door." By the time Reichl was eight years old, she could go grocery shopping and plan menus, like wiener schnitzel, green salad, and brownies, on her own. She often cooked for her family and even took it upon herself to rescue guests from the ill-conceived inedible dishes her mother prepared for dinner parties.

Reichl attended New York City's P.S. 41, then Hunter High School, a public school for the gifted, until the middle of eighth grade. Her mother then abruptly and without warning transferred Reichl to a Collége Marie de France boarding school in Montreal, Canada. Reichl came home from school one day to find that her mother had packed her bag and that she was to leave immediately for boarding school. She was not even allowed to say goodbye to her father or friends. It is not clear whether this decision to send Reichl away was due to a manic whim or to a misguided maternal desire to enrich her daughter's education. Not only was her departure abrupt, but also the school was French-speaking, so Reichl, who was not fluent in French, found herself in a strange school in a strange country surrounded by teachers and students she could not understand. Again, food became a source of comfort, and on weekends and holidays when classmates went home to their families, Reichl roamed Montreal trying out new restaurants.

As she mastered the French language, Reichl developed friendships with many of her fellow students and on one weekend visited the home of a classmate. Her friend's gourmand father was impressed by Reichl's appreciation of food and introduced her to *foie gras*, caviar, lobster bisque, *marrons glacés*, and the proper way to appreciate French Brie: eaten with a fork, rather than with bread. After three years in Quebec, Reichl was not only fluent in French but had even mastered the art of making the soufflé.

Reichl then transferred to a high school in South Norwalk, Connecticut, near her parents' weekend home. They remained primarily in New York City, leaving Reichl to fend for herself yet again. Reichl graduated in 1964 and applied to the University of Michigan, far from home, wanting respite from her mother's overbearing manner, wildly erratic mood swings, and nontraditional parenting style.

Beginning to Write

In addition to her studies at the University of Michigan in Ann Arbor, Reichl worked part-time as a waitress in the French restaurant L'Escargot. There she learned to make classics like steak Diane, crêpes Suzette, and Caesar salad, all prepared tableside. This first foray into the world of restaurants gave her experience in fine French food, which at the time was synonymous with fine American dining. It also taught her about restaurants, from the stresses of the kitchen, and the importance of the waitstaff, to the dining experience from the patron's point of view.

Reichl met artist Douglas Hollis, a fellow student, whom she married in 1970—the same year she graduated with a master's in art history. Traveling with her husband for a time through North Africa and Europe further awakened her palate. During her travels she discovered the cuisines of Greece, Spain, Italy, and Tunisia. Alice Waters recalled, "Ruth celebrates the ethnicity of food." Indeed, this trip shaped a lifelong interest in foods from around the world.

Reichl and Hollis moved back to New York City, where both worked for a time for Reichl's father and shared a loft with the artist Pat Oleszko, a fellow alumnus from the University of Michigan. In her memoir, *Tender at the Bone*, Reichl notes that Pat encouraged her food writing: "You're such a good cook. Why don't you write a cookbook?" Reichl's first professional attempt at food writing, *Mmmmm: A Feastiary*, was published by Holt, Rinehart and Winston in 1972. Recipes ranged from classic American fare, such as pumpkin soup, baked beans, and oatmeal cookies, to dishes she learned as a child, such as Aunt Birdie's Potato Salad. The book also contained unusual foreign recipes, including *coquilles St. Jacques, moules marinieres, spaghetti carbonara*, and pesto. However, it received little critical acclaim or attention and is now out of print.

RESTAURANT REVIEWS

New West

Reichl and her husband moved from New York City to Berkeley, California, in April of 1973, where they lived with a group of five friends in a communal household. Berkeley, in those days the epicenter of both social unrest and pioneering foodways, was where Reichl honed her culinary talents. She initially wanted to be a novelist and supported herself by cooking at the Swallow, a collectively owned and operated restaurant in the University of California at Berkeley Art Museum. The Swallow made everything from scratch, including breads, pies, and soups, something that was a rarity in the 1970s for establishments of that size. "I had to explain even simple terms, like quiche, to customers," recalled Reichl.

Reichl and her husband lived modestly except for a yearly splurge on a fine dinner at Waters's famed Berkeley restaurant, Chez Panisse. Waters had become a pioneer in foodways, embracing locally grown products from small farms, sustainable agriculture, home-made breads, and organic ingredients.

Reichl's career as a restaurant critic began in 1978 at age 30, when a frequent Swallow customer and editor for *New West* magazine, *New York Magazine*'s sibling publication, asked her to review an upscale French restaurant in San

Francisco. This leap from writing a few freelance food articles to reviewing an expensive restaurant was seen as a betrayal by her Berkeley housemates and family. As Reichl, in her memoir *Comfort Me with Apples*, reflected, a housemate and dear friend asked, "You're going to spend your life telling spoiled, rich people where to eat too much obscene food?" Reichl ignored the criticisms and accepted her new calling.

In addition to writing for *New West*, Reichl wrote for magazines such as *New Dawn, Apartment Living* (now *Metropolitan Home*), *Cuisine*, and *Food & Wine*. "But my greatest triumph," notes Reichl, was her assignment for *Ms.* magazine to interview M. F. K. Fisher, whom Reichl considered her hero. Of Fisher, Reichl wrote, "She can make you taste things just by writing about them, but that's not the point. She actually makes you pay attention to your next meal, feel more alive because you're doing that. When you read her you understand that you need to respect yourself enough to focus on the little things of life. She celebrates the everyday by making it seem momentous." However, *Ms.* magazine was not pleased with Reichl's first draft because it wanted the piece to focus on Fisher's struggle as a single working mother. Reichl later admitted, "They sensed that I lacked the requisite gravity to be one of their writers, and they did not offer me a second assignment."

Reichl also wrote about and befriended other California food celebrities, including Wolfgang Puck and Waters. Waters reminisced about her early meetings with Reichl: "Ruth represented all my food values, she liked to talk about the things most valuable to me. She and I both believed that we need to pay attention to what we're eating, and if we make the right choices in food, it is not only delicious but good for the planet and the economy. Ruth is so honest about what she thinks, and isn't afraid to write what she thinks without sweetening it at all. Oh, she uses beautiful language, that naturally sweetens everything she writes, but she doesn't intentionally sugarcoat things."

Reichl's California years exposed her to many new ingredients and cooking styles. The young food writer quickly learned to appreciate *aceto di Modena* (balsamic vinegar), *mozzarella di buffala* (mozzarella made with buffalo milk), and Szechuan peppercorns. Her increased awareness expanded as she wrote about Santa Barbara's excellent quail and the wonderful raspberry and strawberry vinegars produced by California chefs.

As a self-taught food professional and freelance writer, Reichl further developed her palate through travel. For example, in 1978, when she wanted to learn more about wine, she asked a local Berkeley wine merchant, Kermit Lynch, if she could join him on a wine-buying trip through France. In Paris she ate in her first three-star restaurant, Tour d'Argent. Just before a trip to Taishan, China, her father had a stroke. Her mother's reaction was not to console Reichl, but to rant, "What will I do if he dies? I'll just be another sad old lady without a man. How can he do this to me?" Reichl's father, despite being hospitalized at the time, encouraged her to make the trip: "You'll be seeing things no American has ever seen. . . . Promise me you'll go. Even if I am not better. Even if I die. You may never get this chance again."

Reichl went and wrote her father long letters detailing parts of the trip—a bean-curd factory visit, how they dry pig's skin to create imitation bird's nests, and the fact that the secret to Cantonese cooking is chicken fat. While there, Reichl spoke with a Beijing chef who described the nuances of their cuisine as three factors: "The color must be varied and beautiful. The texture is important too; all the pieces must be cut to uniform size. And then, of course, the ingredients must all be seasonal." On her return to the States, Reichl learned that her letters were all unopened. Her father had died during her trip.

Reichl's freelance articles for *New West* and other magazines revealed her quirky charm. In a *New West* article she reviewed three restaurants and focused on the love stories that unfolded before her—a gay couple, an elderly couple, and two platonic friends. In a review of the San Francisco restaurant Roberts, she assigned vaguely secret agent-like monikers "Fingers," "Lady," and "The Saint" to the friends she had asked to join her in the meal and wrote the review as a report to the "Chief." Throughout the review she maintains this whimsical trope of the good guys seeking out evil: "'Don't worry,' says Fingers, 'the snails will be terrible.' He spears one on his fork, pops it into his mouth, 'Well?' we chorus hopefully. He shakes his head sadly, 'They're great. Hot, chewy, the garlic pungent but not overwhelming.' We all turn from him in disgust." In another section, Reichl writes, "Somebody in the kitchen must have been on to us. How else could they have managed not to make a single slip?" The article ends as whimsically as it begins: "As for myself, Chief, I think that you should get rid of the whole bunch of bunglers and get a group of agents who know that if you can't find trouble, you gotta create it. Personally, I'd be willing to make a sacrifice and go to eat at that joint again."

During this time Reichl began an affair with Michael Singer, a journalist. "A man like that you can hate on first sight," she told a friend. "The deep sexual connection I had felt with Michael both thrilled and frightened me," she writes in her second memoir, *Comfort Me with Apples*. Reichl brought Singer along on a visit to M. F. K. Fisher's home for dinner, but the couple ended up staying as her guests for two nights. Though heart-wrenchingly difficult, Reichl and her husband separated.

The Los Angeles Times

In 1984, Reichl became the restaurant critic for *The Los Angeles Times*. Initially reluctant to leave Berkeley for Los Angeles, she eventually accepted the position. Reichl fretted, "At thirty-five I was still a freelance writer. I had no health insurance and no pension and my expense account was twice the size of my meager earnings. This was the first time I had ever been offered a full-time job that paid real money and provided benefits." At that time she was still officially married but had been living with Singer for two years. Singer supported the move to Los Angeles and viewed it as an opportunity for the couple to "start out fresh, with no baggage."

Reichl felt the weight of her new role at California's largest newspaper: "More than a million people were reading my words, and half of them seemed to hate me." Before long she acclimated to the position and won her own new fan base, which included actor Danny Kaye, who called to praise her reviews and invite her to his home for dinner. She was so taken with the design of Kaye's kitchen—"Each counter was precisely calibrated to his height, so that he could stand at the stove and reach anything he might need"—that she followed his design many years later in her weekend home in Columbia County, New York.

Just as she had done in her freelance work, Reichl continued to expand on her own whimsical take in writing reviews. She brought Singer, whom she dubbed "the Reluctant Gourmet," to restaurant visits to serve as a counter-force: "puncturing pretension, questioning authority, taking a skeptical view of the high price of eating out. . . . He was smart, irreverent, and funny, and he could say all the things a restaurant critic could not." However, when she tried writing that the ghost of Gloria Swanson had joined her on a restaurant review, her editor balked and returned the review to her saying, "This won't do. In journalism you have to tell the truth. I'm sorry."

After several years in Los Angeles, Reichl divorced Hollis and married Singer at a small ceremony in their new home with food friends like Danny Kaye, Alice Waters, Andrew Coleman, and Wolfgang Puck in attendance. As she continued writing for *The Los Angeles Times*, she developed friendships with Hollywood celebrities, including Gregory Peck, Kathleen Turner, and Henry Winkler.

After years of unsuccessfully trying to become pregnant, Reichl and her husband began steps to adopt a little girl, Gavi. After many months of developing a strong parental bond, however, the birth mother reclaimed the infant, leading to a heartbreaking time in Reichl's life. Happily, despite being 41 years old, Reichl conceived a child shortly afterward.

The New York Times

Upon invitation by *The New York Times*, Reichl interviewed for a position as the paper's restaurant critic. The request came at a time when "the great Los Angeles restaurant boom came screeching to a halt," observed Reichl. Although not initially interested in leaving Los Angeles, Reichl, with her husband's encouragement, agreed to an interview in New York City. "I wouldn't fit in here," she told an assistant managing editor. When asked why, she gave her impression of the existing reviewers: "They hand down judgments from on high. They seem to think they are right. There is no right or wrong in the matters of taste." Although at first she was trying to convince them not to want her on the *Times*, by the end of a series of interviews she found herself admitting, "My mother died a year ago. I wouldn't have considered living here while she was alive, but now that she's gone, I guess I can come home." She accepted the position of restaurant critic for *The New York Times* in 1993.

As Reichl noted in her third memoir, *Garlic and Sapphires* (2005), she wanted to change the way the *Times* reviewed restaurants and was forthright in sharing her philosophy during her initial interviews, saying, "You shouldn't be writing reviews for the people who dine in fancy restaurants, but for all the ones who wish they could." She wanted to hold restaurants accountable for what and how they served, helping the public make informed choices about where to spend their dining dollars. Reichl went on to influence not only how the *Times* reviewed restaurants but even what sorts of restaurants were reviewed.

Kim Severson, food writer at *The New York Times*, noted that "Ruth led diners into what we see now, a more varied dining landscape in NYC. She made food criticism much more accessible and more proletariat." Severson also wrote, "Craig Claiborne established the star system, which is still widely used today, but Ruth changed what it means to have a star." "She opened up the door for other styles of cuisine to be star worthy."

Reichl spotlighted not only New York City's fancy three- and four-star continental restaurants, but also many small ethnic establishments and informal eateries in the city's outer boroughs, and she was not obsessed with French cooking, like her predecessors were. Also, unlike critics that came after her, she genuinely enjoyed dining out. Chef and restaurant owner Mario Batali believed that "you got the sense that she was cheering for the restaurant industry, not just making stern professorial proclamations. She had an optimist tone, which was a delight for both the *New York Times* reader and for restaurateurs. In reading her first reviews, I realized immediately that her critical strength came because she intimately understood the entire restaurant business, from purchasing goods at the purveyor, to kitchen prep, cooking, and waitstaff concerns, as well as the customer's dining room experience."

Indeed, Reichl's reviews focused on not just the food, but on everything from the wine list to noise level, with special emphasis on how the staff treated customers and the general mood in the room among patrons. Reichl wrote from a common person's perspective, aiming to demystify the world of fine dining and expose pretentiousness and sexist behaviors among management and waitstaff in some of the city's posh establishments.

Being the restaurant critic for *The New York Times* is a powerful position. Batali stated, "*The New York Times* is the gold standard of international restaurant reviewing. If *The New York Times* gets you, your restaurant succeeds, but if they don't, you will almost surely close." One of Batali's restaurants received a glowing review and three stars from Reichl, and Batali readily admitted that "Ruth's review of my restaurant Babbo on August 26, 1998 was the most important of my life!" He was pleased, not only with the praise she heaped on him and his partner in the restaurant, Joe Bastianich, but also with the fact that he thought she truly understood the whimsy behind his food choices. "She gets what the chef is after, from why we plate in a certain way, to what ingredients we choose."

Because it was known that New York restaurants put up pictures of reviewers to alert waitstaff and kitchen staff, Reichl realized she wanted to maintain anonymity to be able to evaluate a restaurant without preferential treatment. To that end, she turned to longtime family friend and acting coach, Claudia Banks, for advice on disguises, which had to be well planned and executed.

DG: Craig Claiborne and Pierre Franey wrote about this epic meal—it cost thousands of dollars, and they had dozens of wines—after bidding $300 for it at a charity auction.

RR: One of my editors asked me if I would find the most expensive restaurant in the world and redo that story. . . . And I said, you know, this has really gotten out of hand. There is something worrisome to me about it. You start thinking about Rome.

DG: Do you ever walk out of a restaurant feeling . . . debauched?

RR: Last night I was at a meal where we had a porterhouse for two for $75 and it came with nothing else. You come outside and you see some homeless person standing on the street, and it doesn't feel great. I wouldn't want to be a person who didn't pay attention to it.
—Dwight Garner, "Ruth Reichl, Palate Revolt." The Salon Interview,
November 1996, Salon.com, http://www.salon.com/nov96/
interview961118.html

Reichl's first disguise was as "Molly," a high school teacher with two college-age children who come into New York City every few months to enjoy the city's theater, shopping, and restaurants. Wearing an Armani suit three sizes too large to accommodate the extra padding needed to camouflage her small frame, Reichl visited the first restaurant she would review for the *Times*—Le Cirque. This famous spot had hired a new chef so it merited a new review. Reichl's review of Le Cirque caused controversy not only because she demoted the restaurant from four to three stars, but also for the review's unconventional format—essentially two reviews, one from the perspective of an "unknown diner" and one as "a most favored patron."

During her six-year stint as restaurant critic for *The New York Times*, Reichl assumed many disguises, including "Chloe," a champagne blonde oozing sexuality; "Brenda," a vintage-clothing-clad sweetie; "Emily," a punctilious restaurant manager; and "Miriam," a recreation of Reichl's own mother, replete with a string of pearls and silver-gray wig. Reichl reviewed hundreds of restaurants, ranging from those owned by celebrity chefs Batali, Rocco DiSpirito, Daniel Boulud, and Jean-Georges Vongerichten, to dumpling parlors, Korean barbeque places, and sushi bars.

Reichl has a distinctive writing style that Batali described as "wonderfully libidinal," written by a "delightfully sensual woman who writes with wonderment about the carnal components of food." Anthony Bourdain, chef and author of the international bestseller *Kitchen Confidential: Adventures in the Culinary Underbelly* (2003), adds, "She comes more out of the Elizabeth David school than the A. J. Liebling school. I appreciate that she isn't a snob, and that she doesn't fetishize ingredients, like so many other writers." Kim

Severson, food writer at *The New York Times*, notes, "The literary quality of her writing moved food journalism and food writing ahead quite a bit. She really set the bar very high for those of us who write about food."

David Kamp from *The New York Times* wrote in April 2005 that "Reichl bestowed multiple stars and high praise to sushi bars and visually nondescript outer-borough Asian joints and wrote novelistic reviews, heavy on the first person and overheard snatches of dialogue from fellow diners, that marked her verdicts more as Ruth Reichl's than the *Times's*. To some readers and even *Times* people, this was an abomination, an upending of all the standards, journalistic and culinary, that had been established by the paper's original poobah of food, Craig Claiborne, in the 1960s, and upheld through the 1970s and 1980s by such writers as Miller, Mimi Sheraton and Marian Burros. To others, however, Reichl's approach was invigorating, just the jolt the food pages needed. Whichever way you felt, if you cared about restaurants, Reichl's weekly review was a compulsory read."

Toward the end of her last year with the *Times*, Reichl became restless. As she noted in *Garlic and Sapphires*, "I'm going to get out of the dining room and go back to the kitchen." She even had imaginary conversations with her long-dead mother, who, she fantasized, grilled her with questions like "Do you intend to spend your entire life practicing this ridiculous profession?" Reichl's *New York Times* reviews earned her three James Beard Awards: in 1996 and 1998 for restaurant criticism and in 1994 for journalism.

Gourmet

Serendipitously, shortly afterward, James Truman from *Condé Nast* contacted Reichl, asking her to interview for the editorship at *Gourmet* magazine. Reichl arrived at *Gourmet* as editor-in-chief in April 1999. "Ruth brought an intellectual rigor to *Gourmet* that it didn't have before," said *New York Times* food writer Kim Severson. Bourdain, who has been called a "cooking's bad boy" by CBS News and others, recalled, "Shortly after she took over at *Gourmet*, she really took a chance and commissioned an article about me, which talked about my past drug use among other topics. As I understand it, the article got a torrent of angry mail from old-school *Gourmet* readers. Many of these readers were used to cutting bundt cake recipes out of the magazine and pasting them into their scrap books, and didn't know what to make of a character like me." Despite that initial controversy, Reichl asked Bourdain to write several articles a year for *Gourmet*. Bourdain continued, "The magazine became a lot less stuffy as soon as she took over. Ruth has made *Gourmet* more accessible, and even made the covers more approachable and less structured, and by extension, she's made the world of fine dining and fine eating more accessible. More people are eating better because of her."

AWARDS AND HONORS

Under Reichl, *Gourmet Magazine* was nominated for 17 National Magazine Awards by the American Society of Magazine Editors and has won three (Photography in 2008, General Excellence in 2004, Photography in 2005) as well as 56 James Beard Award nominations with 18 wins in Food Journalism. Reichl was named "Magazine Editor of the Year" by *Adweek Magazine* in 2007 and also shepherded the magazine to two other *Adweek* awards. *Gourmet* achieved record circulation levels in 2006, and Reichl received the Missouri Honor Medal for Distinguished Service in Journalism, given by the Missouri School of Journalism, in October 2007. She earned the 2008 Matrix Award for Magazines from New York Women in Communications, Inc. She has also won the YWCA's Elizabeth Cutter Morrow Award.

Reichl edited several books for *Gourmet*, including *The* Gourmet *Cookbook* (2004), which appeared on *The New York Times* bestseller list. She also edited *History in a Glass: Sixty Years of Wine Writing from* Gourmet (2007); *Remembrance of Things Paris: Sixty Years of Writing from* Gourmet (2005); Gourmet *Cookies* (2010), which gives recipes for the best cookie of each year of *Gourmet*'s history; and Gourmet *Today*, published in 2009.

TELEVISION SHOWS

Reichl was the executive producer and sometime host of *Gourmet's Diary of a Foodie*, a James Beard Award–winning public television series that premiered October 2006. The program presented a cultural view of the world through its cuisine with topics that ranged from New Zealand's honey to Italy's famed Parmigiano-Reggiano cheese and even featured Reichl herself in brief cooking segments. The third season (2009) of *Gourmet's Diary of a Foodie* focused on travels to such diverse locations as Istanbul, Vermont, and Hong Kong. "It's some of the very best food television ever," said Bourdain, host of *A Cook's Tour* on the Food Network and *Anthony Bourdain: No Reservations* on the Travel Channel. In addition, Reichl hosted *Eating Out Loud*, three specials on Food Network covering New York (2002), San Francisco (2003), and Miami (2003).

Reichl is also executive producer of the forthcoming *Garlic and Sapphires*, a movie based on her memoir.

CONCLUSION

In October 2009, Reichl, in an unexpected conversation with S. I. Newhouse, head of Condé Nast, learned that *Gourmet* and three other magazines would be shut down immediately. The November issue, already at press, was to be the esteemed magazine's last, and Reichl and her staff were to clean out their offices and be gone by the end of the day. It was a sudden and ignominious end for *Gourmet*, which was in its own right an icon of American cuisine. Founded in 1941, the magazine had, over its 68-year history, published such epicurean luminaries as M. F. K. Fisher, James Beard, and Bourdain. It was considered the diamond standard of luxury food and travel writing and offered many of its readers a glimpse into a jet-setting world at the edges of their aspirations. Perhaps this was its downfall. Many readers loved Reich's inclusion of food politics, reflecting the zeitgeist of the 2000s, and palate-challenging exotic ingredients, but many others thought that as her food passions evolved she had made the magazine too snobby and inaccessible for the average reader. Condé Nast cited increasingly disappointing advertising sales and declining subscription rates, and thus elected to close *Gourmet* rather than its other popular cooking magazine, *Bon Appétit*, which targeted the middle-class, home cook. While the demise of *Gourmet* came as a shock to Reichl and her readers, it did not mean the end of Reichl's work with the brand. Two weeks after losing her job with Condé Nast, Reichl's new public television series, *Gourmet's Adventures with Ruth,* premiered. In addition, Reichl continued to tour and publicize her latest book under the *Gourmet* masthead, *Gourmet Today.* She is also writing a book on her 10 years with Condé Nast.

NOTE

1. All quotations are from interviews between Francine Segan and the sources quoted, 2009.

FURTHER READING

Reichl, Ruth. *Tender at the Bone: Growing Up at the Table.* New York: Broadway Books, 1999.

Reichl, Ruth. *Comfort Me with Apples: More Adventures at the Table.* New York: Random House, 2001.

Reichl, Ruth. *Garlic and Sapphires: The Secret Life of a Critic in Disguise.* New York: Penguin, 2005.

Reichl, Ruth. *Not Becoming My Mother: And Other Things She Taught Me along the Way.* New York: Penguin, 2009.

Francine Segan

Marion Rombauer Becker looks over the *Joy of Cooking* with her mother Irma Rombauer, at left. The mother and daughter team coauthored the 1951 edition of *Joy of Cooking*. (AP/Wide World Photos)

Irma Rombauer and Marion Rombauer Becker

Joy of Cooking (1931) is the best-selling and perhaps the most beloved American cookbook of all time. Large, voluminous, and comprehensive, *Joy* was first self-published in 1931 as the brainchild of a widowed St. Louis socialite who was looking to make some extra money in the Great Depression. Against all odds, it grew from these humble origins to sell more than 18 million copies in eight editions, largely due to the giant personality of author Irma Rombauer and the unflagging dedication of her daughter, Marion Rombauer Becker, who took over the "family business" in the early 1960s after her mother's death. *The New York Times* has called *Joy* "the most fabled of all American cookbooks, although not always the most fashionable," and "the Swiss Army knife of cookbooks."[1] It "became the one book you gave young cooks and newly married couples," one reviewer notes—"Glance at your bookshelf: it's probably there."[2]

Yet *Joy of Cooking* is more than just a cookbook. It is a personality in and of itself—a book that manages to encompass everyday convenience and highbrow cooking, and that does so in a manner that feels inviting, unintimidating, and completely self-assured. Equally at home with canned soup and caviar, *Joy*'s longevity and popularity come from the fact that it reflects how people actually cook, covering the entire spectrum of their culinary lives (from Wednesday supper to lavish dinner parties), ready with a recipe or suggestion for any eventuality, from apple pie to sautéed whale.

EARLY YEARS

Irma von Starkloff

Irma Rombauer was born Irma Louise von Starkloff in St. Louis, Missouri, on October 30, 1877, the youngest of four children. She grew up in a large German immigrant enclave filled with recent arrivals fleeing from the failed German rebellions of 1848, which advocated a unified Germany. Cultured, professional, educated, and uninterested in assimilating, this German community proudly retained their language and heritage and saw themselves as separate if not better than the "American" culture in which they lived. Rombauer's father, Max von Starkloff, was a doctor who had served in the Civil War on the Union side as an army surgeon. Her mother, Emma Kuhlmann, had been a kindergarten teacher before becoming Max's second wife and stepmother to his two grown sons.

Rombauer spent her teen years in Europe. Her father was appointed vice-consul of Bremen, Germany, in 1889, and the family lived there for five years. Her education was rather spotty and focused on ladies' pursuits such as reading, music, and art. Though Rombauer took art classes at university when she returned to the States, she never pursued a degree.

Pretty and vivacious, Rombauer "was small and neatly made, with a great flair for wearing clothes and making herself interesting to others, especially men."[3] She had a brief *affaire de coeur* with writer Booth Tarkington before he was famous but then settled down to marry Edgar Rombauer, another member of St. Louis's German elite. They met while acting in a local play. He was an attorney who had not yet made his way in the world and suffered from occasional severe bouts of depression—nervous breakdowns—that required his removal to healthier climes.[4] The couple married October 14, 1899, and settled in St. Louis, near their families. Their first child, Roland, was born in 1900 but died the following year. Both parents were devastated by the loss, and in 1902 Edgar had another breakdown. Yet, on January 2, 1903, the couple had their second child, Marion. In 1907, their youngest son, Edgar Jr., arrived. The Rombauers had also taken in their young nephew, Roderick, after the untimely death of Edgar's brother.

As Edgar's law practice flourished, Rombauer threw herself into the life of a society matron by joining the clubs and associations that gave women power and voice in their communities. She had "blazing, irresistible energy," although she was evidently somewhat Machiavellian. "People ether adored or detested here, or sometimes both," according to one report. "In her clubs, she was usually embroiled in some faction."[5] Rombauer joined the Unitarian Church to be involved in its women's alliance, and she also belonged to the Wednesday Club—the elite women's social and philanthropic club in St. Louis.

Marion Rombauer

Rombauer's daughter Marion, meanwhile, grew up surrounded by her mother's whirlwind of social activity and her father's bouts of depression. She loved dance and studied it on and off during her life, though she was tall and solidly built. She attended the prestigious Mary school in St. Louis and then Vassar, where she studied art history. In 1925, after Edgar had had another breakdown, Rombauer moved the whole family to Europe for an extended stay, with Marion joining them after graduation. Marion, who had suffered from allergies throughout her childhood and wore glasses because of a bout of scarlet fever, suffered most from the cruel taunting of her mother, who called her plain and unattractive. In Europe, Marion studied modern dance, particularly eurhythmics. This experience brought her into the intellectual world of 1920s Munich, where she had an affair with a middle-aged intellectual/philosopher named Ernst Kropp, whose book Marion hoped to translate into English.

On her return to St. Louis, Marion reconnected with her childhood friend John Becker, a handsome, struggling young architect. She found a job at a department store and later worked as a stringer for *Women's Wear Daily*, before teaching art history at the progressive John Burroughs School in St. Louis. Meanwhile, Marion and John fell in love, although circumstances, financial and otherwise, conspired to delay their marriage.

Death of Edgar Rombauer

Late in 1929, Edgar Rombauer suffered another attack of severe depression. The stock market crash and a painful struggle with bladder cancer, combined with his lifelong mental illness, may have been overwhelming. Rombauer, who often dealt with her husband's fits by taking him on vacation, hustled him off to South Carolina, where he seemed to improve. They returned in January 1930, and on February 3, after Rombauer left the house to go shopping, Edgar shot himself in the head.

COOKBOOKS

Joy of Cooking, 1931

Plunged into grief, the Rombauer women soon needed to address their dwindling finances. Edgar had left them only $6,000, some rapidly devaluing stock, and a little property. Although Marion was supporting herself by teaching, Rombauer had no external source of income. She soon seized on the idea to write a cookbook, which seemed a somewhat random choice for a woman who was not especially known for her cooking. However, it was the perfect choice for a woman of Rombauer's social position.[6] Marion remembers that her mother had taught a cooking class for the Women's Alliance of the Unitarian Church, had been a cofounder of the St. Louis Children's Lunch Association, and had taken a cake decorating class at the Chautauqua Institute in Bay View, Michigan, where the family summered.

Rombauer spent the remainder of 1930 collecting, organizing, and testing recipes, and getting Marion and several of her friends to test recipes as well. Marion, known for her artistic paper cutouts, also designed the cover and the art on the chapter title pages. She contacted a printer and arranged to have 3,000 copies printed and bound at her own expense. The enterprise cost $3,000—half of Edgar's legacy. Rombauer managed to sell 2,000 copies and to break even, but the *Joy of Cooking* had not fulfilled its promise of providing financial independence.

Joy of Cooking is relatively straightforward, with none of the long explanatory sections that grace the later editions. In her one-page introduction, Rombauer writes, "I have attempted to make palatable dishes with simple means and to lift everyday cooking out of the commonplace." She continues, "In spite of the fact that the book is compiled with one eye on the family purse and the other on the bathroom scale, there are, of course, occasional lapses into indulgence."[7] The chapters are arranged according to the order of a dinner party, from cocktails to dessert and reflect the way ordinary women probably cooked in 1931. Canned soups, and convenience flavorings like Savita (yeast extract), bouillon cubes, and Kitchen Bouquet (a browning agent), appear frequently and liberally on the pages.[8] In the introduction to her soup chapter, Rombauer writes, "Recently the French government conferred a decoration upon the cook who prepares Campbell's soup. It is regrettable that this distinction could not be made to include all soup manufacturers who have brought to us this good and nutritious product at so low a cost."[9] Yet, while canned and convenience ingredients do seem to dominate the main dishes, the desserts chapter reflects Rombauer's German heritage and what seems to be a real interest in baking and pastry. It has been argued that "the strongest and best material in *The Joy of Cooking* always has been in the realm of cakes, cookies, pies, and assorted desserts."[10] Pages of German Christmas cakes rub elbows with cookies, cupcakes, Lady Baltimore cake, three variants of fruitcakes (with poundage), and all manner of icings, custards, and soufflés—rarely with a canned or convenience food required.

One of the great secrets to *Joy*'s success was Rombauer herself: "The first *Joy* shows Irma still feeling her way. She displays her own personality more tentatively and sparingly than she would in versions to come, when she more consciously understood what it was that she had to offer against the competition."[11] Rombauer was not especially qualified to write a cookbook. Even Marion remembers, "Mother's early housekeeping days, after her marriage to Edgar Rombauer in 1898, gave little evidence of culinary prowess. 'Will it encourage you,' she asked in one of *Joy*'s prefaces, 'to know that I was once as ignorant, helpless and awkward a bride as was ever foisted on an impecunious young lawyer? Together we placed many a burnt offering upon the altar of matrimony.'" Indeed, Marion continues, "It is an open secret that Mother, to the very end of her life, regarded social intercourse as more important than food."[12] It was this social intercourse, and these social connections, along with the tested everyday recipes and company fare, that made the first book a success. As one reviewer and associate of Rombauer's noted in a column in the *St. Louis Post-Dispatch*, "it does not insult my intelligence."[13]

Yet, even with her famed large personality, Rombauer's flashes of wit grace the pages of the first edition only occasionally, as in her introduction to potatoes: "Those who have visited Hirschorn in the sweetly romantic Neckar Valley and who have climbed the hill to the partly ruined castle that dominates the little village, will remember being confronted by a 'Potato Monument,' dedicated piously 'to God and Francis Drake, who brought to Europe for the everlasting benefit of the poor—the Potato.' Please don't say that Sir Walter Raleigh or Governor Lane imported the potato, for it really doesn't matter, does it?"[14]

Bobbs-Merrill

Rombauer was not quite satisfied with either the sales or the text of her book and decided to revise it. Not only did she add new material, but she created a new format for recipes that included the ingredients, typographically distinctive from the rest of the text, within the recipes themselves, in the order in which they were needed. She also decided she needed a proper publisher who could give the book wider distribution.

In 1932 the self-published *Joy of Cooking* fell into the hands of Laurance Chambers, vice president of the Bobbs-Merrill publishing company in Indianapolis, who rejected it in 1933, saying, "The true fact of the matter is that the book trade is in such a low state that we could not get any wider distribution for *Joy of Cooking* than you are doing without our help."[15] By 1935, he had changed his mind, and on December 5, Rombauer signed a contract with Bobbs-Merrill to take over publication of the cookbook. This contract, which assigned copyright to Bobbs-Merrill, not just for the new edition but for the 1931 edition as well, would be the source of years of anger, strife, and conflict between the Rombauer family and their publisher.

Bobbs-Merrill had no real experience with cookbooks, and Rombauer had no real experience with publishers. The preparations for the new edition were contentious to say the least—the publisher wanted to cut Rombauer's "culinary chats" to make way for new recipes, but Irma put her foot down and prevailed. Moreover, the contract stipulated that the author would have to pay for proof corrections over 15 percent, which is unrealistic for cookbooks both then and now.[16] Published in 1936, the first trade edition of *Joy of Cooking* sold through almost 7,000 of its initial 10,000-copy print run within the first six months, prompting Bobbs-Merrill to order a second 10,000-copy run for 1938. Its success also convinced the publisher to sign Rombauer to a second book, focused on convenience foods and quick-cookery, to be titled, *Streamlined Cooking* (1939). It did not sell well and was a "terrible flop"—but Rombauer did manage to salvage much of the material for later *Joy* editions.[17]

By the early 1940s, *Joy* had become a bestseller, and Chambers of Bobbs-Merrill and Rombauer signed up again to do a revision, even though they were barely on speaking terms. This 1943 edition not only meshed *Joy* with *Streamlined Cooking*, but also dealt with war rationing, which other books did not. The new revision became the best-selling book in the United States. It was, coincidentally, the first cookbook Julia Child owned.

With the book's rapidly escalating sales came a period of newfound fame for Rombauer. Politician Wendell Wilkie and his wife Edith praised *Joy*. Food writer Cecily Brownstone became fast friends with Rombauer and introduced her to the foodie community in New York. It has been noted, "At last Irma knew herself a star, and she adored it."[18]

Even though the conflict with Bobbs-Merrill continued, now centered on discount sales and the loss of royalties from unauthorized printings, the company issued a 1946 edition, printed from the same plates as 1943, only with the rationing sections removed. It was now time to start planning a full revision. Cognizant of her age and concerned about her health, Rombauer had inserted a clause into the 1943 contract specifying Marion as the designated authorial heir for any future revisions to the text should Rombauer herself be unable to finish them. Bobbs-Merrill wanted to revise fully the new edition, with color photography. Marion, who assented to helping her mother with the revisions, found herself embroiled in arguing this point with the publisher. For the first time, the Rombauers retained counsel in their battles with Bobbs-Merrill and managed to block the publisher's plan to replace the book's distinctive line drawings with color photographs. More wrangling took place over the book's length and an index that Rombauer and Marion considered atrocious, until it was replaced in the 1953 edition.

While Marion contributed sections on her twin passions, gardening and health food (giving the book what one reviewer calls "a schizophrenic quality"), this was also the last edition of the book that Rombauer herself wrote.[19] The 1951 *Joy* was "Irma's last and Marion's first effort at cookbook writing, lasted until 1962 and is still cooked from today by a handful of aging users."[20] As Marion remembered, "Every transformation of *Joy* means to its authors a 'power and astonishment of work.' But preparing and putting together the edition of 1951 seemed, especially to the senior member of our pair, intolerably irksome. When the last galley had been corrected she told me she felt like the wan and emaciated angel [illustrator] Ginnie Hofmann sent us along with her final drawing. Indeed, after some reflection, she announced that she was, like Ginnie and her winged messenger, 'finished'—reluctantly, but for good. She had planted the acorn and performed a stupendous and winning job of cultivation. The sapling she nurtured had grown to a tree of broad caliper, and she was at last ready to rest in its grateful shade."[21]

Joy of Cooking, 1963

Marion and John Becker had married on June 18, 1932, after the publication of the original *Joy*. They moved to Cincinnati, where Becker worked in a marginally successful firm as an architect. Marion taught art briefly at a girls' school, then took up local liberal causes and organizations, such as the National Association for the Advancement of Colored People, the American Civil Liberties Union, and the League of Women Voters, before becoming, in 1939, the director of the Cincinnati Modern Art Society. The Beckers produced two children, Mark (1937) and Ethan (1945), and in 1936 Becker designed their dream house, which they named Cockaigne. The home's eight-acre lot gave Marion the opportunity to indulge in a newfound passion for gardening, which would later feed her interest in health food and the organic movement.

Rombauer, having finished the revisions for the 1951 version, with its attendant indexing and other corrections resulting in changes to the 1952 and 1953 printings, settled down to live the life of a famous author. She traveled to New York to visit with her food maven friends and to give public appearances. She went to Europe, where she had a chance luncheon with Julia Child, Simone Beck, and Louisette Bertholle while they were in the early stages of writing what would become *Mastering the Art of French Cooking* (1961). She had begun to earn real money from *Joy of Cooking* and liked to spend it, giving presents and money to those she loved. At home in St. Louis, she built a summer cottage in the country and cultivated a circle of younger friends, with whom she liked to drink, talk, study German, and read books. However, her age was starting to catch up with her—she had digestive and cardiac troubles and "had become a heavy drinker, of the sort who is slowly working through a glass of whiskey throughout most of the day."[22]

In the spring of 1955, Rombauer had a stroke. Marion had just been through a radical mastectomy to treat what would become a lifelong battle with breast cancer. Although prospects for recovery initially seemed good, Rombauer continued to decline until she became bedridden and increasingly less able to communicate. Marion likewise suffered from the aftereffects of her surgery, including radiation and lymphedema, which resulted in a swelling so severe she had to keep her arm elevated whenever it flared up.

Nevertheless, even though Rombauer was unable to continue and Marion was in constant pain, Rombauer negotiated with Bobbs-Merrill to bring out a new edition of *Joy*. Marion had been involved with her mother in the previous edition, but she had been less involved editorially than with the legal wranglings between the two parties. Moreover, Bobbs-Merrill had a fairly new editorial and administrative staff, most of whom had no experience with cookbooks and no idea what kind of work had gone into producing the various versions of *Joy of Cooking*. It was the perfect confluence of miscommunication, unclear expectations, and misunderstandings. Marion, for example, thought she could turn in the completed manuscript on index cards, while Bobbs-Merrill neglected to negotiate a contract in advance of the revision.

The relationship rapidly deteriorated. Marion envisioned a wholesale revision of *Joy* that involved the addition of instructional chapters, rearranged material, and the addition of new recipes, all of which made the manuscript much longer than the publisher had planned. Bobbs-Merrill had hired an outside editor, Alice Richardson, to turn the index cards into an actual manuscript, but she and the Beckers were unable to get along. Without knowing how long the book was actually going to be, the publisher began production on it. By 1961, the relationship had deteriorated so badly that M. Hughes Miller, the head of the company, sent a memo to his staff that read, "Alice Richardson is to edit the Beckers' edited galleys, but the Beckers are not to know about this."[23] Bobbs-Merrill then proceeded to publish *Joy of Cooking* in 1962, without Marion's knowledge or even a contract. Marion was furious. While she was considering her legal options, Rombauer, who had suffered not just from her stroke but also from a series of continuing health problems, including seizures, blood clots, and an amputation for gangrene, died on October 14, 1962, mere weeks before her 85th birthday.

On the advice of attorneys, Marion and Bobbs-Merrill agreed that the *Joy* would be reprinted with Marion's corrections. The result was the first manifestation of *Joy of Cooking* versions that today's cooks revere and remember. Marion added all of the fascinating and quirky chapters on technique, such as "The Foods We Heat," and "Know Your Ingredients." She also added the "Abouts" that are scattered through the text, as well as the unique symbols, and the modifier "Cockaigne" (the name of her home), to designate family favorites or special recipes. "Devil's Food Cake Cockaigne," for example, is "the best chocolate cake we know," Marion wrote.[24]

The 1963 *Joy* retained all of Rombauer's charm but saw the flower of Marion's vision for good food, well made at home, by ordinary people who cared about taste and health. It also suggested the end of an era in which middle-class American women lost their cooks and went back into the kitchen. As the introduction offers, "'The cook,' said [writer] Saki, 'was a good cook, as cooks go; and as cooks go, she went.' Indeed she did go, leaving us, whether in charge of established or of fledgling families, to fend for ourselves."[25] Ethan Rombauer calls his mother's freshman effort "one of the most outstanding books in the gourmet revolution of the 1950s and 1960"; it also had the distinction, in 1973, of earning the biggest advance for any paperback book in history after the New American Library paid $1.5 million for the paperback rights.[26]

Joy of Cooking, 1975

After the success of her 1963 *Joy*, Marion turned her attention to writing two books that more closely matched her own interests, *Little Acorn* (1966), a history of the *Joy of Cooking*, and *Wild Wealth* (1971), a tribute to gardening and wild plants that also featured extensive artwork. She and Becker had planned to begin a new revision of *Joy* in 1972. Since her son Ethan had decided he wanted to help, the Beckers sent him to Paris to study at Le Cordon Bleu—he would be the only one in the family to have any kind of professional culinary training whatsoever. Revisions were delayed when Marion discovered that her breast cancer had returned, resulting in another mastectomy and painful course of radiation therapy. Her long-term prognosis was poor. To make matters worse, Becker, who thought he may have had a stroke, discovered an inoperable brain tumor that, like Rombauer before him, turned him into an invalid. Marion had assumed that Becker would outlive her, but he died on October 22, 1974, less than a year after the first appearance of his symptoms. Marion was also embroiled in a lawsuit brought by old family friend Mazie White, who had helped Rombauer through several drafts of early editions of *Joy* and had also helped Marion with the 1963 revision—all without a formal contract.

Writing *Joy of Cooking* had always been a team effort—Rombauer had relied on White, Marion, and other friends through the years to type, test and suggest recipes, and proof and edit the manuscripts. Marion had likewise relied on her husband, White, and other close family friends. Now, with the 1975 revision of the book, she needed her team more than ever. Her relationship with her publisher had improved significantly, and the contract and publication of the book "proceeded without a hitch. The results were everything Marion or Bobbs-Merrill could have desired."[27] The *New York Times* food critic Craig Claiborne called it "the finest basic cookbook available. It is a masterpiece of clarity."[28] Marion died December 28, 1976.

Joy of Cooking, 1997

Marion's 1975 revision of *Joy of Cooking* lasted for over 20 years until Simon and Schuster, which had purchased Bobbs-Merrill, decided to embark on another revision, this time under the direction of Ethan Becker. Marion's last *Joy* had become the best-selling edition to date, and the 1963 edition remained in print as a popular paperback. First Lady Laura Bush named the 1963 version one of her favorite books, essential for pancakes, meats, and "lemon sponge custard." The University of Buffalo included *Joy* on their list of 100 books recommended to students as unrequired reading.[29] Nancy Davis, in thinking about buying a new copy of the *Joy*, wrote lovingly of her four decades with the much-spattered, dog-eared, ripped, and coverless 1946 edition she had received as a young bride, reliving through its marks and annotations an entire lifetime of cooking and memories: "Well, old book, I guess it's time to say goodbye. . . . They'll never find you tossed in a trash can or put in a garage sale. You and I will never part. Should I have you bronzed? No, you'll be retired to a place of honor on my kitchen shelf, right next to the old-time mixer and the cracked fondue pot."[30]

News of a new edition after 20 years filled cooks and critics with a mix of hope and trepidation. Ethan worked with Simon and Schuster's experienced cookbook editor, Maria Guarnaschelli, who assembled a large team of experts to oversee the revision. Guarnaschelli envisioned a total overhaul of the book, which had not been touched in 20 years, to make it both modern and relevant. She also put together focus groups to find out what people wanted from their *Joy of Cooking*. Journalist Molly O'Neill reported, "'What could be wrong with 'Joy'?' asked one of the 12 members of the focus group convened by the publisher in June. Like so many other Americans, she saw 'Joy of Cooking' as a bible—though she hadn't used it in eight years."[31] Clearly, the zeitgeist seemed right for a revision that reflected the changes in culinary taste since the last edition in 1975. In his introduction to the 1997 *Joy*, Ethan writes, "What times these are! Who would have thought twenty-five years ago that cooking would be a noble career choice and one of America's favorite pastimes?"[32]

In many ways, the new *Joy*'s focus on chef-driven recipes, fresh ingredients, and from-scratch cooking also reflected Ethan's experience at the Cordon Bleu. He relied heavily on Guarnaschelli, who wrote that Ethan "did not undertake a revision until he found an editor and publisher whose vision of *Joy* matched his own."[33] Guarnaschelli deleted the canning and freezing sections, as well as the quaint but occasionally necessary information on skinning squirrels and rabbits that had originally entered the book via Edgar Rombauer's interests in hunting and camping. Guarnaschelli assigned individual chapters to such food luminaries as Deborah Madison, Dorie Greenspan, Chris Schlesinger, John Willoughby, Rick Bayless, Betty Fussell, and Bruce Aidells. Never had such an illustrious team worked together to produce what was supposed to be the ultimate manifestation of *Joy*.

However, something went "terribly wrong," according to Ethan. "Recipes from professional food writers replaced many of the book's old standards, food processors whirred a bit too much and the voice of the cookbook became subsumed. In 97 we kind of lost our way."[34] Critics were not overly warm to the revision, which they described as "corporate" in tone, and "the New Coke of cookbooks." Yet, even while declaiming the book for its lack of heart and personality, many of the same critics did find things to like about it, calling it "smart, chef-driven," and "better organized."[35] O'Neill wrote, in the same review, that the new recipes were better than those in the 1975 version, but that at the end of the day, "'Joy,' the icon, is no longer a guide to daily life and an antidote to the worries of its era. The new 'Joy' is a good cookbook. But it is only a cookbook." Even though the 1997 *Joy* sold wildly, the book had clearly lost its soul, and in doing so, had lost its audience. Ethan himself later referred to it as "publisher driven" and seems to have downplayed his involvement in the revision.[36]

Joy of Cooking, 2006

In 2001, Ethan decided to try again. With his wife Susan and a new hand-picked team that included Julia Child before her death, he went back to Marion's 1975 edition of the book to, as Child wrote, "put the joy back in *Joy*."[37] The newest version seems largely to have restored the homey voice to the book, but perhaps at the expense either of timeless or contemporary needs. Reviews of the 2006 edition were mixed; generally cooks seemed happy to have the old favorites from the earlier editions back again, but thought that the book was too nostalgic. In *Slate*, food writer Laura Shapiro called it "an impassioned *mea culpa* for the last edition," noting that, in their quest to restore the book, the editors had instead "antiqued it with a vengeance."[38] Yet, one way in which *Joy of Cooking* has changed with the times is in its portion sizes and calorie counts. Researchers recently "examined seven editions of *Joy of Cooking* published from 1936 to 2006. In 14 of 18 recipes studied, the calorie content had surged by an average of 928 calories, or 44 percent per recipe."[39]

From Joy of Cooking

How good is your sense of values? What is your first thought when you prepare a meal? Is it of a decorated cake or a fancy salad? It should be of the nutritional value of food you plan to serve, not only for the one meal but in relation to the whole day's intake. Gastronomy and nutrition are not synonymous—so don't confound them. Your thought should be of the correct preparation, cooking and timing of the food. It should be an attempt at variety in ingredients, textures and flavors.

If you have little time, choose a menu that may be quickly prepared. Prepare such dishes in advance as are not harmed by early preparation. For all details, consult the cookbook and the index. Know at what degree of heat you are going to cook the food and how long it is going to take.

Start with the dish that takes the longest time to cook and follow it up with the others requiring a shorter time. Set the table in one of the intervals.

Serve hot food hot from hot dishes. Serve cold food chilled from chilled dishes. Keep calm even if your hair striggles and you drip unattractively.

Brush up before serving. Your appearance and the appearance of the food are important but eating in a quiet atmosphere is even more important to the family's morale and digestion.

A meal represents effort and money. It is worthy of a dignified hour.

Your first efforts at cooking may result in confusion, but soon you will acquire a skilled routine that will give you confidence and pleasure. You don't believe it? Will it encourage you to know that I was once as ignorant, helpless and awkward a bride as was ever foisted on an impecunious young lawyer? Together we placed many a burnt offering on the altar of matrimony, and I have lived to serve a meal attractively and well and even to write a cookbook that has proved helpful to others.

—Irma S. Rombauer, "Introduction." *Joy of Cooking,* 1953

CONCLUSION

Nevertheless, for the last 80 years, *Joy of Cooking* has been perhaps the most popular and iconic American cookbook in print. Like Child, Rombauer came to cooking in the second half of her life, wrote a cookbook without really knowing how, and became a unique and influential voice in American cuisine. Like Rachael Ray, Rombauer eschewed food snobbery, and instead privileged good cooking for real people who want to eat well every day. Like Martha Stewart, Rombauer believed that anyone could throw a great party, with a little help from a book. To all this, and her mother's wit and verve, Marion added careful study of technique, ingredients, and process, a legacy now held by Ethan. The many editions of *Joy of Cooking* have reflected Americans back to themselves—how they were, and how they wished to be. It is the quintessential expression of the way Americans actually eat.

NOTES

1. Martin Arnold, "Making Books; A Culinary Fantasy Life," *The New York Times* (October 29, 1998) http://www.nytimes.com/1998/10/29/books/making-books-a-culinary-fantasy-life.html?scp=100&sq=joy%20of%20cooking&st=cse&pagewanted=1; Kim Severson, "Does the World Need Another 'Joy'? Do You?," *The New York Times* (November 1, 2001) http://www.nytimes.com/2006/11/01/dining/01joy.html?_r =1& scp=2&sq=joy%20of%20cooking&st=cse

2. Severson, "Does the World Need Another 'Joy'?"

3. Anne Mendelson, *Stand Facing the Stove: The Inside Story of the Women Who Gave America* The Joy of Cooking (New York: Henry Holt and Company, 1996), 29.

4. Mendelson, *Stand Facing the Stove,* 38.

5. Mendelson, *Stand Facing the Stove,* 45.

6. Mendelson, *Stand Facing the Stove,* 83–86.

7. Irma Rombauer, *The Joy of Cooking* (1998 facsimile edition; New York: Simon and Schuster, 1931), n.p. Note that even though the book was originally published in St. Louis, Bobbs-Merrill negotiated for copyright extending back to 1931, which then transferred to Simon and Schuster upon their acquisition of Bobbs-Merrill.

8. For (yeast extract) information on Kitchen Bouquet, see Kitchen Bouquet in "Practically Edible: The World's Biggest Food Encyclopaedia," http://www.practically edible.com/edible.nsf/pages/kitchenbouquet; on Savita, a yeast extract from the Kellogg company, see "Foods that Build Health Can be Palate Tempting," *National Geographic* (February 1929), in "Modern Mechanix: Yesterday's Tomorrow Today," http://blog .modernmechanix.com/2009/06/22/foods-that-build-health-can-be-palate-tempting/

9. Rombauer, *The Joy of Cooking* (1931), 19.

10. Mendelson, *Stand Facing the Stove,* 142.

11. Mendelson, *Stand Facing the Stove,* 145.

12. Marion Rombauer Becker, "Irma Rombauer," Famous Unitarians, http:// harvardsquarelibrary.org/unitarians/rombauer.html

13. Mendelson, *Stand Facing the Stove,* 96.

14. Rombauer, *The Joy of Cooking* (1931), 95–96.

15. Quoted in "Foreword to the Facsimile Edition," by Edgar R. Rombauer Jr., in Rombauer, *The Joy of Cooking* (1931), n.p.

16. Mendelson, *Stand Facing the Stove,* 153, 158.

17. Mendelson, *Stand Facing the Stove,* 167, 171.

18. Mendelson, *Stand Facing the Stove,* 174–175.

19. "Joy of Cooking: A Listing of the American Editions," http://www.cookbkjj .com/college/joy.htm

20. Mendelson, *Stand Facing the Stove,* 279.

21. Becker, "Irma Rombauer," http://harvardsquarelibrary.org/unitarians/rombauer .html

22. Mendelson, *Stand Facing the Stove,* 195.

23. "*Joy of Cooking* 1963 edition," in Joy History, TheJoyKitchen.com: The Online Home of the *Joy of Cooking,* http://www.thejoykitchen.com/history.lasso?tag=1963; also quoted in Mendelson, *Stand Facing the Stove,* 324.

24. Irma Rombauer and Marion Rombauer Becker, *Joy of Cooking* (Indianapolis: Bobbs-Merrill, 1964), 627.

25. Rombauer and Becker, *Joy of Cooking* (1964), n.p.

26. "The History of the *Joy of Cooking,*" TheJoyKitchen.com, http://www.the joykitchen.com/about.lasso?menu=two; Eric Pace, "Record $1.5 Million for Paperback That Revels in the *Joy of Cooking,*" *The New York Times* (April 3, 1973) http:// select.nytimes.com/gst/abstract.html?res=F40B10F63E5C1A7A93C1A9178FD85F4 78785F9&scp=8&sq=joy%20of%20cooking&st=cse

27. Mendelson, *Stand Facing the Stove,* 393.

28. *Joy of Cooking,* 1975 edition, in Joy History, TheJoyKitchen.com: The Online Home of the *Joy of Cooking,* http://www.thejoykitchen.com/history.lasso?tag=1975.

29. Marian Burros, November 14, 2001, "From the Joy of Cooking to Frida Kahlo," http://www.nytimes.com/2001/11/14/dining/from-the-joy-of-cooking-to-frida-kahlo. html?scp=21&sq=joy%20of%20cooking&st=cse; "A College Reading List of Good If Not Necessarily Great Books," *The New York Times* (September 28, 1993) http://www .nytimes.com/1993/09/28/nyregion/a-college-reading-list-of-good-if-not-necessarily- great-books.html?scp=54&sq=joy%20of%20cooking&st=cse

30. Nancy Davis, "Memories in a Worn Cookbook," *The New York Times* (November 13, 1988) http://www.nytimes.com/1988/11/13/nyregion/memories-in-a-worn-cookbook.html?scp=37&sq=joy%20of%20cooking&st=cse

31. Molly O'Neill, "It's a New Joy, But Is It the Old Love? The Cookbook Now Speaks in a Corporate Tone," *The New York Times* (November 5, 1997) http://www.nytimes.com/1997/11/05/dining/it-s-new-joy-but-it-old-love-cookbook-now-speaks-corporate-tone.html?scp=40&sq=joy%20of%20cooking&st=cse

32. Ethan Rombauer, "Foreword," in *Joy of Cooking* by Irma Rombauer, Marion Rombauer Becker, and Ethan Becker (New York: Scribner, 1997), ix.

33. Maria Guarnaschelli, "Introduction," in *Joy of Cooking* (1997), xi.

34. Jennifer Steinhauer, "The Way We Eat: Ode to Joy," *The New York Times* (October 15, 2006) http://query.nytimes.com/gst/fullpage.html?res=980DEED81330 F936A25753C1A9609C8B63&scp=31&sq=joy%20of%20cooking&st=cse

35. Severson, "Does the World Need Another 'Joy'?"

36. *Joy of Cooking* 1997 edition, in Joy History, TheJoyKitchen.com: The Online Home of the *Joy of Cooking,* http://www.thejoykitchen.com/history.lasso?tag=1997. For sales of the 1997 edition, see Martin Arnold, "Making Books: A Culinary Fantasy Life," *The New York Times* (October 29, 1998) http://www.nytimes.com/1998/10/29/ books/making-books-a-culinary-fantasy-life.html?scp=100&sq=joy%20of%20 cooking&st=cse&pagewanted=1. Simon and Schuster shipped half a million copies in the first six months.

37. Ethan Becker, "A Letter from Ethan Becker," in *Joy of Cooking* by Irma Rombauer, Marion Rombauer Becker, and Ethan Becker (New York: Scribner, 2006), xi.

38. Laura Shapiro, "What *Joy* Is Missing," Slate.com, November 1, 2006, http:// www.slate.com/id/2152620/

39. Tara Parker-Pope, "Who's Cooking? For Health, It Matters," *The New York Times* (March 16, 2009) http://www.nytimes.com/2009/03/17/health/17well.html? scp=72&sq=joy%20of%20cooking&st=cse

FURTHER READING

Mendelson, Anne. *Stand Facing the Stove: The Inside Story of the Women Who Gave America* The Joy of Cooking. New York: Henry Holt and Company, 1996.

Rombauer, Irma S., Marion Rombauer Becker, and Ethan Becker. *Joy of Cooking.* New York: Scribner, 2006.

TheJoyKitchen.com

Elizabeth S. Demers

Martha Stewart poses for photographs in the Katonah model home at the unveiling of her homebuilding and design concept in the Hampton Oaks subdivision outside of Fairburn, Georgia, July 25, 2006. (AP/Wide World Photos)

Martha Stewart

Since 1982, Martha Stewart has changed the way Americans think about, create, and enjoy food. Her influence has been acknowledged in her inclusion in *Time*'s annual "Top 100" list (2005) and five appearances in *Fortune*'s "50 Most Powerful Women" list (1998–2001, 2005), among many other awards for her business acumen. In 2007, she received a Lifetime Achievement Award at the Food Network South Beach Wine & Food Festival.

Through over 30 cookbooks and entertaining guides, several award-winning television programs, a 24-hour satellite radio channel, award-winning monthly magazines, a Web site, and personal appearances, Stewart has harnessed the myriad possibilities of the information age to advise and teach Americans about all aspects of homemaking. Following in a long tradition of 19th-century domestic advisers from Catharine Beecher and Lydia Child and the inventors of home economics, to 20th-century columnists such as Heloise and chefs such as Julia Child, Stewart has energetically pursued perfection, whether in pie crust or in potatoes. Although Stewart's multimedia enterprise comprises many aspects of house care and homemaking, food and cooking remain its central focus.

EARLY YEARS

Family and Childhood

Martha Helen Kostyra Stewart was born on August 3, 1941, in Jersey City, New Jersey, to Edward Kostyra and Martha Ruszkowski Kostyra. All of her grandparents had immigrated to the United States from Poland in the first decades of the 20th century, bringing with them Polish culinary and cultural traditions that would be embraced by their granddaughter. Married in 1937, Edward, a gym teacher, and "Big Martha," as she was familiarly called, raised Martha and her older brother Eric in a small Jersey City apartment until the family moved, in 1944, to the Newark suburb of Nutley, which was 12 miles from New York City and populated primarily by Irish, Italian, and Polish families. The family would grow to include four more children (George, Frank, Kathy, and Laura), all living at 86 Elm Place, a modest three-story, three-bedroom, one-bath Dutch Colonial built around 1930.

Though crowded, the house served as a learning laboratory for "Little Martha." Stewart, as the eldest daughter, aided her mother in cooking, baking, and house-cleaning and learned decorating and gardening from her father. She recalled in 1992 that the house's basement was "full and really very good . . . where we cooked, laundered, did small carpentry projects and worked on hobbies."[1] In her first book, *Entertaining* (1982), Stewart explained to readers that she remembered three kitchens as "places of learning." The first was the eat-in kitchen in which her mother prepared the family meals. Her mother served robust meals, including "sauerbraten, tongue, and galumpkies (stuffed cabbage)," for the large family, who ate supper together every night.[2] Without a dining room, the Kostyra family crammed around the kitchen table for their meals.

Both sides of Stewart's family celebrated daily their heritage through their food practices. Her paternal grandfather, after a stint as a mess hall cook and restaurant employee, opened a butcher shop and later purchased a tavern, at which "pickles, sausage, and sauerkraut" could be purchased "as part of a highwayman's lunch." Stewart's Uncle Joe was also a butcher, and his wife, Mary, made salads to sell in the shop. Another uncle operated a delicatessen with "the best Polish sausage [Stewart] ever tasted, handmade every morning by Aunt Katerin."[3]

Stewart's mother preserved the fruits and vegetables grown by her husband in the family's backyard. Various berry patches supplied the family with seasonal delights. The backyard fig and MacIntosh apple trees were points of pride for Stewart's father, who also grew roses and cultivated a vegetable garden in the two-tiered plot. "Oh, he was always in competition with the neighbor next door to see who could grow the longest string beans and the biggest tomatoes," his wife recalled. "He planted something like ninety tomato plants every year."[4] The lessons of these activities were quickly learned by their daughter. In *Martha Stewart's Gardening* (1991), Stewart wrote this acknowledgement: "Most of all, my thanks to my father, for being my first teacher of gardening. His love of growing things was transferred to me though [*sic*] our gardening together; I will remember what he taught me forever."[5] Her mother's canning knowledge was featured in the pages of the popular monthly periodical *Martha Stewart Living*. Stewart also learned about food preservation from her maternal grandparents during summers spent with them in Buffalo, New York. Her grandparents' kitchen, with its old-fashioned icebox and a black cast-iron stove, was the second "place of learning" in Stewart's culinary education.

A neighbor's kitchen provided the third "place of learning." Stewart recalls fondly her neighbors, "Mr. and Mrs. Maus"—Robert Maus and his wife, Katherine, who lived at 96 Elm Place. Robert, born in Germany in 1883, had been a professional baker. The delights of German baking—"plum and cherry kuchen, raspberry and apple strudels"—enchanted Stewart and her siblings until Maus's death in 1951.[6]

Stewart, in her "Remembering" columns in her popular monthly periodical *Martha Stewart Living*, often portrays her childhood as an idyllic time of curiosity and of living richly by appreciating domestic life and jobs well done, rather than living like the rich. She often recalls her father as an aesthete, a creative and curious man who took up many projects and hobbies. At the same time, however, she writes that many of these endeavors did not succeed or fulfill him. She notes that her father, who had become a pharmaceuticals salesman, found money for his hobbies and for the purchase of expensive clothes, while his wife—who at one time returned to teaching to enhance the household income—and daughters sewed their own garments. Other family members and childhood friends remember Kostyra as a demanding father and unhappy man, rueful of not having achieved career and financial success. The Kostyra children learned to obey their father's demands and meet his exacting standards of order and cleanliness.

The Kostyra family played and prayed together. Both activities involved food. With a large family and a small income, they could rarely afford vacations. Branch Brook Park, designed by Frederick Law Olmsted and the first county park in the United States, attracted the family during the annual spring Cherry Blossom Festival. During the summer, the family enjoyed day trips to the seashore that included picnic lunches and clamming in the shallow waters.

On Sundays, family members donned their best clothes to attend Our Lady of Mount Carmel, a Polish Catholic church. Afterward, the family enjoyed treats at a nearby Polish bakery. At Easter, their priest, Father Czechowski, visited their home to bless their food. More so than other contemporary lifestyle experts, Stewart, in her television programs and in *Martha Stewart Living*, celebrates the eastern European ethnic traditions of Lent and Easter: *chrusciki* (fried dough knots dusted with sugar), *pascha* (a large round loaf of bread), *pierogi*, *pysanky* (decorated eggs), and kielbasa.

Schooling

Stewart attended public schools in Nutley. By all accounts she was a passionate reader and an excellent student, earning top grades. She wrote for the high school's literary quarterly and earned honors in her English classes. Her high school yearbook chronicles her participation in many club activities. She and her father decorated the high school gymnasium for the prom, and she prepared the school's traditional Saturday morning breakfasts for the football team. In *Entertaining*, Stewart describes this "breakfast of heroic proportions" her first "'catered' party."[7] Under her senior class portrait were the words "I do what I please, and I do it with ease." Supplied by the yearbook editorial staff, this sentiment likely represented her classmates' impression of her competence, confidence, and ambition. Stewart graduated from Nutley High School in 1959.

With a superb academic record, Stewart was offered a full scholarship to New York University, yet she chose to attend Barnard College on a partial scholarship. At her father's urging, Stewart had, during high school, taken up modeling. She appeared in print advertisements for such upscale department stores as Bonwit Teller and for Breck and Clairol hair care products, as well as acted in television commercials for Tareyton cigarettes and Lifebuoy soap. In her first semester at Barnard, she lived at home and commuted to campus, but in 1960 she moved to New York City and received room and board in exchange for housekeeping for two elderly sisters in their Fifth Avenue apartment. This arrangement lasted another semester and, with her modeling income and part-time sales positions at area department stores, allowed Stewart to afford tuition. Indeed, Stewart's modeling career allowed her to move into a campus dormitory the next year. A serious student, she undertook a course of study in art and architectural history, earning a bachelor of arts in art history in 1964.

Stewart intensively attended not only to her studies but also to her public image and her private life. In 1961, she appeared in the pages of *Glamour*, a popular American fashion magazine, as one of the 10 best-dressed college girls in the nation. Already well versed in modeling and fashion, Stewart, photographed wearing several borrowed articles of clothing, is described in phrases befitting the era's concepts of domesticity: "life pleases her," the editor observed, "in particular, a young man named Andy, art and architecture." And "she cooks, too."[8]

Marriage, Motherhood, and Homemaking

In her second semester at Barnard in spring 1960, Stewart was introduced to Andy Stewart, a Yale Law School student from a cosmopolitan, nonobservant Jewish family. Within a year the couple were engaged, and they wed on July 1, 1961, at St. Paul's Chapel (Episcopalian) on the Columbia University campus. The newlyweds moved to Connecticut so that Andy could complete the last year of law school; Stewart put her studies on hold. They returned to New York City in 1962, where they worked and attended school: Stewart modeled and reenrolled at Barnard, and Andy worked part-time at a law firm while attending Columbia University for a master of law degree. Both finished their respective degrees in 1964, and on September 27, 1965, Stewart gave birth to Alexis Gilbert Stewart, the couple's only child.

The couple's hectic pace continued to accelerate. Because of the dynamic changes in the modeling business in the 1960s, Stewart's wholesome features and polished look were losing popularity as more exotic looks became fashionable. She turned again to aiding her husband's career, hosting cocktail parties and suppers for his law firm colleagues, and to holiday dinners and celebrations for family members and friends. The necessity of an income to support this lifestyle, however, mandated that Stewart return to the workplace. Influenced by her stockbroker father-in-law, Stewart acquired her stockbroker license in 1968 and was hired by Moness, Williams and Sidel, a Wall Street firm founded only three years earlier. She quickly became one of the firm's top salespersons, at one point earning an annual salary of $135,000.

During this time the Stewarts poured their savings and labor into the purchase, in 1965, of "Middlefield," an 1850 schoolhouse in the Massachusetts Berkshire foothills. Over the next five years, the Stewarts often drove the 400-mile round trip in a weekend to renovate what they planned as a weekend retreat. Stewart's brother George remembers this time as one in which "it was all about going and finding a piece of land and living off it, learning how to get back to nature. . . . We used to have the greatest evenings with a bunch of hospitable people. . . . Martha would make pies and other things for the occasions. Sometimes she would bring a bushel of peas and we'd all shuck them. We would spend hours picking wild blueberries—you know, the little bitty ones. Then when we got back, Martha would make a pie or bread."[9]

The sort of activities in which the Stewarts engaged the friends and family continued at "Turkey Hill Farm," the 1805 "fixer upper" the couple bought in 1971 on Turkey Hill Road in Westport, Connecticut. Weekends would find the

Stewarts and their visitors engaged in a variety of projects: Andy built a chicken coop (the "Palais des Poulet"), George Kostyra and his fraternity brothers scraped and painted white the Federal-style house's exterior, and Stewart planted a vegetable garden. All came together, however, in the preparation and consumption of food. As George recalled, Stewart wished to "live off the land," quoting his sister as saying, "We are going to just buy the basic staples from the food store." They fished and crabbed, ate the garden's seasonal bounty, and, thanks to Stewart's chickens, "ate lots of eggs."[10] This was more than an economic or political statement. As Alexis asserted, her mother "never allowed any junk food in the house. . . . The house contained only ingredients. . . . No finished products, no snack food, no fast food, no nothing. My mom loves using fresh ingredients—not only for the flavor but for the health benefits too."[11]

Closer to New York City and to Andy's employment as assistant in-house legal counsel at Bangor Punta Corporation, a mining company that had moved its headquarters from Manhattan to Greenwich, Connecticut, Turkey Hill Farm was intended to provide the family's stability and lessen the stresses of a career and commute. In important ways, however, the move to Turkey Hill Farm represented a major life change for the Stewart family. In 1973 both the Stewarts changed careers. Andy moved to the Times Mirror Company, where he soon became president and chief executive officer of Abrams Publishing. Stewart resigned her lucrative job because of Wall Street setbacks, the loss of credibility due to poor advice to friends about Levitz Furniture stock, and the strain on her family and herself. Middlefield may have been a dress rehearsal for the more extensive renovation of Turkey Hill Farm, but the house and gardens and outbuildings there would soon serve as the stage upon which Stewart would achieve success.

Cooking, Catering, and a New Career

The parties and dinners Stewart created were also dress rehearsals, of sorts. At those events Stewart attended to every detail, schooling herself in various cuisines and with fashionable foods. In particular, she credits *Mastering the Art of French Cooking* (1961), written by Julia Child, Simone Beck, and Louisette Bertholle, with opening her up to the vast culinary world. At loose ends in Westport, Stewart sought a new career. In 1974, with old friend Norma Collier, whom she had met as one of *Glamour*'s "Best Dressed College Girls" in 1961, Stewart opened a business called the Uncatered Affair. The small business created and delivered food using clients' own cookware, utensils, and serving dishes, as if clients themselves had prepared the food. Despite a growing business, including cooking classes and consultancies, the partnership ended acrimoniously in early 1975.

Stewart continued to cater, building up a clientele and seeking new ways to raise her business profile. Westport's upscale Common Market, offering retail shops and trendy and imported foodstuffs, proved the venue at which Stewart could sell homemade baked goods—especially pies, priced at $20—and other prepared foods. Starting at a table outside a shop, Stewart's endeavor blossomed into a successful shop called the Market Basket. Through the local newspaper, the *Westport News*, Stewart advertised for local bakers and cooks to provide their best baked goods and dishes to the store. Many of the women who answered the advertisement developed long and supportive friendships with Stewart; the opportunity to make money through one's formerly unremunerated domestic skills came at a time when more Americans were working longer hours and did not always look forward to cooking for themselves.

However, the Market Basket venture, although successful, was also fraught with problems. Local health inspectors raised legal issues of food safety and licensing, necessitating the installation of a commercial kitchen on the premises. After several other problems and disagreements, the owners of the Common Market severed their relationship with Stewart.

Nevertheless, with high visibility, a growing clientele, and a well-equipped, if cramped, cellar kitchen at Turkey Hill Farm, Stewart's catering business grew. The year 1977 was one of hope and despair for Stewart and her family. She created Martha Stewart Incorporated in January 1977. In the spring of that year, however, Andy discovered and underwent radiation treatment for cancer. Stewart's father was also ailing from years of drinking that only complicated his heart problems. He would die on August 31, 1979. The period in which Stewart would achieve fame beyond Westport and Manhattan was also one in which her family and herself suffered from life's tragedies.

Stewart Holiday Party

Yet another family tradition began when Andy and I celebrated our first Christmas on Riverside Drive. We had a spacious apartment with a wonderful flow from room to room, and we found that we could easily entertain eighty or ninety for cocktails. That first year, the invitation read "Christmas Carols, Cocktails, and Desserts," and this theme has persisted over the years with the addition of more hors d'oeuvres, and a hearty one-course supper for late departees.

This year, more than 175 guests came for "Christmas All Over the House," to begin at 6 P.M. and end whenever. Hors d'oeuvres were served in the outside kitchen, a buffet supper was laid out in the barn, and champagne, eggnog, and desserts were in the main house. It was a clear night, there was a bit of a moon, and the sky was filled with stars. The paths were lined with hundreds of paper-bagged candles, and the fruit trees and windows shone with little white lights. It was festive, but simple, warm, and welcoming and friendly—all that a gathering of family and friends should be.

—Martha Stewart, *Martha Stewart's Christmas*. New York: Clarkson Potter, 1989, p. 119

PUBLICATIONS AND TELEVISION SHOWS

Entertaining *and the Lifestyle Revolution*

What brought Stewart to the American public's attention was the publication in December 1982 of *Entertaining*, a work based on Stewart's experiences and advice. Her husband drew up the contract and suggested that a professional writer be included in the project. This writer was Elizabeth Hawes, a former *New Yorker* editor. Published by Clarkson Potter in a coffee table size with full-color photographs, this book offered advice as it chronicled the parties and dinners and events that Stewart had planned and catered. In addition, *Entertaining* offered recipes. Not quite a prescriptive guide or a cookbook, but a little of both, *Entertaining* was an instant success because it offered one person's "rags to riches" story as a guide to a lifestyle that could be realized through emulation. The book also appeared as the American economy was on an upswing and elite and luxury goods designers were turning their attentions to the mass market. What was once the privilege of the wealthy could be adapted to the middle class.

With the success of *Entertaining*—30 printings and over 500,000 sold—Stewart Inc. was firmly established. However, although the book's reviews were favorable, *Newsweek* pointed out that two of its recipes originally appeared in Julia Child's work. Former partner Norma Collier also noted in 1991 that "a lot of her recipes were mine."[12] And the well-known cook and restaurant owner Barbara Tropp, the author also of *The Modern Art of Chinese Cooking* (1982), charged Stewart with stealing several of her recipes. Although American copyright law does protect recipes, recipe authors rarely sue. Rather, professional ethics tend to dictate the claims to originality in a recipe. Following accepted professional practice, Tropp is credited as "inspiring" several recipes in later editions of *Entertaining*.

What would become known as Stewart's "empire" was being established. Individuals paid between $900 and $1,200 to spend several days at Turkey Hill Farm, taking seminars on cooking and entertaining. She began to plan and cater events for celebrities and charities as well as large-scale extravaganzas for luxury companies such as Tiffany's. Stewart followed her initial publication with *Martha Stewart's Quick Cook Menus* (1983), *Martha Stewart's Hors D'Oeuvres* (1984), and *Martha Stewart's Pies and Tarts* (1987), a set of videotapes entitled *Martha Stewart's Secrets for Entertaining*, and appearances in special programs on the Lifetime Channel and in the pages of *Bon Appetit*, as well as other magazines. In one decade, the company would grow to a business worth $1 million.

Public Television

Stewart's ability to combine food preparation and presentation, her knowledge of cultural tastes and traditions, and her good looks and business savvy soon garnered more attention. In 1986 Boston's public television channel, WGBH-TV, produced and aired *Holiday Entertaining with Martha Stewart*. *Weddings*, weighing in at five pounds, was, like *Entertaining*, an instant success when it was published in April 1987. In July of that year she also signed a contract to serve as consultant and spokesperson for a line of Martha Stewart products to be sold in over 2,000 K-mart stores. Stewart had become not only a personality but a brand.

At the same time, however, the strains on the Stewarts' marriage caused by her dedication to her career had reached a tipping point. Andy filed for divorce in March 1988, and a marriage of 27 years ended two years later.

Martha Stewart Living

In November 1990 a new monthly magazine appeared on newsstands. *Martha Stewart Living*, published by Time Warner, was an instant success. The product was entirely Stewart's, from content to layout, and featured her image on the cover. The magazine's coverage of food and cooking was distinctive. Readers did not simply find recipes. They found articles about the various characteristics of different types of rice or pasta, fruits, and vegetables. They read step-by-step instructions of how, when, and where to plant and cultivate herbs, vegetables, and fruits, how to raise chickens, and how to compost.

Stewart had gained fame as a caterer by using foods as display items, so it was not surprising to view strikingly stylish photographs of the varieties of a given food. In such a manner readers could learn about new foods that were exotic to them. Stewart was not just recommending, through her experience, good food; rather, she was advising readers on how they could acquire the knowledge with which to create their own dishes. It was one thing to follow a recipe or take advice, and quite another to acquire the skills to understand how each ingredient works. If one understands the properties and actions of a given foodstuff, one can create new dishes. Specialized knowledge is key: as *Martha Stewart Living* editor Stephen Drucker observed, "it's possible to be a connoisseur of anything." The magazine was to become, collected over time, an "encyclopedia of homemaking."[13]

The same logic was applied to other of the magazine's features, from house-cleaning and gardening to entertaining and crafts. By June 1991, Time Warner and Stewart had agreed on a 10-year contract to publish *Martha Stewart Living* and books, to create and market videos, and to create television programs. Although her early appearances on NBC's *Today* program were problematic, the six- to eight-minute segments eventually attracted and kept a viewership. *Martha Stewart Living*—the half-hour television show—on the Lifetime network reached even more women. Her daily show *Living with Martha Stewart*, introduced in 1997, reached 88 percent of U.S. households and was awarded multiple Emmys. This was the essence of a lifestyle empire based on a single life: Stewart "was the message, *she* was the subject matter, *she* was the brand, with the magazine, the TV show, with everything."[14]

Stewart had become so influential that her advice could change the way Americans cooked and baked. For example, in her quarterly magazine, *Martha*

Stewart Weddings, introduced in 1993, Stewart advised her readers to make their own cakes, supplying a variety of cake recipes for all sorts and sizes of wedding receptions. "There are two eras of wedding-cake design," noted Montreal *Gazette* food editor Lesley Chesterman, "BM (Before Martha) and AM (After Martha). . . . In the eyes of pastry chefs, the Martha Stewart cakes were sacrilege, an insult to our years of training. But after reproducing many of these 'English Country' cakes, I fell in love with this casual style, which made the crusty-icing concoctions of the past look old-fashioned. . . . Martha Stewart's cakes changed the wedding-cake landscape."[15]

OTHER ENDEAVORS

Martha Stewart Living Omnimedia

Stewart also changed the business landscape. Seeking sole and uniform control over her multiple and varied enterprises, Stewart, with the help of Sharon Patrick, who had created a strategic management company of her own, was able to acquire the capital to purchase Martha Stewart Living from Time Warner and to create Martha Stewart Living Omnimedia, one of the first companies to take advantage of the Internet "dot.com boom." On October 19, 1999, Stewart served scrambled-egg-stuffed brioche, chocolate croissants, and orange juice to stockbrokers at the New York Stock Exchange as her new company went public. The public offering of stock was a wild success: at the end of the day, Stewart, owning 70 percent of the stock, possessed a personal wealth of $1 billion. The company's stock nearly tripled in value.

The creation of one multimedia company to sell and serve a "living brand" aligned with a stock market boom and with the new information age of the World Wide Web. Martha Stewart Omnimedia manages and cross-promotes publications (books, magazines, videos); creates, markets, and syndicates newspaper columns and television and radio shows (including *ask Martha, From Martha's Kitchen*, and holiday specials); oversees a mail-order product line (*Martha by Mail*) and Web site; and contracts and supervises partnerships and relationships with other companies. As the 21st century dawned, the former homemaker and caterer Stewart was one of the most well-known and successful women in the world. "It's a good thing," her trademark phrase, applied both to her ideas and to her life.

Enduring "Camp Cupcake"

Both beloved and reviled as the "diva of domesticity," in 2002 this "living brand" became known not only for her successes but also as one of many corporate CEOs whose personal greediness had led to unscrupulous business practices. As one of the few women in the high-stakes business world, at a time when the stock market boom went bust and the U.S. economy was in trouble, Stewart's high profile as a "living brand" exposed her life to the public as a "celebrity scapegoat for more egregious, if less glamorous, corporate criminals."[16]

In December 2001, Stewart, on vacation in Mexico, sold 3,928 shares of her friend Sam Waksal's Imclone Systems stock. Her stockbroker, Peter Bacanovic, had left a message with Stewart's assistant that the stock would decrease in trading value, and after discussing the matter with Bacanovic's assistant, Doug Faneuil, Stewart and Faneuil decided to divest. Faneuil had told Stewart that Waksal was selling his stock in the company, and Stewart telephoned her old friend Waksal. The charge of insider trading was the core of the subsequent investigation, since Waksal had been given the news that the Food and Drug Administration would not approve a cancer drug created by Imclone. What Stewart knew and when she knew it became the key questions.

While the government could not find evidence to prove insider trading, the investigation dragged on for over a year, negatively affecting Martha Stewart Living Omnimedia. On June 4, 2003, Stewart was indicted on charges of obstruction of justice, conspiracy, lying to investigators, and securities fraud in New York City.

Stewart stepped down from her position of Omnimedia CEO and president. Still, the company adopted a "business as usual" strategy and Stewart introduced a new magazine, *Everyday Food*, during this time. Food, rather than Stewart, was depicted on the cover, and the monthly magazine featured simple dishes created by Omnimedia's test kitchens as well as by readers, echoing Stewart's early relationship with her workers in her catering firm. Although a plan was in place to divorce the company from its "living brand" in the eventuality of Stewart's retirement or death, the company decided in September 2003 to delete from *Martha Stewart Living* Stewart's "Remembering" column and calendar and to reduce the size of her name on the magazine's cover.

After a much-publicized trial beginning in January 2004, Stewart was found guilty of conspiracy, obstruction of justice, and lying on March 5, 2004. Shares of her company fell in price, and her daily show was taken off the air. On July 17, 2004, the sentence handed down was five months in jail and five months of house arrest plus a fine of $30,000. Although Stewart wished to appeal the verdict, she decided that serving her sentence would be the most expedient way to resolve the issue and save her company. She began serving her term at Alderson Federal Prison for Women in Alderson, West Virginia, on October 8, 2004.

There, in what is termed "Camp Cupcake" for its minimum security and women-only population, Stewart served as a model inmate, cleaning the administrative offices, participating in leisure-time activities, and devising ways to cook meals in the prison dormitory's microwave rather than eat government-issue foods. Her release from prison in the very early morning hours of March 4, 2005, was televised. Visibly thinner and wearing a crocheted poncho made by another prisoner, Stewart's reemergence had already been carefully planned.

The April 2005 issue of *Martha Stewart Living* featured the headline "Welcome back, Martha." Despite house arrest and probation, Stewart plunged again into her business endeavors. Although Stewart's version of Donald Trump's television show, *The Apprentice*, did not succeed, *The Martha Stewart Show*, an Emmy Award-winning daytime television talk show, put her in touch with a studio audience, and the 24-hour Martha Stewart Living Radio on SIRIUS XM and a redesigned Web site, marthastewart.com, which offered more than 10,000 recipes, reached an even larger audience. Americans still saw her as, and preferred her as, a domestic expert first. And they saw a new Stewart: perhaps more humble, gentler, and definitely more willing to engage a larger audience and consumer base than the upper and upper-middle classes she had previously sought to emulate and engage. She could laugh at herself, putting her imprimatur on *Whatever, Martha!* (Fine Living Network), a program using clips of her 1990s show to mock her in the hopes of appealing to younger audiences—and, incidentally, teach some viewers.

CONCLUSION

Martha Stewart Living Omnimedia continues to expand. At the heart of the enterprise is food. In 2009 COSTCO signed an agreement with Hain Celestial Group to produce a retail line of antibiotic-free poultry, as well as pastas and baking mixes made of natural ingredients, all under the Martha Stewart brand. Still, Stewart teaches old-fashioned cookery methods and cookbooks continue to be published yearly. The Martha Stewart Collection at Macy's provides aspiring cooks with the tools they need. Learning how to make pie crust with Stewart in her television kitchen, *People* magazine writer Elizabeth Gleick worried that she did not have the right skills or the right tools. Stewart handed her a better rolling pin, and the lesson commenced. Gleick's advice, after her successful second crust? "Use [Martha's] recipe. . . . And remember what Martha, over and over again, kindly told me: 'It's only dough.'"[17]

NOTES

1. Martha Stewart, *Martha Stewart's New Old House* (New York: Clarkson N. Potter, 1992), 9.

2. Lloyd Allen, *Being Martha: The Inside Story of Martha Stewart and Her Amazing Life* (Hoboken, NJ: John Wiley & Sons, 2006), 41.

3. Martha Stewart, *Entertaining* (New York: Clarkson Potter, 1982), 2.

4. Allen, *Being Martha*, 41.

5. Martha Stewart, *Martha Stewart's Gardening* (New York: Clarkson Potter, 1991), 5.

6. Stewart, *Entertaining*, 2.

7. Stewart, *Entertaining*, 2.

8. Jerry Oppenheimer, *Just Desserts: Martha Stewart: The Unauthorized Biography* (Boca Raton, FL: American Media, 2003), 90.

9. Allen, *Being Martha*, 60.

10. Allen, *Being Martha*, 63.

11. Allen, *Being Martha*, 69.

12. Jeanie Kasindorf, "Living with Martha: Can Decorating Dynamo Martha Stewart Make Herself a Permanent Cover Girl?" *New York Magazine* (January 28, 1991), 26.

13. Stephen Drucker, "Editor's Letter," *Martha Stewart Living* (February 1998), 22.

14. Christopher Byron, *Martha Inc.: The Incredible Story of Martha Stewart Living Omnimedia* (New York: John Wiley & Sons, 2003), 248.

15. Lesley Chesterman, "Wedding-cake Wannabes: Local Pastry Chefs Scramble to Create Martha Stewart Look," *The Gazette* (Montreal) (June 14, 2000), D1.

16. Jyoti Thottam and Michael Weisskopf, "Why They're Picking on Martha," *Time* (June 16, 2003), 44.

17. Elizabeth Gleick, "Making Pie Crust with Martha," *People* (November 3, 2008), 49.

FURTHER READING

Allen, Lloyd. *Being Martha: The Inside Story of Martha Stewart and Her Amazing Life*. Hoboken, NJ: John Wiley & Sons, 2006.

Bland, Elizabeth L., and Janice C. Simpson. "Living: A New Guru of American Taste?" *Time*. December 19, 1988.

Byron, Christopher. *Martha Inc.: The Incredible Story of Martha Stewart Living Omnimedia*. New York: John Wiley & Sons, 2003.

Kasindorf, Jeanie. "Living with Martha: Can Decorating Dynamo Martha Stewart Make Herself a Permanent Cover Girl?" *New York Magazine*. January 28, 1991, 22–30.

Martha Stewart, www.marthastewart.com

"Martha Stewart Roundtable." *American Studies* 42:2 (Summer 2001): 67–138.

Meachum, Virginia. *Martha Stewart: Successful Businesswoman*. Springfield, NJ: Enslow Publishers, 1998.

Oppenheimer, Jerry. *Just Desserts: Martha Stewart: The Unauthorized Biography*. Boca Raton, FL: AMI Books, 2003.

Price, Joann F. *Martha Stewart: A Biography*. Westport, CT: Greenwood Press, 2007.

Stewart, Martha. *Entertaining*. New York: Clarkson Potter, 1982.

Stewart, Martha. *The Martha Rules*. New York: Martha Stewart Living Omnimedia, 2005.

Shirley Teresa Wajda

Renowned chef Charlie Trotter talks about his plans to open a new restaurant in Chicago, Illinois, as part of a new 60-story luxury hotel and condominium project during an interview on November 28, 2006. (AP/Wide World Photos)

Charlie Trotter

At the age of 27, Chef Charlie Trotter opened a restaurant that instantly changed the face of American cuisine and catapulted him to international culinary stardom. Trotter did not grow up with a particular interest in culinary pursuits or in a family with an especially strong food culture. Still, when his restaurant, Charlie Trotter's, opened in Chicago in 1987, it showcased a new paradigm in excellence for the restaurant world. Trotter became known not only for his singular cuisine but also for setting new standards in all facets of the dining experience, from menus and service to ambience and wine pairings.

Trotter is renowned for his intellectual approach to gastronomy. His understanding of cuisine is inspired not only by influential chefs like Fernand Point and Fredy Girardet but also by great literary and philosophical figures such as Fyodor Dostoevsky and Ayn Rand. Trotter's style of cooking is famously improvisational. He attributes its spirit to his long-standing love of jazz music, especially that of trumpeter Miles Davis. A mélange of western European traditions, an Asian minimalist aesthetic, and the freshest local foodstuffs, Trotter's cuisine, like jazz, is uniquely American. His dishes respect the seasonality of ingredients and are characteristically light, clean, and intensely flavorful. The Trotter philosophy is uncomplicated: pursue and inspire excellence. He considers himself an "excellencealist" rather than a perfectionist and defines his cuisine simply as what he likes to eat.

EARLY YEARS

Growing Up

Robert and Dona-Lee Trotter celebrated the birth of their first child Charles on September 8, 1959. His two younger brothers, a younger sister, and eventually the world would know him as Charlie, after jazz great Charlie Parker. Robert Trotter, a jazz enthusiast, said his son could have just as easily been named Miles, after another of his musical heroes. In fact, the elder Trotter would often joke that it was his love of jazz that inspired him to marry his wife because her name is also the title of one of Davis's finest compositions. From the day Trotter was born, jazz has been integral to his identity and provides the sound track to which he composes his plates, career, and life.

The Trotters raised their children in the prosperous bedroom community of Wilmette, a North Shore suburb of Chicago. Food was not a central focus of family life. Trotter's mother's cooking repertoire was limited to about 10 dishes that she served to her family on a weekly basis. At a time when the typical American family ate a great deal of beef, Trotter's mother served fish several times a week. Today at Charlie Trotter's the nightly menus feature a preponderance of dishes with the freshest seafood. The Trotter family rarely went out to eat except for very special occasions; to them fine dining meant a lobster tail with clarified butter.

Trotter's first cooking memory is of baking with his mother. He also remembers following a cookbook with recipes from popular children's literature and says that his signature dish may have been Mad Hatter Meatballs. At the age of 12, his enthusiasm for meatballs had not yet crystallized into anything more than a passing interest. Even as a boy, however, Trotter exhibited his characteristic drive and high energy level. He never sat still and always had projects on which he was working. He loved sports, especially baseball and gymnastics, organized activities for his younger siblings, and had a newspaper route.

The Trotter children never felt pressured by their parents' expectations. The Trotters believed the path to a happy life lies in the pursuit of goals and consistently encouraged their kids to develop their own. Trotter may have inherited his pronounced drive to succeed from his father, who was a self-made millionaire.

As a youth Trotter's father was considered the black sheep of his family. He was a pool-hall hustler with an independent streak and played the trumpet in a jazz group he formed called the Trotter Sextet. No doubt influenced by his own father's insistence on stability and planning for the future, Robert Trotter went on to attend Northwestern University, graduating from its Kellogg School of Management in 1953. Once he had made his millions, he became a generous donor to his alma mater.

In 1962 Robert Trotter cofounded an executive search firm called Source EDP, one of the earliest staffing firms specializing in information technology during the industry's first explosive period of growth. It was a huge success. Source EDP changed its name to Source Services and had established more than 90 offices in the United States and Canada when it was sold in 1998. Trotter considers his father to have had something of a Midas touch, and to this day he says patrons of his restaurant tell him how his father, who died in 1993, changed their lives through Source EDP.

Trotter learned the importance of commitment and follow-through from his father. He considers himself to have been raised by a true entrepreneur but has also observed admiringly that his father's modest and old-fashioned approach to life was not particularly materialistic. The elder Trotter stressed the value of community and personal generosity to his children. The purchase of a new Jaguar every few years was the single extravagance he allowed himself.

In spite of his own success, Robert Trotter never encouraged his children to go into the family business. He wanted his children to always strive to be the best but to chart their own course. Trotter recalls his father advising him not to be afraid of failure and telling him, "Your mother and I will support you no matter what—spiritually, emotionally and even financially if necessary—but you are not coming to work for me. You must choose your own path and be your own boss. It is the most satisfying way to live and the only way you can experience the joy of charting your own course."[1]

Trotter claims never to have considered going into his father's business. When he graduated from New Trier East High School in 1977, gymnastics, not cooking, was his life, and the trampoline, not food, was his passion. A champion trampolinest and star of his high school's team, the 17-year-old Trotter did not yet know what course his life would take. In the fall, he was off to college.

Learning to Cook

At the University of Wisconsin, Madison, Trotter took advantage of the liberal arts curriculum and enjoyed taking a broad array of classes. He chose political science as a major and complemented it with a minor in philosophy. While academically he found his college experience stimulating, socially Trotter felt alienated from most of the student body. Although he studied political science, he did not feel particularly compelled to participate in antiwar and other protests on the campus mall or join any student groups. Fraternity life was decidedly not for him either, and he was no party animal. Feelings of isolation, that there was no one to whom he could relate, began to take root in Trotter's psyche. Then two things completely changed his life: one was a lasagna, and the other was Ayn Rand.

Trotter's cousin Katy, also a college student, recognized her cousin was having something of an existential crisis. Thinking it would help, she sent Trotter her copy of *The Fountainhead* by Ayn Rand (1943). Rand's grand themes of individualism, creative genius, and self-reliance resonated with Trotter, reinforcing beliefs he already had but about which he had felt unsure. He realized that it is acceptable—in fact, heroic—to walk alone and that it is easy to become jaded but much harder to maintain a sense of wonder and curiosity in the world. Trotter formulated a credo that he would adhere to for many years to come: anything less than the pursuit of excellence is a crime.

While Rand helped Trotter to gain confidence in his convictions, his college roommate helped him to find a new direction in life via lasagna. This fellow student made sausage, pasta, bread, and lasagna from scratch and shared his creations with Trotter and their friends. Both roommates had an interest in wine. Trotter's curiosity was piqued; he began making soups, chili, and lasagna and sharing them with his fellow students at dinners in their apartment. Soon the two began taking turns making dinner and competing with each other to see who could make the best five-course meals and choose the best wines to accompany them. Of this pivotal time in his life, Trotter says, "I soon realized how much fun I was having and decided to pursue cooking further. So I went out and bought several cookbooks and started to try many different types of dishes. Some turned out great, but others were, well . . . it probably would have been better if I had figured out before the fire department arrived that blackened fish meant to blacken the spices, not the ceiling in my kitchen."[2]

Trotter bought cookbooks by culinary greats like Julia Child, James Beard, and Craig Claiborne. During his first few intense months of learning and experimentation, Trotter says he approached cooking much the same way he solved a math problem. Choosing a recipe from *The James Beard Cookbook*

(1959), Trotter followed it to the letter, leveling each quarter of a teaspoon of spice and eyeballing every half-cup of water. It was the beginning of his storied gastronomical journey.

Prompted by his experiences in the kitchen and around the table in his student apartment, Trotter decided to work at a restaurant. His first restaurant job was not in the kitchen but in the dining room as a waiter and bartender. Trotter was "impressed with the energy level and dynamism of restaurants." He had acquired the restaurant "bug."[3]

After graduating from college in 1982, Trotter moved back to Wilmette and with his parents' support got a job in the dining room of Sinclair's Restaurant in Forest Hill. The restaurant was named for and by chef and restaurateur Gordon Sinclair, whose acclaimed restaurant, Gordon, was credited with keeping Chicago at the cutting edge of contemporary American cuisine. At the helm of Sinclair's kitchen was Chef Norman Van Aken. Despite his lack of professional culinary experience, Trotter convinced Van Aken to take him on as part of his kitchen crew at a rate of $3.10 per hour. On his first day of work in the kitchen at Sinclair's, Trotter realized that he had found the life he wanted for himself. He was 22.

At 23 Trotter began to chart his own course. He decided to attend culinary school to catch up to his peers, and once again his parents were supportive. They did not understand their son's goal of one day opening a restaurant, however, and Trotter's father was particularly puzzled by his son's attraction to all things culinary. The elder Trotter's perception of the restaurant industry was that those who worked in it were unreliable, wild, and crazy. Nevertheless, he told his son that when he was ready to open his own restaurant, he would be there for him. With the blessing of his parents and the experience gained under Chef Aken, Trotter moved to San Francisco to enroll at the California Culinary Academy. He explained to his parents that if he failed, at least it would be on his own terms.

Feeling stifled at the academy and eager to live, learn, and work in the restaurant world, Trotter dropped out after four months. Over the next four years, from 1983 to 1986, he worked in dozens of restaurants and eventually created his own culinary curriculum. Trotter decided he would work until he could not learn anything more. In each establishment in which he worked, he was committed to giving back more than he had taken, working extra hours and holding himself to a higher standard than was asked of him. At job interviews, he never asked what the position entailed or what it paid. The most important thing to him was gaining skill and knowledge. If Trotter did not agree with the way a restaurant was run, whether it was due to poor sanitation or poor-quality foodstuffs, he would leave after as few as five days. He considered it a personal failure if, after leaving a restaurant, they did not need to hire two or three people to replace him.

During these industrious years, Trotter also read incessantly, mostly cookbooks, dined out at restaurants as much as possible, and traveled. He planned trips to New York City specifically to eat at the nation's most highly rated and talked-about restaurants. He was, for the most part, underwhelmed by the cuisine and service but charmed by restaurants housed in converted brownstones. Trotter liked the fact that passersby may not even realize they were passing such a restaurant, as well as the intimate ambience the brownstones offered in contrast to the sterility of more famous restaurants housed in skyscrapers and hotels.

Trotter also traveled to Europe to explore the culinary world on the other side of the Atlantic. He spent several months on the continent eating at some of the best restaurants in the world, two of which particularly influenced him. He describes his dinner in Vienne, France, at legendary chef Fernand Point's landmark restaurant, La Pyramide, as magical and his experience in Crissier, Switzerland, at Girardet, named for the restaurant's famed chef, Fredy Girardet, as transcendent. Trotter refers to Girardet as his philosophical mentor and to Point as his spiritual mentor. He considers Girardet the great poet of the kitchen and admires the way he captures the sense of being in the moment with food. He is profoundly impressed by the way Girardet brought together the four elements of the dining experience: cuisine, wine, service, and ambience. Trotter recognized that no element was neglected or considered most important; each received the same extraordinarily high level of attention.

Point, whose wife kept La Pyramide running into the late 1980s, is known for his hugeness of heart and generous spirit, which shone through in his cuisine and pervaded the spirit of his restaurant even years after his death. Trotter has often said that if he could keep only one book in his kitchen it would be Point's masterpiece, *Ma Gastronomie*. Together, La Pyramide and Girardet proved to Trotter that a restaurant can be more than the sum of its parts and that dining can occur on a spiritual level.

Back in the United States, Trotter worked under two prominent and award-winning chefs who played particularly important roles in his development. Chef Bradley Ogden, a pioneer of New American Cuisine, hired Trotter to work at the Campton Place Hotel in San Francisco. New American Cuisine refines traditional, regional American food using a combination of classic and cutting-edge techniques, organic farm-fresh ingredients, and ethnic dishes made with creative twists. The movement was coming into its own in California at the time. When Trotter left Chef Ogden's kitchen, he reunited with Chef Van Aken, who was making strides in defining New World Cuisine, a fusion of Latin American, Caribbean, Asian, African, and American flavors. He moved to Juniper Beach, Florida, to help Aken open another Gordon Sinclair venture, Sinclair's North American Grill, and later moved on to Key West to assist Aken in opening his own restaurant, Louie's Back Yard. It would be the last restaurant Trotter would work for that did not have his own name on it.

Stepping Out

Trotter had worked, learned, traveled, and tasted, and by 1986 he considered himself ready to open his own world-class restaurant. Drawing inspiration from French American chef Jean Banchet, who was making world-class cuisine at his restaurant Le Français in Wheeling, Illinois, Trotter set out to put Chicago on the culinary map. Robert Trotter agreed to bankroll his son's entire project. From the beginning of their partnership, Trotter and his father were involved in every detail, acting as consultants, architects, and construction contractors. Trotter says that working alongside his father, both toward opening the restaurant and in the subsequent years running it, was one of the best parts of his career. He feels that he has earned his MBA from working with his father. While his father made him a businessman, he made his father an unlikely restaurateur.

The business partners had to find a Chicago location for their restaurant. In Trotter's mind the ideal area would have a high population density, lots of business travelers, and the potential for him to develop a sophisticated clientele. Trotter also knew that he wanted to convert an old townhouse like the iconic brownstones of New York City for the restaurant site. He and his father looked at 40 buildings in various neighborhoods. In the end, because of arcane Chicago zoning laws, only two of the properties could be used as commercial establishments. One such law forbids a business to be located within 90 feet of a house of worship. At just 100 feet from the Greater Little Rock Baptist Church in Chicago's Lincoln Park neighborhood, the building at 816 West Armitage Street barely passed muster, but it would be the site of Trotter's future restaurant.

It was a two-story, single-family home built in 1908. Trotter and his father had the building completely gutted, leaving only the outer walls. After years of gang violence, general neglect, and dilapidation, the mid-1980s found the Lincoln Park section of the city in the midst of gentrification and revitalization. The stars seemed to be aligning for father and son.

The Trotter family venture soon began to stir up attention in Chicago. However, not all of the notices were good. People in the neighborhood and in the industry were talking about "some rich kid who is opening a restaurant and his father is paying for everything."[4] Of his critics, Trotter says nothing they said ever bothered him. At the time he leaned on the philosophical teachings of St. Augustine, from whom he learned to look inward to find truth. And like the idiot in Dostoevsky's famous novel of the same name, Trotter would remain self-confident and faithful to the course he had chosen, leap from the cliff and figure out how to land on the way down. He recalled all the restaurants he had left after only a few days on the job. Trotter thought he could do at least as well as those operations. He remembered the extraordinary places where he had eaten and especially the fluidity and naturalness of his Girardet experience.

Trotter wanted to attract both affluent and budget-conscious diners. To court the latter, he would open the restaurant with an a la carte menu that included moderately priced items. To woo the affluent crowd, he catered a slew of parties at the homes of Chicago's social and business leaders. In addition to establishing a clientele before the restaurant even opened its doors, this strategy created a buzz around town. These catering engagements also let Trotter refine his technique and develop his style. He had his knowledge base and was slowly starting to build on it by changing ingredients and flavor combinations and having the confidence to find inspiration in the moment. It was the beginnings of his jazzlike, improvisational, intuitive approach to cooking.

Trotter also drew inspiration from a French-born chef named Raymond Blanc, who was gaining fame in England. He had read an article about Blanc in which he talked about opening a restaurant and finding one's own voice as a chef. In the several months leading up to the opening of a restaurant and for at least a year after, Blanc would stop dining out and reading culinary publications. Trotter decided to do the same. "I do not want to be the best at what I do, I want to be the only person who does what I do," he declared.

As the stage was set for the opening of the restaurant, it seemed Trotter and his father had taken care of every detail—except for what to call it. At first Trotter was against naming it after himself, but a marketing consultant convinced him that to do so would be in the tradition of many of the great restaurants he admired, like Girardet. Trotter conceded. His mission was to create a dining experience that would surpass all his guests' expectations. Trotter says that is still his mission decades later.

THE RESTAURANT

Opening Charlie Trotter's

After seven months and $1.7 million worth of luxury renovations to a small, converted townhouse in Lincoln Park, a restaurant seating 68 people opened its doors to offer the public an a la carte menu created by a relatively unknown, certainly young chef. Trotter was ready for the onslaught of reviews: "I have always believed that if you are going to open your doors and charge diners full price, there should be no grace period. Why should a restaurant learn at the public's expense?" In August of 1987 the first guests arrived to be seated at Charlie Trotter's.

Charlie Trotter's front doors open to a short staircase leading up to a two-story reception area and an eight-seat bar. A massive, vertical wine storage wall is situated behind the bar, to the side of which is the first of two sleek and stylish dining rooms with thirty-four seats. The floors are Brazilian cherry wood laid in an intricate design. The tables are set simply with white cloth tablecloths, and the chairs are black, lacquered leather. Banquettes are covered in fabric with a Viennese print, and there are subtle splashes of gray, mahogany trim and beige stitched wallpaper. Art by the likes of Joseph Muller hangs from the walls. A small staircase at the far end of the first dining room leads to the second, intimate 34-seat dining room decorated in the same fashion. Trotter aspired to French refinement without its formality. He wanted the food to be the focus, not the décor, and for his guests to be comfortable.

In the back the kitchen staff stood ready on opening day for the first orders of the evening. Trotter's crew included five women and three men and sous-chef Geoff Felsenthal, three years Trotter's senior. The kitchen, designed by

Trotter, was as large as the main floor. This design ran counter to the trends of the time, which allowed for restaurants with oversized, grand dining rooms and a small kitchen space. Because Trotter wanted his servers to take pride in their jobs and appear approachable to diners, they wore suits rather than uniforms. He wanted his dining room to be an intimate space with a touch of Midwestern wholesomeness.

On opening night Trotter's guests were his friends, family, and many prominent fellow chefs, including Rick Bayless of Frontera Grill and old friends and former bosses Norman Van Aken and Gordon Sinclair. Trotter's wife of one year, Lisa, was in the kitchen. She had put off law school to don an apron and apprentice to the pastry chef to learn how to make desserts. Charlie Trotter's opened on their first wedding anniversary.

The menu on the first night offered crayfish consommé, terrine of leeks with smoked salmon salsa, warm quail and *foie gras* salad, saddle and rack of lamb, a variety of small-portion desserts, and wines from around the world. Trotter was attempting to put flavors and textures together in a way not seen before. The prices for appetizers, salads, and desserts ranged from $3.00 to $6.50 and for entrees from $13.00 to $17.00. Diners were also offered the option to choose a *prix fixe* menu for two for $70.00.

Although Trotter's cuisine has become more singular, at first it was considered a part of the New American movement. Trotter's food was distinguished by his scant, practically nonexistent use of fats and creams, which, according to Trotter, block and mute flavors. As a result, flavors came through more cleanly and clearly and dishes were lighter. He also emphasized vegetable cookery as the most interesting part of any cuisine. His innovative way of saucing a dish became characterized by the use of vegetable-based vinaigrettes, light emulsified stocks and purees, delicate broths, and light meat and fish essences. According to Trotter, "I do not want guests walking out of the restaurant feeling as if they have over-indulged because of excessive cream, butter and alcohol. I want them to feel stimulated and alert, knowing that they will be able to look forward to breakfast the following morning. Food does not have to be rich to taste good."[5]

Trotter's guests and critics agreed. The restaurant began receiving rave reviews from the very beginning. The few complaints leveled at Charlie Trotter's were about particulars like an overly sweet dessert, an overcooked piece of fish, a mistake by a server, and the fact that the wine list had few bargains and no classics. None of these infractions became a habitual problem. Paul A. Camp, food critic for *The Chicago Tribune*, gave Charlie Trotter's three out of four stars in his first review, only to name it restaurant of the year "hands down" in a later column. Trotter was also voted second meanest man in Chicago but shrugged it off, as he came in second to Michael Jordan and Mayor Daly ranked third. In an extraordinarily short period of time, Trotter had put Chicago on the culinary map.

Trotter was also setting trends in the way he acquired his foodstuffs. He used many purveyors from the region and throughout the country and the world to guarantee the highest quality in products such as line-caught fish and farm-fresh organic vegetables. In a particularly bold move, he designed his kitchen, which has been renovated only once since its opening, with no walk-in refrigerators to ensure that fresh ingredients will arrive and be used every day.

A Distinctive Style

In addition to setting new trends in restaurant style, cuisine, and service, Trotter also changed the way people eat by changing what menus look like. After three years, Trotter took his love for eating many different things in small portions to the American public through the creation of his nightly tasting menus: the Grand, the Vegetable, and the Kitchen Table menus. The Kitchen Table menu is actually served to guests at a table in the kitchen. It is more of an idea than a menu because guests are served whatever Trotter feels inspired to make for them.

Over time, Trotter's constantly changing menus have become ever more streamlined and minimalist, with more small, light courses laying the foundation for the next, each one emphasizing only two or three ingredients per plate. Trotter compares every menu and dish to a jazz composition: in their spontaneity and openness to improvisation, they come out different each night. It is estimated that Trotter created nearly 25,000 distinct menus between 1987 and 2009. His trademark was to be a world-famous chef without a signature dish.

AWARDS AND HONORS

Charlie Trotter's continues to maintain world-class quality in its cuisine, wine, service, and ambience. Trotter has accumulated numerous accolades. He is a member of the elite Traditions & Qualite, received a Mobile Five Star rating and a AAA Five Diamond rating, and won 10 James Beard Foundation Awards, including "Outstanding Restaurateur" and "Outstanding Chef." Charlie Trotter's was named "The Best Restaurant in the World for Wine & Food" and "America's Best Restaurant" by *Wine Spectator*. Trotter has also authored 14 cookbooks and three management books and has hosted the award-winning PBS cooking series *The Kitchen Sessions with Charlie Trotter*. The show was filmed in a study Trotter built next to his restaurant. United Airlines even offered menus created by Charlie Trotter to its elite travelers. He also has produced a line of organic-based food products.

OTHER ENDEAVORS

By 2009 Trotter was operating three additional restaurants with another venture in the works: Trotter's to Go in Lincoln Park, Restaurant Charlie and Bar Charlie in Las Vegas, and a forthcoming restaurant located at One Madison and Park in New York City. He was also involved in numerous charities and established his own philanthropic organization, the Charlie Trotter Culinary Education Foundation, for which he has received awards from both President George W. Bush and General Colin Powell.

CONCLUSION

Of retirement Trotter says, "I still sometimes have the feeling 'What else is there?' I enjoy what I do but many of the great books are unread still. I try to find time to devote to the life of the mind. I also have the responsibility of employing one-hundred people. If I closed the restaurant, a lot of talented, hard working people would be out of luck. I have to weigh those things against each other."[6] Whether or not his restaurant remains open, Trotter has influenced restaurants across the globe to provide impeccable service, intimate dining rooms, and light multicourse tasting menus. His cuisine and improvisational style, however, are forever his own.

NOTES

1. Jennifer Iannolo, *An Interview with Charlie Trotter,* www.theatlasphere.com (December 15, 2003).

2. Edmund Lawler, *Charlie Trotter's* (New York: Lebhar-Friedman Books, 2000), 27.

3. Lawler, *Charlie Trotter's,* 29–30.

4. www.charlietrotters.com, *Cuisine* section, 2009.

5. Michael Washburn, *Chewing the Fat with Charlie Trotter,* The Illinois Humanities Council, 2009, www.prairie.org/humanities-resources/detours/q-amp-chewing-fat-charlie-trotter

6. Michael Washburn, *Chewing the Fat with Charlie Trotter,* The Illinois Humanities Council, 2009, www.prairie.org/humanities-resources/detours/q-amp-chewing-fat-charlie-trotter

FURTHER READING

Clarke, Paul. *Lessons in Excellence from Charlie Trotter.* Berkeley, CA: Ten Speed Press, 1999.

Dornenburg, Andrew, and Karen Page. *Becoming a Chef.* New York: Van Nostrand Reinhold, 1995.

Lawler, Edmund. *Charlie Trotter's.* New York: Lebhar-Friedman Books, 2000.

Lawler, Edmund. *Lessons in Service from Charlie Trotter.* Berkeley, CA: Ten Speed Press, 2004.

Trotter, Charlie. *Charlie Trotter's.* Berkeley, CA: Ten Speed Press, 1994.

Trotter, Charlie. *Gourmet Cooking for Dummies.* Foster City, CA: IDG Books Worldwide, 1997.

Trotter, Charlie. *The Kitchen Sessions with Charlie Trotter.* Berkeley, CA: Ten Speed Press, 1999.

Trotter, Charlie. *Vegetables.* Berkeley, CA: Ten Speed Press, 2004.

www.charlietrotters.com

www.chefs-story.com

Sean Kenniff

Alice Waters, the grand dame of the "slow food" movement, looks on during an interview in her kitchen in Bolinas, California, August 6, 2008. (AP/Wide World Photos)

Alice Waters

In a 2009 CBS *60 Minutes* broadcast entitled "Alice Waters' Crusade for Better Food," reporter Lesley Stahl interviewed 65-year-old Alice Waters and introduced her as a Prius-driving, latte-sipping mother of the fresh food movement. Stahl further described Waters as a steamroller for the anti-industrial food cause who had changed more about how Americans eat, cook, and think about food than any chef since Julia Child. Waters became an American food icon as a chef, a 1970s pioneer of the food revolution, a Slow Food missionary, a cookbook author, an advocate of "edible education," and a co-owner of the Chez Panisse and Café Fanny restaurants in Berkeley, California.

Before Waters's Chez Panisse credo of fresh, local, and seasonal produce became the international standard for high-end cuisine, most restaurants depended on canned, frozen, and imported ingredients for their meals. Waters's story is of a woman with no formal training as a chef, few skills as a businesswoman, and little experience as a writer who became the mascot, spokeswoman, and figurehead for what would become known as "California Cuisine" and its call for seasonal, locally grown, small-farmed, organic, fresh foods aimed at countering the ill effects of industrial agriculture and agribusiness.

EARLY YEARS

Margaret Hickman Waters and Charles Patrick Waters of Chatham, New Jersey, welcomed their second daughter, Alice Louise, into the world on April 28, 1944. As good food enthusiasts, her parents had cultivated their own World War II victory garden. During the 1950s Waters and her three sisters (Susan, Ellen, and Laura) and their mother followed their father's Prudential Life Insurance career as it first took them to Indiana and finally to southern California. During Waters's formative years, her mother's strong sense of social conscience provided the girls with empathy for the poor and underprivileged. The girls later laughingly recalled attending their elementary school classes wearing campaign buttons for Harry Truman and Adlai Stevenson.

Waters proved to be a good student with a propensity for fun. While attending Van Nuys High School, she ran with a more intellectual crowd and, like many teenagers of that era, discovered alcohol and partying. Directly out of high school she attended the University of California at Santa Barbara for two years, where she joined a sorority and took full advantage of the laid-back beach party spirit. Waters, like many in her baby-boom generation, embraced the revolt against white male–dominated big government and big business. Armed with a new intellectualism, she resisted traditional politics. In looking to broaden her world perspective, she elected to do her junior year (1965) abroad at the Sorbonne in Paris. There she encountered a new world of food and wine and quickly adapted to French traditional foodways. Waters later recalled that her climactic food moment occurred when she and some friends ate a dinner of local trout amandine and restaurant garden vegetables in a rustic Breton stone house restaurant. Her love affair and obsession with food had begun.

While Waters was experiencing her food metamorphosis in France, America was undergoing a major political and social realignment that sparked police arrests of hundreds of Berkeley students in the free speech sit-ins, civil rights demonstrations, racial turmoil and rioting in the Los Angeles neighborhood of Watts, farm worker strikes, escalation of the Vietnam War, Students for a Democratic Society (SDS) war protests, U.S. invasion of the Dominican Republic, the start of LBJ's "Great Society," astronaut Edward White's "walk" in space, the Voting Rights Act of 1965, and a cadre of anti-authority hippie youth espousing free love, drugs, and the simple life. Upon her return to the United States, Waters and her Alpha Phi sorority sister Eleanor Bertino decided to transfer to the University of California Berkeley for their senior year so that they could be part of the revolutionary spirit for which the campus had become famous.

With Waters's blossoming left-wing passions for all things anti big business and big government, and her fascination with the free speech movement and its folk hero Mario Savio, Berkeley seemed like a perfect fit. In a short time Waters volunteered for the election campaign of New Left antiwar radical Robert Sheer, *Ramparts Magazine* editor, where she met David Goines, an artist and printer with the Berkeley Free Press. Goines and Waters fell in love and, in the free-love antimarriage spirit of the age, they moved in together. With neighbors Charles Shere (music critic for the radical radio station KPFA) and his wife Lindsey, they hosted numerous dinner parties for fellow free speech movement leaders, many of whom had been friends with Savio during the sit-ins and mass arrests of the previous years. Through all of this radicalization, Waters, now a French cultural history major, never lost her obsession with all things French and prided herself in the cooking of Julia Child's recipes from *Mastering the Art of French Cooking* (1961) and her television shows on PBS.

Waters combined her newfound passions both for food and left-wing political beliefs and joined like-minded people to declare war on the big-business and government policies of fast food and agribusiness. Finding sympathetic foodies was relatively easy in the Bay Area, which was the home of national health enthusiasts like Jerome Irving and his *Organic Farming and Gardening* publication, and natural diet proponent Euell Gibbons. The community thus had deep roots in a culture of sustainability. Local support for her new ideals also found fertile ground within the newly formed North Berkeley area, referred to as the Gourmet Ghetto, which included Peet's Coffee and Tea and the Cheese Board Collective.

Like most college students, Waters wandered a bit after graduation as she tried to figure out what she wanted to do with her life. In 1967, she worked at the Quest, a second-rate French restaurant in Berkeley, and wrote food columns titled "Alice's Restaurant" (after Arlo Guthrie's antiwar song) for Free Speech Movement colleague Bob Novick's *San Francisco Express Times*. That fall, Waters became an assistant teacher at the Berkeley Montessori School and so enjoyed the progressive alternative-style education that she decided in

August of 1968 to attend the International Montessori Center in London. Waters and Goines spent eight months in London while Waters earned a degree in Montessori education and Goines studied calligraphy.

Upon return to the States, Waters continued to write her *San Francisco Express Times* food articles and Goines used her recipes to publish a wood-block series and book entitled *Thirty Recipes Suitable for Framing.* In 1970, with profits from the book, he purchased his employer's Berkeley print shop. Soon thereafter Waters and Goines amicably parted ways. In a short time, Alice moved in with Tom Luddy, the manager of the Telegraph Repertory Cinema in Berkeley. The couple quickly became famous for their dinner parties with guest lists that included Susan Sontag, Abbie Hoffman, and Huey Newton. During their time together, Luddy introduced Waters to the 1930s films of Marcel Pagnol and the character of sailmaker Panisse, who married his friend Fanny after he learned that she was pregnant by another man. Waters became so enamored with the films that she began wearing the vintage clothing from the era.

RESTAURANTS

Modern Western restaurant traditions, for the most part, are a French creation dating back to the mid-18th-century *haute cuisine* of Antonin Carême and Paris soup merchant Monsieur Boulanger. Formal restaurants date back to the 1860s and French chef Georges Auguste Escoffier's *chef de partie* system. Escoffier's classic French kitchen functioned as a military brigade: a man who wished to be a cook worked his way through the ranks via a series of stations. American eateries developed around this system, and in the post–World War II decades, Francophile Americans, led by the likes of James Beard, Craig Claiborne, and Julia Child, frequented high-end eateries based on New York French immigrant Henri Soule's model of *haute cuisine* and excellent service. To accommodate the needs of America's new growing middle class and their demand for restaurants in their price range, restaurateurs, for the most part, turned to new advances in market-driven business efficiency and new, inexpensive scientific industrial foods to cook extravagant meals with price points that would maximize their profits.

The Chez Panisse Revolution

Waters ventured into this restaurant world in 1970 when boyfriend Luddy's film buddy and University of California Berkeley professor Paul Aratow convinced her to open a restaurant and offered to arrange for the start-up money to launch the project. They purchased a run-down Berkeley house on Shattuck Street near the university and the Gourmet Ghetto. To keep costs down, the partners hired local hippies for the remodeling labor and then employed inexperienced Berkeley Ph.D. candidate Victoria Kroyer as the first chef. Lindsey

Shere became the pastry chef, and Waters served as the front house hostess and kitchen coordinator. Waters named the restaurant Chez Panisse after Pagnol's film character, and on August 28, 1971, the restaurant opened with a fixed menu, a limited California and French wine list, nonprofessional staff without uniforms, local fresh ingredients, and recipes from Elizabeth David's *French Provincial Cooking* (1960) book.

Waters soon found herself turning people away on a regular basis as the restaurant ran out of food. From the start, menu prices were well out of the range of most of the area's young counterculture activists, and in protest some of the Cheese Board members accused the new restaurant of being "capitalist villains." They streaked naked throughout the restaurant in protest.

Perhaps because of her initial success, the inexperienced Waters focused her entire life on the restaurant and subsequently drove herself and the staff into the ground. She continually overspent her budget, and within the first year she lost her cook and broke up with Luddy, and even her financial backer Aratow lost interest in the business. Waters then moved in with her new boyfriend, waitstaffer Jerry Budrick, and assumed some of the cooking duties to help ends meet. The counterculture spirit ran high in the restaurant, and rumors of staff indulgences in sex, drugs, and rock 'n' roll flourished. Problems aside, the clientele grew and a 1975 favorable *Gourmet* magazine article brought the restaurant national attention. Yet, by the end of the year, the business fell onto hard times and could not meet payrolls, bills went unpaid, and continued unbridled extravagance drove menu prices up.

Then kitchen staffer Gene Opton joined the business as a partner. His business sense, along with some of his money, helped turn the financial situation around. Additional support emanated from the French Escoffier-style kitchen and high-end cuisine of chef Jeremiah Tower, which brought new loyal customers to the restaurant. A short time later, Waters created the business corporation Pagnol et Compagnie, which purchased Opton's share and regained control of the restaurant.

While trying to define her food philosophies, Waters sought the guidance of other food leaders. Cecilia Chiang, owner of the San Francisco Mandarin Restaurant, recalled Waters coming into her restaurant: "She asked me questions and said, your food is quite different to me. What is it? Is it the vegetables you serve? I said, 'In the old days in China, we didn't have anything that went through refrigeration. We just bought it from the market and cooked it right away. We tried to keep the original flavor, original color and texture. The whole thing is just fresh.'"[1] Chiang also remembered that Waters's circle of culinary advisers included Beard, Marion Cunningham, Ruth Reichl, Chuck Williams, M. F. K. Fisher, and many others who helped her define her food goals.

Waters inspired many local chefs, regional farmers, and employees to venture out on their own as suppliers for the restaurant. The Chez Panisse high-end meals, replete with the freshest and finest ingredients, required snubbing the processed foods on which most restaurants had grown to depend. To adjust to this shift, Waters began courting local farms like the Amador County organic farm and started the practice of placing farmer or ranch names on the menu. Meyer lemons or, as the menu called them, "backyard lemons," were picked in Berkeley neighborhood backyards. Waters went as far as helping busboy Steve Sullivan start up the Acme Bread Company in Berkeley. In 1978 Waters traveled through Europe with Cunningham and Chiang and upon her return used her travel experiences to reinvigorate the menu with new recipes that drew raves from a *San Francisco Chronicle* reviewer.

In 1979 *The New York Daily News* named Waters an up-and-coming chef, and *Playboy* magazine named Chez Panisse one of the top 25 restaurants in the United States. To meet expanding diner demands, Waters created an upstairs café, installed a wood-burning oven, featured Sonoma County Laura Chenel goat cheese, and hired new chef Joyce Goldstein. Further success came in 1981 when *The International Herald Tribune* published an article titled "New Wave California Cuisine: A Marriage of Many and a Mime of None" and named Chez Panisse as an example of the new restaurant model.

COOKBOOKS

But just as success and financial stability seemed within reach, a major fire in the restaurant threatened to end the enterprise. Undaunted, the self-driven and indefatigable Waters rebuilt the facility with insurance money. She met and moved in with artist Stephen Singer, 11 years her junior, and, with ex-boyfriend Goines as illustrator, published the successful *Chez Panisse Menu Cookbook*. Despite the ups and downs, the restaurant again quickly stabilized with the hiring of new chef Paul Bertolli, who brought farm connections, better business practices, and stellar reviews in *House and Garden, Vogue, Newsweek*, and *The San Francisco Chronicle* to the restaurant.

OTHER ENDEAVORS

Pushing Local Food

With the restaurant finances again stabilized, Waters began transforming the business into a vehicle for her personal politics. In 1983 she brought in her first forager, Sibella Kraus, to supply the restaurant daily with fresh seasonal local produce. Kraus, a University of California Agriculture Economics graduate, helped Waters start the Farm Restaurant Project to bring local farmers and chefs together. Waters became a salad pioneer, introducing exotic greens such as sorrel, mâche, baby greens, and radicchio to her menu. To get these unheard-of greens, she convinced locals to grow them for her in home gardens and started contracting local small farmers to grow and provide them to her restaurant.

Waters also pushed the idea of thinking locally and began featuring local products like Spenger's Tomales Bay bluepoint oysters, Monterey Bay prawns,

Sebastopol geese, and Big Sur trout. The menu now reflected producers' names like Bob's turnips and DeeAnns garden greens. Waters planted a restaurant garden on property in Amador County. French wines now came through Berkeley importer Kermit Lynch, and bread was supplied from the Acme Bread Company. Waters's idea of California cuisine became fully realized at Chez Panisse.

Food Educator

New life directions during the 1980s forced Waters to realign her food passions to coordinate with new family responsibilities. Her new food path expanded to include roles as a food educator and cookbook author. In 1983, Waters celebrated the birth of her daughter Fanny, and two years later she married Singer. New responsibilities as a mother moved Waters to allow others to take control of the restaurant, and by 1985 her father computerized the Chez Panisse business operations while Singer took control of the restaurant's wine list.

This additional time allowed Waters to reflect on how she wanted her daughter to learn her mantra of local, organic, seasonal, and sustainable foodways. She quickly brought past political beliefs on food passions together to begin attacks on diabetes, obesity, pesticides, industrial processed foods, unhealthy school lunches, and overuses of corn syrup. First, she made the restaurant menu completely sustainable by demanding that all meat dishes be from humanely treated, hormone-free, and organically fed animals. In an attempt to treat her workers better, she moved Chez Panisse from tip sharing by all the staff, in the old French service *compris* system, to a shared fixed charge on the final tab.

Adding to the credibility of Waters's spokesperson role were numerous awards and starlike recognition for her and the restaurant. In 1991 the James Beard Foundation named Chez Panisse Restaurant of the Year and named Waters Chef of the Year. Waters quickly learned to take this fame and use it as political capital for her food cause. She cooked for numerous Bill Clinton fundraisers, and in 1993 cooked for Clinton himself at Chez Panisse. Food became her politics, as exemplified by the fact that she had earlier refused to cook for President Ronald Reagan at the White House. The contradiction was that her foodie paradise, with its high prices, always seemed to be out of reach of the common people.

In 1995, Waters broadened the audience for her foodway philosophy by establishing the Martin Luther King Middle School Edible Schoolyard program in Berkeley. The idea of school children raising food dated back to 1909 when Berkeley professor Earnest B. Babcock published "Suggestion for Garden Work in California Schools." Waters stated, "Give me any kid. In six weeks, they'll be eating chard."

An attempt to take her cause international by opening a restaurant and interactive food museum in the decorative arts wing of the Louvre in Paris never came to fruition. Like all things in her life, Waters had one speed when she started a new endeavor: full throttle. This all-encompassing food passion helped lead to her divorce from Singer in 1997.

Mentoring a New Food Royalty

In 1971, when Waters opened Chez Panisse, little did this left-wing Berkeley activist realize that she had helped spark a national food revolution against industrial foodways. In a few short decades, her philosophy of seasonal, local, fresh, farmer-contracted ingredients cooked in a simple manner helped shift the national food paradigm. In turn, her mentorship of people with like philosophies helped launch the careers of numerous food giants, such as Jeremiah Tower (Stars Restaurant), Judy Rodgers (Zuni Café), Deborah Madison (Greens), Mark Miller (Coyote Café), Paul Bertoli (Oliveto and Fra Mani Salumi), Joyce Goldstein (Square One), Christopher Lee (Eccolo), Charlie Hallowell (Piazziaola), Catherine Brandel (chef and later instructor at the Culinary Institute of America at Greystone), David Lebovitz (Monsoon Pastry Chef), Paul Johnson (founder of Monterey Fish Market), Jesse Malgren (executive chef at Madrona Manor in Healdsburg), Gayle Ortiz (Gayle's Bakery & Rosticceria in Capitola), Mark Peel (Campanile Restaurant and

---

On Chez Panisse

What I knew was what I read in a book that I came across by Arthur Bloomfield, and this is back in the early seventies. He wrote a wonderful little paperback guide that was published by Chronicle books about San Francisco restaurants. It was really more than that, it was San Francisco and local Bay Area. He had a couple from the East Bay, one was Narci Davids's, where I ended up working part time while I was waiting for something to come up at Chez Panisse where I ended up staying for ten years. He had a wonderful description of Chez Panisse and what they were trying to do and of some meals he had had there. It just captured me in a way that made me and my friend who, I was traveling with, go there. That was 1974. We had a wonderful meal and it was something that changed my view of the world a little bit. It was so simple and so delicious and so well done. Delicious food cooked wonderfully, but in a casual atmosphere. That was a change from the old days where you went to these temples of gastronomy and you had to get dressed up and the waiters were very formal. I don't even remember the meal I had, but it was transformative.

—Christopher Lee, former Chez Panisse cook and restaurateur,
from oral history interview conducted by Kirstin Jackson in 2004,
Regional Oral History Office, The Bancroft Library,
University of California, Berkeley, 2006

the La Brea Bakery), Lindsey Shere (Downtown Bakery in Healdsburg), Peggy Smith (co-owner of Cowgirl Creamery in Point Reyes Station and Artisan Cheese in San Francisco), Michel Troisgros (three-star restaurant in Roanne, France), Jonathan Waxman (Michael's in Santa Monica, Jam's and Hulot's in New York), Diane Wegner (food consultant for the Mount Diablo schools and for the Berkeley Unified School District), Victoria Wise (Pig-by-the-Tail charcuterie in Berkeley), and Mary Canales (Ici Ice Cream shop). Waters also helped launch the local farms Niman Ranch, Hoffman Chicken Farm, Chenel Goat Cheese, Chino Ranch, Laughing Stock Farm, and Star Route Farm (California's first certified organic farm) and the career of Sibella Krauss, who founded Sustainable Agriculture Education (SAGE) and the San Francisco Ferry Plaza farmers' market.

The Chez Panisse philosophy became a standard for what many considered to be California Cuisine or American-style terroir, based on the French concept of *terroir,* whereby climate, soil, farming, regional cuisine, and tradition determine how people eat and live. The movement also influenced the Colorado-based Celestial Seasonings in 1972, Ithaca, New York's, Moosewood in 1973, the 1977 Los Angeles Mrs. Gooch's Natural Foods Market (now Whole Foods Market), and Ben and Jerry's ice cream in 1978. Marketing for the new cuisine meant reeducating the palates and minds of Americans in new cookbooks such as Julee Rosso and Sheila Lukin's 1977 *Silver Palate Cookbook*, new television cooking shows, growing numbers of newspaper food writers, and the marketing of food consumer goods by Williams-Sonoma, Cuisinart, and Crate and Barrel.

Reaching Pioneer Status

In the 1980s, the movement against industrial foods found international support when Carlo Petrini of Piedmont, Italy, conceived of the Slow Food movement. Petrini, who despised industrial food, led a rally to block the store entrance of American industrial food giant McDonald's when it opened a franchise in Rome. Thus began an international movement to fight the mediocrity and bland uniformity of industrial food—what Petrini labeled the McDonaldization of food. In 1988, Petrini ate at Chez Panisse and started a friendship with Waters, which resulted in her becoming active in forming an American Slow Food movement.

As Fanny matriculated through Berkeley schools, Waters tenaciously advocated for better food and food education for K–12 students and sought to formalize food education. In 1996 she began the Chez Panisse Foundation to support food-related educational programs such as the Edible Schoolyard. Over the course of the next two years, Berkeley educators wrote a garden curriculum for science, math, and social studies classrooms. The mantra of a local, seasonal, organic, and sustainable supply of food for school lunches became a reality in July of 2004 when the Berkeley Unified School District and the Chez Panisse Foundation signed an agreement to create a formal district-wide food curriculum.

To free up more time for political and educational action, Waters selected Gilbert Pilgram in 2000 to serve as general manager of the restaurant. In 2001, as Fanny entered Yale University, Waters took her cause eastward to help Yale establish a Sustainable Food Project for students. Closer to home, she talked San Francisco mayor Gavin Newsom into supporting a "slow food" festival outside City Hall, which attracted 85,000 people. The centerpiece of the event was an urban victory garden in front of City Hall, in which Waters had planted a grand variety of vegetables.

On Alice Waters

Alice Waters has also told us that her daughter is at Yale. When she first went with her daughter [to visit Yale], she met the university president. Her daughter was, I don't think, even embarrassed, because she knew it was coming, and Alice said, to the president, "There's terrible food in the dining room," or something like that, "and you should have better food, and grow stuff." So they did. In one house, at least, they started out a pilot program for improving the food and growing their own things, and so on. So, it's amazing that she's very persuasive. I don't know if education is her thing, as much as a means to convey to people that everything should be local and fresh and instant and not to use things out of season.

—Doris Muscatine, food writer, from oral history interview conducted
by Victor W. Geraci in 2004, Regional Oral History Office,
The Bancroft Library, University of California, Berkeley, 2006

Detractors

Not everyone agreed with Waters's food philosophy or her methods, and many rejected the claim of her being a leader in the food movement. Detractors believed that her ideology could not provide enough food for the world's billions of inhabitants. In fact, many outwardly criticized Waters's food philosophy and Chez Panisse as an elitist luxury in a calorie-starved world. These critics believed the restaurant had become a place to be seen as a sort of food Mecca. Mary Risley, owner of the San Francisco Tante Marie Cooking School, reflected, "I have always had good food at Chez Panisse, but it's become a kind of a tourist restaurant."

Waters defended her beliefs by explaining that people make daily decisions on how to spend their resources. If health can be enhanced by quality food, then consumers should be willing to forego useless goods and spend more on food purchases. Karen Christensen, global produce buyer for Whole Foods Market, backed Waters up while at the same predicting that sustainable produce could drive costs up by 20 percent. Slow food enthusiasts argued that government subsidies for agribusinesses had created a false sense of inexpensive food and drove small farmers out of business. Further support for this argument came from Frederick Kirschenmann, senior fellow at the Leopold Institute for Sustainable Agriculture, Iowa State University, who believed that in the long run industrial foodways would be more expensive because of the costs of governmental agricultural subsidies, tax breaks, and cleaning up environmental damage resulting from the production of cheap food.

Others have attacked Waters for taking too much credit for the new food movement. Former food critic for *The New York Times* Mimi Sheraton believed that the fashion for local food and fresh ingredients did not have its roots at Chez Panisse but with restaurants such as the Four Seasons in New York, which had offered seasonal cooking since the early 1960s. Further attacks from the likes of former Food Network star Anthony Bourdain emphasized that Waters's food ideas would not necessarily give Americans more affordable good food. Bourdain declared that his priority was to deliver taste, not necessarily local, seasonal, or organically grown foods.

Despite the detractors, Waters held steady in the political battle for sustainable foodways. She appeared at benefits such as the Center for Land-Based Learning, a nonprofit started by Craig and Julie McNamara that seeks to interest young people in careers in agriculture. Her work against industrial food also featured a speaking tour to promote the documentary *Food Inc.*, an exposé of the food industry coproduced by Eric Schlosser, author of *Fast Food Nation*. As President Barack Obama took office, Waters convinced First Lady Michele Obama to plant a 1,100-square-foot garden on the White House South Lawn to promote the sustainable food cause. Waters had also offered to help the Obamas select a White House chef with a devotion to the ideals of healthy nourishment for all citizens, environmentalism, health, and conservation.

CONCLUSION

Waters served as an activist spokesperson for the Slow Food philosophy of fresh, seasonal, local, and sustainable produce in the United States, and her food ideals ushered in many changes in restaurant cuisines. Before Chez Panisse, most restaurants used industrial, processed foods for efficiency and profitability. Yet, according to the National Restaurant Association, by the new millennium over 60 percent of the best American restaurants featured organic ingredients on their menus. In 2008, Waters supported the federal organic law and helped create new U.S. Department of Agriculture guidelines for school lunches. Many restaurants also follow the Chez Panisse management style of a board of directors for business decisions, employment of a full-time forager with relationships with local farmers and food producers, benefits for employees, and shared chef positions so that workers can have a life outside the kitchen.

Waters's food passions and ability to draw upon the California bounty helped create the early wave of what many called California Cuisine. Chuck Williams of Williams-Sonoma remembered a time when Californians saw limited fresh produce in local markets and almost no farmers' markets. He credited the California Cuisine craze with the ability to overcome transportation and distribution problems while at the same time ensuring profitability for boutique farmers. But Williams went a step further by adding that California Cuisine was not "cooking a dish in any special way. It was just a matter of providing those kinds of ingredients to cook with. Here in California, it was coming from a different direction of not cooking things so long, and cooking them a little better."

But the changes influenced by Waters extended beyond the food she served. Christopher Lee, past Chez Panisse forager and chef at Berkeley's Eccolo Restaurant, also believed that Waters changed the way Americans eat in high-end restaurants. No longer did well-dressed diners flock to temples of gastronomy featuring waiters in tuxedos; now food was allowed to be the transformative part of the dining experience. Of equal importance was the fact that women were now being recognized for their excellence in the kitchen and restaurant worlds. Waters had become the unofficial pioneer, spokesperson, and gatekeeper for those wishing to succeed in the new American *haute cuisine*.

NOTE

1. All quotations are taken from oral history interviews with Charles Williams, Mary Risley, Christopher Lee, Doris Muscatine, and Cecilia Chiang from the UC Berkeley Regional Oral History Office Food Series, The Bancroft Library, University of California, Berkeley. See Further Reading below.

FURTHER READING

Publications by Alice Waters

Chez Panisse Cooking, with Paul Bertolli. New York: Random House, 1988.
Chez Panisse Desserts. New York: Random House, 1994.
Chez Panisse Menu Cookbook. New York: Random House, 1995.
Chez Panisse Pasta, Pizza, Calzone. New York: Random House, 1995.
Chez Panisse Vegetables. New York: William Morrow, 1996.
Fanny at Chez Panisse: A Child's Restaurant Adventures with 46 Recipes. New York: William Morrow, 1997.
Chez Panisse Cafe Cookbook. New York: William Morrow, 1999.
California Fresh Harvest: A Seasonal Journey through Northern California, with Gina Gallo. Nashville, TN: Favorite Recipes Press, 2001.
Chez Panisse Fruit. New York: William Morrow, 2002.
Waters, Alice, Caro Petrini, and William McCuaig. *Slow Food: The Case for Taste: Arts and Traditions of the Table: Perspectives on Culinary History*. New York: Columbia University Press, 2003.
The Art of Simple Food. New York: Clarkson Potter, 2007.

Slow Food Nation's Come to the Table: The Slow Food Way of Living. San Francisco: Modern Times, 2008.

The Edible Schoolyard. New York: Chronicle Books, 2008.

In the Green Kitchen: Techniques to Learn by Heart. New York: Clarkson Potter, 2010.

Works on Alice Waters

Chiang, Cecilia. "Cecilia Chiang: An Oral History." Interview conducted by Victor Geraci, 2005–2006, Regional Oral History Office, The Bancroft Library, University of California, Berkeley, 2007.

Kamp, David. *The United States of Arugula: How We Became a Gourmet Nation.* New York: Broadway Books, 2006.

Lee, Christopher. "Bay Area Restaurateur." Interview conducted by Kirstin Jackson and Victor W. Geraci, 2004, Regional Oral History Office, The Bancroft Library, University of California, Berkeley, 2006.

McNamee, Thomas. *Alice Waters and Chez Panisse: The Romantic, Impractical, Often Eccentric, Ultimately Brilliant Making of a Food Revolution.* New York: Penguin, 2007.

Muscatine, Doris. "Food and Wine Writer." Interview conducted by Victor W. Geraci, 2004,

Regional Oral History Office, The Bancroft Library, University of California, Berkeley, 2006.

Risley, Mary. "Food Educator and Proprietor of the San Francisco Based Tante Marie's Cooking School." Oral history interview conducted in 2004 by Victor W. Geraci, Regional Oral History Office, The Bancroft Library, University of California, Berkeley, 2006.

Williams, Chuck, and Howard Lester. Volume II, Williams-Sonoma: Mastering the Homeware, 1994–2004. Oral history interview conducted in 2004 by Victor W. Geraci, Regional Oral History Office, The Bancroft Library, University of California, Berkeley, 2005.

Victor W. Geraci

Chuck Williams, founder of Williams-Sonoma Inc., stands outside his very first storefront as a plaque is unveiled to mark his company's 50th anniversary in Sonoma, California, March 20, 2007. Williams started the nationwide specialty retailer of high-quality home products at the site in 1956. (AP/Wide World Photos)

Chuck Williams

In 1956, Chuck Williams founded the Williams-Sonoma kitchenware chain of stores that introduced post–World War II American homemakers and cooks to French kitchen staples such as the soufflé dish, the madeleine mold, the bain marie, the sauté pan, and the hefty chef's knife. His merchandising success emanated from a personal dedication to creating a service-oriented store that sold only quality cookware for foodies. In an era when customer service diminished as corporate department stores prospered, Williams-Sonoma targeted upscale shoppers who, in Williams's words, "enjoyed patronizing a shop that gave good service, and did not mind paying extra for the service."[1] As the American middle class grew, Williams's cookware stores helped provide the tools and cookbooks necessary to model the cooking styles pioneered by foodie revolutionaries Julia Child, James Beard, and Alice Waters.

Williams persevered over poverty and family tribulations caused by the Great Depression and learned to use his eclectic work experiences with wealthy West Coast people to achieve personal security. He emerged from these experiences a man grounded in the simple pleasures of the table and versed in the nuances of high-end consumerism. He used skills learned from hardship to create a merchandising expertise based on quality and service to become a pioneer in the California and American food revolutions.

Williams operated his business out of his San Francisco corporate headquarters, where he served as the buyer, creative genius, and standard bearer for the company. His corporate office's test kitchen produced and tested the thousands of recipes in the company's catalogs and cookbooks. During his long career he served as either an editor or contributor and orchestrated the publication of more than 100 cookbooks.

Williams's philanthropic and personal involvement in food education and promotional activities helped define the growing success of American foodways. His many contributions included mentoring and providing scholarships for promising students in the field of culinary arts at the Culinary Institute of America. Promotion of the field included dedication of his personal time as a member of the Board of the American Institute of Food & Wine and financial support of events sponsored by the International Association of Culinary Professionals.

EARLY YEARS

The Depression

On October 2, 1915, Ohio native Nettie Marie Shaw Williams, housewife and office manager, Charles Edward Williams, Rhode Island auto mechanic, and their two-year-old daughter celebrated the birth of Charles Edward ("Chuck") in their Jacksonville, Florida, home. When Williams was three years old, the family moved to Saranac Lake in upstate New York, where his father was to serve as the chauffeur for a wealthy family. The new job provided a mediocre standard of living for the family, so they moved back to Jacksonville, which was booming in the hot 1920s economy. The elder Williams first worked for a Cadillac agency, then quickly seized opportunities to open his own Cadillac and Lincoln auto repair and painting business, which faltered during the Great Depression. In a desperate search for job opportunities, the family first moved to Beaumont, Texas, and then to Banning, California, where the young Williams supplemented the family income by picking cherries and almonds. In 1933 Williams's unemployed and disheartened father abandoned the family.

For as long as Williams could remember, food was an important part of his life. His maternal grandparents instilled a respect for food in their grandson at a time when people cooked at home and had a more personal relationship with what they ate. Williams remembered his grandmother's stories of how she had owned a restaurant in Lima, Ohio, and how her kitchen functioned like a business, serving three simple meals a day, based on regional and seasonal fruits and vegetables. He recalled that she taught him how to cook stews and soups and always let him assist in the baking of pies or cakes, even encouraging him to take the leftover batter and bake something for himself. Williams fondly remembered that "she cooked all these great meals without a cookbook because there weren't many cookbooks in those days outside of the *Fannie Farmer* (1896) cookbook or recipes in newspapers and in magazines like in *Ladies Home Journal*." Williams's grandfather loved to eat good food and also taught his grandson traditional foodways. Williams remembers him coming home once with a butchered pig and how they dressed, cooked, and ate the whole hog in times before refrigeration.

In keeping with this family food knowledge and skill base, Williams's mother turned to food as a source of income to support her son and daughter during the Depression. She moved the family to San Antonio, Texas, where she opened a small restaurant. Almost immediately the business failed, and in 1933 the family moved back to California. Williams recounted: "I remember the Depression very well. It was a catastrophe as far as I was concerned. It's had a lasting effect on me, I know. Growing up under those circumstances, having it hit at the age it hit me, 15 or 16 years old, and not having the advantage of finishing school properly, going to college, or having a job—not having anything, and then having your family fall apart. Being on your own made it even worse—having to make your own way."

In their new home in Indio, California, Williams found employment in Dr. and Mrs. Sniff's ranch, roadside shop, and mail-order date and grapefruit business. The Sniffs loved the hardworking young man and even wanted to adopt him. They sent him to high school in the mornings, and he worked in the afternoons. Williams's mother and sister moved to Palm Springs as household servants. Food again became an integral part of his life as Mrs. Sniff taught Williams further appreciation of cooking and food.

This Indio date ranch experience heavily influenced Williams's approaches to retail sales and the concept of service to customers. Palm Springs was a desert winter resort area replete with luxury hotels and resorts. Williams remembered serving the San Francisco wealthy Magnin (of I Magnin Department Stores) and Fleishhacker (banking and philanthropy) families who wintered in Palm Springs. He learned a lot about service in those days because the shop and mail-order business were built on service, and those kinds of wealthy, influential people paid for and demanded assistance. In Williams's words, "When I think back over it today, it was the same sort of mail-order business that I established here—the same sort of clientele, upper class. And the business I started in San Francisco, where I located, did attract an upper-class clientele."

But tragedy struck Williams's family again. His sister died in 1933 from a brain injury after being hit in the head with a baseball, and his mother decided to return to Florida. Williams, on the other hand, decided to stay in California because he "felt there was nothing for me to go back to Florida for, so I might as well stay in California and make my own way. I felt I could better myself that way." His intuitions proved correct, and over the next three summer off-seasons he met people who provided life-enhancing experiences for his future. Part of one summer he stayed in Los Angeles with a family of professional photographers who had photographed well-known places like Yosemite, Yellowstone, Glacier National Park, and Crater Lake. During another summer his connections to the family that owned the Bullock's Department Store chain landed him a job in Los Angeles in the window-trimming department. After finally finishing high school and armed with these work experiences, Williams worked two years in the Hollywood and Wilshire I Magnin store, where he advanced to the head of the shipping and receiving department.

Entering the World of Food

As the national economy braced to support America's European allies fighting Germany in World War II, Williams took a job with Lockheed Aircraft as a riveter for repair of British warplanes. In these pre–Pearl Harbor 1941 days, he took a risk and signed up to work in Massawa, Eritrea, as part of a secret U.S. government project designed to aid the British war effort. After a two-year stint in Eritrea, the company transferred him to India, where he spent the next two years repairing and servicing Allied planes fighting in the Burma Theater of operations.

As the war ended, Williams, along with many others, returned home to face the task of restarting his life. This was not easy for a product of the Depression who feared poverty and "was concerned about my security more than anything else." In his words, "I never, never want to be poor again. Not that I couldn't cope with living meagerly. I can. I suppose in lots of ways I'm very selfish in being very careful in what I spend. I have always done everything the cheapest way I could, which is not always the best way to do it. I wasn't much of a gambler. I didn't have anything to fall back on. I always worried about that."

Williams returned home in the latter half of 1946 and rejected a safe, secure job at Lockheed for work helping a Porterville, California, friend and overseas colleague build a home. After completion of his friend's home, Williams moved to Sonoma, California, where he took his savings and purchased a piece of cheap land to build a house for himself. In less than six months, the American housing boom allowed him to flip the house for a profit. Thus, he started his new career as a contractor. Sonoma proved to be a lucrative location for a contractor, as wealthy retirees, escaping the city and suburbs, built homes in the rural outskirts of the San Francisco Bay area. Over the next few years, Williams built several homes, remodeled many others, and built a home for himself and his mother, whom he had brought from Florida.

In 1952, the security-minded Williams decided that he needed to have a profession rather than just drift from job to job building and remodeling homes. The idea for this new path came to him after a 1953 trip to England, Holland, Germany, France, Spain, Denmark, and Norway with two friends. He decided to act on his dreams of financial security by focusing on his new love of travel and his old passion for food.

These Sonoma years not only reignited Williams's food passions but also introduced him to the newly fashionable American craze for French food. A few of his neighbors had banded together to form a dinner club where members cooked for each other. The leader of the group was Franco-American Therese Bacon, who loved to cook French country food. Another member, Ola Tryon, from San Francisco, had moved to Sonoma and built a beautiful house replete with an enormous living-room kitchen and a restaurant stove. Tryon's French food finds, along with the new gourmet cookbook era and *Gourmet* magazine's inaugural issue, provided a learning platform for Williams.

Other wealthy Sonoma foodies, usually retired professionals, joined their food group during the 1950s. Central to the group was Gordon Tevis, scion of old California money from multigenerational landholdings, who bought the Spreckel family (California Sugar Refinery) de Bretteville mansion and remodeled it for his lavish dinner parties. During these parties, Tevis demonstrated his cooking skills in his kitchen and showcased an exquisite collection of French pots and pans. The group also frequented the growing numbers of fine restaurants throughout the San Francisco Bay area.

Participation in the cooking group's activities opened many opportunities for Williams. Arthur Bacon, a Sonoma friend, worked in an antique shop in San Francisco and had done home decoration and design work. Bacon's acquaintance, Elena Teller of the Folger Coffee family, had a summer home in Sonoma, and she wanted to help a friend plan a debutante party for his daughter. Teller approached Bacon, who in turn brought Williams on to make wooden table centerpieces, a chandelier, and wall sconces for the tent in the front yard of the Hillsborough home. Through the party, Williams met about 450 people who became his future customers. It would be during this period of his life that Williams learned from his wealthy acquaintances how to market French culture to American Francophiles.

THE STORE

Opening

In 1954, Williams made a bold move and decided to purchase and remodel a large, old-fashioned hardware store by dividing it into three smaller shops for rental income. He kept the hardware store, later named Williams-Sonoma, and stocked it with brooms, mops, imported European kitchenwares, and general hardware. He rented the other two smaller shops out to a florist and beautician. From the start of his new endeavor, his Depression era upbringing, insecurities of coming from a broken family, and eclectic work experiences converged to influence his approach to selling quality merchandise and outstanding service, aimed at a new generation of Americans with increasing amounts of disposable income.

By 1958, many of Williams-Sonoma's first customers lived in nearby San Francisco. As word of the store spread, it became apparent that a move to the city would allow Williams to introduce more people to the cookware he had discovered overseas. With no real business plan, he chose a location a few blocks from Union Square, the center of San Francisco's shopping district, with a staff that included himself and one other person. In his words, he "was just starting a little business of selling French cookware and French tools for people that liked to cook and that would like to learn about French cooking." He did not realize at the time that he had secured an amazing location. The Sutter Street building was within two blocks of major medical buildings, across the street from the Francisca Club, the most prestigious women's club in San Francisco, and on the same block as Elizabeth Arden's beauty salon and fashion store. As a result, his new location had constant foot traffic from many of San Francisco's well-to-do women.

When the store opened, it became a magnet for fashionable upper-crust ladies, restaurant chefs, and businessmen. The store also attracted counterculture types who, Williams recalls, "found in the store large French pots essential for preparing communal meals." Williams provided free local delivery, like his business neighbors I. Magnin, Saks Fifth Avenue, and Tiffany, and provided in-house credit for customers. In those years, Williams did everything from sweeping the sidewalk, stocking, buying, designing displays, and selling; he remembered that he was "never any good at delegating other people to do things. It was much easier for me to just do it myself. That certainly isn't the type of person that would be thinking of growing and increasing a business." In the first few years, Williams's business expanded to suit the needs of new economic and social trends predicated on the ever-increasing disposable income of large groups of Americans. Despite this new wealth, the custom of having private cooks began to disappear from the homes of the wealthy, and more homemakers rediscovered their kitchen and began to cook and entertain for their families and friends.

Included in this change was the 1960s renaissance in the way Americans thought about and prepared food. A new trend of returning to natural and simple ways drew attention in the Cold War world of nuclear tensions. In San

Francisco, this zeitgeist was partly expressed with a passion for preparing food. The times were right for a small San Francisco kitchen store to supply newly educated cooks as they read recently released cookbooks by the likes of James Beard, Helen Brown, and Elizabeth David. Also fanning the flames of the new passion was the publication of Julia Child's cookbook *Mastering the Art of French Cooking* (1961) and her subsequent hit television cooking shows. Further adding to the glamour of the new French trend was the adaptation of French cuisine by the First Family, the Kennedys. Jackie Kennedy adored French cooking and hired a French chef for the White House.

Merchandising Cooking Supplies for the Food Revolution

By the early 1970s, Williams and his store had become a haven for the disciples of the regional California Cuisine and the fermenting food revolution. Williams defined California Cuisine as being about the use of fresh vegetables, fruits, and nuts supplied by local farmers who used the state's Mediterranean climate. Near-perfect agricultural conditions allowed farmers to grow a wide variety of ethnic fruits and vegetables to meet the needs of diverse ethnic communities in the state's urban centers of San Diego, Los Angeles, and San Francisco. To Williams, it was not about cooking a dish in any special way but more a matter of using fresh, seasonal ingredients. Most amazing was the fact that Williams never thought he had the business sense to expand his operation.

Williams's past experiences with wealthy patrons and pioneering foodies bought him membership in the new California food scene and the early roots of the Slow Food cause. During this time, he befriended American cookbook author Marion Cunningham, who was James Beard's assistant, a *San Francisco Chronicle* columnist, and a 1993 winner of the Grand Dame award from Les Dames d'Escoffier. In the next three decades, the two became frequent dinner companions. Cunningham later described Williams as a kind, fun-loving person who supplied quality cookware that he used in his own kitchen.

By 1970 Williams's profitable local business had become his entire life. He also quickly began to realize that to maintain future profitability he would need to expand his operation and feared more than ever that he did not have the expertise and needed capital to do so. In an attempt to accrue the expansion capital, he approached his longtime bank, Wells Fargo, for a loan, only to have them turn his application down. Williams recalled, "I had no credit rating, I had never borrowed money before." What he did know is that he had a "good eye" for quality cookware and understood the needs of the fledgling high-cuisine food revival.

OTHER ENDEAVORS

A Mail-Order Business

Despite the initial expansion problems, 1972 proved to be a banner year for the growing business. That year Jackie Mallorca, a customer and copywriter for a local San Francisco advertising agency, approached Williams with the idea of producing a catalog for the store. Williams's only experience with catalog sales had been from his years with the Sniff's date ranch. Feeling the need for business advice, Williams turned to his business acquaintance, Edward Marcus, director of the Neiman Marcus catalog, who encouraged him to move forward with the idea. Mallorca helped create the first catalog, and with the in-house mailing list of 5,000 names, a new era began for Williams-Sonoma. Mallorca continued to work on the company's catalogs for over 30 years.

Yet, success proved to be a two-edged sword for Williams. Increased sales required a larger operation and more business management skills than he possessed. He later recalled telling Marcus, "'It's gotten to the point that after the store closes at night, I go to the back room and sit down and have a glass of wine.' I said, 'Doing everything myself, not being able to delegate other people to do things, what should I do? I am going to become an alcoholic or I am going to have a heart attack over it, one or the other.'" Marcus agreed that this was a problem and offered to form a business partnership with him. In a short time, the two incorporated the store as Williams-Sonoma, Inc., and with Marcus's contacts borrowed expansion money from local banks.

At first, the credit-based expansion went well. The borrowed money funded new stores in the California upscale communities of Beverly Hills, Palo Alto, and Costa Mesa and later an out-of-state store in Dallas, Texas. By 1976, the catalog business had outgrown the small basement offices in the San Francisco store and forced them to move the operation just across the bay from San Francisco to a new warehouse in Emeryville, California. But deep inside, Williams, with his Depression-era background, was uncomfortable with the idea of this business expansion through loans. It was an outside-the-box move for a man who had never borrowed any money from anyone and who feared debt and losing control of his business.

By the late 1970s, his fears had become reality. The task of running a large business outstripped Williams's abilities, so Marcus again stepped in and convinced a Dallas friend, who worked for a catalog company, to run the mail-order sales for Williams-Sonoma. With new leadership and dreams of increasing catalog sales, the company again borrowed large amounts of money. This time the expansion costs did not generate the expected revenues and the company had insufficient assets to pay off loans. Making matters worse, Marcus, the business mind for the corporation, died. Williams faced losing his operation and his home, which he had mortgaged for the expansion.

Branding a National Chain

In 1978, the company regained its footing when Howard Lester, a twice-retired entrepreneur from Oklahoma, sought a new business opportunity after deciding that he disliked retirement. While traveling through California, Lester had stopped in the Beverly Hills Williams-Sonoma store and was impressed with what he saw. He arranged a meeting with Williams and within a few months had purchased the company with a friend. Lester assumed control as president and CEO of Williams-Sonoma, Inc., and the agreement allowed Williams to stay on board as a vice president for buying, for the cookware catalog, the cookbooks, and in a preferred role as brand ambassador.

During the early 1980s, Lester's new company flourished and expanded into many other areas. First came the purchase of Gardeners Eden, a catalog company that sold plants, tools, and garden supplies. By 1983, Williams-Sonoma had regained its financial footing, and Lester decided to expand even further. He took advantage of the booming stock market and took the company public on the New York Stock Exchange. Sales of WSM stock yielded the needed funds for expansion, and in 1984 the company completed construction of a larger distribution center in Memphis, Tennessee, to meet the needs of the growing number of customers on the East Coast. Next came the 1985 purchase of Hold Everything and the 1986 takeover of the failing Manhattan-based Pottery Barn stores, which sold dinnerware, ceramics, and a few pieces of furniture. The purchase of the Chambers Catalog in 1989 rounded out the decade.

The rapid expansion continued through the 1990s and into the new millennium. In 1991 the stores began a computerized Bridal Registry system, and starting in 1996, customer care centers opened in Las Vegas, Nevada, Oklahoma City, and Camp Hill, Pennsylvania, to serve both store and catalog customers. In 1999, the company began online shopping and opened Pottery Barn for Kids. In the first few years of the 2000s, the Williams-Sonoma lineup expanded to include the Bed, Bath and Beyond Catalog, West Elm, and PB Teen, as well as the expansion of brick-and-mortar stores in Canada.

COOKBOOKS

Over his lifetime, Williams acquired a vast knowledge, arguably more than many professional chefs, about the kitchen and cooking. Yet, it was not until 1986 that he published his first cookbook, *The Williams-Sonoma Cookbook with a Guide to Kitchenware*. Since then, Williams has written or edited more than 100 cookbooks, including the best-selling *Williams-Sonoma Kitchen Library* series.

As a boy Williams remembered that people bought one cookbook, such as the *Fannie Farmer Cookbook*, with the idea that it would be the only book they would ever need.

Williams believed that his customers' needs changed over time. When he started his business, most people cooked at least two meals a day and had a basic familiarity with the kitchen, cooking techniques, and foods. But as women entered the workforce and workers commuted longer distances, people had less time to prepare complicated meals. Yet, these same people had not abandoned good food, and most of them wanted to cook on weekends or to entertain for friends and family. These weekend cooks actively sought advice on how to prepare and serve fine meals. In Williams's words, "Now they buy a cookbook—I mean, it's not just one cookbook that they buy, that they think, 'Well, this is going to change my way of cooking.' They have the feeling that if they get one or two recipes out of that book, it's well worth it. So that's when they are cooking. And they need recipe books for that. They are trying, and you know, if you are cooking for entertaining, you're cooking for other people, you're not cooking for yourself, so they're trying to cook something they think will impress their friends, which is natural."

With this belief about modern cooks, Williams began publishing his cookbook series. The idea grew to fruition when a small publisher from Australia approached him with the ideas of doing single-subject books, like *Pasta* or *Salad*, with distribution through the store and catalogs. The resulting Time-Life *Williams-Sonoma Kitchen Library* series grew to include 40 volumes and sold over 10 million copies. Williams also served as the sole author of the Time-Life/Williams Sonoma books *Simple Cooking*, *Simple American Cooking*, *Simple French Cooking*, and *Simple Italian Cooking*.

AWARDS AND HONORS

Magazine writers have dubbed Williams the "captain of cookware," "a kitchen revolutionary," and "the guru of cookware." Most of his colleagues laud his genius as a buyer and enjoy recounting stories of his perfectionism. Yet, the quiet and unassuming Williams, by his own admission, lacked the financial and managerial skills to create his houseware empire. His true talent emanated from his passion for cooking and cookware and the belief that anyone could learn about and share food. Clark Wolf, an old friend and restaurant consultant, believed that Williams's true business acumen was his "good eye" for quality cookware. The American public learned to treasure Williams's food sense and purchased new foodwares and food items endorsed by Williams.

In 1992, food peers named Williams "Retailer of the Year" at the San Francisco Gourmet Products Show. In the following year, the James Beard Foundation named Williams to the "Who's Who of Food and Beverage," and in 1995 they honored him with a Lifetime Achievement Award. The honors continued with presentation of the Lifetime Achievement Award from the International Association of Culinary Professionals in 2001 and his subsequent induction into the Culinary Institute of America's Hall of Fame in 2002. In 2006, Williams was honored as a Visionary Retailer at the seventh annual Giants of Design Awards presented by House Beautiful in New York City.

CONCLUSION

Williams expresses his own ideas about his contribution in these words: "I think that I would like to be known for introducing Americans to good cookware, good tools, and for encouraging them to cook. I also like to think that I have contributed to their appreciation of good food and what good food can be if it's properly cooked."

NOTE

1. This profile is written using content and quotes from the following two oral history interviews with Chuck Williams: Charles E. Williams, Williams-Sonoma Cookware and the American Kitchen: The Merchandising Vision of Chuck Williams, 1956–1994, an oral history conducted in 1992–1994 by Lisa Jacobson and Ruth Teiser, Regional Oral History Office, The Bancroft Library, University of California, Berkeley, 1995; and Chuck Williams, Williams-Sonoma: Mastering the Homeware: 1994–2004, an oral history conducted in 2004 by Victor W. Geraci, Regional Oral History Office, The Bancroft Library, University of California, Berkeley, 2005. Complete transcripts are available at http://bancroft.berkeley.edu/ROHO/projects/food_wine/food.html.

FURTHER READING

Saekel, Karola. "Chuck Williams at 90." *The San Francisco Chronicle*. October 5, 2005.

Williams, Charles E. Williams-Sonoma Cookware and the American Kitchen: The Merchandising Vision of Chuck Williams, 1956–1994. An oral history conducted in 1992–1994 by Lisa Jacobson and Ruth Teiser, Regional Oral History Office, The Bancroft Library, University of California, Berkeley, 1995.

Williams, Chuck. Williams-Sonoma: Mastering the Homeware: 1994–2004. An oral history conducted in 2004 by Victor W. Geraci, Regional Oral History Office, The Bancroft Library, University of California, Berkeley, 2005.

Victor W. Geraci

Tim and Nina Zagat share dessert at Gabriels restaurant in New York, November 28, 1995. The couple publishes the *Zagat Survey*, a series of guides in which consumers review restaurants and other services, including hotels, resorts, airlines, and car rental companies. (AP/Wide World Photos)

Tim and Nina Zagat

Tim and Nina Zagat (pronounced zuh-GAT) are husband-and-wife entrepreneurs and founders of Zagat Survey, a publisher of consumer survey-based guides for restaurants, hotels, and other leisure activities. Begun by the couple as a hobby in 1979, the Zagat Survey has grown to become an influential force in the world of dining and leisure. Their collection of more than 50 pocket-sized annual guidebooks in a distinctive vertical format (8.5 inches tall by 3.75 inches wide) and their companion Web site, Zagat.com, provide ratings and reviews on restaurants, hotels, spas, golf courses, nightlife, shopping, and other attractions, covering more than 100 countries worldwide.

The *Zagat Restaurant Survey*, with its trademark crimson cover, was the original focus of the New York–based company and remains the flagship of its publishing empire, with an estimated 650,000 copies of the New York City guide sold annually. The *Survey*'s appeal is based in part on the democratic notion of creating restaurant ratings and reviews based on volunteer feedback from thousands of consumers instead of the opinions of individual professional food critics. Each review—available in printed guidebook form as well as a variety of other media platforms, including the Web, cell phones, in-car and personal navigation devices, television, and radio—features ratings for food, décor, and service, as well as pithy comments culled from responses provided by more than 350,000 volunteer reviewers worldwide. The prominence of the brand and its influence on millions of daily dining decisions position Tim and Nina Zagat as powerful figures in the food world.

EARLY YEARS

Budding Gourmands

Born Eugene H. Zagat Jr. on May 13, 1940, Tim Zagat spent his childhood in New York City. Nina Zagat (née Safronoff) was born August 12, 1942, and grew up on Long Island. Upon graduating from college—he from Harvard, she from Vassar—both pursued law degrees at Yale Law School in New Haven, Connecticut. The couple met in 1963, during their first year in law school when they shared a Contracts class and started studying together over Nina's home-cooked dinners. They discovered their personalities matched—Tim's outgoing and loquacious nature to Nina's quiet discipline and reserve—and two years later, they married. After graduation in 1966, they each took positions at prominent Wall Street law firms, Tim as a corporate attorney and Nina specializing in estate law.

When Tim's firm offered him an assignment in Paris, Nina requested and received a transfer from her firm, too. Originally thinking their stay would be for only six months, the couple eagerly explored the culinary attractions of the city, often referring to European restaurant guidebooks such as the *Guide Michelin* for advice. They regularly shared meals with a small group of friends at both popular and out-of-the-way Paris restaurants, where they evaluated their experiences, compared their observations to the established guidebooks, and exchanged recommendations for future dining. In a prescient move, they kept a list of these Paris restaurant experiences and ratings, a project they wryly dubbed the "Guide de Guides." Adding to their gastronomic adventure, Nina enrolled in classes at the famous Cordon Bleu cooking school. The couple ultimately spent two years working and dining in the French capital. Although they did not recognize it at the time, their years of research laid the foundation for their later culinary enterprise.

In 1970 the Zagats returned to the United States, ready to explore the evolving world of New York City restaurants. They joined a monthly food-and-wine group, the Downtown Wine-Tasting Association, which held monthly dinners with fellow food enthusiasts. During one 1979 raucous dinner, with heated debate over a *New York Times* restaurant critic (suspected to be Mimi Sheraton) and her unreliable restaurant reviews, the idea for the Zagat Survey emerged. Tim suggested compiling reviews from friends and colleagues, arguing that multiple opinions are better than a single viewpoint. The result was a survey of food, service, and décor for approximately 100 New York City restaurants, based on input from nearly 200 food-loving volunteer reviewers. The compilation was published as a simple double-sided mimeographed sheet of legal-size paper, but every contributor received a copy and it soon became an underground sensation, passed along to thousands.

THE GUIDEBOOK

A Hobby Becomes a Business

The annual gastronomic project expanded, and by 1982 about 300 New York restaurants were reviewed by approximately 600 individuals. The survey's popularity and reputation continued to grow, particularly among banking and business executives, who frequently sought good restaurants for business meetings or to host important guests. Growth created challenges, however, as the Zagats' hobby became more and more costly. By 1982, Nina—the more fiscally attentive member of the duo—calculated that the survey was costing them about $1,000 a month, since they had to hire an outside firm to compile and tabulate the results; moreover, they were supplying more than 5,000 free copies a year. The expense calculations also did not include one of the central elements of their research—the cost of their own dining out. They determined it was time to sell the guide to nonparticipants and to establish a publishing company. As experienced attorneys, they were aware of the tax advantages of becoming a business and recognized that even if the project broke even, at least they could deduct their expenses.

In 1983, they decided to publish the restaurant survey as a guidebook for sale in bookstores and other retail outlets. Traditional publishers, however, declined interest, arguing that similar guides had fared poorly in the American marketplace. After receiving numerous rejections—including even one from Tim's uncle, who had his own publishing company—the Zagats chose to self-publish. They filled the back of their brown Toyota Corolla station wagon with books and persistently made the rounds of bookstores in the New York City area, urging booksellers to stock the publication. The 1983 guide, officially titled the *Zagat New York City Restaurant Survey,* rated 317 restaurants and sold 7,500 copies. The company broke even that year, mostly due to participating reviewers who each received a complimentary copy but purchased additional guides for friends and colleagues. By 1984, sales had climbed to 18,000 copies and more than doubled by 1985 to 40,000 copies.

A major turning point occurred with the 1986 edition of the restaurant guide, thanks in large part to a *New York* magazine cover story. The article, titled "The Food Spooks," appeared in the Thanksgiving food-focused issue of the magazine and showcased the *1986 Zagat New York City Restaurant Survey* as the "insiders' guide" to local dining. It featured a brief overview of the genesis of the *Survey* and its rating system alongside a photo spread of 43 prominent New Yorkers who served as Zagat reviewers. Dressed in fedoras and raincoats, and photographed at tables in the elegant Petrossian restaurant in Manhattan, the individuals in the large group shot were identified only by their work title or affiliation (for example, trustee, Museum of American Folk Art; real-estate executive; vice-chairman, hospital fund-raising committee; gallery owner). The approach piqued the interest of status-conscious New Yorkers, who were keen on detecting the full identities of the Zagat reviewers. Furthermore, the magazine featured a selection of 48 restaurant reviews from the 632 included in the 1986 survey. Readers were introduced to the Zagat rating system and the pithy reviewer comments that are hallmarks of the guide. The article also included lists of the 50 favorite restaurants, the 26 most expensive restaurants, and 39 "Super Buys." Spread over nine pages of the magazine, the story created widespread visibility for the *Zagat Survey* and attracted thousands to join the ranks of reviewers. The publicity also skyrocketed book sales in the month following the article to 75,000, nearly double the *Survey's* sales for the entire previous year.

Other publications, including *The New York Times* and *People* magazine, soon followed with feature articles of their own. The extensive media coverage transformed the Zagats' time-consuming and expensive sideline into a fast-paced entrepreneurial venture. Tim soon left his position as chief litigation counsel for Gulf & Western to lead the company, Zagat Survey, which the couple incorporated in December 1985, and they hired their first full-time employee. Nina left the Shearman & Sterling law firm to join him in 1990.

The publicity and increasing sales and visibility of the "burgundy bible" also launched the couple as celebrities in their own right in the late 1980s, and they became increasingly powerful arbiters of dining choices in New York City. Tim's burly figure was ubiquitous on the restaurant scene, as he visited dozens of restaurants a night, checking on food and promoting the guidebooks. His pockets were always filled with extra copies so that maitre d's who did not recognize him could quickly respond when he flashed a copy and announced, "I do this."[1] Choice tables and fawning service usually followed, whether the couple were dining ensemble or Tim was scouting solo. With every guidebook sold and every night out, the couple knit themselves into the tight fabric of the New York City food establishment.

OTHER ENDEAVORS

New Cities, Topics, and Formats

With the success of the original *New York City Restaurant Survey*, the Zagats quickly expanded their efforts to include other cities and additional topics. Major metropolitan areas with active dining scenes were a natural extension, and restaurant guides were created for Chicago, San Francisco, and Washington, D.C. In 1986 the first guide for Los Angeles appeared, joined by Boston and New Orleans the following year. In 1987, surveying of hotels, resorts, and spas began, and in 1990, international editions debuted with a Canadian restaurant survey. Movies received the Zagat survey treatment in 2002, and a year later the company expanded into shopping, CDs, and Broadway theater. The company hired the noted design firm Pentagram to refresh the guides' layout in 2007 and continues to pursue new survey topics. For example, the Zagat Survey *Disneyland Resort Insider's Guide* debuted in 2009, presenting an overview of 279 rides, attractions, dining, shopping, hotels, and amenities rated by 3,122 theme park visitors.

From the earliest days of their publishing empire, the Zagats leveraged their corporate contacts to sell customized publications for business clients in tandem with their retail guidebooks. Banks and other commercial institutions have been longtime supporters of the *Zagat Survey*, dating back to the original mimeographed compilation, which Citibank copied and circulated to more than 3,000 people. Soon after the debut of the self-published version of the guide, Citibank ordered 10,000 copies of the book as a premium for its banking clients. Over the decades, companies from numerous industries have used customized Zagat guides for marketing purposes such as direct mail premiums, loyalty rewards, purchase incentives, or promotional and sales tools. These custom editions contribute an important revenue stream and source of prestige affiliation for the company. By the early years of the 21st century, Zagat Survey had secured agreements with approximately 3,000 companies, ranging from MasterCard's purchase of 50,000 copies to give to its credit card customers to the 5 million copies of the *Zagat Movie Guide* ordered by Bank of America in 2004. Deluxe edition covers can be imprinted in silver or bound in leather, have silver-edged pages, and carry a corporation's name, logo, and marketing message. Recent corporate sales offerings also include maps, wallet guides, gift cards, and customizable apparel such as chef's coats and aprons that carry the Zagat logo.

Zagat.com

The Internet profoundly transformed both the Zagat surveys and the company. The founders embraced the Internet more quickly than many of their contemporaries and struck content licensing deals with several early online services, including CompuServe, Prodigy, and AOL. In the late 1990s, the company invested $1 million to create their own site, Zagat.com, which launched in May 1999. Within the first two weeks, the site recorded more than 7 million hits, far surpassing anticipated online traffic estimates and planned server capacity. In the site's early stage, individuals were signing up to be online Zagat reviewers at the rate of 2,000 a day. Within six months of launch, the site claimed more than 180,000 registered voters, far surpassing the total number of Zagat surveyors in the entire 20-year company history. These ranks would swell by the early years of the 21st century to 250,000 reviewers. Today, more than 350,000 individuals from around the world cast votes in the surveys.

Part of the site's early appeal stemmed from the decision to place all of the *Zagat Restaurant Survey* content online for free and to generate revenue from other sources, including licensing, corporate sponsorship, an online restaurant reservation system, ecommerce, restaurant-branded items such as knives, and business-to-business services. Initially eschewing an ad-sponsored business revenue model, the company experimented with offering online subscriptions to access its ratings and reviews. In October 2002, it began charging $14.95 per month for access; by 2006 this had dropped to $25 per year. The current membership model features two options: free and paid. All visitors to the Zagat site have access to general information on more than 40,000 restaurants and leisure sites, including street and Web addresses, phone numbers, maps, menus, and comments provided by registered members. Premium Member plans are subscription-based and provide access to the full *Zagat Survey* guidebook numerical ratings and edited reviews for restaurants, nightspots, hotels, and attractions worldwide, as well as discounts on publications and other items from the online store.

The *Zagat Survey* creates a rich database of information that can be referenced in multiple ways. Visitors can browse the restaurant listings or create instant lists of establishments based on location, style of cuisine, or dozens of features such as "business dining" or "celebrity chef." For example, a few clicks of the mouse can create an instant list culled from the New York City master roster to find all Italian restaurants in Greenwich Village that are local favorites. Premium Members can set additional parameters for minimum or maximum ratings in food, service, décor, or cost. In addition, the site offers multiple "Top Lists" of restaurants noted for specific qualities, such as "Top Burgers," "Power Scenes," or "Best Buys."

An increasingly popular option is to access Zagat.com from laptop computers or Web-enabled mobile phones. The Zagats recognized the potential of creating mobile access to their data shortly after the Zagat Web site went online in 1999, when they traveled to Japan to launch a Tokyo Zagat guide on Nippon Telephone and Telegraph's wireless i-mode service on Japanese cell phones. Zagat Survey had been invited to create the guide as a way to get people to accept the new phone. Once Nina—who displays strong technological savvy—saw how users could push a button and be shown the five nearest restaurants with Zagat ratings, she quickly recognized the opportunity to innovate much more quickly with Zagat content. In addition to its offerings on Zagat .com, today the company has online alliances with other popular sites, including Facebook, Google, and Priceline.

Everyone's a Critic

The fundamentals of the *Zagat Restaurant Survey* methodology have changed little over the years, although online voting has replaced paper ballots. Hundreds of thousands of amateur reviewers—or Zagateers—rate a restaurant on its food, décor, and service based on a scale of 0–3. A rating of 0 means poor to fair; 1, good; 2, very good; and 3, excellent. They also estimate the cost per person of a dinner with one drink and tip. The scores are then multiplied by 10, aggregated and tabulated by computer, and rounded off to the nearest whole number. The results become the trademark Zagat 30-point rating: 0–9 means poor to fair; 10–15, fair to good; 16–19, good to very good; 20–25, very good to excellent; 26–30, extraordinary to perfection. In the concise write-up for each restaurant, these three numbers are displayed in columns for Food, Décor, and Service. A fourth column, Cost, indicates the average price of a single dinner with one drink and tip, based on the surveyors' estimates.

The *Zagat Surveys* pack a remarkable amount of information into each one-inch-high guidebook entry. Numerical figures contribute only part of the reviews. Many believe that it is the pithy reviewer comments—often filled with puns and witty expressions—that supply the personality of the Zagat publications. Each review features a brief (approximately 50-word) paragraph of descriptive text brimming with reviewer evaluations in quotation marks and a telegraphic style. A sample review might rave about a "'glamorous' and 'upbeat' setting that's 'star-studded' yet 'touristy'" or that "there's 'no better place' for 'elegant, formal dining' than this 'unforgettable' 'temple of gastronomy.'" From hundreds, or perhaps thousands, of individual reviews, Zagat editors select comments that provide insight about a restaurant as well as create a lively reading experience for guidebook buyers and Zagat.com Premium Members. Each entry also includes basic information such as name, address, Web site, and telephone number of the restaurant; its hours, indicating whether it is open on Sunday and/or Monday, for lunch, or after 11 P.M.; and whether it accepts credit cards. The Cost column carries one of four abbreviations: I (Inexpensive), M (Moderate), E (Expensive), and VE (Very Expensive). In 2009 most of the guidebooks retailed for $15.95.

REVIEWS

Cheered and Feared

The widespread popularity of the *Zagat Restaurant Survey* instills both enthusiasm and fear in restaurant owners and chefs. Because it influences millions of dining decisions, the *Survey* has become a powerful economic force in the American restaurant industry. Owners and chefs await each annual issue with anticipation and trepidation. Based on past experience, they know that the ratings and reviewer comments can impact a restaurant's reputation—and by extension, revenue—in dramatic ways. In many cities, the Zagat guides are considered more influential than all other restaurant review sources. A few restaurants have even initiated lawsuits claiming damages for low ratings in the guide, although it appears that none has been successful. In 2003 one restaurant consultant estimated that a top position in the New York City guide could be worth up to $3 million in additional revenue to a restaurant that could capitalize on the Zagat ranking.[2]

Some restaurateurs consider the guides an important barometer for gauging public opinion about their food, service, and dining environment. Others dismiss the surveys as an entertaining collection of public commentary that often does not reflect a professional assessment of a restaurant's culinary capabilities. Detractors cite the *Survey*'s lack of transparency and flawed methodology, stating that the reviews assume a democratic stance but that the populist approach only maintains the status quo. In contrast to more scientific polling that randomly selects respondents, they argue, Zagat reviewers are self-selected. Many are thought to vote each year, thereby reinforcing existing rankings. This has led to a bias that *New York Times* critic Williams Grimes in a 1999 column dubbed "The Zagat Effect." Grimes believes the highest-ranking restaurants retain their spot because the public flocks to them and "convinced they are eating at a top-flight establishment, cannot bring themselves to believe otherwise."[3] The result, critics assert, is a reinforcing cycle of the same restaurants attaining the best ratings and highest rankings.

Others have noted additional weaknesses in the Zagat methodology. In a November 2000 article in *Commentary* magazine, attorney and food writer Steven Shaw points out that the numerical averages based on a simplified four-point scale can be misleading, and that the *Survey* leans toward rankings based on popularity and average tastes rather than quality.[4] Small pools of voters who give inflated ratings to a particular restaurant can also skew the *Survey*. As a result, modest neighborhood restaurants can receive stunningly high ratings, as a storefront restaurant in Brooklyn did in the 2004 edition. Ratings for The Grocery, a one-room, 30-seat establishment, placed it among the Top Ten restaurants in New York City in the *Survey*, alongside acclaimed four-star perennials such as Le Bernardin, Daniel, and Jean Georges. The ranking for the self-proclaimed "true mom-and-pop restaurant in the modern sense" generated considerable attention in the restaurant industry and a front-page story in *The New York Times*.[5] It is suspected that the restaurant's avid following (60 to 70 percent were regular customers) catapulted the restaurant to its lofty rank by a focused *Zagat Survey* voting effort.

Other criticisms center on the validity of the responses. For example, survey-ors are not required to substantiate that they actually ate in the restaurants they reviewed. Ballot stuffing on behalf of a favorite restaurant is possible, although never proven and strongly denied by the Zagat organization. The edited reviewer comments sometimes emphasize pithiness over substance, leaving the reader with a chuckle but only vague guidance. The Zagats defend their work in the face of this criticism, citing the hundreds of thousands of votes cast each year in the survey. Even this aspect of the process is problematic, however, since the company does not disclose how many votes were cast for any particular restaurant, and survey respondents can vote for as many or few as they wish. In theory, the rating of a popular restaurant could be based on thousands of responses, while another may be calculated on a few dozen, and it is never revealed how many votes are required to be listed in a guide. Oth-ers are dismayed by a ratings creep, noting that in the first *Survey*, the average for all New York City restaurants was 16.5; by 2004 the average food rating had climbed to 19.93.

Industry Influencers

In spite of concerns about the Zagat methodology, the *Zagat Restaurant Survey* has sustained its popularity with both the casual diner and dedicated food-lover, and Tim and Nina Zagat remain prominent figures in the culinary world. From their perch atop a mountain of popular opinion data, they hold power over both sides of the restaurant equation, influencing individuals on where to spend their dining dollars and impacting restaurant chefs and owners who seek to increase their reputations and build their enterprises. The Zagats are familiar ambassadors throughout the global restaurant community, particu-larly in New York City, where Tim continues to visit multiple establishments a night. His fast-paced forays keep him current with the menus, customer traffic, staff, and ambiance at classic venues as well as up-and-coming restau-rants. He clearly relishes the frenetic pace and public attention, in contrast to the more reserved Nina, who enjoys escaping to the quieter environment of their weekend home, a 19th-century farmhouse nestled on 160 acres in the Hudson Valley.

Today the Zagat domain extends to partnerships with leading restaurants on special projects, such as the series of "vintage dinners" featuring 19th-century dishes at some of the finest New York City restaurants held in late 2008. The couple are also active in New York Restaurant Week, a promo-tional event that Tim cofounded in 1992 and that is run by the city's tourism board. They make frequent media appearances, including on Food Network shows such as *The Iron Chef*. They contribute monthly commentary to a food-focused online forum hosted by the *Atlantic* magazine, and to the *Food Channel*. Tim serves as a board member of the Partnership for NYC and the World Travel & Tourism Council and has twice served as chair of NYC & Company, the official marketing, promotion, and tourism arm of New York City.

AWARDS AND HONORS

Tim and Nina Zagat have received numerous awards for their leadership and contributions to the food and hospitality industries. In 2000 Ernst & Young recognized them as Entrepreneurs of the Year, and in 2001 the couple were inducted into New York University's Entrepreneurship Hall of Fame. They are Fellows of the Culinary Institute of America, inductees of the Hospitality Industry Hall of Honor, and have been part of the White House Conference on Travel and Tourism. Tim received l'Ordre de Merite from the French government for his role in responding to the events surrounding 9/11. Nina was named one of the Leading Women Entrepreneurs of the World by Star Group in 2001 and has twice been honored by *Crain's New York* magazine: as one of Crain's Top Tech 100, the most influential people in technology, in 2001; and as one of *Crain's New York* Most Influential Women in 2007.

CONCLUSION

From their corporate offices overlooking New York City's Central Park, Tim and Nina Zagat remain secretive about future plans for their family-operated company, including whether the firm ultimately will be sold. In February 2000, a group of private and institutional investors purchased an equity stake in the enterprise for $31 million, which at the time was valued at more than $100 million. The technology bust a few months later derailed plans for an initial public offering of stock in the company. In early 2008, the company hired banking firm Goldman Sachs to seek a buyer for the company, which was valued then at more than $200 million. By June, however, the decision was rescinded, and the company ended its effort to sell.[6]

A recent advertising tagline—"Eat. Drink. Play. Stay."—captures the company's expanding reach into leisure-related fields, with guides for hotels, spas, golf courses, movies, and nightlife accompanying the core restaurant focus. The Zagats also have explored adapting their *Survey* ratings and reviews methodology to other industries. In a move beyond traditional leisure topics, in early 2009 Nina Zagat introduced the *Zagat Health Survey* for the medical profession. In a joint project with WellPoint, the nation's largest health benefits company, the *Survey* asks individuals to review and evaluate their physicians on four distinct criteria: trust, communication, availability, and office environment. An additional comment section allows individuals to provide feedback on their experience with a physician. Information about medical expertise or other factors, such as malpractice settlements, is not included. Responses are summarized and edited by WellPoint and can be viewed only by WellPoint customers. Although many physicians voiced opposition to the idea, the Zagat organization has plans to introduce the program in collaboration with WellPoint across all of the health insurance company's markets, ultimately reaching 35 million members.

As Zagat Survey enters the second decade of the 21st century, it faces increased competition from the burgeoning number of food-related Web sites and blogs that offer free content, including restaurant reviews, and a youthful spirit. While the challenges of staying nimble and relevant are formidable, Zagat remains a dominant global brand for communicating standards of fine dining and quality leisure pursuits. The Zagat name and iconic crimson-covered guidebooks are embedded in modern American culture, shorthand for public opinion surveys and witty, quote-filled commentary about restaurant experiences. In building their publishing empire, the Zagats rode the wave of interest in—and played a fundamental role in contributing to—the revolution in American food and dining.

NOTES

1. Toby Young, "Tim Zagat," *The Evening Standard* (April 29, 1996) http://www.nosacredcows.co.uk/profiles/368/tim_zagat.html (accessed April 10, 2009).
2. Florence Fabricant, "A Little Restaurant Elbows the 4-Stars in Zagat's New List," *The New York Times* (October 30, 2003), A1.
3. William Grimes, "A Face Lift for a Polished Performer," *The New York Times* (October 20, 1999), F1.
4. Steven A. Shaw, "The Zagat Effect," *Commentary* (November 2000), 49.
5. Fabricant, "A Little Restaurant."
6. Andrew Ross Sorkin, "Zagat Family Is Putting Guide Empire on Market," *The New York Times* (January 14, 2008), C1.

FURTHER READING

Adler, Carlyle. "Still Hungry after All These Years." *Fortune Small Business*. December 1, 1999, 56.

Apple, R. W. "Zagat at 20: Populist, and Powerful." *The New York Times*. November 11, 1998, F1.

Bensinger, Ken. "Zagat Math." *Smart Money*. March 2007, 76.

Fickenscher, Lisa. "Zagat Eats Up the Competition." *Crain's New York Business*. December 18, 2006, 1.

Frumkin, Paul. "Tim & Nina Zagat." *Restaurant News*. January 1995, 223.

Gimein, Mark. "Table for Mr. Bigfoot." *Fortune*. January 12, 2004, 46.

Lowry, Tom. "The Zagat Guide to Just About Everything." *Business Week*. December 9, 2002, 44.

McMath, Quita. "The Food Spooks." *New York*. November 25, 1985, 61–74.

Stross, Randall. "How Many Reviewers Should Be in the Kitchen?" *The New York Times*. September 7, 2008, BU4.

Weinstein, Bob. "Rave Reviews." *Entrepreneur*. August 1996, 120.

Zagat, Nina, and Tim Zagat. "Diary." *Slate*. June 4, 1999. http://www.slate.com/id/29583

Zagat Web site, http://www.zagat.com

Terri Lonier

About the Editors and Contributors

THE EDITORS

VICTOR W. GERACI is the Associate Director and Food and Wine Historian at the University of California Berkeley's Bancroft Library's Regional Oral History Office.

ELIZABETH S. DEMERS is senior editor at Potomac Books in Chicago.

THE CONTRIBUTORS

BONNIE S. BENWICK is deputy food editor and recipe editor of *The Washington Post*.

LENORA BERENDT, a former librarian, is pursuing a Personal Chef and Catering Certificate in the School of Culinary Arts at Kendall College in Chicago.

CYNTHIA D. BERTELSEN is a culinary historian and independent scholar in Blacksburg, Virginia. She writes about food and culture for several publications.

DIANE TODD BUCCI is Associate Professor of English Studies at Robert Morris University.

JOANN E. CASTAGNA has been a restaurant reviewer in Chicago and Iowa City and is now a writer.

CHRISTINE CRAWFORD-OPPENHEIMER is the Information Services Librarian and archivist at The Culinary Institute of America. She has written about food history.

MEREDITH ELIASSEN is the operations manager for Special Collections at the J. Paul Leonard Library at San Francisco State University.

MILDRED JACKSON is Associate Dean for Collections at The University of Alabama Libraries.

SEAN KENNIFF is a writer/editor and chef and consultant for the Unilever Corporation developing food and beverage products.

TERRI LONIER wrote her New York University Ph.D. dissertation on the history of entrepreneurial food marketing in the United States and the origins of global food brands.

TAMARA MANN is a Ph.D. candidate in American History at Columbia University.

SIGNE ROUSSEAU is a researcher and part-time lecturer at the University of Cape Town, South Africa. Her doctoral thesis, "From Chef to Superstar: Food Media from World War II to the World Wide Web," focused on the cult of the celebrity chef from its nascent post-war period to the fully fledged industry of today.

FRANCINE SEGAN, a New York City based food historian and lecturer, is the author of four cookbooks including *Opera Lover's Cookbook* (2006) and a James Beard and IACP awards finalist.

TABITHA Y. STEAGER is a Ph.D. candidate in Interdisciplinary Studies at the University of British Columbia Okanagan. Her ethnographic research uses food as a means for understanding how and why people react the way they do to dominant global socioeconomic and social systems.

LEENA TRIVEDI-GRENIER is a San Francisco Bay-based food and travel writer. She writes the food blog, Leena Eats (www.leenaeats.com/blog) and teaches cooking classes.

MICHAEL TWITTY is webmaster of www.afrofoodways.com, a Web site to devoted to African American historic foodways. He is also a consultant for the Landreth Seed Company and is the curator of the first marketed collection of African American heirloom vegetables and herbs, partly based on Edna Lewis's recipes from *A Taste of Country Cooking*.

KIMBERLY WILMOT VOSS is an assistant professor of journalism at the University of Central Florida. She specializes in telling the stories of women's page journalists from the 1950s and 1960s, including food editors and fashion writers.

SHIRLEY TERESA WAJDA is a cultural historian specializing in American material culture, photography, and consumption. She was the coeditor of *Material Culture in America: Understanding Everyday Life* (ABC-CLIO, 2008).

Index